THE COMING OF ZION'S REDEEMER

The Prophecies of Haggai, Zechariah, and Malachi

RONALD HANKO

REFORMED
FREE PUBLISHING
ASSOCIATION

Jenison, Michigan

Scripture cited is taken from the King James (Authorized) Version

Cover design by Christopher Tobias/www.tobiasdesign.com
Interior design by Katherine Lloyd/www.theDESKonline.com

Reformed Free Publishing Association
1894 Georgetown Center Drive
Jenison, Michigan 49428
616-457-5970
www.rfpa.org
mail@rfpa.org

ISBN 978-1-936054-41-1
Ebook ISBN 978-1-936054-42-8

LCCN 2014940910

This book is dedicated to my children,
who by the grace of God have been and continue to be
committed to the work of building Christ's church
both in their own families
and in the congregations to which they belong
while they wait for the return
of Zion's Redeemer.

And the Redeemer shall come to Zion,
and unto them that turn from transgression in Jacob,
saith the L*ORD.*

—Isaiah 59:20

Contents

DESIRE OF ALL NATIONS
THE PROPHECY OF HAGGAI

PRIEST UPON THE THRONE
THE PROPHECY OF ZECHARIAH

MESSENGER OF THE COVENANT
The Prophecy of Malachi

Foreword

Pastor Hanko's commentaries on the books of Haggai, Zechariah, and Malachi are written not mainly *to be referred to* while seeking an answer to some challenging biblical question, but more particularly *to be read and assimilated* by believers who seek greater understanding of God's word. Two of the commentaries were initially published serially by the *Standard Bearer* and thus were set forth to be read, albeit incrementally. The other commentary is published here for the first time but is written in the same readable style.

The full commentary on each book may be read with great profit by virtue of the author's trained, experienced, and studied insights. Three perspectives stand out: first, a living picture of Judah in the generation following the return from the Babylonian captivity with her special charge to reform true worship of God; next, a sharp delineation of the truth that these ancient prophecies especially have direct and significant application to us as the church today; and finally, a humble bowing in living fearfulness before the one only true God of heaven and earth, Jehovah of the scriptures, who sovereignly carries out his absolute rule over all to its culmination in the unconditional, covenantal salvation of his church, all to his own honor and glory alone.

One simple acknowledgment should be made related to the author himself. He was called to the pastoral and missionary ministry in the Protestant Reformed Churches thirty-five years ago, and it pleased God to raise him up on the shoulders of a paternal grandfather now in heaven after following a lifelong commitment to that same ministry, and on those of a father who, now in a kind of "restless retirement," surely from time to time glances back on his own life calling as a pastor and professor in these same churches. This is a remarkable manifestation of God's covenantal faithfulness through the generations and adds unusual depth to these commentaries.

Joel Sugg
Member of Hope Protestant
Reformed Church in Redlands, California,
and former parishioner of the author

Preface

The last three prophets of the Old Testament have always intrigued me, living and working as they did in the latter days of that Testament, with the first coming of Christ just over the horizon of history. Their messages individually and together seemed very pertinent to the last days in which we live, with Christ's coming again very near. Closer study of the three prophecies has reinforced my belief that the message they bring is intended for and needed in the last days of the New Testament.

In addition, the prophecies of Haggai and Malachi attracted me by their wonderful prophecies of the coming of Christ and by their vivid language. Zechariah's difficult and sometimes obscure symbolism was also intriguing, as were its obvious similarities to Revelation, although the similarities were much greater than ever I realized before studying the book.

The work on the prophecies of Haggai and Malachi began with a series of sermons on those books, and the work of Zechariah followed as a matter of course and by way of completing a study of these three books.

May God bless and use these feeble efforts that only touch on the glory of Christ, the desire of all nations, the great priest-king and the messenger of the covenant. He, Zion's redeemer, is the one for whom we are still waiting.

Introduction

The three prophecies of Haggai, Zechariah, and Malachi form a unit, not only because these three and they alone are the prophets of the restoration, that is, of Judah's return from exile in Babylon, but also because they have the same general theme and purpose. That one great purpose is the preparation of God's covenant people for the coming of Christ.

In the days of Haggai and Zechariah that long-awaited event was five hundred years in the future; in Malachi's day it was even closer. While waiting for Christ's coming, the covenant people had to learn to look away from the Old Testament types to the fulfillment of all the types in him who was promised. Each of these three prophecies, in its own way, taught them to do that.

Thus these prophecies continue to be of value to the covenant people of God, for the church is still waiting for the realization of God's promises concerning the coming of Messiah, promises that will not be entirely fulfilled until he returns at the end of the ages. Though the types and shadows of the Old Testament have already vanished, the people of God must still be reminded to lift up their heads and see that their redemption draws near (Luke 21:28). They need to look away from a perishing world and be watching and waiting for the coming of a kingdom that will never be moved.

Each of these three marvelous prophecies heralds the coming of Christ in a different way. Haggai points to him in the central passage of his prophecy as the great *king* and temple builder, the desire of all nations (2:6–9). Zechariah, in chapter 6:9–15 of his prophecy, shows him to be a *priest* upon the throne, the one in whom the counsel of peace is realized and the glory of God's house guaranteed. Malachi foretells his coming as the messenger of the covenant, the great *prophet*, the one by whom the sons of Levi are purified and healed and made acceptable to the Lord (3:1–4).

The focus of these prophecies, then, is on the offices of Christ. He is forevermore the chief prophet, only high priest, and eternal king of his people. There are many other similarities between these books. Especially in Haggai and Zechariah, who were contemporaries, there are many of the same themes, emphases, and even many similar expressions, but the unity of all three lies in what they teach about the offices of our Savior. They belong together and are like different movements of one great symphony that swells to its climax in the truth that Jesus Christ is everything to his church: that beside him the church has need of nothing. In him we are complete (Col. 2:10).

The three prophecies focus on Christ's offices by focusing on the men who held these offices in the closing days of the Old Testament: Zerubbabel, of the royal family of David, Joshua the high priest, and Malachi the prophet. Zerubbabel is the figure of Christ the king and temple builder, Joshua of Christ the enthroned priest, intercessor, and justifier of his people, and Malachi of Christ the messenger of the covenant.

These men appear in the three prophecies, but only to fade into the background as Christ reveals himself through them. Indeed, the offices these men held, the Old Testament offices of prophet, priest, and king, were fading and would soon pass away. Zerubbabel, though descended from King David, was only a local ruler under the Persian monarchs. Joshua, though high priest, was a priest without a temple, and Malachi the prophet was the last lonely prophetic voice of the Old Testament.

The fading of these offices was part of the fading and vanishing of all the Old Testament types and pictures, something that had to happen as the coming of Christ loomed. The types had to make way for the reality to which they pointed, which was nothing less than Christ and his everlasting and peaceable kingdom. That fading and vanishing of the types and shadows of the Old Testament had to take place for the sake of God's people as well. They had to look away from those temporary and perishing things to Christ himself, something they found very difficult to do. God helped them to do that by making those types much less attractive in these closing days of the Old Testament.

One of the most important of those types was the temple, and so the three prophecies are concerned also with the rebuilding of the temple (Haggai and Zechariah) and the worship of God in the temple (Malachi). The people had to be called to the work of rebuilding, had to be encouraged in that work, and, when it was built, had to be reminded that the temple was the house of God, a place to be kept holy. To be faithful in these duties they had to look away from that earthly temple to Christ who is the true temple builder and to the spiritual house that he would build.

So it is that the three prophecies not only testify to us of Christ, but call us to service in Christ's kingdom. The true temple of God, the church, is still being built, and though Christ is the great builder, we have the calling to build also. George Ophoff says:

Yet there is a sense, a very actual sense, in which the believers do and shall build the temple. The temple of the first covenant was a shadow...It symbolized the indwelling of the triune Jehovah in His church through Christ in His Spirit...It is plain in what sense God's believing people of this day do and shall built the temple. They may be said to build the temple when they bring to manifestation in this world the body of Christ through their chosen officebearers and place themselves under their jurisdiction in obedience to Christ. Thus they build the temple when they submit themselves to the ruling and teaching ministry that Christ has instituted in the church and receive their word and admonition. They build the temple when through these ministries as their organs they faithfully expound the Scripture and vindicate sound doctrine against heresies and errors. They build the temple when they lay off sin, put on Christ and walk in newness of life and fight the good fight. We saw how displeased God was with His people of old for their neglect of His temple. Not to be for Christ is to be against Him. Not to build the temple is to destroy it. Let then God's people build the temple which they do by His mercy. Let them not fear but let their hands be strong. For their labors are not vain in the Lord.[1]

May our study of these prophecies bring the greater honor to Christ's blessed name as we too wait for him. May we, when the days are as dark as they were in the years after the restoration, look for this kingly Desire of all nations, this Priest upon the throne, this mighty Messenger of the covenant,

---

1 George M. Ophoff, "The Prophecy of Zechariah," *Standard Bearer* 33, no. 5 (Dec. 1, 1956): 106.

and see that he will bring salvation to Zion when he comes again. May we faithfully build in the house of our God, until that day when in the heavenly Jerusalem, there will be no need of a temple, when the Lord God Almighty and the Lamb are the only temple for God's people (Rev. 21:22).

The Years following the Return from Captivity in Babylon

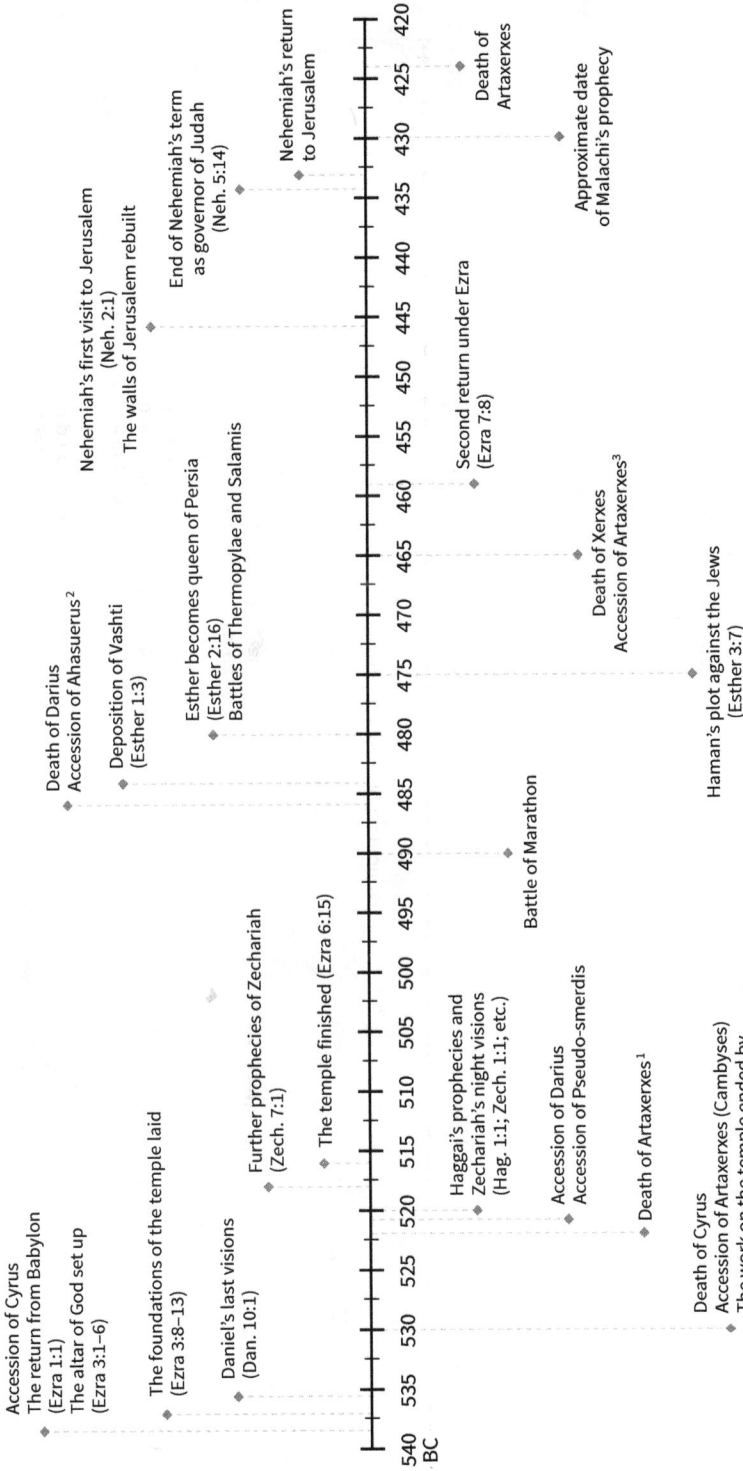

Timeline scale (BC): 540, 535, 530, 525, 520, 515, 510, 505, 500, 495, 490, 485, 480, 475, 470, 465, 460, 455, 450, 445, 440, 435, 430, 425, 420

Events along the timeline:

- Accession of Cyrus
  The return from Babylon
  (Ezra 1:1)
  The altar of God set up
  (Ezra 3:1–6)

- The foundations of the temple laid
  (Ezra 3:8–13)

- Daniel's last visions
  (Dan. 10:1)

- Death of Cyrus
  Accession of Artaxerxes (Cambyses)
  The work on the temple ended by
  the king's decree
  (Ezra 4:6–24)

- Death of Artaxerxes[1]

- Accession of Darius
  Accession of Pseudo-smerdis

- Haggai's prophecies and
  Zechariah's night visions
  (Hag. 1:1; Zech. 1:1; etc.)

- Further prophecies of Zechariah
  (Zech. 7:1)

- The temple finished (Ezra 6:15)

- Battle of Marathon

- Death of Darius
  Accession of Ahasuerus[2]

- Deposition of Vashti
  (Esther 1:3)

- Esther becomes queen of Persia
  (Esther 2:16)
  Battles of Thermopylae and Salamis

- Haman's plot against the Jews
  (Esther 3:7)

- Death of Xerxes
  Accession of Artaxerxes[3]

- Second return under Ezra
  (Ezra 7:8)

- Nehemiah's first visit to Jerusalem
  (Neh. 2:1)
  The walls of Jerusalem rebuilt

- End of Nehemiah's term
  as governor of Judah
  (Neh. 5:14)

- Nehemiah's return
  to Jerusalem

- Approximate date
  of Malachi's prophecy

- Death of
  Artaxerxes

1 Also known in history as Darius I, Darius Hystaspes, and Darius the Great.
2 Called Ahasuerus in the book of Esther but known in history as Xerxes.
3 Known in history as Artaxerxes I or Artaxerxes Longimanus.

xv

The Prophecies of Haggai and Zechariah during the Reign of Darius (521 BC to 486 BC)

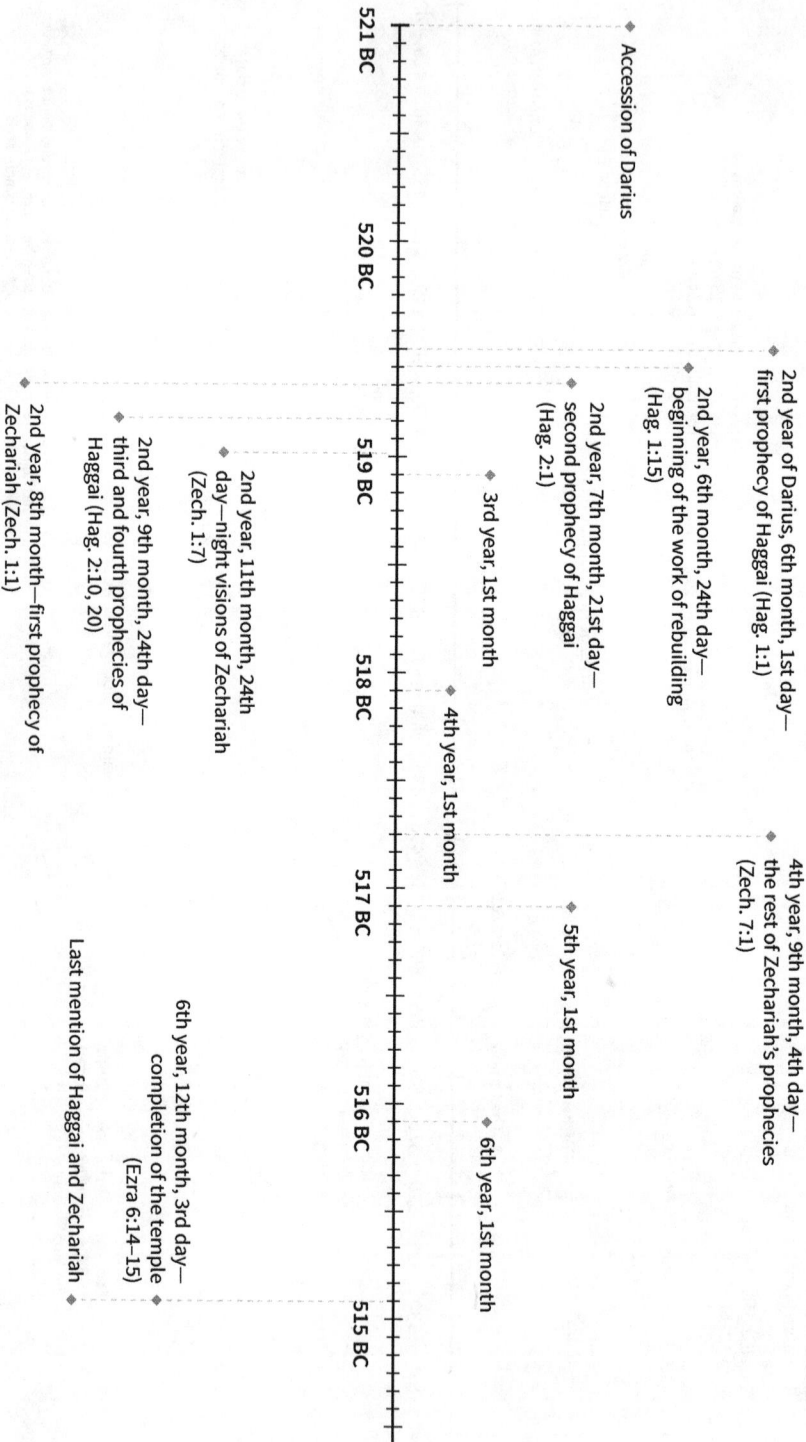

Accession of Darius

521 BC — 520 BC — 519 BC — 518 BC — 517 BC — 516 BC — 515 BC

2nd year of Darius, 6th month, 1st day—
first prophecy of Haggai (Hag. 1:1)

2nd year, 6th month, 24th day—
beginning of the work of rebuilding
(Hag. 1:15)

2nd year, 7th month, 21st day—
second prophecy of Haggai
(Hag. 2:1)

2nd year, 9th month, 24th
day—night visions of Zechariah
(Zech. 1:7)

2nd year, 9th month, 24th day—
third and fourth prophecies of
Haggai (Hag. 2:10, 20)

2nd year, 8th month—first prophecy of
Zechariah (Zech. 1:1)

3rd year, 1st month

4th year, 1st month

4th year, 9th month, 4th day—
the rest of Zechariah's prophecies
(Zech. 7:1)

5th year, 1st month

6th year, 1st month

6th year, 12th month, 3rd day—
completion of the temple
(Ezra 6:14–15)

Last mention of Haggai and Zechariah

DESIRE
OF ALL
NATIONS
THE PROPHECY
OF HAGGAI

For thus saith the LORD *of hosts;*
Yet once, it is a little while,
and I will shake the heavens, and the earth,
and the sea, and the dry land;
And I will shake all nations,
and the desire of all nations shall come:
and I will fill this house with glory,
saith the LORD *of hosts.*
—Haggai 2:6–7

Introduction to Haggai

The prophecy of Haggai, though little known, is a book of enormous value not only as a record of God's dealings with his people in the Old Testament, but also as a prophecy of God's regard for and faithful care of his church in the New Testament. Haggai is a book about the church, about the calling that every member has in the church, and about God's faithfulness to his church. It is therefore a book that very much needs to be read and understood in times such as these, times in which the church is despised and neglected and fallen into spiritual ruin.

Haggai is about the church because it is about the temple, and the temple is one of the great Old Testament figures and types of the church, as Ephesians 2:19–22 says:

> 19. Now therefore ye are no more strangers and foreigners, but fellow-citizens with the saints, and of the household of God;
> 20. And are built upon the foundation of the apostles and prophets, Jesus Christ himself being the chief corner stone;
> 21. In whom all the building fitly framed together groweth unto an holy temple in the Lord:
> 22. In whom ye also are builded together for an habitation of God through the Spirit.

The prophecy concerns the rebuilding of the temple following Judah's return from captivity in Babylon. Though that might seem to have little bearing on our life and calling in the New Testament, it is a vivid and unforgettable reminder of the truth of the Reformation slogan that describes the church as "reformed and always reforming." When the church is reforming its doctrine and life according to the word of God and being built up in holiness, it is being built like the temple was in Haggai's days. The calling that Judah had to rebuild God's house is ours also therefore, and it is a calling that continues until the Desire of all nations comes again as he has promised.

The book of Haggai, however, is not just about the church, but about Christ. He is the true temple, the living temple of God in which God lives with his people in one house as their God and Father. He is the one in whom dwells all the fullness of the Godhead (Col. 2:9), as well as the one in whom we are complete (v. 10). "Destroy this temple," he said to the Jews, "and in three days I will raise it up," referring to the temple of his body (John 2:19–21). In that temple we dwell by faith, "for we are members of his body, of his flesh, and of his bones" (Eph. 5:30), and there, in Immanuel, God dwells with us. It is no surprise, then, that the central prophecy of Haggai concerns him as the desire of all nations, the true temple of God.

But he also appears in Haggai as the head and builder of the church (Matt. 16:18; Eph. 1:22–23) through the figure of Zerubbabel as the great temple builder, without whom nothing can be accomplished. The prophecy of Haggai, then, is more about Christ than about the church. It speaks of the church only in relation to him, and that is the way it should be. Calvin summarizes Haggai's message in this way: "Christ also would at length come to secure the perfect happiness and glory of the Church."[1]

The Author

Haggai is the first of the three prophets of the return. He began prophesying about two months before Zechariah, and the two of them prophesied about ninety years before Malachi. There can be no doubt that he is the author of these prophecies, since he is named nine times in the book and twice in Ezra. He worked as a prophet in Judah bringing God's word about the rebuilding of the temple, as confirmed in Ezra 5:1–2:

1. Then the prophets, Haggai the prophet, and Zechariah the son of Iddo, prophesied unto the Jews that were in Judah and Jerusalem in the name of the God of Israel, even unto them.
2. Then rose up Zerubbabel the son of Shealtiel, and Jeshua [also called Joshua] the son of Jozadak, and began to build the house of

---

1 John Calvin, *Commentaries on the Twelve Minor Prophets*, trans. John Owen (Grand Rapids, MI: Eerdmans, 1950), 4:316.

4

God which is at Jerusalem: and with them were the prophets of
God helping them.

He is also mentioned in Ezra 6:14:

And the elders of the Jews builded, and they prospered through the
prophesying of Haggai the prophet and Zechariah the son of Iddo.
And they builded, and finished it, according to the commandment
of the God of Israel, and according to the commandment of Cyrus,
and Darius, and Artaxerxes king of Persia.

Some suggest that although Haggai is the author of the prophecies,
this does not necessarily mean that he actually *wrote* the book, since he is
referred to in the third person throughout. Three times, however, we read
literally that the word of the Lord came "in the hand of Haggai" (1:1, 3; 2:1;
see also Gal. 3:19; Col. 4:18; and 2 Thess. 3:17), which would indicate that
he is both the one through whom these prophecies came and the one who
wrote them down.

That the prophecies of the book are the word of the Lord by the hand
of Haggai reminds us of what we believe concerning the inspiration of the
scriptures. In this book too, God used a man to preserve his word in writing
for all ages, while insuring that what was written remained "the word of the
Lord," infallible and perfect.

We know nothing about Haggai, except that he prophesied about
twenty years after the return from Babylon as a contemporary of the prophet
Zechariah, when Zerubbabel was governor of Judah and Darius was king
of the Persians. Haggai is not mentioned elsewhere in scripture, except in
Ezra, and neither his prophecy nor the book of Ezra gives us any information
about him.

As far as we know, he delivered only four prophecies, each of which is
marked in the book of Haggai by a date. Those four prophecies were given over
a period of just under four months (fifteen weeks). There is the possibility that
Haggai's career as a prophet was longer than this short span of fifteen weeks.
Ezra 6:14 may mean that Haggai continued to prophesy until the temple was
finished, but whether Haggai's career as a prophet lasted longer, and whether

there were other prophecies besides these four, we really do not know. If there were other prophecies, the wisdom of God has not given them to us.

That we know so little of Haggai is of some significance. What he says is the word of God, and the man himself matters very little in light of that important fact. As the word of God and not the words of a man, his message must be heard by God's people in every age. It is a divine message, the relevance of which has not changed though many hundreds of years have passed and though the circumstances of the church are ever so different.

That Haggai apparently prophesied for only a very short time speaks also of the Lord's sovereignty in his dealings with his people. The men he uses to bring his word are merely instruments of his sovereignty and grace, to be used as he sees fit, even if it is only for a few months and to speak a few words.

The Date

The book dates itself to the second year of Darius, king of Persia. This is confirmed in Ezra 4:24: "Then ceased the work of the house of God which is at Jerusalem. So it ceased unto the second year of the reign of Darius king of Persia."

This Darius is not the same man as Darius the Mede, the conqueror of Babylon, mentioned in Daniel 5:28. He had died about twenty years earlier and had been followed by Cyrus the Great, who sent the Jews back to Judah, and by several other kings. The Darius of Haggai's days is almost certainly Darius I Hystaspes, also known as Darius the Great, who ruled Persia from 521 to 486 BC. Haggai, then, prophesied around 520 BC, approximately twenty years after the return from captivity and during the early years of Darius's rule.

In secular history Darius is the Persian king who first tried to conquer Greece and whose armies were defeated at the battle of Marathon. It is striking that, great king though he was, none of his exploits are mentioned in scripture. Scripture's bare mention of him tells us that God judges greatness by a different standard than men do. Those who are great in the world are usually of little account in the kingdom of God, and those who are unnoticed and who die unremembered in the world, like Haggai, are often of great account before God.

In the book of Haggai Darius is important only insofar as the rebuilding of the temple is dated to his reign. The important event on God's calendar in those days, that which in his eyes was worthy of note and a great event of history, was the rebuilding of the temple, not the accession and power of this famous world ruler.

The History

The book of Haggai highlights the rebuilding of God's house as the main reason for the return from captivity. God was concerned more than anything else with his house and the glory of his own name in that house. Even the return of his people from captivity and their reestablishment in the promised land was only a means to that end. In New Testament terms, this is God's way of saying that the church is more important than the salvation of the individual members or their well-being, though in God's purpose the two are connected.

What a testimony Haggai is against the spirit that pervades Christianity today, the selfish idea that makes our own salvation and blessedness the most important thing of all and that relegates the church and the members of the church to a lesser place in the lives of believers. This is the spirit that permits believers to abandon the church altogether, or to float around from church to church looking for something that moves them or warms their hearts. It is the spirit that encourages passivity in the members of the church even when the church is declining. They shrug their shoulders, refuse to work at church reformation, and suggest that because they themselves are saved it matters not that the church goes to ruin.

That the rebuilding of the temple took place many years after the return is the reason Haggai had to bring the word of God to God's people in Judah. It was twenty or more years after the return, and the temple was not yet completed. The work had been started almost as soon as the Jews had first returned to Judah. Seven months after the decree of Cyrus they were back in Canaan, and the next year they were already busy with the rebuilding of the temple and had laid its foundation (Ezra 3:8–13).

In the years that followed, however, very little more was done, so that at the time of Haggai's prophecies the temple was still unfinished. Originally the work had stopped because of the interference of Judah's enemies. Those enemies, especially the Samaritans, had hired counselors (something on the order of lawyers) who did all they could to stop the work (Ezra 4:4–5). Their efforts had been unsuccessful while Cyrus and his successor, Ahasuerus (not the husband of Esther but a man known to secular history as Cambyses, Ezra 4:1–6), were still living. When a man named Artaxerxes (known in history as Pseudo-smerdis) became king, they were able to have the work stopped (Ezra 4:6–24).[2] Artaxerxes listened to the charges of these enemies, concluded that the rebuilding of the temple would be an occasion for rebellion, and ordered the work halted.

Nevertheless, as God pointed out through Haggai, the interference of these enemies was not the only reason the temple remained unbuilt. The work God had given Judah to do had been neglected. God admonishes that neglect through Haggai's prophecies, urging the Jews to finish their work on the temple and promising them his blessings when they obeyed.

The Jews did obey, and the work on the temple was finished five years later, in the last month of the sixth year of the reign of Darius (Ezra 6:15). Apparently Haggai was still living or prophesying when the work was finished since he is mentioned in Ezra 6:14, but his concern was getting the work underway and encouraging the people to continue. Once that was accomplished, he faded from the scene of biblical history. God's word through him, however, remains and continues to be of value to the church.

The Divisions

These prophecies of Haggai are four, each identified by the date on which it was brought, all of them in the second year of Darius. The first is dated to the first day of the sixth month and is found in Haggai 1:1–15. The second came less than two months later, on the twenty-first day of the seventh month, and is found in Haggai 2:1–9. The third and fourth were another two months later, on the twenty-fourth day of the ninth month, and include Haggai 2:10–19 and 2:20–23.

Most scholars agree that the dates in Haggai can be determined with quite a degree of accuracy from Babylonian records.

---

2 See the timeline of the years following the return from Babylon on page xv for a list of these kings and the years they ruled.

REFERENCE	DARIUS'S YEAR	MONTH	DAY	CALENDAR DATE
1:1	2	6	1	29 August 520 BC
1:15	2	6	24	21 September 520 BC
(this is not a new prophecy, but the date the work began anew)				
2:1	2	7	21	17 October 520 BC
2:10	2	9	24	18 December 520 BC[3]

That the dates can be worked out so accurately is further testimony to the importance of the temple in this period of Israel's history.

Haggai and Zechariah

There are many similarities between Haggai and Zechariah. Both mention Zerubbabel and Joshua by name. Both are concerned with the rebuilding of the temple. Both mention the *mountain* of the Lord's house. Both are concerned with God's covenant, and in both the Spirit is promised, a rather rare promise in the Old Testament. Both describe the overthrow of the heathen nations, Judah's oppressors. Both are concerned with current events and reach to the end of time and the return of Christ as redeemer and judge. Where Haggai speaks briefly, Zechariah speaks at more length. What Haggai only mentions is more fully revealed in Zechariah. Nevertheless, they bring the same message of comfort and hope. They, with Isaiah, had the commission, "Comfort ye, comfort ye my people, saith your God. Speak ye comfortably to Jerusalem, and cry unto her, that her warfare is accomplished, that her iniquity is pardoned: for she hath received of the LORD's hand double for all her sins" (Isa. 40:1–2).

The two prophets are similar because they were contemporaries, they both prophesied about the rebuilding of the temple, and their message is really the same. Concerned with the rebuilding of the temple, they are also both concerned with the realization of God's covenant in Christ, for the temple was the place of God's covenant in the Old Testament and a picture of the church as God's dwelling place in the New. The two together promise God's continual presence among his people and his unchangeable faithfulness to them in that temple/church. Thus it is that they speak so plainly to

---

3 See J. Alec Motyer, "Haggai," in Thomas Edward McComiskey, ed., *The Minor Prophets: An Exegetical and Expository Commentary* (Grand Rapids, MI: Baker Books, 1998), 3:967.

the church of the New Testament as well as to the church of the Old, and though couched in Old Testament language are like the books of the New Testament.

The Four Prophecies

We have seen that the book of Haggai contains four prophecies, each introduced by the date on which it was delivered. The first prophecy is a call to be busy with the work of building the temple, accompanied by a warning against further neglect of the work. In that warning God points out the sins of his people and shows them how he was punishing them for those sins. Though they did not recognize the fact, many of the troubles they were suffering in Judah were God's chastisement.

Attached to that first prophecy is a historical notice of the people's obedience to God's word and a further word of encouragement to them in their work of rebuilding. Haggai does not tell that part of the story, but after restarting the work, the Jews, to the consternation of their enemies, obtained a decree from the king allowing them to build and providing them with the necessities for building and for the worship of God in the temple (Ezra 5:3–6:13).

The second prophecy, found in chapter 2:1–9, is the most important of them all. In it God addresses the discouragement of the people, who could see, now that the work was progressing, that the temple they were building did not compare to Solomon's temple. God not only encourages them with the promise that he would live in the temple as in old times, but also points them forward to the coming of Christ, to the building of the true temple, and to its glory, which would be far greater than the glory of Solomon's temple. This second prophecy, therefore, concerns the future history of the temple and carries us all the way to the end of the world, to the day when all things will be shaken and destroyed and only the true temple will remain.

The third prophecy is a reminder to the people, through an example taken from the law of Moses, that because the work was God's work, they must be holy and work with holy hands. The warning is reinforced in chapter 2:13–19, with a reminder of God's former judgments and a promise of future blessing.

The fourth of these prophecies speaks again of the coming of Christ as the one who would build the true temple. Christ is spoken of in the figure of Zerubbabel, the governor of Judah, and under that figure God guarantees the building of his house and at the same time promises his people complete deliverance from their enemies. All this, in the fourth prophecy, is grounded in God's great and eternal love for his people, the motive for all his dealings with them.

Thus these prophecies take us into the New Testament and have to do not only with Old Testament events but with the first coming of Christ, as well as with those things that are now taking place between Christ's coming as the desire of all nations and his return to shake all things. The book of Haggai is only quoted once in the New Testament, in Hebrews 12:26, but it is very much a book for New Testament believers, a book that may not be neglected and forgotten, a book that concerns the church of Jesus Christ in the world and the calling of believers in relation to the church.

Chapter 1

THE FIRST PROPHECY: HAGGAI 1:1–15

1:1   In the second year of Darius the king, in the sixth month, in the first day of the month, came the word of the LORD by Haggai the prophet unto Zerubbabel the son of Shealtiel, governor of Judah, and to Joshua the son of Josedech, the high priest, saying,

1:2   Thus speaketh the LORD of hosts, saying, This people say, The time is not come, the time that the LORD's house should be built.

1:3   Then came the word of the LORD by Haggai the prophet, saying,

1:4   Is it time for you, O ye, to dwell in your cieled houses, and this house lie waste?

1:5   Now therefore thus saith the LORD of hosts; Consider your ways.

1:6   Ye have sown much, and bring in little; ye eat, but ye have not enough; ye drink, but ye are not filled with drink; ye clothe you, but there is none warm; and he that earneth wages earneth wages to put it into a bag with holes.

1:7   Thus saith the LORD of hosts; Consider your ways.

1:8   Go up to the mountain, and bring wood, and build the house; and I will take pleasure in it, and I will be glorified, saith the LORD.

1:9   Ye looked for much, and, lo, it came to little; and when ye brought it home, I did blow upon it. Why? saith the LORD of hosts. Because of mine house that is waste, and ye run every man unto his own house.

1:10   Therefore the heaven over you is stayed from dew, and the earth is stayed from her fruit.

1:11   And I called for a drought upon the land, and upon the mountains, and upon the corn, and upon the new wine, and upon the oil, and upon that which the ground bringeth forth, and upon men, and upon cattle, and upon all the labour of the hands.

1:12   Then Zerubbabel the son of Shealtiel, and Joshua the son of Josedech, the high priest, with all the remnant of the people, obeyed the voice of the LORD their God, and the words of Haggai the prophet, as the LORD their God had sent him, and the people did fear before the LORD.

1:13   Then spake Haggai the LORD's messenger in the LORD's message unto the people, saying, I am with you, saith the LORD.

1:14   And the LORD stirred up the spirit of Zerubbabel the son of Shealtiel, governor of Judah, and the spirit of Joshua the son of Josedech, the high priest, and the spirit of all the remnant of the people; and they came and did work in the house of the LORD of hosts, their God,

1:15   In the four and twentieth day of the sixth month, in the second year of Darius the king.

1:1. In the second year of Darius the king, in the sixth month, in the first day of the month, came the word of the LORD by Haggai the prophet unto Zerubbabel the son of Shealtiel, governor of Judah, and to Joshua the son of Josedech, the high priest, saying,

The first of the month was a Jewish feast or holiday (Num. 28:11–15). It is possible, therefore, that this first prophecy was given in the temple area. This would have meant that Haggai had a large audience and could point to the unfinished temple itself as evidence of the people's failure to honor and obey God.

The mention of Darius is a reminder that the Jews, at the time of Haggai's prophecy, were no longer an independent nation but under the dominion of foreign and heathen kings. They even dated events now by the reigns of these strange kings who ruled from far-off Persia. The fact that this king is not the same king who sent them back to Judah shows that many years had passed and the work of the temple was not yet finished. It was Cyrus who had sent them back, and now another king named Darius was on the throne of Persia and the temple was still in ruins. It was also a reminder that circumstances had changed once again and they could no longer use the hostility of former kings as an excuse for their neglect of God's house.

There is some controversy about whether the sixth month was the sixth month of the reign of Darius or the sixth month of the Jewish year, but the question is of little significance. The main reasons for carefully dating each of the prophecies are threefold: first, to show how long the people had been remiss in their calling; second, to show their quick obedience to God's command when rebuked for their sloth and indifference; and third, to show God's faithfulness in encouraging them and helping them in the work. He always immediately encouraged their willingness to work and was quick to see their troubles and discouragements and to assist them. The date is otherwise unimportant.

Most important, the word Haggai brings, whether a word of rebuke or of encouragement, is God's word, literally "the word of *Jehovah*," Israel's covenant God, the one whose covenantal faithfulness never fails. The phrase "saith the LORD" is found over and over again in Haggai, as often as three times in the same verse (2:4, 23). Judah had to know that their calling to rebuild the temple did not depend on the whims of earthly kings, however great they might be, but came from the King of kings himself. Nothing and no one might stand in the way of their obedience. God, not Cyrus or Darius, had commanded the building of his house and commanded it as the God of the covenant.

The idea that the word Haggai brings is really God's word is prominent here. Literally we read that the word came "in the hand of" Haggai, a rather unusual expression in the Old Testament, but it emphasizes the truth that Haggai was only a channel for this message from God—only the carrier of it.

That emphasis on the word of God is very important today. The calling to rebuild God's house is for us the calling to labor faithfully in and for the church. We will do so, as Judah did, only when we are certain our calling comes to us from God himself and concerns his house. If we do not understand that the calling is from God, we will be as neglectful and indifferent as Israel was before the word of God came to them through Haggai. If we think the church is only a human institution and that we work in the church only on our own behalf, then indifference will follow.

A quick glance at the book of Haggai will show that God most often identifies himself in the book by the name Jehovah and that Jehovah is used many times in this very short book, thirty-four times in thirty-eight verses. The name very often appears as "the LORD of hosts," or more literally, "Jehovah of hosts." In comparison, the only other name used is the name "God," and that only three times.

God uses his name Jehovah to teach Judah and us that the temple, called here his house, is a part of his covenant with his people. There he chooses to live with his people, to reveal himself as their God, and to take them as his own. That living together is what his covenant is all about, and so he uses his covenant name time and time again.

This first word of God is addressed especially to Zerubbabel the governor (also called Sheshbazzar in Ezra 1:11; 5:14, 16) and Joshua the high priest (also referred to as Jeshua). That does not mean that God is not speaking to the rest of the people. He addresses all of them through their leaders. Zerubbabel was a descendant of King David and the grandson of Jehoiachin, the second-to-last king of Judah. He would have been king himself if Judah had been an independent nation and if the throne of David had not fallen from its former glory. He is mentioned in 1 Chronicles (3:19), Ezra, Nehemiah, Matthew (1:12), and Luke (3:27). In Matthew and Luke he is identified as one of the ancestors of Jesus. Joshua was a descendant of Aaron and is mentioned also in the prophecy of Zechariah (3:1–9; 6:11).

The mention of these two men is evidence of God's faithfulness to Judah, a faithfulness that makes their unfaithfulness all the more inexcusable. God had preserved the lines of both David and Aaron through the awful years that led to and followed the Babylonian captivity. He had preserved those lines not because there was any merit in the house of David or of Aaron, but that his promises, especially the promise to live with his people and to be their God, might not fail.

More importantly, these men in their offices of priest and governor represent Christ himself. It is really through him and from him that this word of God concerning the temple comes, and it is by his grace that the word of God through Haggai bears the good fruit of obedience in the hearts and lives of God's people. Even in the Old Testament he was the great temple builder, and nothing could or would be done without him.

Christ, then, is the governor or king by whom the true temple of God is built. It is as king that he describes the building of the true temple in John: "Destroy this temple, and in three days I will raise it up" (2:19). He is also the great high priest in the house of God (Heb. 3:1–3; 8:1–2), through whom and in whom God is worshiped in his temple and the worshipers themselves are sanctified. Through Zerubbabel and Joshua as figures of Christ, this word of God comes to God's people to insure their obedience.

1:2. Thus speaketh the LORD of hosts, saying, This people say, The time is not come, the time that the LORD's house should be built.

To understand the book of Haggai and its relevance to the New Testament church, we must see that the Old Testament temple, called here the "LORD's house," prefigures the institute or visible church. The institute church is the church on earth manifested in different congregations and denominations. It is the church organized according to the rules of God's word with its pastors, elders, deacons, and members—the church busy with the work of preaching the gospel, administering the sacraments and church discipline, worshiping God, and living together in fellowship.

That this church is the spiritual reality of which that temple was a figure or type is clear from the witness of the New Testament. In 1 Timothy 3:15, the institute church, the church in the world, is given the *same name* as it is here in Haggai: "But if I tarry long, that thou mayest know how thou oughtest to behave thyself in the *house of God*, which is the church of the living God, the pillar and ground of the truth" (emphasis added).

We know that Paul is speaking of the institute church in 1 Timothy 3:15 because he recommends proper behavior in the church, in this case the church or congregation of Ephesus, where Timothy was minister. That church, not the building but the members and officers organized according to the rules of God's word, is the house of God. Of that church Haggai is speaking when he speaks prophetically of the house of God.

Why do the Old Testament temple and the New Testament church have the same name in scripture? They are both called the house of God because they are the place of God's covenant, the house where God and his people live together under one roof and as one family—where he is their Father and Jesus is their elder brother through the communion of the Holy Spirit. This identity of temple and church is our point of contact with the prophecy of Haggai.

God had promised that the temple would be his house, the place of his covenant, in the Old Testament:

> 44. And I will sanctify the tabernacle of the congregation, and the altar: I will sanctify also both Aaron and his sons, to minister to me in the priest's office.
> 45. And I will dwell among the children of Israel, and will be their God. (Ex. 29:44–45)

That promise was first fulfilled when God in the cloud of glory came to the tabernacle in the wilderness.

For the same reason the church is called the house of God in the New Testament. It is the place above all others where God lives with his people in blessed and close covenantal fellowship. It is the place where the family of God meets together, eats together the bread of life, and does the work of God's kingdom and covenant.

If the temple is not the church prefigured and typified, the book of Haggai has nothing to say to us as New Testament Christians. Even if it is true, as the dispensationalists believe, that the Old Testament temple will be rebuilt in Jerusalem during a thousand-year period preceding the end of the world, that temple and the book of Haggai are still of no significance for us. The temple and sacrifices were Jewish and will remain so even if the temple is rebuilt. In that case our interest in Haggai can only be that of idle curiosity.

If the temple is the same as the church in the New Testament, the calling to rebuild the temple is our calling—the calling to be always busy building and rebuilding the church. Of that calling we will speak more fully as we go on, but that calling is carried out in the New Testament in all the work of the church, as well as in the way of church reformation. It is the constant calling of every believer, something the great Protestant Reformation recognized in its description of the true church as "reformed and always reforming." It is the work all God's people do when they are working for the cause and kingdom of God.

Here, in Haggai 1:2, God points out that the reason for the unfinished work on the temple was not the interference of enemies or even the decree of the king, but that the people had given up in the face of many difficulties. They had not entirely forgotten God's command, but they were suggesting that the work should be left to some future and more propitious time. As Calvin suggests, their reasoning was along these lines:

> It is indeed true that the worship of God is deservedly to be preferred to all other things; but the Lord grants us this indulgence, so that we are allowed to build our own houses; and in the meantime we attend to the sacrifices. Have not our fathers lived many ages without a Temple? God was then satisfied with a sanctuary [the tabernacle]: there is now an altar erected, and there sacrifices are offered. The Lord then will forgive us if we defer the building of the Temple to a suitable time. But in the meantime every one may build his own house, so that afterwards the Temple may at leisure be built more sumptuously.[1]

When in Babylon the Jews had sung:

---

1 Calvin, *Commentaries on the Twelve Minor Prophets*, 4:324.

By Babel's riverside we sat in tears,
Rememb'ring Zion's pride in former years,
While on the weeping willows there were hung
The harps our grief had silenced and unstrung.

For they who led us there a captive throng
Required that we prepare for them a song;
Yea, there our captors asked for mirth and praise,
Required a song of Zion's happy days.

O how shall we thus sing at their command
Songs of the Lord, our King, in this strange land?
O Zion, if I e'er forget thy woe,
Let my right hand its skill no longer know.
Yea, let my tongue, I pray, all silent be,
If I do not alway remember thee;
If I prefer not thee, though in thy grief,
Above all other joys my very chief.[2]

But how quickly they had forgotten Zion when once they were back in their own land and busy once again with their plowing, planting, and decorating!

The decree of Artaxerxes and the efforts of the Samaritans to halt the work had been taken by the Jews as a sign that God did not really mean them to be rebuilding the temple at that particular time. They had done what so many do today: taken what they thought was a sign from God and used that as an excuse to neglect God's explicit command. Christians today are also quick to find signs in circumstances that allow them, they think, to live in disobedience to God's explicit commands in the scriptures. If their disobedience is pointed out, they excuse themselves by saying, "But God showed me that this is what I must do." Further inquiry will usually reveal that God's showing them what to do is nothing more than their taking some event in their lives as a sign from God.

---

2 No. 380:1–4, in *The Psalter with Doctrinal Standards, Liturgy, Church Order, and Added Chorale Section*, reprinted and revised edition of the 1912 United Presbyterian *Psalter* (Grand Rapids, MI: Eerdmans, 1927; rev. ed. 1995).

We must remember that God's word is our only guide and rule for faith and life. Nothing from God will ever contradict his word or allow us to live in disobedience to his word. That is not to say that God does not guide us through circumstances, but we must be very careful that we do not misinterpret circumstances and providences, something we most certainly are doing if our understanding of those circumstances leads us into disobedience to God's revealed will in the scriptures.

A young person who is considering marriage might think on the basis of circumstances that God is showing him whom to marry by the fact that God has brought another person into his life to whom he is attracted and who has come to depend on him and be his friend. But if that other person is an unbeliever, the command of God in 1 Corinthians 7:39 stands: "only in the Lord," and no circumstance may be interpreted in such a way that it allows anyone to disobey that rule.

The clearest and perhaps the only way that God guides us through circumstances is when he makes something impossible or does not give us what we have asked of him. Even that, however, is open to misinterpretation, as the example of these Jews showed. Especially the decree of Artaxerxes suggested that it was impossible to build the temple at that time. Nevertheless, they had the command of God, and at no time may difficulties, however great, come into conflict with such a command.

That God calls himself here the Lord of hosts is a reminder that he controlled King Artaxerxes and all their enemies and that the difficulties they faced in the work were really from him. The name Lord of hosts, used twelve times in this book, refers to the fact that all creatures in heaven and on earth—men, angels and devils, righteous and wicked, even inanimate things—are God's army or host, which he commands and through which he brings to pass his own sovereign and unchangeable will.

Here God is reminding the people of Israel that the difficulties they faced were not outside of his control and most certainly should not have allowed them to think they could disobey his command to rebuild the temple. When he refers to them through Haggai as "this people," and not "my people," he evidences his displeasure with their disobedience.

What the Jews were saying to excuse their disobedience, then, was nothing more than pious-sounding hypocrisy that was not much different from what many do and say today. No one will argue that the church today very much needs rebuilding. Its worship is often profane and conducted with no thought for the glory of God, its members are wayward if not completely worldly, its witness is weak and faltering, and its work is misdirected. Yet instead of working to correct these things and to rebuild the church on a more biblical foundation, many point to the times in which we live, which are evil, and use them as an excuse for forsaking the church and its work altogether, or for sitting back and waiting for someone else to fight the battles and do the work that needs to be done.

Many people do not even realize that every Christian is called to that work, as all the Jews were in this verse. Not only the leaders but also the *people* were rebuked for sloth and indifference by Haggai. In that respect too, things are not very different today. The people may not lay all the blame on the ministers, elders, and deacons of the church for the sad condition of the church, when they themselves are not willing to take up the work that needs doing.

1:3. Then came the word of the LORD by Haggai the prophet, saying,

1:4. Is it time for you, O ye, to dwell in your ceiled houses, and this house lie waste?

The Jews had pleaded the difficulties they faced as an excuse for their failure to carry out God's command to rebuild the temple. They pled their poverty, the hostility of the Samaritans, and the decree of Artaxerxes as proof that the time had not come to build God's house. God rebuked them for that, but he also points out in Haggai 1:3–4 the real reason for their failure: a gross materialism that revealed itself in a greater concern for their own houses than for God's house. Worse, their lack of concern for God's house was really a lack of regard for God himself and for the covenant he had established with them.

When they had first arrived back in Judah, they had immediately begun the work of rebuilding the temple and had shown a greater concern for it than for their own homes and farms, though those homesteads were ruined and overrun with weeds and wild beasts. That had changed so that they were now living in homes of their own, but God's house was still waste. God says to them, "You have a place to live and I don't."

We must not misunderstand. That God lived in the temple in the Old Testament does not mean that he was confined to it. Solomon had confessed at the dedication of the temple, "Behold, the heaven and heaven of heavens cannot contain thee; how much less this house that I have builded?" (1 Kings 8:27). God's living in the temple meant that he revealed his glory there as the God of his people, spoke to them there, and kept his covenant with them there. So until the temple was finished there was no place for God to reveal himself to Judah. Judah's lack of concern for the temple reflected, therefore, their attitude toward God and his covenant.

Verse 4 makes it clear that the temple was far from finished at this time. God speaks of it as lying waste. That alone shows that there was much more to all of this than just the difficulties they were using as an excuse. The decree of Artaxerxes forbidding the work had only been passed about five years earlier, but twenty years had passed since the return and little had been done beyond the laying of the foundation. They just did not care about God's house and had spent their time working on their own homes.

Not only was the temple unfinished but, as the words "lie waste" suggest, the site had been largely abandoned, the worship of God at the temple site had ceased, and the work that had been done previously had fallen again into decay and ruin. All that belonged to the temple was no longer of any concern to Judah.

When God speaks of their ceiled houses, the idea is not just that their houses were finished and could now be lived in, but that they had even had time to decorate and furnish their houses. The word used is the same as that used to describe Solomon's work on the inside of the temple and of his own palace (1 Kings 6:9; 7:3, 7). God describes their houses as "ceiled" to show how little concern they had for his house. It was not just that they needed roofs over their heads and places to live, but that their only interest was in their own comfort.

God puts them in their place by the double "you" of verse 4. He is reminding them that he is their savior and they are his people whom he brought out of Babylon and took safely back to the land of Canaan. The words therefore express a certain incredulousness that they, who owe so much to God, should have so little care for his house and have such selfish regard for their own: "*You*, you of all people, let my house lie waste?" May we never be like them.

That the Israelites to whom Haggai preached showed more concern for their own homes than for the house of God is a recurring problem in the church. All too often God's people seem to be concerned only for their own homes and families in their finances, in the use of their time, in their goals, and in their efforts. They have time for everything but the work of the church, so much so that sometimes it is difficult to find men to serve in the offices of the church and to take the lead in building up the church. Families can afford everything but the church budget. Recreations and holidays take priority over worship. Work and other responsibilities keep members from the Bible studies and other meetings of the church. Membership is considered of very little importance, and even where Christians are members of a church, their membership involves very little commitment to God, to his word, or to the work of the church. We, like the Jews, live in ceiled houses while God's house lies waste.

T. V. Moore says it well.

> Men are always prone to put religion off with scraps and leavings, and serve God with what costs them nothing. In the outward things of religion they are much more disposed to work for themselves than for God; and if they have time that cannot be otherwise used, or funds that are not very current, to give them to the treasury of the Lord, and if any larger expenditure of either is urged, to plead that "the time has not come" to do this work. In the inward things of religion the same spirit is shown. The young, the middle aged and the old, all alike procrastinate the great work, on the plea that "the time has not come," the convenient season that, like the horizon, recedes as we advance.[3]

The result is that the church institute is broken down and ruined as the temple was in Haggai's times. Preaching, sacraments, and discipline have fallen on hard times. Worship is seldom carried on in obedience to God's word. The members, instead of being built up, have their faith undermined and weakened. The church is hardly recognizable as the church instituted by

---

3 Thomas V. Moore, *A Commentary on Haggai, Zechariah and Malachi* (Edinburgh: Banner of Truth, 1979), 65–66.

Christ and, if not entirely ruined, resembles more an entertainment facility of some sort, a club, or a social services agency.

The lament of Psalm 74 is as true today as in the Old Testament.

Remember Thy inheritance,
Thy Church, redeemed by grace;
Remember Zion's mount profaned,
Thy ancient dwelling place.
In ruin long Thy temple lies;

Arise, O God of grace,
And see the ruin foes have wrought
Within Thy holy place.

Amid thy courts are lifted high
The standards of the foe,
And impious hands with axe and fire
Have laid Thy temple low.

They have profaned the holy place
Where Thou hast set Thy Name,
The sanctuaries of our God
Are given to the flame.

We see no signs of power divine,
No prophet speaks for Thee,
And none can tell, and none can know,
How long these woes shall be.[4]

All this does not mean we should have no concern for our own houses, whether the building or the lives that are lived there, but God insists that his house is more important than ours and that we can be blessed in ours only when our first concern is for his. That may appear to be very selfish of God and show a lack of love for us, but it really is not so. God's own glory and honor are the most important things and ought to be most important to

---

4 No. 205:2–6, in *The Psalter*.

us, not the least because we cannot be blessed apart from him. Knowing his own glory and our need for him, he insists that his house must be built and that we love it more than our own houses.

1:5. Now therefore thus saith the LORD of hosts; Consider your ways.

1:6. Ye have sown much, and bring in little; ye eat, but ye have not enough; ye drink, but ye are not filled with drink; ye clothe you, but there is none warm; and he that earneth wages earneth wages to put it into a bag with holes.

Having pointed out and rebuked the sins of Judah, God now calls them to self-examination and repentance. He wishes them to see that their ways are sinful and displeasing to him by acknowledging their sin and turning from it. Though God does not explicitly call for repentance, that is what he has in mind. There is no value in considering our ways if this does not lead us to turn to ways that are pleasing to God. It is much the same with God as with an earthly father who says to his child, "Look what you've done." He means, "Do you not see that you have done wrong? You must acknowledge it and turn from your wrongdoing."

We should note too that dealing with our sins always involves a consideration of our ways and a turning from the old ways of sin. The person who considers his ways but goes on in them has not truly repented of his sins. This becomes abundantly clear in verses 7–8, where God does call Judah to new ways of obedience.

This call for repentance and conversion is addressed not only to Judah but also to us. If we have neglected the house of God, the church, or have shown a lack of care for the church as the place of God's covenant, we too must consider our ways and turn from whatever evil we have done. We must consider our ways and see that Judah's sins are ours and that God is speaking to us as well as to them. If we do not, we are as blind and ignorant as they were before this word of God came to them.

God enforces that call to self-examination and repentance by telling Judah that he had been punishing them for their sins, though they were unaware of it. Among the troubles they had suffered were famine, crop failure, bad weather, drought, and disease (see also 1:10–11; 2:17). These troubles had come from God as chastisement for their sin. Not all their problems, therefore, could be blamed on their enemies or on the decree of Artaxerxes. God makes sure that they see these things as his judgment and not as an excuse for forsaking the work of rebuilding.

God says that their crops had been small, so no one had enough to eat and drink or even sufficient clothing. These are the judgments that had been threatened in Deuteronomy as punishment for disobedience: poor crops in Deuteronomy 28:38, lack of food in Deuteronomy 8:10, and insufficient clothing in Deuteronomy 10:18; and God was fulfilling his own word in sending them. Under these judgments it had been as though everything they earned was put in a bag full of holes. And so it is always. Those who will not obey God cannot be and are not blessed and do not prosper.

All this raises the question concerning the relationship between obedience and material prosperity. Especially in the New Testament, is it true that those who live in obedience to God can expect material prosperity or receive it when it comes as a sign of God's favor and blessing? That is a question that needs answering.

Material prosperity, according to scripture, can be an evidence of God's blessing. That would be impossible to deny. In the Old Testament this was far truer than in the New Testament. God made it clear to Israel that prosperity in the land of Canaan was evidence of his good pleasure and that drought and enemies were signs of his displeasure. Even in the Old Testament, however, this was not true absolutely. The book of Job is a lengthy lesson otherwise and shows that prosperity does not equal blessing on a personal level. In the Old Testament therefore, prosperity was a sign of God's blessing *nationally*, but not *individually*. Times of national prosperity did not mean that everyone in the nation was blessed by God, and times of trouble did not mean that every individual was under God's curse.

What is more, there were times when God sent enemies and other troubles for reasons of his own and not because the nation as a whole was living wickedly. Had Hezekiah and Judah been unfaithful when God sent Rabshakeh and the Assyrians against them? There is no evidence that they had. The people of God, therefore, needed the prophets and the word of God to interpret their circumstances and to tell them that God was pleased or displeased with them.

What was true individually in the Old Testament continues to be true in the New. Individual prosperity or the lack of it cannot be interpreted as a sign of God's favorable or unfavorable attitude. God can, as Psalm 73 so clearly teaches, send prosperity as a curse or send evil things for our good, so that all things work together for good to those who love God (Rom. 8:28). There is no common grace or favor or mercy of God in things, and those who think so have no explanation for God's giving prosperity and earthly gifts to the ungodly whom he will send to hell, or for his sending cancer and other ills to those he loves.

However, we often *feel* that God is displeased with us when we are not living in obedience to God and when he, in those circumstances, sends trouble and grief into our lives. It is also possible that, walking in sinful ways, we have all we want and prosper in our wickedness. That is not proof of God's blessing but of God's setting us in slippery places (Ps. 73:18) or filling our mouths while he sends leanness in our souls (Ps. 106:15).

The only nation of God that now exists is a spiritual nation, the church. No earthly nation, not the USA, not Scotland, not the Netherlands, can claim to stand in the favored position that Israel had in the Old Testament, and even Israel in its favored position was a type and foreshadowing of the church. That the church is that favored nation is taught in 1 Peter 2:9: "But ye are a chosen generation, a royal priesthood, an holy nation, a peculiar people; that ye should shew forth the praises of him who hath called you out of darkness into his marvellous light."

The prosperity that God gives his church when she is faithful and obedient is not crops and good weather and freedom from hunger and disease, but spiritual prosperity. The church that is being blessed by God is not necessarily the wealthiest church, but the church in which the members are enjoying all the riches of God's grace and salvation. When the church is not prospering spiritually, when the people of God go spiritually hungry and thirsty, and when they are like the church of Laodicea, spiritually poor and blind and naked, they may certainly conclude that there is something desperately wrong and they must consider their ways.

Let us then, as members of the church, be always busy considering our ways. Let us observe the spiritual condition of the church and not be blind to the fact that God may very well be sending his judgments on the church for her unfaithfulness. Certainly we must not think that because the members of the church are prosperous in material things and because the church has many members and enough in the offerings to pay for all sorts of programs, these things are evidence of God's blessing. The church is blessed when the members of the church are clothed in the spotless robes of Christ's righteousness and when they have the bread of life as the food of their souls and the water of life as their refreshment.

1:7. Thus saith the LORD *of hosts; Consider your ways.*

1:8. Go up to the mountain, and bring wood, and build the house; and I will take pleasure in it, and I will be glorified, saith the LORD.

As in verse 5, the Lord again admonishes his people and calls them to self-examination and repentance with the words, "Consider your ways." We are so sluggish that the word of God must come repeatedly before we are roused from our sloth and begin to do what God requires. In this we are no different from Judah. That God does continue to send his word and its admonitions is itself an evidence of his faithfulness and mercy. Instead of saying, "Enough is enough," he continues to call.

In this second call we see another side of repentance and conversion: that it is not only a turning from sin, but also a returning to God's ways and to God himself. God shows this by calling the people back to the work of building his house and by promising that he will bless them if they do what he requires.

We may never think, though, that God's call, this or any other, implies that we have in ourselves the ability or power to do what God says. There are those who draw that conclusion, but the biblical doctrine of total depravity, that we can of ourselves do no good, and the words of scripture in Galatians 5:17 prove that it is not so, not even with Christians. Of ourselves we can do nothing.

The power to obey is in the command, and it is there because the command comes from Almighty God. Augustine understood this when he said that the command *was* the grace. This is an important truth for us all. It is important for the preacher and elders, lest they begin to think that the power of their preaching and admonitions lies in them, or that the power to obey lies in the members of the church. Then they will begin to preach unsound doctrine, use unbiblical practices, and think themselves to be more than they are. This truth is important for those who hear the word, for they must look to God for the grace and help they need and receive the admonitions of his word.

Here God calls Judah to make the necessary preparation for their work by gathering the timber and stones needed for the work of building. For us, that house is not made of timber and stones; it is a spiritual house. Therefore, the work and the tools that belong to the building of that spiritual house are also spiritual. Nevertheless, to think of the church as a building helps us to understand how we fulfill our calling to build.

When scripture describes that spiritual house, the church, it tells us that the foundation is sound doctrine, the doctrine of the apostles and prophets. The cornerstone is Jesus Christ (Eph. 2:20–22). Believers are the living stones out of which the house is built (1 Pet. 2:4–8), and the love of the brethren is the cement that binds the stones of that house together (Col. 3:14).

Building that spiritual house means, therefore, that we ensure that the foundation is well laid in relation to Christ the chief cornerstone. That foundation is laid through the preaching of the gospel, through prayer for the ministry of the gospel, through our hearing, receiving, and submitting to the truth of the gospel, and through reading and studying the word of God both publicly and privately. In that way every member has a firm foundation for his faith and for his relationship to the other members.

Christ must be the cornerstone in all that word. The preaching must be Christ centered. Prayer must be made in his name and for his sake. The gospel must be believed and obeyed in relation to him. Through the gospel, as well as by worship, prayer, Christian fellowship, admonition, the sacraments, and church discipline, every member of the church is gathered, cut, and shaped like timber and stone and built up in faith and holiness, and all the members built up in relationship to one another.

To this work of building belong both the instruction of the church's children and the work of evangelism, including both the gathering and teaching of new converts. It is not at all difficult to see that these are essential to the work of building the church. Through them the church has the assurance that she not only is well-built for the present but also will continue to be well-built in the future.

To the building up and rebuilding of the church belongs the work of the elders and deacons, each in their offices. When properly carried out, their work of ruling the church and of caring for the needs of the widows, the orphans, and the poor builds up the congregation in which they perform their labors. It becomes another means by which each member grows and all grow together, so that the church is strong and faithful and stands like a fortress against the assaults of Satan.

Even the work done by godly parents in the home fulfills the calling that God lays on his people in Haggai 1, as Paul so eloquently shows in the last chapters of Ephesians. That book describes the church as the body of Christ, and the closing chapters, which have to do with marriage and family life as well as with our daily work and walk in the world, are not unconnected to the rest but are part of what the Spirit has to say about the church. The man who fears Jehovah and walks in his ways will not only experience family blessedness and happiness, but also will see the good of Jerusalem, the church, all the days of his life and will experience peace in Israel (Ps. 128:5–6).

When the church has fallen into ruin and when its foundations are crumbling, the church needs to be rebuilt in the way of church reformation, whether that comes through purifying a church or through leaving an apostate church for one that is faithful. That happened in the sixteenth century through the work of Luther, Calvin, and many others. It has happened on a smaller scale at other times. It is a constant need. It is very much needed today.

The word *edification*, used so often in connection with the preaching and teaching of the church, means "building up" and refers to the strengthening and blessing of each individual believer so that through him the whole church is built up, strengthened, and blessed. Everything that is done in the church must be for "edification" (Rom. 15:2; 1 Cor. 10:23; 1 Thess. 5:11).

The calling to build belongs to every believer. Even the preaching of the gospel and church discipline are the responsibility of everyone, not just of the leaders. All are to be builders in the house of God. None may leave the work to others or be too busy with his own affairs to have any time for God's house.

31

This call God urges upon Judah and upon us, upon Judah in its Old Testament typical form and upon us in its New Testament reality. He urges this call with the promise that he will take pleasure in the house and be glorified in it. For Judah that was the promise that he would reveal himself in the temple they were building as he had done in the days of Moses and of Solomon—that he would be present in all of his power and grace and goodness as the savior of his people.

For us the promise is that the church will be the place of God's covenant, where he is the God of his people and is worshiped and glorified as God. It is the promise that the church will serve the purpose for which God chose her and saved her, the glory of his own great name. It is the promise that he will rejoice in his people and they in him; that he will be their God and Father. Such encouragement is always needed. By such encouragement God himself draws us into and along the way of obedience, not as dumb beasts, but as those who have learned to know him and love him.

The reference to the mountain in verse 8 is an important part of this call to obedience. The mountain is not the place where timber for the building of God's house was to be found, but the place where God's house had to be built. The other prophets also speak of that mountain as the place where the house of God was built (Isa. 2:2; Zech. 8:3).

That mountain in scripture not only symbolizes strength and safety (Ps. 11:1), but it also testifies that the place where God dwells with his people is very high, high above this world and the things of this world. That mountain is symbolic of heaven as the real dwelling place of God with his people. Here too that is the case. God is saying to his people, "Build my house, but build it not only as the place where I will now live among you: build it in the hope of heavenly glory and of life everlasting. Build it as a place in which you are very near heaven and as a place that makes you think of heaven and look toward heaven."

1:9. *Ye looked for much, and, lo, it came to little; and when ye brought it home, I did blow upon it. Why? saith the LORD of hosts. Because of mine house that is waste, and ye run every man unto his own house.*

1:10. *Therefore the heaven over you is stayed from dew, and the earth is stayed from her fruit.*

1:11. And I called for a drought upon the land, and upon the mountains, and upon the corn, and upon the new wine, and upon the oil, and upon that which the ground bringeth forth, and upon men, and upon cattle, and upon all the labour of the hands.

In this closing section of the first prophecy, God elaborates on what he had told the Jews in verses 4–6. He reminds them of their sin, now described as the sin of every man running to his own house. That is really no different than their living in ceiled houses, but it emphasizes Israel's complete abandonment of the work God had given them to do. They had forsaken God's house for their own materialistic attempts to establish for themselves a place in Canaan and to become prosperous (Prov. 1:16; Ps. 119:32). Here the verb "run" is in the present tense and indicates that at the time God spoke they still had not turned from their sins. They were still running every man to his own house.

We may learn from this how difficult it is for us to see our sins. By nature we are blind especially to our own sins and can see them only when they are repeatedly pointed out by God. That is the result of our natural depravity. We ought to remember this whenever our sins are brought to our attention, whether it be by others or by God himself through his word.

God also speaks in more detail of the troubles the Jews had suffered for their sins. He explains their lack of material prosperity by telling them that the drought they had suffered was from him. Later on he speaks of other judgments (2:17), but apparently it was a drought that was the chief cause of poverty and starvation among them. The word "drought" is a play on words not evident in English. The word so translated is the same word used to describe the ruined condition of God's house in verse 9. In effect God says, "My house lies *waste*, and therefore I have called for a *waste* upon the land." In that way he connects the punishment with the sin and shows how the one fits the other.

God even suggests in a figure of speech that the heavens and earth agree with him concerning Judah's sin. Literally verse 10 says, "The heavens over you refrained from dew and the earth refrained from its fruit," as if the creation itself understood Judah's sin and held back its gifts from an ungrateful and unrepentant nation. It was as if the creation had more regard for God than did his own people. How sad it is when we are so spiritually insensitive to the admonitions of the gospel that even the creation becomes a witness against us by its desire to glorify God while we have no such desire.

God is showing the Jews that the drought they suffered was his judgment for their sins. Not only are all things from God, who by his providence controls and directs even the forces of nature, but they are also used to accomplish his sovereign purpose. In this case he had specifically called for a drought upon the Jews and upon their land so they might learn to obey and to see that only through obedience could they enjoy the blessing of God. This drought had been so severe that all the produce and work of their hands had been affected by it. How long it had lasted we do not know, but it had affected the cattle as well as the crops, and even the work of those who did not live as farmers and herders.

Haggai expressly mentions that this drought was a result of God's *call*. The call he speaks of is not the call of the gospel, but what is known in theology as the *vocatio realis*, the call of God through the things that are made. That call of God in the creation is one of the ways in which he makes himself known even today. Paul speaks of that call in Romans 1:19–20:

19. Because that which may be known of God is manifest in them; for God hath shewed it unto them.
20. For the invisible things of him from the creation of the world are clearly seen, being understood by the things that are made, even his eternal power and Godhead; so that they are without excuse.

As we learn from these verses and in the word of God through Haggai, that call, or witness of God in the creation, is a witness against the wickedness of men and has no saving power. Apart from God's grace and the saving work of the Holy Spirit, that call only leaves men without excuse. Here, in order that his people might not only be reminded of their sins but also might obey and turn from their wickedness, that call of God through the creation is accompanied by the call of the gospel through the mouth of Haggai.

For us in the New Testament church, the drought suffered is not a lack of dew and of the fruits of the ground, but a spiritual drought and famine, such as the word of God describes in Psalm 106:15 and in Amos 8:11: "Behold, the days come, saith the Lord God, that I will send a famine in the land, not a famine of bread, nor a thirst for water, but of hearing the words of the Lord." This kind of famine and drought came on the church of the Old Testament in the period between Malachi and the coming of Christ. For four hundred years or more the word of God was not heard in Israel. It comes also on the church today when she does not heed God's word and has no care for his house.

Such famine is common in the church. There was a long spiritual famine in the years before the Reformation. There have been periods of famine in more modern times, especially in the nineteenth century, when apostasy and liberalism held sway in the churches. It is not uncommon these days, for in some places and in some churches the word of God, read, sung, and preached, is hardly to be heard. Sermons, even where they are not open heresy or the words of men, are not biblical—no longer God's word to his people. The Bible is little read and less studied and its fountains of living water little desired, and folk are so dull and so unspiritual that few realize the days of famine prophesied by Amos have come. Certainly they do not see in such famine the judgment of God for disobedience and neglect of his house and covenant.

All this is summed up in the opening words of verse 9: "Ye looked for much, and, lo, it came to little; and when ye brought it home, I did blow upon it." How true that is in these last days. Every Christian expects much when he reads the promises of God's word, but how little profit and blessing there really is. How little peace and happiness, how little knowledge of God, how little enjoyment of the riches of grace and salvation! How little godliness and piety, how little blessing in family life and in marriage! God blows upon our spiritual harvests and leaves us impoverished and hungry.

Insofar as the word of God is still heard and read and prayer offered, little comes of it because for the most part the church is disobedient to God and almost completely disinterested in seeing his house built up. God will not allow us to enjoy the blessings we do have and the spiritual privileges that still remain if we neglect his house and the glory of his name in that house.

1:12. Then Zerubbabel the son of Shealtiel, and Joshua the son of Josedech, the high priest, with all the remnant of the people, obeyed the voice of the LORD their God, and the words of Haggai the prophet, as the LORD their God had sent him, and the people did fear before the LORD.

This historical notice, the first of two in the book of Haggai, is the occasion for a renewed promise of blessing. The obedience of the people to the word of God through Haggai is recorded in this verse and is the reason for the four words of encouragement (two words in Hebrew) that follow in verse 13, "I am with you." The blessing of God is experienced and enjoyed only through obedience to his commands: a simple lesson, but not often learned.

Zerubbabel and Joshua are mentioned first because they took the lead in obeying God's word. They were so important to the work that Ezra 5:2 does not even mention the people but these two men only. Their leadership, however, is not only an example of what every leader in the church, minister, elder, or deacon, ought to do and how he ought to lead the people in obedience to God. It also reminds us that ultimately it is Christ himself who leads us in obedience to God, not only by his own example, but also by giving us the grace of obedience. These men, in their offices, are pictures of Christ as the king and priest of God's people, who atones for all their disobedience and sends them his Spirit to lead them in the right way.

We should note that the name Joshua is really the same name as Jesus, Joshua being the Hebrew version of the name, and Jesus the Greek version. And we should remember that Zerubbabel was of the royal line of David and an ancestor of our Lord. Not only as David's heir but also as governor of God's people he foreshadows him who governs the church in perfect righteousness.

The people are described as the remnant, not as "this people." When they were disobedient they were "this people," but when obedient they are "the remnant." By the name remnant God shows that he still cares for them just as he had when he brought them back from Babylon, even though they were few in number (fewer than fifty thousand had returned from Babylon). He reminds the people that he was aware of their small numbers and their difficulties. For us that name remnant is a reminder that the church is always only a little flock, but that her size and condition are known to God, who helps and preserves her. Her size and insignificance, however, do not in any way excuse her from her calling to be built up as a spiritual temple and a dwelling place of God.

Of this remnant one commentator says:

> Those who are trying to obey God's Word and put it into practice in these days are the faithful remnant. So many who think of themselves as God's people are just asleep to God's voice. They will not stir themselves to leave their "Babylon". They are comfortable in their surroundings. They are not bothered by the ungodliness of their associates. They see no need to obey the call to "come out from them and be separate" (2 Corinthians 6:17).
>
> But the remnant today are characterized by a concern to listen carefully to God's Word and a desire to apply it to their church and personal lives. They are not happy to allow the thinking and desires of the ungodly world to dominate their lives and their Christian fellowships. They are concerned to maintain a purity of doctrine in their churches and they want to do all they can to follow the teaching of the Word of God. Above all, they repent deeply of their past complacency and endeavor to place God's Word at the centre of their thoughts and actions.[5]

That God speaks to the people as well as to the leaders is a striking reminder of the calling that every believer has toward the church. Very often the members think the work of the church is solely the responsibility of the leaders, and the members are content merely to fill the pews and go along with whatever the leaders decide, or to blame them when things go wrong. Especially in the New Testament, because we are all priests and kings (Rev. 1:6), we are all equally responsible for the life and work of the church. We are all builders.

Church discipline is a good example. Long before sins come to the attention of the elders and through them to the attention of the whole congregation, it is the responsibility of every member to be busy admonishing his fellow believers and to be heeding their admonitions. Even when

---

5 Michael Bentley, *Building for God's Glory: Haggai and Zechariah Simply Explained* (Darlington, UK: Evangelical Press, 1989), 43.

a particular sin comes under the formal discipline of the church, it is the responsibility of every member to be praying for the errant brother and admonishing him to turn from his sin and repent. If that is not done, discipline is incomplete, even if the elders fulfill their responsibility and the sinner is excommunicated. Indeed, if it is not done, there is little chance that the elders will continue to do their work in admonishing, censuring, and excommunicating the wayward, or that the wayward sinner will respond to discipline and repent.

That all the people are commanded to be busy with this work of building is striking because in the Old Testament, generally speaking, the ordinary people of God were far less responsible than we. For the most part the work of the Old Testament church belonged to the kings, priests, and prophets whom God gave them, and the people were largely passive spectators in worship, prayer, sacrificing, and serving God.

God tells us again that he sent Haggai, a fact as important today as it was then. Those whom God chooses to bring his word must be sent. Romans 10:15 asks, "How shall they preach, except they be sent?" Unless they are commissioned and sent by God himself, they have no right to expect that the people will listen to and obey the word of God through them.

In the New Testament that commissioning is not direct, as it was in the Old Testament, but comes through the church. Paul and his fellow laborers did not begin their work as missionaries until they were sent by the church in Antioch, and by the Spirit through the church. Those who are not so sent have no commission from God.

When the people feared before the Lord, they understood that God was speaking through Haggai and that they must obey him or perish. This fear is not the terror the ungodly experience when they come face to face with God's wrathful judgments, but an awe and reverence of God, mixed with the love of God, that recognizes one's own sin and creatureliness and the great glory and holiness of God, trembles before him, and obeys him.

Obedience to God is always rooted in the fear of God. Obedience is such a rare virtue in the church because God in all his glory is not known, nor his judgments understood. He is viewed for the most part, if known at all, as one like us, who can be spoken of as we speak of our fellows and who can be met and talked to as one meets and speaks to a casual acquaintance.

Only when the fear of God is born again in the hearts of God's people will obedience to God follow.

The fear of God has his approval and blessing. He proves that in Isaiah 66:2: "To this man will I look, even to him that is poor and of a contrite spirit, and trembleth at my word." The fear of God is pleasing to him because it is always the fruit of his own grace. He cannot and does not despise his own work in his people.

Obedience and fear are produced by the word of God. The word "then" suggests this: "*Then*...[they] obeyed the voice of the Lord their God" (v. 12, emphasis added). The word of God has that power because it comes from God. Its power is the same as the power of God's creative word by which he called the things that were not as though they were (Rom. 4:17). The word of God is its own power and produces that which it requires. That is always a reason the word of God must be preached, and only the word.

1:13. Then spake Haggai the LORD's messenger in the LORD's message unto the people, saying, I am with you, saith the LORD.

The word of encouragement Haggai brings to the people, who were now obeying God's command to rebuild the temple, is simple and short but contains all that the people needed to hear. It is for Judah the promise that the temple, though far less glorious than Solomon's, would be the house of God himself, who would live among his people there, bless them from that place, and keep covenant with them.

God speaks in the present tense and says, "I am with you."[6] He promises to help them and to bless them, but even suggests that his presence preceded their obedience—that he had never truly left them. In no other way could they possibly have obeyed or been stirred up out of their sloth.

The word "then" reinforces the truth that blessing and obedience are inseparable. We like to think we can have God's blessing while going our own way, but it never happens. God is not mocked by sin. What a man sows he also reaps (Gal. 6:7). Blessing is only for those who obey, and the sooner we learn such an important truth the better off we will be. Obedience does

---

6 The word "am" is not in the Hebrew (note the italics), but that is certainly the idea here, as the King James Version (KJV) suggests.

not earn God's blessing, but God works no other way than in the way of teaching his people to obey and then blessing them.

The promise God gives them is the formula for the covenant in scripture. That covenant, the relationship between God and his people, is always described in such terms: that God is the God of his people and is with them and that he takes them as his people. That promise is realized fully in the new heavens and earth (Rev. 21:3), but it is enjoyed now in the church as the body of Christ and the house of God and through obedience to God's commands.

The Lord fulfilled that promise as well. Ezra tells us that the eye of the Lord was on them to protect them from their enemies and to turn the heart of the king to favor their cause, so that the things they needed for the work were provided by his decree. God's words of encouragement are not empty as ours are but are the powerful, helping, saving words of the Almighty. These words are like the words of blessing with which many New Testament books begin. Like them, these words actually bring God's richest blessing to his people.

The words Haggai brought are the heart of every word of encouragement God gives us. He does not tell us what is ahead; he never tries to reassure us by minimizing future difficulties or by promising that there will be none. All he ever really says is this: "I am with you." We must remember his promise in our work and not judge the value and profit by visible results, by the presence or lack of difficulties, or by our own perceptions of the work.

This encouragement is given especially for the church and is given because God loves his church for Christ's sake. Article 27 of the Belgic Confession says this and states:

> This Church hath been from the beginning of the world, and will be to the end thereof...[and] is preserved or supported by God against the rage of the whole world; though she sometimes (for a while) appear very small, and, in the eyes of men, to be reduced to nothing.[7]

---

7 Belgic Confession 27, in Philip Schaff, ed., *The Creeds of Christendom with a History and Critical Notes*, 6th ed., 3 vols. (New York: Harper and Row, 1931; repr., Grand Rapids, MI: Baker Books, 2007), 3:417.

Notice too that this encouragement is given immediately upon evidence of repentance. God does not put his people on probation when they repent of their sins but blesses them without delay, a great encouragement to repentance.

Haggai is called here the Lord's "messenger" and his word of encouragement the Lord's "message." The word "messenger" or "message" is, in the Old Testament, the same word often translated as "angel" (Gen. 16:7; 19:1; etc.). It can therefore be used as a general term for any messenger or for those special messengers who live in the presence of God in heaven. That "messenger" is used here for Haggai is somewhat surprising, because he is always elsewhere referred to as a prophet. It says that the message of comfort he brings is heavenly.

1:14. And the LORD stirred up the spirit of Zerubbabel the son of Shealtiel, governor of Judah, and the spirit of Joshua the son of Josedech, the high priest, and the spirit of all the remnant of the people; and they came and did work in the house of the LORD of hosts, their God,

1:15. In the four and twentieth day of the sixth month, in the second year of Darius the king.

The recorded date is not merely a historical record but proof that the obedience of Judah was without delay, as all obedience to God ought to be. Within a month's time the people were once again busy with God's work after a lapse of about twenty years. Their previous disobedience and sloth had proved them unwilling and unable to obey. The credit for their new obedience must therefore be given to the grace of God, supplied through his prophetic word and worked by his Spirit in the hearts of his people. Haggai's contemporary Zechariah speaks of that in chapter 4 of his prophecy: "Not by might, nor by power, but by my spirit, saith the Lord of hosts" (v. 6).

Nor did the people wait until the decree of Artaxerxes was repealed. The story is told in Ezra 5 and 6. Tatnai, the governor of the territory in which Judah was found, investigated the news that they were building again and wrote the king, suggesting that it would be in his best interest to have the work stopped. He also reported the words of the people who had said that Cyrus had sent them to rebuild the temple. When investigation was made in Babylon, it was discovered that the Jews had spoken the truth. Cyrus had decreed the rebuilding of the temple and sent them to Judah to do it, and so Darius not only forbad the governor from interfering, but also commanded him to give the people everything they needed for the work and for sacrifices. Thus God showed he was with them. But the people did not wait for the matter to be investigated or for the decree of King Darius, but began and continued the work in obedience to God.

That is the nature of true obedience always. It does not wait for men, not even for kings and rulers, nor does it fear them and their decrees, but insists that God has spoken and what he has said must be done, no matter what the consequences. Such obedience has brought much suffering to God's people, but it is the only kind of obedience that is pleasing to God. Obedience that waits for a favorable season or for the approval of men is no obedience at all.

Such obedience is always the fruit of God's own grace, as evidenced in the testimony of these verses. The people and their leaders obeyed because God stirred up their spirits. He did that by his word through Haggai and by the internal work of the Holy Spirit. His word is always quick and powerful and is the way in which he gives his grace to us, not only at the beginning of our Christian life but also daily. May he ever so stir up the spirits of his people to obey and to come and work in the house of the Lord their God, that is, in the church, which is the house of God, the pillar and ground of the truth (1 Tim. 3:15).

A stirred-up spirit is characterized by the fear of the Lord. Such fear is not the slavish terror of those who hate God and who come under his judgments, but a fear that trembles in awe and reverence before the presence of his majesty. Such fear is sadly lacking among Christians today, and this is the result of a lack of knowledge of God and his glory. Such fear is necessary if ever we are to understand the importance of his house and the urgency of our calling to work in his house.

Judah showed this fear of God when they once again put his glory and his house first and set it above their earthly concerns. They showed the fear of God when they turned to God in repentance and conversion, seeing in the Lord's holiness a reason to turn from sin.

A stirred-up spirit is also characterized by quick and ready obedience. That was so in the case of the people of Judah. It is the case also now. A stirred-up spirit does not make excuses, does not procrastinate, does not continue idle, indifferent, and careless, but immediately does what God requires. Such stirred-up spirits are a great necessity in the church of Jesus Christ, for without them, the people of God will continue to run to their own houses.

Such stirred-up spirits are the work and gift of the Holy Spirit and are given when the Holy Spirit applies Christ and his work to God's people. The Spirit, in other words, does not stir up their spirits by some secret and hidden operation but by showing them the loveliness of Christ and of the grace of God in Jesus Christ. God does that here by the promise, "I am with you," a promise that is really the promise of Immanuel, God with us.

Stirred-up spirits are much needed and seldom found in the church today. People are often stirred up, but by the wrong things and for the wrong ends. They can be much stirred up about turning the church into a soup kitchen, about entertaining the young folk, about speaking in tongues and doing miracles, but few are stirred up at the thought of fellowship with the living God or by a desire to see his house built and prosperous, to see him worshiped there as he commands in his word. These Jews, as we ought to be, were stirred up by a desire to obey God, to work in his house, and to enjoy once again the fellowship and blessedness of his covenant in that house. May God by his Spirit so stir up ours.

Note, finally, that for the first time in the prophecy God identifies himself as the God of his people, "their God," not because his favor and relationship to them depend on their obedience, but because it is only in the way of obedience that his people know and can believe that he is "their God." How wonderful, after all his former threats and judgments, to know again and be reassured that he looks with favor on his people and accepts them as his own!

Chapter 2

THE SECOND PROPHECY:
HAGGAI 2:1–9

2:1   In the seventh month, in the one and twentieth day of the month, came the word of the LORD by the prophet Haggai, saying,

2:2   Speak now to Zerubbabel the son of Shealtiel, governor of Judah, and to Joshua the son of Josedech, the high priest, and to the residue of the people, saying,

2:3   Who is left among you that saw this house in her first glory? and how do ye see it now? is it not in your eyes in comparison of it as nothing?

2:4   Yet now be strong, O Zerubbabel, saith the LORD; and be strong, O Joshua, son of Josedech, the high priest; and be strong, all ye people of the land, saith the LORD, and work: for I am with you, saith the LORD of hosts:

2:5   According to the word that I covenanted with you when ye came out of Egypt, so my spirit remaineth among you: fear ye not.

2:6   For thus saith the LORD of hosts; Yet once, it is a little while, and I will shake the heavens, and the earth, and the sea, and the dry land;

2:7   And I will shake all nations, and the desire of all nations shall come: and I will fill this house with glory, saith the LORD of hosts.

2:8   The silver is mine, and the gold is mine, saith the LORD of hosts.

2:9   The glory of this latter house shall be greater than of the former, saith the LORD of hosts: and in this place will I give peace, saith the LORD of hosts.

2:1. In the seventh month, in the one and twentieth day of the month, came the word of the LORD by the prophet Haggai, saying,

2:2. Speak now to Zerubbabel the son of Shealtiel, governor of Judah, and to Joshua the son of Josedech, the high priest, and to the residue of the people, saying,

The twenty-first day of the seventh month would have been the last day of the feast of tabernacles (Lev. 23:34). This was a very appropriate day for Haggai's prophecy that goes on to speak so clearly of the coming of Christ as the true tabernacle of God (2:9). God's word to his people is always timely.

The feast of tabernacles celebrated Israel's deliverance from Egypt. God makes reference to their deliverance in the verses that follow. Their deliverance would have been on their minds, therefore, and must have made the people wonder whether God was really with them as he had been in the days when they came out of Egypt. Then they were a great host; now they were a remnant. Then they had been on their way to a land flowing with milk and honey; now they were having difficulty even subsisting in the land. God assures them in this prophecy that a day would come when he would give such glory that all their years in the wilderness of this world would be forgotten.

His word to them was timely too because it came nearly a month, that is, twenty-seven days, after the people had begun working again on the house of the Lord, and nearly two months after the first prophecy. It came, as will be seen, in response to their discouragement with the work. That it came so quickly is a wonderful testimony to God's watchful care for his people and to his mercy. He no longer chides them for their previous sins or keeps them on probation for those sins, but immediately comes with a necessary word of encouragement through Haggai.

The encouragement God gives has two parts. In the first part God compares the temple they were building to the past temple of Solomon. In the second part he speaks of the temple in the future and of its future glory. In both parts God is reassuring them that the temple they were working on was necessary in the historical development of his house from the time when it was only a tent in the wilderness to the time when Christ would come as the true temple of God, when the tabernacle of God would be with men and he would live with them forever (Rev. 21:3, 22).

The prophecy is addressed not only to Zerubbabel and Joshua but also to the people because they were doing the actual work. They were the ones who faced so many discouragements in that work. God wishes them, therefore, to hear his gracious words directly, not through the mouths of their leaders.

Zerubbabel and Joshua are also named, however, because this prophecy concerns Christ as the one through whom the temple of God would be filled with glory greater than the glory of Solomon's temple, and these men in their offices were the representatives and pictures of Christ to the people. God not only speaks to them and to the people about Christ, therefore, but also holds Zerubbabel and Joshua up as prefiguring Christ. Their glory, though very dim in those days, was still part of the glory God had given in Solomon's days and a hint of the glory that would follow when a greater than Solomon appeared.

2:3. Who is left among you that saw this house in her first glory? and how do ye see it now? is it not in your eyes in comparison of it as nothing?

There are those who think these words are proof that Haggai was among those who had seen and still remembered the temple of Solomon (Ezra 3:12–13), but that cannot be demonstrated either from this verse or from other passages. Nor is it the point of this verse. Haggai is not speaking of himself, but of the people and their discouragement in the work of rebuilding the temple. That they *were* discouraged is clear from the exhortation to "fear ye not" (2:5).

Haggai's words show how the people, having begun the work of rebuilding, were able to see that this temple would be neither as beautiful nor as glorious as Solomon's. It may have been larger than Solomon's (the decree of Cyrus in Ezra 6:3–4 stipulated a temple of sixty cubits wide by sixty cubits high as compared to the twenty cubits wide and thirty high recorded of Solomon's temple in 1 Kings 6:2), but it had nothing of the richness of Solomon's temple.

Solomon's temple had been covered with gold and silver on the inside, and much of the furniture and many of the vessels had also been of precious metal. This was impossible in Zerubbabel's temple because of the poverty of the people. God himself alludes to this lack of ornament in Haggai 2:8. Even that, however, was not the chief cause of the people's discouragement, but rather the lack of some important things from Solomon's temple. Most importantly, the ark of the covenant was not there.

The Jews traditionally listed five things lacking in the second temple: the ark with its mercy seat; the holy fire burning perpetually in the candlesticks and on the altar (Lev. 6:8–13; 24:2); the cloud of glory (1 Kings 8:10–11); the spirit of prophecy; and the Urim and Thummim (Ezra 2:63). Four of these five were indeed lacking (the spirit of prophecy did not depart until after Malachi's work was finished); the glory of this temple was not what it had been. This was evident already when the foundation was laid. Then the older people who had seen and remembered Solomon's temple wept bitterly (Ezra 3:12–13).

Of all these missing items, the ark of the covenant was the most important because it symbolized God's presence with his people in the way of mercy and atonement for sin. Without the ark, it must have seemed to the believing Jews that the temple they were building was worthless.

We know the ark was not in the second temple because it is not listed in Ezra 1:7–11 among the items that the Jews took back with them to Jerusalem. All they took back were some small dishes and other relatively unimportant items. The ark is never mentioned again in scripture, and Jewish tradition confirms that after the captivity the only thing that stood in the holy of holies was a large rock. Probably the Jews did not dare rebuild the ark without an express command from God.

The ark symbolized the presence of God in the house and among his people in the way of blood atonement, for it was there the blood was sprinkled on the great day of atonement. The people must have feared, therefore, they were building the house in vain—that God would not be there and dwell with them there, for he could live among them only in the way of atonement for sin. This prophecy reassures them on exactly that point.

The other ways in which this temple lacked beauty were not unimportant, however. The beauty and glory of Solomon's temple and the gold and silver that adorned it were originally ordered by God for the purpose of reflecting his glory and showing him to be the one who promised to live in the temple, the sovereign lord and owner of all, the King of kings and Lord of lords. This temple lacked all that. Zerubbabel's temple has been described by one commentator as "drab and utilitarian."[1] The people's fears and discouragement were well-founded, and Ezekiel's prophecy of a more glorious temple did not help them.

Instead of glossing over these things, God reminds the people of them through the words of Haggai, all but rubbing their noses in the fact. Thus he shows that he knows their hearts and the fears that were troubling them. The matter was important to him. As he tells the people more plainly in the verses that follow, it was his will that the glory of his house be less than in former times.

This word of God through Haggai ought to touch a sensitive nerve in every member of the church who loves God's house in the New Testament. Everyone who is spiritually sensitive can see that what was true in Haggai's day is also true today. The house of God, the church in the world, is also much less glorious today than it was in former days. Compared to the church in the days of the apostles or in the days of the great Reformation of the sixteenth century, the church today is nothing.

We see the church splintered and divided. We see the glory of her worship waning as the emphasis in worship is less and less on God and more and more on the worshipers. We see worship changed to entertainment and socializing. We see the preaching and sacraments despised and misused and discipline nonexistent. Even the glory of the members, those living stones of which God's house is built, appears as nothing, for their glory is the glory of holiness and that too is departed in these last days. We can understand the feeling of these Jews and their need for encouragement. Their need is also ours.

Lest we be discouraged, God tells us that he is aware of these things and addresses both Judah and us with words of encouragement that keep us busy with the work of building his house, even when, humanly speaking, there seems so little point to it. Those words of encouragement are found in verses 4–9 and consist in a number of distinct though connected promises.

God first encourages them by speaking of the temple they were building as a continuation of Solomon's temple. Though less glorious, it was nevertheless the same house. Both are referred to as "this house." In that way God tells the

---

1 Motyer, "Haggai," 3:987.

people that whatever may be lacking in this rebuilt temple, it is still his house, the same that he commanded to be built in the days of David and Solomon.

God promises also that he will be with his people and dwell among them as in former days (vv. 4–5). He promises a greater glory for his house than that of the house Solomon had built. And he promises that he will give his people peace and deliverance from their enemies in that house, when its glory finally transcends the glory of Solomon's temple. Included in these promises are the promise of the coming of the Holy Spirit, the promise of Christ's coming both in Bethlehem and at the end of all things, the promise of a new heavens and earth, and the promise of the salvation and glorification of his church.

Why was it, though, that God was satisfied with a house that was only a poor shadow of the house Solomon had built? We might think God would want the most beautiful temple possible, and that he would have supplied the Jews with gold, silver, precious stones, and valuable wood, making sure his house would be more beautiful than any kingly palace. Why did he remind the Jews of the poverty of this house and do nothing to enrich it?

The answer to these questions is, Christ was coming and the people had to start looking away from the earthly types and shadows to Christ himself. It would be only a little while before the Desire of all nations would come, and they had to be ready. Haggai 2:9 is a promise of the coming of Christ. He is the true temple of God because he is Immanuel, God with us, the fulfillment of all God's promises to dwell with his people. The people had to stop thinking so much of the earthly house they were building and look for that true temple and its coming.

In verse 3, then, God is reminding the people of the poverty of the temple they were building. He was doing that because Christ's coming was only a little while away, less than five hundred years in the future. To help these Old Testament believers look for his coming, God began to take away the pictures and types, in some cases by removing them altogether, as with the ark, and in other cases by taking away their glory and beauty, as with the temple building. This was necessary because the pictures and types were so attractive that the Jews sometimes became enamored of them. At the time of Jesus' death, for example, they were so enamored of the types and shadows that they could eat the passover lamb the night before Jesus was crucified and never recognize him as the Lamb of God who takes away the sins of the world. They continued to bring their sacrifices without seeing the sacrifice of Christ in them. They continued to worship in the temple without recognizing him as the true temple.

Perhaps God is doing the same today. Perhaps he is taking away whatever external glory the New Testament church once had, making her smaller and more insignificant in the world, in order to prepare us for the second coming of Christ. That would not be at all surprising in light of the fact that this prophecy speaks of the lesser glory of God's house in the latter days. On the basis of this prophecy we have no reason to expect that in the last days the church will become the dominant force in human society, controlling politics, education, and the other areas of human life. Before Christ comes again the New Testament church will be reduced to nothing. Jesus prophesies it when he asks, "Nevertheless when the Son of man cometh, shall he find faith on the earth?" (Luke 18:8).

The wonderful thing is, though, that when the glory of the church is reduced to nothing, as it shall be in the coming days, we have every reason to hope that Christ will soon appear. As Jesus says, "When these things begin to come to pass, then look up, and lift up your heads; for your redemption draweth nigh" (Luke 21:28). The lesser glory of God's house in these latter days, though no excuse for sloth and indifference, is a sign that our final redemption is near.

2:4. Yet now be strong, O Zerubbabel, saith the LORD; and be strong, O Joshua, son of Josedech, the high priest; and be strong, all ye people of the land, saith the LORD, and work: for I am with you, saith the LORD of hosts: 2:5. According to the word that I covenanted with you when ye came out of Egypt, so my spirit remaineth among you: fear ye not.

In these verses God is promising his people that he would reveal his presence and glory in the temple they were building, even though the building itself did not compare to the temple of Solomon. His promise was bound up in the words, "I am with you," words always at the heart of God's covenant with his people, the covenant symbolized and typically realized in the Old Testament temple.

God's covenant is above all a relationship between God and his people that flows from and is part of the relationship between the three persons of the Trinity. The covenantal relationship is consistently summarized in scripture by the promise, "I will be your God, and ye shall be my people," a kind of formula for the covenant in scripture. His promise is expressed in different ways, among them the promise of God to be with his people or to dwell among them.

The relationship between God and his people was symbolized by the temple as the house of God. It was in God's house, through the ministry of the priests as mediators, that God lived with his people, revealing himself as their father and taking them under his fatherly care and counting them as his children.

God has this covenant in mind here, as is clear from the triple use of the name Jehovah in verse 4. Jehovah is preeminently his covenant name, for it speaks of his unchangeable faithfulness to his people. It was also the name that he first revealed when he brought them out of Egypt. It was a name that proved that he was their God and they his people. When he in verse 4 calls himself the Lord of hosts, he simply reminds them that he rules all things as their covenant God.

The reference to God's covenant is further confirmed by the language God uses. He says literally that he "cut" his word with his people when they came out of Egypt, language that is ordinarily used of the covenant in scripture. The Hebrew for making a covenant is almost always "cutting" a covenant, in reference to the solemn ceremony of cutting animals in pieces as part of covenant making (Gen. 15).

God speaks of his covenant also in verse 5, when he describes the promise of Exodus 29:45–46 as the word he had "covenanted" with them: "And I will dwell among the children of Israel, and will be their God. And they shall know that I am the Lord their God, that brought them forth out of the land of Egypt, that I may dwell among them: I am the Lord their God" (Ex. 29:45–46).

Not only does his promise in Exodus include all the elements of the covenant, God's promising to be the God of his people and to dwell among them, but also it was given in connection with the setting up of the tabernacle and the promise of God to meet with the children of Israel there and to speak with them (Ex. 29:42–44). His promise was all the people of Judah needed as an answer to their discouragement. They had to understand, and did understand if they were spiritually minded, that the size and glory of the building they were working on were of little account. What mattered was God's presence.

God's covenantal promise, even today, remains the hope and blessedness of the church. If God is not present in the church, nothing else matters, not the number of members, not the many programs and ministries that are carried on in the church, not the approval of the membership, not the growth of the church. If God is not present, the worship of the church is a sham, its preaching is vain, and membership in it is of no more account than membership in any other worldly organization. Nothing matters so much as the presence of God, the covenant God of his people.

That presence of God is proved in the New Testament church by the pure preaching of the gospel, biblical worship and sacraments, and the carrying out of Christian discipline, what are sometimes called the marks of the true church. Really, though, they are marks not of the church but of God's presence in the church through Jesus Christ. That is the reason too that membership in the visible church is so important. It is not just a matter of loyalty to one or another group of Christians, but a matter of God's presence in Christ.

The promise of this second prophecy is not only the promise of Christ, but is also a promise of the Spirit. Just as it is only through Christ that God is the God of his people and dwells with them, so it is only by the Holy Spirit that the promise is realized. When God, therefore, speaks of his Spirit in verse 5, he is speaking of the Holy Spirit as the one through whom and by whom he dwells in his church and of the coming of the Spirit to the New Testament church at the time of Christ's ascension into heaven.

That does not mean that the Spirit was not present in the church of the Old Testament. God makes it clear that his Spirit always was and always would be among them. He would remain among them. Nevertheless, it is only in the New Testament, through the outpouring of the Spirit as the Spirit of the risen Christ, the one who testifies of Christ crucified and risen, that the promise is fully realized.

The promise of the Spirit here brings us closer to the New Testament, however, for in the New Testament it is through the Spirit and not through types and shadows that God dwells among his people. The word of God reminds us of this in Ephesians 2:22, where the church is described as a habitation of God through the Spirit. Now, in Haggai's time, after the return, the types and shadows through which God was present with his people were beginning to vanish, and he promises to dwell among them by his Spirit, just as in the New Testament.

That promise of the Spirit parallels the promise of Jesus at the last Passover, when he said the presence of the Spirit was so important that it was expedient for him to go away. The Spirit had to come (John 16:7). The Spirit is the one who works in our hearts, giving us what Christ earned for us on the cross. It is by the Spirit that our hearts are stirred up and we fear God. It is by the Spirit that we obey God's commands, and by the same Spirit that we labor in God's house as builders.

So God tells Judah not to fear enemies or other discouragements, but rather to be strong—strong in faith—and to continue with the work he had given them to do. We must understand, though, that God does not just say so, but by this word gives them the hope and faith and strength they needed. His word is always his own power unto salvation and gives what it requires. His word is that for us also.

2:6. For thus saith the LORD of hosts; Yet once, it is a little while, and I will shake the heavens, and the earth, and the sea, and the dry land;
2:7. And I will shake all nations, and the desire of all nations shall come: and I will fill this house with glory, saith the LORD of hosts.

This passage is the key to the whole prophecy of Haggai, not only because it speaks of Christ, but because it reveals the future history of God's house all the way to the end of the world. It says that through Christ the house of God will become ever more glorious until in the new heavens and earth its glory entirely eclipses the glory of Solomon's temple. This takes place through the shaking of all things and through the coming of the Desire of all nations. These two are related, therefore, the coming of the Desire of all nations being the cause of the shaking of all things, and the shaking of all things accompanying the coming of the Desire of all nations and being the means by which God's house receives its greater glory in the latter days.

The shaking includes not only earthquakes and the great earthquake that will destroy this present creation, but also political and social disturbances that God uses to shake the nations and the hearts of men. The destruction of Gog in Ezekiel 38:14–23 is described as a shaking and so is the destruction of Egypt in Psalm 68:7–8. Isaiah too describes the overthrow of Babylon and the return of Israel to Canaan as a shaking (Isa. 13:13–19).

The shaking to which this passage refers takes place in "once…a little while," which Hebrews 12:26–27 interprets to mean "yet once more." The first shaking was at Mount Sinai when God's voice shook the earth only. This shaking would take place once more and in a little while in the overthrow and destruction of the Persian empire by Alexander the Great, but the "yet once more" refers especially to the shaking that takes place in the New Testament in connection with the coming of Christ. This will be shaking of all things in earth and heaven, temporal and spiritual.

Hebrews 12:27 clearly indicates that the final shaking takes place at the end of the world, for when it happens, Hebrews says, the things that are made shall be removed and only those things that cannot be shaken shall remain. However, it is clear from Haggai that this shaking also takes place in connection with the incarnation of Christ, for the coming of the Desire of all nations is first fulfilled then. It was this shaking especially that the Jews looked for in Haggai's days.

How can that be? We should understand that the coming of Christ in scripture is always viewed as one event that includes his incarnation, his coming through the Spirit (John 14:16–18), and his coming at the end of the world. They are in principle one because through the coming of Christ God accomplishes his one purpose in the salvation of his church and the judgment of the world. It was from this perspective that the Old Testament prophets did not even see the different events that are part of the coming of Christ. Joel, when he spoke of blood and fire and smoke and darkness (Joel 2:30–31), did not realize that he was prophesying both of the coming of the Spirit (Acts 2:16–21) and of the end of the world (Rev. 6:12–14).

In reading the prophets one must think of the whole New Testament as one day on God's time clock, the one day in which he finishes his work and cuts it short in righteousness (Rom. 9:28). It is difficult for us, for whom over two thousand years of New Testament history have passed, to grasp that, but the passage of time means nothing to God. One day with him is as a thousand years and a thousand years as a day (2 Pet. 3:8).

There is, then, a progressive fulfillment of this prophecy as there is of most prophecy. It must be so, since to say that prophecy has only a single fulfillment at one point in history is really to say that the prophecy is of no significance for the people of God living at other times. A progressive fulfillment of prophecy means that prophecy is always relevant and always applies to the times in which we live. We live, therefore, in the middle of the fulfillment of the prophecy of Haggai concerning this shaking.

Haggai's "yet once more" is the whole New Testament, and the shaking that takes place once more is fulfilled again and again in the events of the New Testament until finally the word of God in Hebrews 12:27 is completely fulfilled and the things that are made are shaken to pieces and removed. It is fulfilled in the shaking of Herod's heart at the time of Christ's birth, in the shaking of the nations that brought the wise men to Bethlehem, in the preaching of the gospel to the Gentiles when hearts and minds are shaken by the truth concerning Christ. It is fulfilled in the shaking of the earth at the crucifixion, in the outpouring of the Spirit on Pentecost, in every earthquake that shakes this present world, and in the great earthquake at the end of the ages (Isa. 24:19–20; Rev. 6:12).

This shaking, as Hebrews 12 teaches, destroys everything but the things that cannot be shaken (v. 27). It shakes this present creation and all the works of man to pieces so that only God's work remains. It does that in the judgments and destruction that destroy the ungodly and their world and that leave only God's work of grace in the hearts of his people unshaken. But even in them, that which is sinful is removed and only God's work remains, and then they are translated by means of this shaking into the everlasting kingdom of Christ (v. 28).

We must not set our hearts on or labor for those things that can be and shall be shaken and removed. We must seek those things that cannot be shaken, the things of the everlasting and enduring kingdom of Christ, the kingdom that cannot be moved, the kingdom that is centrally the church. Even that shall be shaken, however, and much that does not really belong to the kingdom of Christ shall fall away and be destroyed: those who are hypocrites, the sin of God's people, as well as those things that belong now to the life of the church in the world but will not be necessary in the life to come.

Of this shaking every earthquake is a sign. Each is a beginning tremor of the great earthquake that shall shake the dry land and the sea, the earth and the heavens. Even the nations are and shall be shaken by this earthquake. All but God's work through Jesus Christ shall be shaken to pieces and destroyed. What a thing it is to experience an earthquake in the light of this prophecy of Haggai! An earthquake is a frightening experience in any case, when the ground beneath our feet becomes unstable and unsafe. How much more frightening when it is seen as the beginning of that greatest of all quakes.

This shaking, then, takes place as a revelation of God's righteous judgments on the world in which we live and on those who live in it. Through that judgment comes salvation, however (Isa. 1:27; 1 Pet. 4:17–18), for those things that cannot be shaken shall remain, the things of salvation and of eternal life (Heb. 12:27–28).

Although Hebrews interprets Haggai's words to mean "yet once more," the "yet a little while" of Haggai is also true. Always, beginning with the coming of Christ in Bethlehem, it is but a little while and this shaking is felt again. From Bethlehem to the cross is but a little while; from the cross to Pentecost, from Pentecost to the gathering of the Gentiles, from the ingathering of the Gentiles to the return of Christ, each is but a little while. Even the whole period from the first to the second coming of Christ is but a "little while": just one day, the day of the Lord, in biblical terms.

This shaking accompanies and is caused by the coming of the Desire of all nations. We take this phrase, as in Handel's *Messiah*, to be a reference to the coming of Christ, first in his humiliation and then in his glory as the judge of the living and the dead. The grammar, however, is quite difficult and has caused much controversy and led to very different interpretations of the passage. The Revised Standard Version (RSV) translates, "The treasures of all nations shall come in"; the New King James Version (NKJV), "They [the nations] shall come to the Desire of All Nations"; and the New International Version (NIV), "What is desired by all nations shall come." These are just a few samples of the many differences in translation that are the result of the grammatical difficulties.

The difficulties are two. The word translated in the KJV as "desire" is feminine and plural, so that literally the phrase would read: "The *desires* of all nations shall come." This is the reason some versions and commentators do not find in it a reference to Christ but to the precious things, the gifts, that the Gentiles bring when they come into the kingdom of Christ (Isa. 60:6). The other difficulty is that the verb "shall come" is singular and masculine and does not seem to fit with the word "desire." That second difficulty is not solved, however, by making the subject, "desire," refer to the Gentiles and their gifts instead of to Christ.

Without going into a detailed explanation of the grammar, I believe that the word "desire" does refer to Christ. That the word is plural must refer to all the riches of his glory and grace. The masculine singular verb confirms that the passage is a reference to him alone. It is difficult to see how the passage could refer to anything or anyone else, since the glory of the temple, which is the main subject here, is not in its members but in him.

That he is called the Desire of all nations is a reference to his being lovely to the people of God in his saving grace and power. They say of him: "He is altogether lovely. This is my beloved, and this is my friend, O daughters of Jerusalem" (Song of Sol. 5:16). They say this only by grace, for without grace he is not lovely but despised and rejected. He is called the Desire of all nations especially, however, because he is the fulfillment of everything the temple represented: the covenant and fellowship with God as members of his family under one roof.

He is the "desires" (plural) of the nations because all pleasant and desirable riches are found in him. One of the early church fathers, Ignatius, says of him:

Hungerest thou and desirest food? Long for Jesus! He is the bread and refreshment of Angels. He is manna, containing in Him all sweetness and pleasurable delight. Thirstest thou? Long for Jesus! He is the well of living water, refreshing, so that thou shouldest thirst no more. Art thou sick? Go to Jesus. He is the Saviour, the physician, nay, salvation itself. Art thou dying? Sigh for Jesus! He is the resurrection and the life. Art thou perplexed? Come to Jesus! He is the Angel of great counsel. Art thou ignorant and erring? Ask Jesus; He is the way, the truth and the life. Art thou a sinner? Call on Jesus! For He shall save His people from their sins. To this end He came into the world: This is all His fruit, to take away sin. Art thou tempted by pride, gluttony, lust, sloth? Call on Jesus! He is humility, soberness, chastity, love, fervor: He bare our infirmities, and carried, yea still beareth and carrieth, our griefs. Seekest thou beauty? He is fairer than the children of men. Seekest thou wealth? In him are all treasures, yea in Him the fullness of the Godhead dwelleth. Art thou ambitious of honors? Glory and riches are in His house. He is the King of glory. Seekest thou a friend? He hath the greatest love for thee, Who for love of thee came down from heaven, toiled, endured the Sweat of Blood, the Cross and Death; He prayed for thee by name in the garden, and poured forth tears of Blood! Seekest thou wisdom? He is the Eternal and Uncreated Wisdom of the Father! Wishest thou for consolation and joy? He is the sweetness of souls, the joy and jubilee of Angels. Wishest thou for righteousness and holiness? He is the Holy of holies; He is everlasting Righteousness, justifying and sanctifying all who believe and hope in Him. Wishest thou for a blissful life? He is life eternal, the bliss of the saints. Long then for Him, love Him, sigh for Him! In Him thou wilt find all good; out of Him, all evil, all misery.[2]

He is, as David says, "all my salvation, and all my desire" (2 Sam. 23:5). He is the "chiefest among ten thousand" (Song of Sol. 5:10), the Wisdom of God who is more to be desired than rubies (Prov. 8:11).

Christ is desirable as the one described in Psalm 45:2: "Thou art fairer than the children of men: grace is poured into thy lips: therefore God hath blessed thee for ever." He is desirable as the one in whom are hid all the treasures of wisdom and knowledge (Col. 2:3), as the one who is the only begotten Son of God come in the flesh, as the savior of sinners whose blood is more precious than gold or silver. He is desirable in his person, in his works, and in his gifts—as the one in whom we are chosen of God, as redeemer, deliverer, intercessor, and judge. There is nothing undesirable about him, and the unbelief of many who do not desire him is not a reflection on his glory but a testimony to their blindness.

---

2 Quoted in E. B. Pusey, *The Minor Prophets: A Commentary Explanatory and Practical* (Grand Rapids, MI: Baker Book House, 1974), 2:312–13.

Because the temple in the Old Testament was the place of God's covenant, it was sometimes referred to as the desire of God's people. Thus Ezekiel 24:21: "Speak unto the house of Israel, Thus saith the Lord GOD; Behold, I will profane my sanctuary, the excellency of your strength, the desire of your eyes, and that which your soul pitieth." And Psalm 84 says the same though in different terms: "How amiable are thy tabernacles, O LORD of hosts! My soul longeth, yea, even fainteth for the courts of the LORD: my heart and my flesh crieth out for the living God. For a day in thy courts is better than a thousand. I had rather be a doorkeeper in the house of my God, than to dwell in the tents of wickedness" (vv. 1–2, 10).

Of that temple and house of God Christ is the reality to which the pictures pointed, the true temple of which the Old Testament temple was a shadow. That he is that true temple is clear from John 2:21. There the word of God adds to Jesus' words concerning the destruction and rebuilding of the temple this explanation: "But he spake of the temple of his body." He is the true temple because in him God dwells with his people and is their God. As Paul says in Colossians 2:9–10: "In him dwelleth all the fulness of the Godhead bodily. And ye are complete in him." Literally, in John 1:14 we read that when he came in the flesh he "pitched his tabernacle among us." In the new Jerusalem he is the only temple (Rev. 21:22). He is the "desire of all nations."

The body of Christ that is the true temple of God is not only his own flesh and blood, assumed through the incarnation, but also his church. We are, Paul says in Ephesians 5:30, "members of his body, of his flesh, and of his bones." That is, as Paul also admits in verse 32, a very great mystery, but it is the mystery of Christ and the church. The prophecy of Haggai 2:7 therefore is a prophecy of the rebuilding of the temple not as a house made with hands, but in its true spiritual reality. It is a prophecy of Christ as Immanuel, God with us. It is a prophecy of the realization of God's covenant in Christ.

Thus God's house is filled with glory that far transcends the splendor of Solomon's temple. The glory of that true temple is that of the living God revealed in Jesus Christ as the God of his people. The Lord of hosts guarantees it. As Lord of hosts he uses even Herod and Pontius Pilate, the Jews and the Gentiles, in their rebellion against him and his Son, to ensure that

THE COMING OF ZION'S REDEEMER

that house is built on everlasting foundations and each stone of that house is built chosen and precious in relation to the chief cornerstone.

Because he is the Desire of all nations, the true house of God, that spiritual temple called the church, will be the place of God's covenant not for one nation, the Jews, but for all the nations of the world, for God's elect out of every nation. In that way too, God will add to the glory of his house in the latter days until its glory will outshine the glory of Solomon's temple as the light of the sun outshines a little flickering candle. God prophesies through Haggai the gathering of the Gentiles and the building of a house in which the Gentiles will be no longer strangers and foreigners but fellow citizens, a house built on the foundation of the apostles and prophets and on Jesus Christ the chief cornerstone, a habitation of God through the Spirit.

In all this God speaks as the Lord of hosts, his principle name in the books of Haggai and Zechariah. The word "hosts" in this name refers to all created things (Dan. 4:35) in heaven and on earth, and to the fact that they are all God's great army that serves him willingly or unwillingly, knowingly or unknowingly, and through which he accomplishes his own sovereign purpose. In this case those "hosts" include the heavens, the earth, the sea, the dry land, and the nations, as well as the wealth of the creation. As Lord of hosts he shakes all things. He sends the Desire of all nations.

2:8. The silver is mine, and the gold is mine, saith the LORD of hosts.

Having spoken of the future glory of his house, God reminds the Jews and us that the glory of his house is not in externals but in Christ. When he says that the gold and silver are all his, he refers to all the gold and silver the world contains and asserts his sovereign ownership of them as Creator. He tells Judah that if he had wanted this earthly temple they were building to be decorated with gold and silver, he could very well have seen to it. When he did not give them gold and silver as he had given Solomon, he proved that he did not want this house to be externally glorious. Solomon had used six hundred talents of gold just in the holy of holies in the first temple. This temple was plain and unadorned.

Yet God did provide for them in other ways. When the Jews began again to build, they were confronted by the provincial governor. Tatnai asked what they were doing. Instead of ceasing the work, they continued, and when a formal inquiry was made by Darius, they answered him by letter and told the story of how Cyrus had sent them back for the express purpose of rebuilding the temple. Their letter initiated a search through the records of Babylon that confirmed what the Jews had written, and Darius, instead of ordering the work stopped, commanded Tatnai to leave the work alone and to provide the people with money for the building and with animals and other commodities for the sacrifices (Ezra 5–6).

God did not provide enough gold and silver to make this temple as glorious as Solomon's, but he did prove in these events that he was able to do so if he wanted to. That he did not was a lesson for the people.

There is a lesson there for us as members of the New Testament church. Even now the glory of the church is not to be determined by the number of her members, though the elect will be in glory an innumerable multitude, nor by pomp and circumstance and elaborate liturgies. It is not in a multitude of programs and ministries, not in earthly wealth and power, not in expensive buildings, but solely in the truth that the church is the body of Christ, joined in him to God himself, and beloved of God.

2:9. The glory of this latter house shall be greater than of the former, saith the LORD of hosts: and in this place will I give peace, saith the LORD of hosts.

The latter house to which Haggai refers is not the building that the Jews were erecting, but the true temple, called in verse 7 the desire of all nations. The earthly house built in Jerusalem in the days of Haggai never had any earthly glory. It remained an empty shell, without ark or holy fire or cloud of glory. Some say the earthly building was made glorious when Christ walked in it. The temple in which Christ walked, however, was really a different temple, usually referred to as Herod's temple. Even Christ's presence in it could not make it anything more than it was, an earthly building that was little used for the true worship of God and often used as a den of merchandise.

God, therefore, was teaching his people to look for the coming of Christ by taking away the external and earthly splendor of the temple. Because it would be a little while until the coming of the Desire of all nations, the earthly house, which had been Israel's desire through all its history, had to begin to decrease that he might increase. The attitude of the Jews who lived at the time of Jesus' earthly ministry showed why this was necessary. They were so enamored of the building that they did not recognize or want him who was the true temple of God. They rejected and crucified him, though he was the fulfillment of everything their beloved temple pictured, and so, in the end, God took even the earthly building away from them.

The glory of the true temple would be the promised peace of which God speaks through Haggai. For the Jews peace came through God's protection from their enemies the Samaritans, whom God forced to provide the things necessary for the temple and its worship. The Jews' peace, however, would not last forever, and indeed it soon departed from them. We see that God had a better peace in mind, the blessed peace he gives us through Jesus Christ when he delivers us from our great spiritual enemies, the devil, the flesh, and the world. Indeed, he not only delivers us from their power, but uses them also to provide what is necessary for the building of his house. It is by their hands that the stone rejected and despised becomes the head of the corner. The glory of the true temple for us is the peace we have with God through our Lord Jesus Christ.

That God reduced the external glory of his house in the days of the return, so that the people might look for the coming of Christ, is true today also. In these last days of the New Testament, just as in the last days of the Old, the church is reduced to a remnant and is poor and despised, retaining none of her former glory as in the days of the apostles or of the sixteenth-century Reformation. But God has his purpose in that as he did with Judah. We too, seeing the lesser glory of God's house, must not be discouraged and despair and cease our work. We must continue in the confidence that the Desire of all nations shall soon come and through his coming the house of God will receive all the glory that God has promised, for through his coming the tabernacle of God will come from heaven and God will dwell with us and be our God and we shall be his people (Rev. 21:2–4).

The lesser glory of God's house in the latter days is not a reason for discouragement, then, but a reason for hope, for it is the proof, for us also, that him whom we desire above all will soon come again. Nor may we, as we witness the beginning of the shaking of all things that shall accompany his coming, cease our labors and simply wait for him, but "receiving a kingdom which cannot be moved," we must serve God with reverence and godly fear (Heb. 12:28).

Chapter 3

THE THIRD PROPHECY:
Haggai 2:10–19

2:10   In the four and twentieth day of the ninth month, in the second year of Darius, came the word of the Lord by Haggai the prophet, saying,

2:11   Thus saith the Lord of hosts; Ask now the priests concerning the law, saying,

2:12   If one bear holy flesh in the skirt of his garment, and with his skirt do touch bread, or pottage, or wine, or oil, or any meat, shall it be holy? And the priests answered and said, No.

2:13   Then said Haggai, If one that is unclean by a dead body touch any of these, shall it be unclean? And the priests answered and said, It shall be unclean.

2:14   Then answered Haggai, and said, So is this people, and so is this nation before me, saith the Lord; and so is every work of their hands; and that which they offer there is unclean.

2:15   And now, I pray you, consider from this day and upward, from before a stone was laid upon a stone in the temple of the Lord:

2:16   Since those days were, when one came to an heap of twenty measures, there were but ten: when one came to the pressfat for to draw out fifty vessels out of the press, there were but twenty.

2:17   I smote you with blasting and with mildew and with hail in all the labours of your hands; yet ye turned not to me, saith the Lord.

2:18   Consider now from this day and upward, from the four and twentieth day of the ninth month, even from the day that the foundation of the Lord's temple was laid, consider it.

2:19   Is the seed yet in the barn? yea, as yet the vine, and the fig tree, and the pomegranate, and the olive tree, hath not brought forth: from this day will I bless you.

2:10. In the four and twentieth day of the ninth month, in the second year of Darius, came the word of the LORD by Haggai the prophet, saying,

This third prophecy comes a little over two months (sixty-three days) after the previous, at a time when the people were busy at work on the temple. They would not be finished with the work for nearly four years, so this prophecy comes very early on in the work. It is couched in the form of two questions about the law, really an admonition to the people to keep themselves holy in the work they were doing, and concludes with a promise of blessing should they do so.

As with the previous prophecies, God identifies himself as Jehovah, the covenant God of his people. He does so because they were at work on his house, the Old Testament place of his covenant and of the covenantal fellowship that he enjoyed with them. The name amounts therefore to a reassurance that he would dwell in the house as he had promised and continue his covenant with them (1:8; 2:4–5).

2:11. Thus saith the LORD of hosts; Ask now the priests concerning the law, saying,

Haggai is commanded to go to the priests with a question concerning several points of law, the law of Moses. He asks the priests these questions because they were the official interpreters and teachers of the law. Malachi speaks of the priests and the law in Malachi 2:6–7:

> 6. The law of truth was in his mouth, and iniquity was not found in his lips: he walked with me in peace and equity, and did turn many away from iniquity.
> 7. For the priest's lips should keep knowledge, and they should seek the law at his mouth: for he is the messenger of the LORD of hosts.

Haggai's particular questions are not specifically answered in the law of Moses. In other words, there is no verse that can be quoted as an answer to Haggai's question, but the answer could easily be deduced from the teaching of the law regarding cleanness and uncleanness. The priests to whom Haggai brought his questions apparently had no difficulty finding answers.

However, they answer these questions not only as a matter of personal interest for Haggai, or even for themselves, although the matter certainly had to do with them, but also for the benefit of the people who were doing the work. That is clear from verse 14, where the lesson from the law is applied to the people in the form of a rather sharp word of God concerning the personal holiness of the people in the work they were doing.

That Haggai addresses this matter of holiness does not mean that the people had turned away from God once again and were living sinfully. Of that there is no evidence in the text or in the other accounts of the work. In fact, the blessing that God promises in verses 15–19 is proof that God was pleased with them and with the work they were doing. Nevertheless, the matter of their holiness was so important that it had to be addressed as it must always be addressed in the church of Christ.

2:12. If one bear holy flesh in the skirt of his garment, and with his skirt do touch bread, or pottage, or wine, or oil, or any meat, shall it be holy? And the priests answered and said, No.

The two questions are very similar. The first concerns the meat of the sacrifices, especially of the sin offerings (Lev. 6:25–26) that were offered in the temple. Haggai calls that meat "holy flesh." That meat was apparently carried at times by the priests in the skirts of their robes, perhaps to the altar to be burned there, or from the altar to be eaten by the priests or the people. When they were carrying the meat, Haggai asks, would contact with the robe in which they carried the meat make other things holy? He mentions other food especially. That is, if the robe brushed against other food, would the holiness of the sacrificial meat be transferred to the items that were touched by it or by the robe in which it was carried?

The priests were able to answer that question correctly with the simple answer no. Leviticus 6:27 indicates that the garment itself or any other vessel in which the meat was carried would be holy, but the rest of the priests' answer, that the holiness would not be transferred from garment or vessel to other things, is not specifically given in the law. They must have deduced their answer from those passages in the law that indicated that the people, who often ate the meat of the sacrifices, were not themselves necessarily made holy by the holy food they ate. It was possible for them to eat and to remain unholy though they were in contact with the holy meat of the sacrifices.

Haggai is talking about ceremonial holiness, the holiness of things that were set apart and kept separate for the worship of God. Ceremonial holiness was a picture of true spiritual holiness, for true holiness is being set apart and dedicated to the service and worship of God. Haggai, then, is pointing out through this question and its answer that holiness is not transferred by mere external contact with holy things.

The Jews often fell into that way of thinking. They thought that because they had the temple and the sacrifices and the worship of God, and because they attended faithfully on those things, they were different and better than the nations around them. They thought they were holy merely because they were in contact with holy things. In thinking this way they were not unlike Christians today.

The principle is a very important one in the New Testament, for it applies to the bread and wine of the Lord's supper and to the water of baptism. It also applies to any circumstances in which we have external contact with holy things: worship, the scriptures, prayer, church membership, the preaching. In all of these circumstances we come into very close contact with holy things, but the holiness of those things, which is the holiness of God himself, is not transferred by mere external contact.

We must think of the holy flesh in terms of the sacrifice of Christ that alone redeems and sanctifies, the Spirit of the living God, and God's own divine saving power. These things are carried to us in the preaching of the gospel, the sacraments, prayer, church membership, and all of the other means God uses to give his saving grace to his people, just as the holy flesh was carried in the priest's garments. The holy things of God are wrapped in these things, and we come into contact with them only through these "wrappings."

The holiness of the things of God lends a certain holiness and separateness to the external forms in which they are wrapped, but the holiness is not further transferred by mere contact with those forms and wrappings. Hearing the preaching, attending the worship of God, being a member of the church, does not make someone holy. This first question and its answer therefore add up to a warning against formalism and dead orthodoxy in worship and church membership.

The principle that is illustrated by this first question and answer also applies in other everyday circumstances and relationships of life. In marriage between a believer and unbeliever, for example, the believer must have no expectation that his own holiness will be transferred to the unbeliever simply by virtue of their marriage. Those who sin by marrying unbelievers often justify what they do on the ground that their marrying the unbeliever will have a good influence on the unbeliever, but that is a vain hope in light of this word of God. Holiness is not transferred in that way.

We learn that same principle in the rearing of our children. Our own personal holiness and the holiness of godly and pious family life are not automatically transferred to every child who is born in a covenantal home. Holiness does not come in that way, no more than it did in the case that Haggai cites to the priests. There are those who seem to think so, who seem to think that being born and raised in a covenantal home automatically makes the children of that home holy and guarantees their salvation. But that is not what the promise of the covenant, "I will be your God and the God of your children," means.

Holiness comes only as a gift of God purchased by the blood of Christ and given through the Holy Spirit. The Lord hints at that in verse 14 when he points out that the people of Judah were in themselves and in all the works of their hands unholy. Even their sacrifices were not holy without the work of God's Spirit and the blood of Jesus that was symbolized by those sacrifices. Nothing but the blood of Jesus applied by the Spirit of holiness makes anyone holy.

2:13. Then said Haggai, If one that is unclean by a dead body touch any of these, shall it be unclean? And the priests answered and said, It shall be unclean.

The second question Haggai asks of the priests is really the opposite of the first. He asks concerning ceremonial uncleanness. There were many ways in which a Jew could become ceremonially unclean, all of which made it impossible for him to enter the temple or present his sacrifices. One way a person could become unclean was through contact with a dead body (Lev. 22:4). In that case a person had to wash himself and was unclean for the rest of the day (vv. 6–7).

Haggai's question concerns contact with someone or something that had become unclean. Would the uncleanness be further transferred by contact with something or someone who had become unclean? The answer of the priests, the opposite of the previous answer, was that the uncleanness would be transferred. The person who had become unclean would make everything he touched unclean, even the food he ate.

To understand the point of the answer, we must see that the ceremonial uncleanness of which the law spoke was a picture of the defilement of sin. The laws about uncleanness certainly were used by God to protect the physical health of his people, but the main reason for them was to teach spiritual truths, in this case to teach them about the pollution of sin. Anything that made a person unclean pictured the uncleanness of sin, and contact with death made a person unclean because death is the punishment of sin.

The point of the question and its answer, then, is that while holiness is not transferred by external contact with holy things, there is the real danger that the pollution and defilement of sin is so transferred. To use an example, one drop of filth will pollute much water, but many added drops of clean water will not make a container of filthy water clean.

The application of this is best seen in scripture's commands to God's people to keep themselves separate from the ungodly (2 Cor. 6:14–18). The danger is always that they become polluted and unholy. They must therefore maintain what is sometimes called the antithesis, their spiritual separation from the ungodly and from their ways.

This separation means they may not marry the ungodly (1 Cor. 7:39), may not be joined to them in any equal union (2 Cor. 6:14), and ought not have fellowship with them (Eph. 5:7–12). They need not go out of the world altogether as Rome teaches (1 Cor. 5:10), but there must be a clear separation between them and the world, especially of a spiritual character. If that separation is not maintained, it is not the unholy that will be made holy, but the holy that will be profaned and made unclean.

This principle applies to marriage and is the basis for the forbidding of marriage between believer and unbeliever (1 Cor. 7:39). It applies to friendships and business relationships and is the reason that in these relationships the believer may not be unequally yoked with the unbeliever (2 Cor. 6:14). It applies to the places one goes and the company one keeps, to a person's recreations and endeavors. It is the fundamental principle of the antithesis and the reason the believer must always "come out from among them, and be...separate" (2 Cor. 6:17).

2:14. Then answered Haggai, and said, So is this people, and so is this nation before me, saith the LORD; and so is every work of their hands; and that which they offer there is unclean.

God now comes to the point of this lesson from the law. The people, in spite of the fact that they often thought otherwise, were not holy by virtue of their contact with the ordinances and types in which the holy things of God were wrapped up: the sacrifices, the priesthood, the worship of God in the temple, even the temple itself.

God is especially concerned, however, with the "work of their hands." That work includes their agricultural labors. It also includes their religious labors, especially the work they were doing in the temple. Unholy themselves, they would certainly pollute everything they touched. They had to learn that they were not holy, not acceptable to God, by virtue of anything in them or by their own works.

There is an important principle here. Without holiness of heart and life, even our ordinary labors are polluted and defiled and unacceptable to God. That is the other side of the biblical principle that all things must be done for his glory. How much more, then, the efforts we put forth in religious and spiritual matters. Holiness is not optional. It is essential, and a lack of holiness among Christians is without doubt the reason the work of the church so often does not prosper but fails.

That leaves the question, how could they be holy? That question is not directly answered by Haggai but only implied. Holiness was necessary, for unless they were made holy, their polluted and unclean hands would defile and make unholy everything they touched, including the house of God they were building and the sacrifices they would be offering in that house.

How then might they be holy? The answer is implied in what God says about their sacrifices. Those sacrifices had no value in themselves and could not make the worshipers holy (Heb. 10:1–2). Nevertheless, God had commanded them and required them because they pointed to the one sacrifice of Jesus on the cross, a sacrifice that not only justifies (provides forgiveness), but also sanctifies (v. 10). Only by that sacrifice is the work of our hands holy and acceptable to God, and that includes the work we do in his house as builders.

The answer is further implied in the last verse of this prophecy, to which we will come in due course. There God promises his blessing, and it is by that blessing alone that we have anything at all, including holiness. His blessing comes through the sacrifice of Christ, offered once for all. It is the payment for sin and the purchase price of every blessing of salvation, including the holiness without which no man can see the Lord (Heb. 12:14).

2:15. And now, I pray you, consider from this day and upward, from before a stone was laid upon a stone in the temple of the LORD:

God tells the Jews to look back to the time four months before when they were still neglecting the house of God and the work of building the house, to the time before one stone had been laid on another in the temple, when only the foundations had been laid and nothing more done. He tells them not only to think back but also to "lay it to heart." He is going to remind them once more of the judgments they had suffered through drought and crop failure, and in verses 18–19 he is going to promise a good harvest and renewed blessing.

He wants them to know that disobedience brings wrath and that his favor and blessing come only in the way of obedience. God's people like to think they can have it both ways. They think they can enjoy the blessing and favor of God while continuing in ways that are displeasing to God. They think that their salvation and status as people of God guarantee them uninterrupted enjoyment of God's goodness.

It is not so. Salvation itself cannot be lost, but the enjoyment of it can be lost when we disobediently and hardheartedly go our own way and refuse to hear the warnings of God's word. The lack of true happiness and peace that is the lot of so many Christians today, the terrors of conscience they suffer, their troubled lives, mental anguish, and coldness are more often than not the result of their not laying to heart what God says here.

That he says it again is due to our forgetfulness and constant inclination to backslide and return to our old ways. Never does it happen that God's people are without the need for the admonitions and warnings of God's word. By those admonitions he draws them on in the way of obedience and does not let them fall back into neglect, carelessness, and sin.

2:16. Since those days were, when one came to an heap of twenty measures, there were but ten: when one came to the pressfat for to draw out fifty vessels out of the press, there were but twenty.

2:17. I smote you with blasting and with mildew and with hail in all the labours of your hands; yet ye turned not to me, saith the LORD.

Now God speaks more fully of the judgments that he had sent Judah, making it clear that they had suffered not only drought, but also inclement weather and various crop diseases that had left them unable to maintain themselves in the land. Harvests that were half or less than half of the expected amounts would have made it nearly impossible for them to live. God speaks especially of the grain and the wine, the two staples on which they subsisted, and of the fact that even these harvests had failed.

He speaks in more detail because the Jews now recognized that the drought, the mildew, and the hail had all come from him as judgments. He reminds them of those judgments not only to warn them against backsliding, but also by way of contrast to direct them to the blessing that would follow. He would give them an abundance that, in contrast to their previous poverty and struggle, would very obviously and clearly represent his blessing and prove to them beyond doubt that their obedience was the way of blessing.

God reminds them too of their former blindness and insensibility under his judgments, not because they were again guilty of these sins, but because there was always the danger that they would lapse again into them. That this is always the tendency of God's people the long and sad history of the Old Testament church abundantly proves. Yet by the grace of God these Jews had learned their lessons, and God who is merciful does not hold their former sins against them but promises the things that they needed.

We learn these same lessons not so much when God sends drought and crop failure as when he sends spiritual drought and a dwindling harvest of souls, as well as storms of trouble and the corrupting mildew of growing sinfulness in the church and in our own lives. The nation today is the church, and the blessings of God are no longer represented by national prosperity, but by spiritual prosperity and wealth.

2:18. Consider now from this day and upward, from the four and twentieth day of the ninth month, even from the day that the foundation of the LORD's temple was laid, consider it.

2:19. Is the seed yet in the barn? yea, as yet the vine, and the fig tree, and the pomegranate, and the olive tree, hath not brought forth: from this day will I bless you.

The twenty-fourth day of the ninth month was the date of this prophecy, at the beginning of the work that was being done on the temple. It was also the day that the foundation of the temple had been laid, many years previously. God tells the people to consider the period of time from the laying of the foundation of the temple to the present and all that had happened during that time. Then they would see that they were blessed in building God's house and unblessed in neglecting that work.

At this time Zechariah had also begun to prophesy. His first prophecy is dated to the previous month (Zech. 1:1), and a few months later he would come with further words of encouragement in his night visions. God's people, then, were well provided for in help and assurances of blessing.

Haggai reminds them of their former neglect to establish beyond doubt that the sufferings they had endured in the land were all due to their failure to build the temple—that God could not and would not bless them as long as they did not finish that work. The temple, after all, was his house, the place where he revealed himself among them as their covenant God and Savior. And though God does not dwell in temples made with hands, yet in the Old Testament, because the true temple had not yet been built in Christ and in his death and resurrection, this earthly house was the symbol of his presence. So much was this true that without it he would not and could not dwell with them.

He speaks to them when the harvest had not yet been gathered. The question about seed is a rhetorical question through which God reminds them of the coming harvest. The produce of the vines and the fig trees was not yet gathered. Yet God promises to bless them, and to bless them from the day that they had begun to work in his house. This prophecy would have been delivered in December, just after the early rains and the sowing, so there would have been no evidence as yet of God's blessing on the fields, and in the light of previous years' experience, little hope for a good crop.

He would not let them forget the close relationship between his house and their blessedness. Nor may we. Though the church of God is nothing like she was in former days and is often despised and forsaken by her own members, she is still the place of God's covenant, the place where our great God reveals himself as the God and Savior of his people. No more than the Jews, then, can we be blessed when the house of God lies in ruins. Then we do not have the preaching of the gospel as the food of our souls, nor the shelter of his gracious presence from the storms that threaten to destroy our spiritual prosperity, nor protection from the spiritual diseases that corrupt our lives and destroy the harvest of blessing he has promised.

We need not expect the church ever again to be as glorious as she was in the days of the Reformation or in the days of the apostles, though we may certainly pray that she will be. The book of Haggai emphasizes the lesser glory of God's house in the latter days, as does the prophecy of Zechariah (4:10). Yet our calling to labor in building and rebuilding does not cease until Christ comes and builds his everlasting and glorious kingdom in the new heavens and the new earth. To neglect that calling is to neglect the command of God and to show that we care little for his gracious presence among us, and so to forfeit his blessing.

Let us labor faithfully and diligently, each in the place God has given, in prayer, in the preaching of the gospel, in the reading and studying of God's word, in the instruction of our children, in missions, and in all the other ways God's spiritual house is built, its stones gathered and shaped and fitted into place, and it built up as a habitation of God through the Spirit. We have the promise of God's blessing to encourage us and to show us that he is pleased with the labors of our hands. We have that blessing in the outpouring of the Spirit, who comes as rain upon dry ground to refresh our souls. We have it in the great harvest of the blessings of salvation, in the fields white for harvest, in shelter from the winds of change that blow in church and state, and in protection from the enemies of the church.

What an encouragement! Well may we sing the words of Psalm 126 as we wait for the harvest God has promised us.

Although with bitter tears
The sower bears his seed,
When harvest time appears
He shall be glad indeed;
For they that in the sowing weep
Shall yet in joy and gladness reap.[1]

_____

1 No. 358:4, in *The Psalter*.

Chapter 4

THE FOURTH PROPHECY:
Haggai 2:20–23

2:20   And again the word of the Lord came unto Haggai in the four and
       twentieth day of the month, saying,

2:21   Speak to Zerubbabel, governor of Judah, saying, I will shake the
       heavens and the earth;

2:22   And I will overthrow the throne of kingdoms, and I will destroy the
       strength of the kingdoms of the heathen; and I will overthrow the
       chariots, and those that ride in them; and the horses and their riders
       shall come down, every one by the sword of his brother.

2:23   In that day, saith the Lord of hosts, will I take thee, O Zerubbabel,
       my servant, the son of Shealtiel, saith the Lord, and will make thee
       as a signet: for I have chosen thee, saith the Lord of hosts.

2:20. And again the word of the LORD came unto Haggai in the four and twentieth day of the month, saying,

Haggai's fourth and last prophecy comes on the same day as the previous word of God, nearly four months after Haggai began his work. It is addressed to Zerubbabel, the local civil ruler of the returned captives, and is a word of promise that concerns the coming of Christ as the king of God's people and the great temple builder.

That this prophecy comes on the same day as the last means that it also is a promise of blessing. By this final promise God shows how he will give and increase the blessings promised in the previous prophecy. The prophecy therefore looks ahead to even greater blessings that would come through Christ as king.

Motyer gives a very beautiful overall view of this final prophecy:

> The final verses of his book reveal Haggai as the literary equivalent of an impressionist painter—he gives general tone and effect without elaborate detail. His colors are the thunderstorm and the earthquake (2:21), revolution (2:22a), clashing armies (2:22b-c), and civil conflict (2:22d). As in a carefully composed picture, where every stroke is designed to lead the eye to what is central, so here too the focus is like a shaft of sunlight illuminating one item—a ring shining on a finger (2:23).[1]

2:21. Speak to Zerubbabel, governor of Judah, saying, I will shake the heavens and the earth;

There is some question about Zerubbabel's father. He is usually identified as Shealtiel, or Salalthiel, but there is one passage in the genealogy of 1 Chronicles where Zerubbabel is identified as the son of Pedaiah (1 Chron. 3:17–19). There are different possibilities with regard to this difficulty; perhaps the most likely is that Pedaiah was Zerubbabel's actual father, but that after he died, his widow married Salalthiel or Zerubbabel went to live with

---

1 Motyer, "Haggai," 3:1000.

Salalthiel, who would have been his uncle. When God continually identifies him as the son of Shealtiel, he reminds us of his descent from David.

That is the important thing. Zerubbabel was of the royal line of David through Jeconiah (1 Chron. 3:16, Matt. 1:11–12), more familiarly known in scripture as Jehoiachin (2 Chron. 36:8–9). This king, himself a wicked man, was the grandson of King Josiah of Judah, and he only ruled for three months before he was taken away to Babylon and imprisoned there. It was through him, though, that the royal line of David was continued. Zedekiah, the last king of Judah, a brother of Jehoiachin, was blinded and had all his sons killed when Jerusalem was taken and destroyed by Nebuchadnezzar. Of him we hear no more in scripture, but Jehoiachin was released from prison by the Babylonian king Evil-merodach and given a position of authority in Babylon (Jer. 52:31–34). It was then and there that he must have married and had children, thus preserving the royal seed of David as God had promised. Zerubbabel was his grandson, born in Babylon.

Zerubbabel as a descendant of David and heir to the throne of David is addressed here. There is a recognition of his royal prerogative in his identification as governor of Judah, and the promise that God makes him is really a promise to restore the throne and power of the line of David. In doing this, God says, he will overthrow all earthly thrones, particularly those that had taken captive and oppressed David's descendants.

Zerubbabel functions in this prophecy as a type of Christ. In his office and as the seed of David, he foreshadows the great ruler of God's people and the Seed of David *par excellence*. Christ is the servant of Jehovah who is addressed here through Zerubbabel, and it is Christ more than Zerubbabel who will be made like a signet on the hand of God. It is he who is chosen by Jehovah of hosts to defeat those who have made war against God's people and he whose throne will be over all.

God's first word to Zerubbabel connects this prophecy with the second, for once again God speaks of the great earthquake that will destroy this present world, the earthquake that would accompany the coming of the Desire of all nations. That earthquake would begin at the first coming of Christ and would culminate in the complete destruction of all things.

The shaking of all things has as its purpose the removal of temporal things, so only those things that are God's work may remain. Here that shaking is the occasion for raising the throne of David from the low condi-tion into which it had fallen and making it glorious above all other thrones and kingdoms.

That the result of this shaking would be the restoration of David's throne shows that this prophecy is about Zerubbabel only as a type of Christ, for in the lifetime of Zerubbabel the throne of David was never restored to its former glory. He was only governor, and he is so identified in the prophecy. Though that was a fairly high position in the Persian empire, he was nev-ertheless under the rule of the Persian kings, and his position was of little account in comparison to that of David, his illustrious ancestor.

Before Christ came, the throne of David would lose even the little glory that it had in the days of Zerubbabel and be reduced to nothing. By the time Jesus was born, the line of David had been reduced to one woman (Luke 1:34), and the descendants of David had no authority or power any lon-ger. At that time some of the Jews, the Herodians (Matt. 22:16; Mark 3:6; 12:13), had given up on the line of David and become supporters of bloody and cruel Herod and his family as the God-appointed rulers of Israel and the continuation of God's promises to David.

2:22. And I will overthrow the throne of kingdoms, and I will destroy the strength of the kingdoms of the heathen; and I will overthrow the chariots, and those that ride in them; and the horses and their riders shall come down, every one by the sword of his brother.

Now God says that the prophesied shaking would be the judgment and destruction of the nations. They and their thrones would be removed by this shaking, and only the throne of Christ, which cannot be shaken, would remain. God is speaking here of all earthly kingdoms, as is clear from the description of them as the kingdoms of the heathen. There are no other kinds of kingdoms that belong to this present world. They will all be destroyed.

The reference to horses and chariots is a reminder of the temporal might of these kingdoms. Such indications of earthly power were forbidden to the Jews (Deut. 17:16; Ps. 20:7). Their trust and strength was Jehovah him-self, who here foretells the ruin and fall of all the kingdoms that depend on earthly might.

The shaking began at the first coming of Christ. Even Herod recognized the threat Christ posed to the kingdoms of this world, as did Pilate. This shaking was fulfilled in principle at the cross, which is the judgment of this world, and it is finished in the destruction of all things and the judgment of the nations that takes place at the end of the world when Christ returns.

God accomplishes this shaking throughout history by keeping the nations at war with one another. Persia was the ruin of Babylon, and Greece of Persia, and Rome of them all. Even the kingdom of antichrist, which God will use to bring down all other power and authority, will be destroyed in this way. Those kings and kingdoms that give their power to the Beast will in the end turn against the Beast and the whore and make them desolate and naked (Rev. 17:16–18).

The warfare among the nations, through which the kingdoms and their power come down, every one by the sword of his brother, is not only the means by which God controls and directs these kingdoms and prevents their premature development. It is also the way in which he brings his judgment on the nations, culminating in the great battle that will immediately precede the coming of Christ (Rev. 16:14; 20:8).

That shaking, God says to Zerubbabel, would be the way in which he would once again exalt the throne and power of David and bring all nations under the sway of David's scepter. Only, of course, God is speaking not of David personally, nor of David's descendant Zerubbabel, but of Christ, in whom all the prophecies of David and his throne have their fulfillment: "He shall be great, and shall be called the Son of the Highest: and the Lord God shall give unto him the throne of his father David: And he shall reign over the house of Jacob for ever; and of his kingdom there shall be no end (Luke 1:32–33).

Christ is the king who rules forever on that throne. His kingdom alone is everlasting. He is Lord of lords and King of kings.

2:23. In that day, saith the LORD of hosts, will I take thee, O Zerubbabel, my servant, the son of Shealtiel, saith the LORD, and will make thee as a signet: for I have chosen thee, saith the LORD of hosts.

If the day referred to, the day of the shaking of all things, is indeed the great day of the Lord, the day that begins with Christ's coming in the flesh and ends with his return for judgment, the reference here is not so much to

Zerubbabel as to Christ. Indeed, it must be so, for this is a promise of the restoration of the kingdom and of the royal rule of David's descendants, something that did not happen during the days of Zerubbabel but only happened when Christ came, born of the seed of David, destined to rule forever on the throne of David.

The signet that God speaks of is a royal ring used to seal documents, both to make them tamper-proof and to indicate that they contained the decrees and statutes of the king. It is in the reference to a signet that we find the evidence that God is indeed speaking of the royal line and throne of David, really the line and throne of Christ. The description of Zerubbabel, and of Christ in him, shows his royal power to be the power of God himself. Zerubbabel and all David's descendants were nothing more than that—signets on the hand of the King of kings, evidences of the power of him who had given the throne to David in the first place and the one to whom the throne and all its power belonged.

This promise reverses a previous threat made to Zerubbabel's grandfather, Jehoiachin (also called Jeconiah or Coniah): "As I live, saith the LORD, though Coniah the son of Jehoiakim king of Judah were the signet upon my right hand, yet would I pluck thee thence" (Jer. 22:24). There we see not only that this signet is on the hand of God, whose power and authority the kings of Judah represented, but we see also God's faithfulness to David. To pluck the ring from his hand would be to take the kingdom away from David, and though he removed from David all the trappings and power of the kingdom, he never abandoned his promise but fulfilled it, and in a way unlooked for: in Christ.

In the verse, Zerubbabel, the political leader of the Jews, is both the person addressed and the subject of the prophecy. Insofar as this promise applies to Zerubbabel himself, it is a promise that Zerubbabel will be God's representative, the representative of his own divine rule among the people, and that God will use him in the work of rebuilding.

That God is speaking to and about Christ under the figure of Zerubbabel is also clear from the prophecy. Zerubbabel is referred to not only as a signet, but also as the servant of Jehovah and as his chosen. Both of these are important names for Christ, especially in the prophecies of Isaiah to which Haggai very obviously has reference (Isa. 41:8–9; 43:10; 44:1–2).

A passage that very obviously refers to Christ as the chosen servant of the Lord is Isaiah 42:1–3, which is quoted in reference to Christ in Matthew 12:18–21:

1. Behold my servant, whom I uphold; mine elect, in whom my soul delighteth; I have put my spirit upon him: he shall bring forth judgment to the Gentiles.
2. He shall not cry, nor lift up, nor cause his voice to be heard in the street.
3. A bruised reed shall he not break, and the smoking flax shall he not quench: he shall bring forth judgment unto truth.

Such passages prove beyond any doubt that it is not finally Zerubbabel but Christ of whom the prophet was speaking.

That Christ is spoken of as a signet ring on the hand of God means that he is the representative of the kingly majesty and power of God. He is such in a way Zerubbabel could never be, for Zerubbabel was a man, and Christ is the one in whom dwells all the fullness of the Godhead bodily (Col. 2:9).

There is a passage in the New Testament that comes very close to describing Christ in the same terms used here. Hebrews 1:3 speaks of Christ as the express image of the person of God. Those words "express image" literally describe the stamp or impression left by a signet ring. That is what Christ is as God's Son come in the flesh, as the bodily representative of God himself.

God speaks of Zerubbabel and through him of Christ as king to show how completely he would provide for his people and fulfill the promises he had made to them. Not only would Christ be the true temple, the desire of all nations, but he would also be the great temple builder. To rebuild and keep in repair the house of God was the role of Solomon and of every king of Judah. Solomon fulfilled that task by building the first temple. Men such as Jehoshaphat and Asa kept the temple open and in repair, and later kings such as Hezekiah and Josiah restored it when it had fallen into disrepair.

We see in Zechariah 4:7–9 that God has Zerubbabel in mind as the builder of the temple:

7. Who art thou, O great mountain? before Zerubbabel thou shalt become a plain: and he shall bring forth the headstone thereof with shoutings, crying, Grace, grace unto it.

8. Moreover the word of the LORD came unto me, saying,

9. The hands of Zerubbabel have laid the foundation of this house; his hands shall also finish it; and thou shalt know that the LORD of hosts hath sent me unto you.

Now God assures his people not only that the temple would be built and that its glory would be complete, but also that he would take the responsibility for seeing to it that the work was finished. He would do so not only in this earthly house that they were working on, but also in the true temple, the body of Christ, the church. We have then in this closing prophecy of Haggai God's word to the church of all ages that he, through our Lord Jesus Christ, builds his church. That does not take away the calling we have in his house, nor leave us idle, but the work is really his and is accomplished through his Son, even when he uses us in that work.

That Christ is both temple and builder is somewhat difficult to understand but reminds us that he is everything. He is both altar and sacrifice, both sacrifice and sacrificing priest, both priest and temple, both temple and temple builder. That he is both temple and builder is clear from John 2:19, 21: "Jesus answered and said unto them, Destroy this temple, and in three days I will raise it up. But he spake of the temple of his body." There is no other name but his.

He builds the temple in all of his work. In his death and resurrection he lays himself as the cornerstone; through his Spirit he gathers the living stones of which that house is built and builds them on himself. He preserves his church in the world and brings her to perfection in glory, where his house is built unmoveable and everlasting. In that house he is the one in whom and through whom God dwells with his people as one family, taking them as his people and revealing himself as their God and giving them the blessed vision of his own face in the face of his beloved Son.

The promise of Christ under the figure of Zerubbabel is the encouragement needed by every temple builder from now until the house of God is finished. It is the guarantee that our labors are not in vain in the Lord

(1 Cor. 15:58). It is the assurance that we too are chosen and precious in God's sight and that we will receive from him every blessing necessary for the work he has given us to do. It is the assurance that God's promises are not failing even when it looks so to us—when all appears hopeless and the cause of God is very small in the world, left like a hut in a garden of cucumbers and like a besieged city (Isa. 1:8).

In Zerubbabel the Jews could no longer see anything of the former splendor and power of the throne of David. Zerubbabel was nothing more than a minor official under a foreign king. And because he had none of the power of David, there was in him no assurance that the temple would be built, and when built, be preserved. It is little different in these last days, now that Christ has gone away for a while and his church is left alone in the world, small and despised. No wonder so many have abandoned and given up on the church and forsaken her to run to their own homes. They have, however, forgotten that nothing depends on us, that God has promised to build his church through our Lord Jesus Christ, and that in him our labors are not in vain.

God promises to raise up the throne of David once again, not in Zerubbabel, but in him who is to come. God will make him the visible representative of the power and dominion of God himself and thus ensure the building and preservation of his house. That promise we have as we take up in the New Testament, in the work of the church and of church reformation, the building and rebuilding of the house of God.

Let us not be slothful in these latter days, but build as we have been commanded—build in the assurance that the true temple, the Desire of all nations, will come soon and that God will build his church with a view to that coming day of Christ, when the church shall be, as the body of Christ, part of that true temple. Let us build in the hope that the true temple of God will remain when heaven and earth and all things in them are shaken and removed.

May our prayer be the prayer of Calvin as we consider what Haggai, through the inspiration of the Spirit of God, has written for our admonition, upon whom the ends of the world are come.

Grant, Almighty God, that...as thou hast favoured us with so great an honour as to make us the framers and builders of thy spiritual temple, may every one of us present and consecrate himself wholly to thee: and, inasmuch as each of us has received some peculiar gift, may we strive to employ it in building this temple, so that thou mayest be worshipped among us perpetually; and especially, may each of us offer himself wholly as a spiritual sacrifice to thee, until we shall at length be renewed in thine image, and be received into a full participation of that glory, which has been attained for us by the blood of thy only-begotten Son. Amen.[2]

---

2 Calvin, *Commentaries on the Twelve Minor Prophets*, 4:326.

PRIEST UPON THE THRONE

THE PROPHECY OF ZECHARIAH

Thus speaketh the LORD of hosts, saying,
Behold the man whose name is The BRANCH;
and he shall grow up out of his place,
and he shall build the temple of the LORD:
Even he shall build the temple of the LORD;
and he shall bear the glory,
and shall sit and rule upon his throne;
and he shall be a priest upon his throne:
and the counsel of peace shall be between
   them both.

—Zechariah 6:12–13

Introduction to Zechariah

Zechariah's prophecy is one of the most remarkable writings of the Old Testament, remarkable for its amazing prophecies of Christ and its similarities to the book of Revelation, which it also matches in difficulty of interpretation. There is no other book of the Old Testament like it in its involved symbolism, its prophetic unveilings of the glory of Christ, and its view of the last times. These unique characteristics are, however, the reason the prophecy was and is of such enormous importance to the people of God.

In its prophecies of Christ it continues to remind us that Christ is everything to us, a message much needed in days when the Christ of the scriptures is again "despised and rejected" (Isa. 53:3). In its symbolism it carries us all the way to the end of the ages and shows us what may be expected then regarding opposition to the kingdom of Christ and God's preserving and protecting grace. This too we must know as we watch and wait for our Lord's return.

In prophesying of Christ, the whole book speaks of him who is "all our desire" (2 Sam. 23:5), but there are especially three passages that stand out and that are the "hinges" on which the rest of the book turns.[1] These passages are historical because they focus on real historical persons, but they are nonetheless prophetic. The passages are chapters 3:1–10, 6:9–15, and 11:1–17, where Christ is presented in turn as the justified one, the royal priest, and the rejected shepherd. These passages will be referred to in this commentary as "story passages" since each of them tells a story.

The main theme of the book, however, is found in chapter 6:9–15, where Christ in the figure of Joshua the high priest is shown to be the great

---

1 *Hinges* is the word used to describe these passages in Meredith G. Kline's *Glory in Our Midst: A Biblical-Theological Reading of Zechariah's Night Visions* (Eugene, OR: Wipf and Stock, 2001). The book must be used with care, however, since it is seriously marred by Kline's concessions to higher criticism and his insistence on reading the Old Testament in the light of heathen mythology and legal practice. Indeed, I am reluctant to mention him and his book at all, since his heretical views of creation are responsible for the demise of that biblical doctrine in Westminster Seminary and the churches it serves. His analysis of the structure of the book is useful, however, and was helpful to me in my study of Zechariah.

priest-king of his people, the embodiment of the counsel of peace, and the reason for every revelation of God's wrath against the nations and of his faithfulness to his people. In this especially the book of Zechariah is different from Haggai and Malachi, for the focus of Haggai's prophecy is Zerubbabel as a type of Christ the king and temple builder, while Malachi's prophecy focuses on Christ the great prophet and messenger of the covenant.

The Author

Zechariah was a contemporary of Haggai but probably younger. Though among those who returned from exile in Babylon about seventeen years before his prophecies, he is still identified in chapter 2:4 as a young man. Perhaps this is also the reason his prophetic career was longer than Haggai's, Haggai's lasting for under three months and Zechariah's for twenty-five months.

He is said to be the son of Iddo (Ezra 5:1; 6:14) and the son of Berechiah the son of Iddo (Zech. 1:1). Since the Hebrew does not distinguish between father and grandfather, Berechiah must have been his father and Iddo his grandfather, but it is impossible to determine why his father, Berechiah, is not mentioned in the book of Ezra. Some think his father died before the return, others that his father was banished from the priesthood, but since scripture does not tell us anything about Berechiah it is useless to speculate. In any case, Zechariah's ancestry is mentioned several times in his prophecy to establish his credentials as a prophet and therefore as one whose prophecies had to be received as the word of God. They also confirm his place in the priesthood as one who could speak with authority on matters that concerned the priesthood and the temple.

He is not the same Zechariah the son of Barachiah of whom Jesus speaks in Matthew 23:35. That Zechariah, identified in 2 Chronicles as the son of Jehoiada the priest, lived at the time of Joash king of Judah and was a martyr during the reign of Joash (24:20–21). He lived about three hundred years before the author of this prophetic book.

The author of the prophecy and Iddo his ancestor are identified in Nehemiah 12:16 as priests who came to Jerusalem with Zerubbabel, and Zechariah as one of the chief priests (Neh. 12:1, 12). It may even be, though the record is not clear, that he was a near relative of Joshua the high priest. In any case his priestly ancestry explains his emphasis on the priesthood and on priestly matters. Yet the fact that we know so little about him is important too, for it shows that he, personally, is of very little importance in comparison to Christ, the eternal priest-king.

The references in Ezra show Zechariah to be a contemporary of Haggai and concerned, as Haggai was, with the rebuilding of the temple in the years after the return to Jerusalem. Ezra says, "And the elders of the Jews builded, and they prospered through the prophesying of Haggai the prophet and Zechariah the son of Iddo" (Ezra 6:14). Zechariah's concern, though, is not as much with the rebuilding of the temple as it is with the priests who served in the temple and who were pictures of Christ, the eternal high priest of his people.

Zechariah's name means "Jehovah remembers," but since no importance is attached to his name in the prophecy, it is best not to place too much emphasis on it. Since scripture interprets itself, it is usually best not to attach too much significance to things that scripture does not single out, though the book certainly does show that Jehovah, the God of the covenant, always remembers his people.

There are those who argue that the last half of the book of Zechariah was written by someone else. In support of such contentions, mention is made of unique words found in the second part of his prophecy and of the different character of that last half of the prophecy. Nevertheless, for those who believe in inspiration, the fact that his name is found at the beginning of each half of the prophecy is enough (1:1 and 7:1). All speculations concerning another author can immediately be dismissed as the idle fancies of those who do not believe the inspiration and infallibility of scripture.

The Date

The book dates itself to the second and fourth years of Darius, king of Persia (1:1, 7; 7:1). This is confirmed in Ezra 4:24: "Then ceased the work of the house of God which is at Jerusalem. So it ceased unto the second year of the reign of Darius king of Persia," at which point Ezra speaks of the work of Haggai and Zechariah.

A comparison of Haggai and Zechariah shows that Zechariah began to prophesy about two months after Haggai. Haggai's first prophecy is dated to the sixth month of the second year of Darius, Zechariah's first prophecy to the eighth month of the second year of Darius. Haggai was first because it was his business to stir up the people to the work of rebuilding God's house, while Zechariah's work was encouraging them in what they were doing. This Zechariah does with many wonderful promises.

Darius king of Persia is not the same man as Darius the Mede, the conqueror of Babylon, mentioned in Daniel 5:28, 31. He had died eighteen years earlier and had been followed by Cyrus the Great, who sent the Jews back to Judah. Cyrus had, in turn, been succeeded by several other kings.

The Darius of Haggai's and Zechariah's days is Darius I Hystaspes, also known as Darius the Great, who ruled Persia from 521 to 486 BC. Zechariah prophesied around 520 to 518 BC, about twenty years after the return from captivity, during the early years of Darius's rule.

The first half of the book is dated to the second year of Darius and the second half to the fourth year of Darius. This explains the similarity between the two halves, for though the first part is in the form of symbolic visions, its message is repeated in the second half of the book. Zechariah brought the same message twice, the first time in his symbolic visions and the second time as a kind of interpretation and reinforcement of those visions.

At the time of his visions the temple was not yet built. Zechariah 4:9 says, "The hands of Zerubbabel have laid the foundation of this house; his hands shall also finish it." For this reason Zechariah is mentioned in Ezra as one of the prophets whom God used to encourage his people in the work of rebuilding. Nevertheless, Zechariah's main concern is not with the temple, but with the priesthood. Thus, though Zerubbabel, prince of the house of David and heir to the throne of David, is not absent from the book (4:1–10), Joshua the high priest appears more often (3:1–10; 6:9–15).

Zerubbabel appears because Zechariah is concerned with the union of the priestly and kingly offices and Zerubbabel was a descendant of King David, but it is especially Joshua the high priest who appears in the book as the type of Christ, the great priest-king. He, the type, and Christ whom he represents are the guarantee that God's temple will be rebuilt and will forever be the center of the worship of the true God.

The Arrangement

The structure of the book of Zechariah is far more complex than that of Haggai and Malachi. The book is divided into two main parts, the first part including Zechariah's visions (1:1–6:8) and the second part in the form of more straightforward teaching and exhortations called "burdens" (7:1–14:21). In each of these main parts of the book the theme of the church's salvation is developed, first in the seven visions and then again in the two burdens.

These two parts are interrupted three times by story passages, first the story and vision of the reclothing of Joshua the high priest (3:1–10), then the story of the crowning of Joshua (6:9–15), and finally the story of the rejected shepherd (11:1–17). In each of these Zechariah is a participant, his participation increasing with each story until in the third he is the central figure.

The first story, which is also a vision, divides the other six visions into two groups of three. The second story separates the visions and the burdens, and the third divides the two burdens. These stories tie the whole book together chronologically and thematically by focusing the attention of the reader on Christ and his work, since he is really the main figure in the book of Zechariah. These stories prefigure Christ as the priest "clothed in righteousness," the great priest-king, and the rejected shepherd-priest. He is the link therefore that ties the different parts of Zechariah's prophecies together; the one who makes these prophecies the gospel of the grace of God.

Each of the visions is introduced by a reference to seeing: "I saw...," "I lifted up mine eyes and looked...," "he shewed me...," and so on, and especially by the word "behold," a word that reminds us each time it is used that what Zechariah saw was symbolic and wonderful.[2] The two burdens are introduced with the same words, "The burden of the word of the Lord..." Each of the story passages is identified by its historical content and by Zechariah's participation in the action.

There is further parallelism between the visions and the burdens, since each of the burdens falls into three parts that each have the same message as one of the visions, though not always in the same order. I have tried to show this parallelism in the chart on page 92. But as is often the case in our English version of the Bible, the chapter divisions do not reflect the actual structure of the book, and this is reflected in the chart.

---

2 The word *behold* is not found at the beginning of the fourth vision, which is also the first story passage, the vision of Joshua's reclothing. It is not used there because the vision is as much historical as symbolic.

PARALLELISM IN THE PROPHECY OF ZECHARIAH	
THE VISIONS	*THE BURDENS*
Introduction to the visions (1:1–6)	Introduction to the burdens (7:1–8:23)
First three visions (1:7–2:13)	First burden (9:1–10:12)
First vision: Christ on a red horse (1:7–17)	Part two: Christ on a donkey (9:9–10)
Second vision: judgment on the heathen (1:18–21)	Part one: judgment on the heathen (9:1–8)
Third vision: restoration of God's people (2:1–13)	Part three: restoration of God's people (9:11–10:12)
Second story: the crowning of Joshua (6:9–15)	
Fourth vision and first story: the reclothing of Joshua (3:1–10)	Third story: rejection of Zechariah as shepherd (11:1–17)
Last three visions (4:1–6:8)	Second burden (12:1–14:21)
Fifth vision: the Spirit promised (4:1–14)	Part two: the Spirit promised (12:10–13:9)
Sixth vision: judgment on apostate Israel (5:1–11)	Part one: judgment on apostate Israel (12:1–9)
Seventh vision: everlasting blessedness (6:1–8)	Part three: everlasting blessedness (14:1–21)

The first three visions as well as the first burden focus on the deliverance of God's covenant people from their enemies and the gathering of the church out of all nations as part of this deliverance. The last three visions as well as the second burden focus on the purifying and sanctifying of the covenant people. In each case the historical incidents or stories that interrupt these different parts, Joshua in his filthy garments and the rejection of the shepherd, explain the need for this work of grace.

It is as though God says in the first three visions and the first burden, "I will deliver my people from the nations that oppress them and will even save a remnant out of these nations." Then in the fourth vision and the story of the rejected shepherd he says, "But my people are in themselves no better than the heathen into whose hands I have given them. I will therefore work by my grace and Spirit upon them and make them both righteous and holy." And that is the message of the last three visions and the second burden.

In these last three visions and the second burden the emphasis falls not only on Christ, but also on his Spirit. These are the only parts of the book of Zechariah that mention the Spirit, and there he is spoken of more often than in any of the other minor prophets. Nevertheless, even in these parts Christ, whose Spirit he is, remains the central figure. Christ is the one through whom God works. Christ, seen typically in the persons of Joshua and Zechariah and more plainly in some of the prophecies, is the fulfillment of all the types found in the prophecy of Zechariah. Zechariah preaches the gospel of Christ to all ages.

Zechariah and Revelation

It is impossible not to notice the similarities between the books of Zechariah and Revelation, and indeed, Revelation borrows more than any other book from Zechariah's prophecies, both by direct quotation and by using its symbolism. Revelation opens with a quote from Zechariah 12:10 (Rev. 1:7) and borrows Zechariah's symbolism in nearly every chapter, ending as Zechariah does with a vision of the new Jerusalem. There is not only parallelism in the structure and content of Zechariah, therefore, but also parallels between Zechariah and Revelation.

Among the many parallels are the references in Zechariah to a measuring line (1:16; 2:1), horns (1:18–21), the seven eyes of Jehovah (4:10), the woman whose name is wickedness (5:7–8), the red, black, white, and piebald horses of chapter 6:1–8, and many elements in the descriptions of Jerusalem in chapters 8 and 14. The more extended parallel sections are Zechariah 2:1–13 and Revelation 11:1–2, both of which describe the measuring of Jerusalem; Zechariah 4:1–14 and Revelation 11:3–14, both of which focus on the two olive trees and candlesticks; Zechariah 5:1–11 and Revelation 18:1–24, both of which record the destruction of the great whore, Babylon; Zechariah 6:1–8 and Revelation 6:1–8, where we read of the different colored horses by which God executes his sovereign decrees in all the earth; and Zechariah 8 and 14 and Revelation 21 and 22, which describe in graphic terms the future glory of the church, the new Jerusalem.

Besides such obvious parallelism, there is also a parallel in Zechariah's presentation of the enemies of Zion in his early visions: the heathen nations and the horns they lift up against God's people (visions 1 and 2), the woman whose name is wickedness who is taken away to the land of Shinar (vision 6), and Satan himself (vision 4). These are the same enemies that appear in the second half of the book of Revelation: the antichristian world power under the form of horned beasts (Rev. 13), the great whore and false church whose name is "Babylon the great" (Rev. 17), and the great red dragon (Rev. 12). In both books scripture not only shows us these enemies of Christ and his church, but also shows us their destruction.

Zechariah's prophecies must therefore be interpreted in connection with those of John the apostle. The clearer light of the New Testament shines back on the Old Testament prophecies of Zechariah and helps us to understand them. At the same time, Zechariah's Old Testament prophecies provide a historical foundation for the book of Revelation and help us to see that the prophecies of Revelation reach backward as well as forward—that the things prophesied there have always been fulfilling in him who is and was and is to come (Rev. 1:8).

Chapter 5

THE INTRODUCTORY EXHORTATION:
Zechariah 1:1–6

1:1   In the eighth month, in the second year of Darius, came the word of the Lord unto Zechariah, the son of Berechiah, the son of Iddo the prophet, saying,

1:2   The Lord hath been sore displeased with your fathers.

1:3   Therefore say thou unto them, Thus saith the Lord of hosts; Turn ye unto me, saith the Lord of hosts, and I will turn unto you, saith the Lord of hosts.

1:4   Be ye not as your fathers, unto whom the former prophets have cried, saying, Thus saith the Lord of hosts; Turn ye now from your evil ways, and from your evil doings: but they did not hear, nor hearken unto me, saith the Lord.

1:5   Your fathers, where are they? and the prophets, do they live for ever?

1:6   But my words and my statutes, which I commanded my servants the prophets, did they not take hold of your fathers? and they returned and said, Like as the Lord of hosts thought to do unto us, according to our ways, and according to our doings, so hath he dealt with us.

The first six verses of chapter 1 are an introduction to the visions that follow as well as to the whole of Zechariah's prophecy. These opening words speak of Judah's sins, of her need for conversion, and of the permanence of God's word. Judah had not listened to God's word through his prophets and had gone into exile. God's mercy had brought her back again, but she had fallen back into sin and needed God's unchangeable word through the prophet Zechariah. The new generation of returned captives had to turn from their sins and be converted to God, or they too would come under God's judgments.

Implicit in these opening words is that God did not expect the present generation to be any different from previous generations. Indeed, there were already indications that the hardheartedness, deafness to the word of God, and disobedience, characteristic of the generation that went to Babylon, were still to be found among the descendants of that generation.

Over against such a sad background of apostasy God continues to reveal his faithfulness and mercy and to comfort his people through Zechariah's visions. Before he gives them those comforting visions, however, he calls the people to repentance in order to show them that his mercy and comfort are only for those who repent and turn from wickedness. Hengstenberg suggests it was necessary for Zechariah to begin with a call to repentance "in order that these consolations might not be usurped by any to whom they did not belong, and abused to the increase of their carnal security."[1] Luther says, "Because this prophet purposes to administer comfort very freely, therefore he strikes a very sharp and earnest note at the outset."[2]

As the prophecies of Zechariah unfolded, it became increasingly evident that the majority of the people were unfaithful and wicked and only a small remnant remained faithful. The wickedness of the majority was finally revealed in the rejection of Zechariah as shepherd (chapter 11), a rejection that foreshadowed the rejection of the great Shepherd himself. For that

---

1 E. W. Hengstenberg, *Christology of the Old Testament and a Commentary on the Messianic Predictions*, trans. Theod. Meyer and James Martin (1872–78; repr., Grand Rapids, MI: Kregel Publications, 1956), 3:271.

2 Quoted in H. C. Leupold, *Exposition of Zechariah* (Grand Rapids, MI: Baker Book House, 1974), 19.

majority these opening words stand as a very sharp warning. God's warning word had gone unheeded in previous generations, but it had come to pass nevertheless. The same would happen again.

1:1. In the eighth month, in the second year of Darius, came the word of the LORD unto Zechariah, the son of Berechiah, the son of Iddo the prophet, saying,
1:2. The LORD hath been sore displeased with your fathers.

Zechariah's ancestors are mentioned by way of establishing his authority as a prophet and his right, as priest and descendant of priests, to speak of priestly matters. The important thing, though, is that he brings the word of Jehovah ("the LORD"), the unchangeable one, whose word remains the same in every generation, both in judgment and in mercy. He is the unchangeable judge of those who do not hear and obey his word and the unchanging covenant God of his people, unfailingly faithful and of never-ending mercy.

These opening words, therefore, called the people to hear and obey or suffer the consequences. And because Zechariah brought the unchanging word of Jehovah, these opening words are as much for us as for the Jews. We too must hear and obey "the word of the Lord" through Zechariah.

The prophecy begins with a reference to God's great anger against Israel, a rather shocking way to begin! Zechariah says, "God has been very angry. He was very angry with your fathers, and therefore you had better be sure that you are not like your fathers. Many in your fathers' days thought themselves secure in their Jewishness and false piety and said, 'The people of God, the people of God, are we.' Yet God was angry with them and sent them into exile. Beware, then, that the same judgments do not come on you."

What a warning to all those who are complacent and at ease in Zion, who think their formalism and outward religiosity are pleasing to God, and who pride themselves on their Christian upbringing or some conversion experience, but who do not truly repent of their sins. This warning is as much needed today, perhaps even more so, as it was in the days of Zechariah.

The anger of the Lord is often misunderstood. On the one hand some find in it proof that God's attitude toward his people and the unrepentant wicked is forever changing. He is the God of predestination, of election and reprobation, but he nevertheless reveals himself in the gospel as one who loves the reprobate wicked and desires their salvation and who is capable of hating his people, at least until they come to repentance and conversion.

On the other hand, some think that electing love means the Lord cannot be angry, very angry, with his people and punish them in anger. They find in scripture's teaching concerning election an excuse for their carelessness and wickedness. They think that God's unchangeable love for his people means that he overlooks their sin, is never angry with them, and will not punish them for their evildoing.

Anyone who has experienced a parent's love for his children knows that love can be and often is very angry, although love itself does not change. Anger does not necessarily mean that the person who is angry hates the one with whom he is angry, although the object of that anger may think so (Isa. 49:14–16). In Israel God had revealed his anger by sending his people into exile. That anger, although it revealed his hatred of the reprobate element in Israel and resulted in their scattering among the nations, was nevertheless an anger that chastised and restored the elect, brought them back to their own land, and was merciful to them—a loving anger.

God had showed his anger in the destruction of Jerusalem and the temple. In doing so he had, in effect, cast the people out of his presence and destroyed the place where he had promised to live among them. Were it not for his unchanging faithfulness, Judah could well conclude that he had annulled his covenant with them.

Moore vividly describes the result of Jehovah's anger:

The land that once flowed with milk and honey was now lying in widowed desolation and barrenness. The hills on whose green terraces once hung the climbing vine and the generous olive, were now bare and rugged. The cities and villages once echoing to the busy hum of a happy people, were now in ruins, and all over their once beautiful land had God written Ichabod.[3]

3 Thomas V. Moore, A *Commentary on Zechariah* (Edinburgh: Banner of Truth, 1958), 41.

1:3. Therefore say thou unto them, Thus saith the LORD of hosts; Turn ye unto me, saith the LORD of hosts, and I will turn unto you, saith the LORD of hosts.

As the word "therefore" indicates, the Lord's displeasure is expressed in the call to conversion that comes in the words "turn ye unto me." In the Old and New Testaments the English words *converted* and *conversion* are simply translations of words that mean "to turn." Turning or conversion must follow when the displeasure of the Lord is made known.

It is necessary, though, to show from the word of God what true conversion is, since most Christians today have very wrong ideas about it. Some see it as a kind of emotional experience or sudden dramatic upheaval in a person's life that somehow proves that he is a child of God and that becomes the content of his testimony. A Christian is even expected to be able to put a date and time to his conversion. Most think, therefore, that conversion only happens once in a person's life, at the beginning of his salvation. Conversion is thought of only in terms of what happened to the apostle Paul on the way to Damascus, and a person who cannot speak of something similar in his own life is considered to be still unconverted.

True conversion is turning *from* sin and turning *to* God. In this verse the prophet speaks of turning or returning to God, in the next verse of turning from sin, from evil ways and evil doings. That is the whole of conversion. But conversion must be both, for the person who puts away a certain gross sin but does not turn with all his heart in repentance and faith to God is not truly converted, no more than the person who appears to have turned to God and been saved but never turns away from his old wicked life. The so-called carnal Christian, the man or woman who claims to have returned to God but who remains carnal, is a fiction, invented to explain why numerous converts of evangelistic campaigns show little or no further interest in the gospel, the church, or Christianity. Those who conduct such campaigns will not admit that the majority of those who come forward to "accept Jesus Christ as their personal savior" are not in fact saved at all.

Conversion, then, is not something that happens only once in the life of a Christian. Rather, it ought to happen every day. As long as we are sinners, that is, all our life long, we must be turning from our sins in repentance, in a daily struggle against sin, and in hatred of sin. We must be always turning to God in love and obedience. Any person who is not turning to God in repentance every day is unconverted. Anyone who is not *always* turning to God in prayer, in love, in obedience, is unconverted.

If we come to salvation later in life, our first turning from sin to God may indeed be something sudden and dramatic, as in the case of the apostle Paul. Nevertheless, it is not always so. There are those whose turning is long and gentle, who find themselves completely turned around in their thinking, experience, and relation to God without realizing at first what has happened to them.

That first turning, when it is sudden and dramatic, may be remembered all one's life with gratitude to God, for one has been plucked as a brand from the burning, but even then it is not the true test of a person's conversion. The real test is whether a person is *still* turning from sin and turning to God today.

Because conversion is a lifelong turning, the person who claims a conversion experience many years ago but now lives in sin is not converted. And the person who cannot name a day and date but lives a holy life with God as its focus is converted though he cannot name a day and date. The real question in conversion is not *when* were you converted? but are you being converted *now*?

We see the call to continued conversion when we remember that Zechariah's call comes two months after Haggai called the people to conversion (Hag. 1:2–11). In response to God's word through Haggai, the people had repented and returned to the work of rebuilding the house of God. If conversion were not continual, there would have been no need for a further word of God through Zechariah. But God's people are always inclined to lapse into sin and sloth, and so the word of God constantly calls them to conversion.

In calling Judah to conversion, God three times names himself Jehovah of hosts, his favorite name in the prophecies of Haggai, Zechariah, and Malachi.[4] By the name Jehovah of hosts he reminds Judah that he is the God of the covenant whose delight it is to live in fellowship with his people,

---

4 The name LORD (Jehovah) is used 35 times in the book of Haggai, 132 times in Zechariah, and 47 times in Malachi, and LORD of hosts 14 of 35 times in Haggai, 53 of 132 times in Zechariah, and 24 of 47 times in Malachi. In comparison the name God is used only 3 times in Haggai, 13 times in Zechariah, and 9 times in Malachi, and the name Lord (Master) only 4 times in Zechariah and 2 times in Malachi. The NIV translates very inadequately the name LORD of hosts as Lord Almighty.

THE INTRODUCTORY EXHORTATION

but who cannot have fellowship with sin (Ps. 5:4). As Jehovah of hosts, however, he is not only the one who calls to conversion, but the one who sovereignly and powerfully brings his people to conversion: who first turns them in order that they may also turn to him. They have to learn the prayer of Jeremiah: "Turn thou me, and I shall be turned; for thou art the LORD my God" (Jer. 31:18).

Here God promises to turn to those who turn to him. His promise does not mean that we are first in this business of conversion. If God does not first turn us, we will never be turned. Nor does God's turning to us depend on our turning to him. He is always first in salvation and also in conversion. We turn only because he first turns to us and in turning to us turns us to himself. He works in us both the willing and the doing of true conversion (Phil. 2:13).

Nevertheless, Zechariah emphasizes an important point. Though our conversion is God's work, it is only in the way of conversion that we experience and enjoy his fellowship. Our experience is always that he who seemed far off and an enemy while we continued in sin is, in the way of conversion, one who turns to us in mercy and restores us to his fellowship.

Canons 5.5 testifies of this in speaking of the falls of God's people:

By such enormous sins, however, they very highly offend God, incur a deadly guilt, grieve the Holy Spirit, interrupt the exercise of faith, very grievously wound their consciences, and sometimes lose the sense of God's favor, for a time, until on their returning into the right way by serious repentance, the light of God's fatherly countenance again shines upon them.[5]

It is as though we experience our turning to him as his returning to us. We should never forget that. Only through conversion, that is, through repentance, through battling against sin and hating sin, through seeking God and worshiping him rightly, can we enjoy his favor and blessing. How many times does not his word tell us that! Yet the lesson is difficult to learn and long in learning. Judah had to be put out of God's presence and sent to Babylon before they even began to learn the lesson of these verses.

---

5   Canons of Dordt 5.5, in Schaff, *Creeds of Christendom*, 3:593.

1:4. Be ye not as your fathers, unto whom the former prophets have cried, saying, Thus saith the LORD of hosts; Turn ye now from your evil ways, and from your evil doings: but they did not hear, nor hearken unto me, saith the LORD.

As he so often does, God grounds his warnings in his past dealings with his people. The lessons of sacred history, though often forgotten, teach us that God's ways are always the same. For that reason we New Testament Christians ought to know the Old Testament and its history.

The fathers of whom God speaks are the ancestors not only of the returned captives, but our ancestors also. There is only one people of God in the Old and New Testaments—Israel is the church (Acts 7:38) and the church is Israel (Rom. 2:28–29), and therefore their fathers are our fathers.

This is taught in some remarkable ways in scripture. In Romans 2:28–29, the word of God makes it clear that those who are only physical descendants of Abraham are not Jews at all, but that those who are justified by faith as Abraham was and who believe in Abraham's God (Rom. 4) are true Jews, whether or not they are Jews physically and outwardly. They are Jews inwardly, the only kind of Jew God recognizes.

In Philippians 3:1–3 Paul focuses especially on circumcision and says that a person who is only interested in the outward rite of circumcision is a mere slasher (the concision). But speaking to a church that was almost exclusively Gentile, he says, "Ye are the circumcision, who worship God in the spirit, and rejoice in Christ Jesus, and have no confidence in the flesh."

Dispensationalism denies this and entirely separates the Old and New Testaments and in its classical form not only makes of Israel and the church two separate peoples, but also even proposes two different ways of salvation for them. The teaching that Israel and the church are one is also a dilemma for the Baptists. Even those Baptists who reject dispensationalism are forced in their defense of believer's baptism to make a principle separation between Israel and the church as far as God's covenant is concerned and to teach that the sign of the covenant is different in each testament.

Any separation between Israel and the church, between the two testaments, destroys the applicability of the word of God in the Old Testament to us as New Testament Christians. The Old Testament is not the record of

God's word to a people who were in a different covenantal relationship to God, but is God's word to us. Zechariah speaks to us as well as to them. They are our fathers.

The lesson for all who hear Zechariah's words, therefore, is this: those who do not turn to God with all their hearts will come under his wrath and judgments. Coming from the Old Testament the lesson is especially forceful, for the whole nation went into captivity, though not all were guilty of idolatry. There is in the church of God a certain corporate responsibility as well as personal responsibility. We cannot sit comfortably in a church or denomination that is unfaithful, saying and doing nothing, and escape responsibility for what happens when that church or denomination departs from the living God. Not only we but also our children will certainly go into spiritual captivity with those who are guilty of leading the church astray.

What happened to heedless Judah is what will happen to us if we do not hear God's word through Zechariah and turn from every evil way. They were told time and again by the former prophets, Elijah, Isaiah, Jeremiah, Joel, Micah, and many others, that God was angry, but they paid no attention. Thinking themselves to be the people of God, carnally secure in the mistaken belief that God's promises were for them no matter what they did, foolishly thinking that he could not possibly be speaking to them, they were finally scattered and destroyed as a people. So will we be if we do not give heed but with a false sense of security think that God's sovereign grace allows us to continue in our own ways.

The popular idea that God's promises are for all (conditionally) promotes carnal security. It feeds in the foolish hearts of men and women the wrong conviction that they are God's people no matter what, that they can do as they please, and it even increases their false sense of security by leaving with them the impression that they can themselves at any time accept or reject those promises as their own.

1:5. Your fathers, where are they? and the prophets, do they live for ever?

1:6. But my words and my statutes, which I commanded my servants the prophets, did they not take hold of your fathers? and they returned and said, Like as the LORD of hosts thought to do unto us, according to our ways, and according to our doings, so hath he dealt with us.

God in these verses speaks more plainly of what happened to carnal, unbelieving Judah in years past. Thus the first question of verse 5: "Your fathers, where are they?" The answer is, of course, they died in slavery in Babylon. God had warned them of the consequences of their sin, they had not listened, and they had found to their dismay that God's word was true. Now God tells another generation that his word is irrevocable and stands, and he uses what happened to their fathers as proof. The fathers and the prophets were gone, but the same word of God was coming to Judah through Zechariah and others, including threats of judgment not unlike those their fathers had heard and disregarded.

The main thought of these two verses, however, is that God's word is powerful not only in judgment but also in salvation. If it were not so, Judah's situation would have been hopeless, for these returned captives had already proved themselves to be no better than their fathers. What hope, then, was there for them?

Their hope lay in the almighty and unchangeable word of God, which had produced repentance and conversion in the hearts of some of their fathers and would continue to do so with them. Always by the power of God's word there had been those who said, "Like as the LORD of hosts thought to do unto us, according to our ways, and according to our doings, so hath he dealt with us." These people not only believed that God keeps his word for good or ill, but also returned to him, forsaking their sins and seeking him as he commanded.

The reference is to the conversion of some, a very small remnant, who "returned" both from sin and from exile. In returning both from sin and from exile they show us that only in the way of true conversion can we have possession of that delightful land God has promised. We also through conversion will return to our own land, not anymore the earthly type, but the eternal and spiritual reality of which Hebrews 12 speaks: "But ye are come unto mount Sion, and unto the city of the living God, the heavenly Jerusalem, and to an innumerable company of angels, To the general assembly and church of the firstborn, which are written in heaven, and to God the Judge of all, and to the spirits of just men made perfect" (vv. 22–23).

The word "returned" in verse 6 is the same word used in verses 3–4, where God calls Judah to conversion. The reference here is not just to the return of the captives from Babylon, but also to God's wonderful grace through which some profited from the lessons God had taught. They accepted the chastisement they received and were converted to him.

This power of the word of God is something little understood today. If it were understood there would not be a mad rush to replace the preaching of the gospel with all sorts of other things, nor such widespread dissatisfaction with the preaching of the word, nor such neglect of the scriptures. Yet the powerful word of God remains the hope of God's people, who are, in themselves, not different from the fathers whom God addresses in these verses. Foolish, wayward, disobedient, heedless, and careless, there would be no hope for them or for the church if God's word did not by its own power produce the good fruit of conversion in some.

Chapter 6

THE SEVEN VISIONS:
ZECHARIAH 1:7–6:8

Having called the people to conversion, the word of God through Zechariah very abruptly turns to visions. That abrupt switch from plain warning to symbolic vision must not obscure the connection between the two. The reassurance that God's almighty word will accomplish the conversion of his people leads directly into the visions that are designed for the comfort of those who have turned to God. They bring comfort by focusing on Christ, in whom are all the promised blessings of conversion.

There is some question about the number of visions. The more traditional division finds eight visions in chapters 1:7–6:8, all of them climaxing in the crowning of Joshua in chapter 6:9–15.[1] This view finds two visions in chapter 5, the visions of the flying roll and the woman in the basket. Meredith Kline finds only seven visions, combining all of chapter 5 into one vision.[2] He argues that all the other visions except the central vision of chapter 3, the reclothing of Joshua, are introduced by the phrase, "I saw and behold," a phrase that is absent from Zechariah 5:5 "where many commentators would begin a separate vision." He adds, "The phrase we find instead at

---

1   Ralph L. Smith, "Zechariah," in Word Biblical Commentary, vol. 32, *Micah-Malachi* (Waco, TX: Word Books, 1984); McComiskey, *Zechariah*; Theo. Laetsch, *Bible Commentary on the Minor Prophets* (St. Louis: Concordia, 1956); Leupold, *Exposition of Zechariah*; Moore, *A Commentary on Zechariah*. Moore counts nine, but only because he counts chapter 6:9–15 as an additional vision, though it is not a vision at all.
2   Kline, *Glory in Our Midst*, 241–56.

v. 5 is like one which marks the middle, not beginning, of a vision at Zech. 2:3."[3] I agree with Kline.

The visions focus on Christ as the great priest-king of his people. This is especially true of chapter 4, where Christ appears in the person of Joshua. But he is present in the other visions as well, especially as the angel of Jehovah, whom we know from the rest of the Old Testament to be the incarnate Christ revealed long before his coming in the flesh. We learn that this angel is God in Judges 6:11–24 and 13:8–23. We learn that he is the savior of God's people from Isaiah 63:9: "In all their affliction he was afflicted, and the angel of his presence saved them: in his love and in his pity he redeemed them; and he bare them, and carried them all the days of old." He is Christ in the Old Testament.

The seven visions show us Christ as the great ruler of the nations (1:7–17), the avenger of the oppressed people of God (1:18–21), the builder of the temple (2:1–13), the justifier of the ungodly (3:1–10), the giver of the Spirit (4:1–14), the executioner of God's curse and the enemy of the unfaithful (5:1–11), and the coming judge (6:1–8). These seven revelations of Christ climax in chapter 6:9–15, where he appears as the enthroned priest, the great priest-king.

---

3 Ibid., 177.

Chapter 7

THE FIRST VISION:
Zechariah 1:7–17

1:7   Upon the four and twentieth day of the eleventh month, which is the month Sebat, in the second year of Darius, came the word of the Lord unto Zechariah, the son of Berechiah, the son of Iddo the prophet, saying,

1:8   I saw by night, and behold a man riding upon a red horse, and he stood among the myrtle trees that were in the bottom; and behind him were there red horses, speckled, and white.

1:9   Then said I, O my lord, what are these? And the angel that talked with me said unto me, I will shew thee what these be.

1:10   And the man that stood among the myrtle trees answered and said, These are they whom the Lord hath sent to walk to and fro through the earth.

1:11   And they answered the angel of the Lord that stood among the myrtle trees, and said, We have walked to and fro through the earth, and, behold, all the earth sitteth still, and is at rest.

1:12   Then the angel of the Lord answered and said, O Lord of hosts, how long wilt thou not have mercy on Jerusalem and on the cities of Judah, against which thou hast had indignation these threescore and ten years?

1:13   And the Lord answered the angel that talked with me with good words and comfortable words.

1:14   So the angel that communed with me said unto me, Cry thou, saying, Thus saith the Lord of hosts; I am jealous for Jerusalem and for Zion with a great jealousy.

1:15   And I am very sore displeased with the heathen that are at ease: for I was but a little displeased, and they helped forward the affliction.

1:16   Therefore thus saith the LORD; I am returned to Jerusalem with mercies: my house shall be built in it, saith the LORD of hosts, and a line
shall be stretched forth upon Jerusalem.

1:17   Cry yet, saying, Thus saith the LORD of hosts; My cities through prosperity shall yet be spread abroad; and the LORD shall yet comfort
Zion, and shall yet choose Jerusalem.

1:7. Upon the four and twentieth day of the eleventh month, which is the month Sebat, in the second year of Darius, came the word of the Lord unto Zechariah, the son of Berechiah, the son of Iddo the prophet, saying,

This first vision comes approximately three months after the first word of God through Zechariah (1:1–6). Once again, because of the time lapse, he is identified in detail, both to establish his credentials and to establish the word he brings as the word of Jehovah.

The date of his vision is also important, not because the year and month are symbolic of anything, but because these were important days for Judah. His first vision follows Haggai's last recorded prophecies by exactly two months, so it was given at the time the people were busy with the work of rebuilding God's house, at the time the foundation of the temple had been laid. Indeed, the twenty-fourth day was of special importance for the returned captives. On the twenty-fourth day of the sixth month the work of rebuilding the temple had resumed (Hag. 1:15). On the twenty-fourth day of the ninth month the foundation of the temple had been laid (Hag. 2:18), and on that same day Haggai had brought his last two prophecies (Hag. 2:10, 20). Now on the twenty-fourth day of the eleventh month, Zechariah receives his visions. By giving the vision on that date God shows his approval of the work the Jews were doing.

Because no further date is given in the visions, it is assumed by many commentators that all the visions were received the same night. That is certainly a possibility but cannot be proved one way or the other.

In this first vision, Zechariah sees a man riding on a red horse accompanied by other red, speckled, and white horses. This rider stands among the myrtle trees, and the place where he stands is described in the KJV as "the bottom." It should be obvious that there is some connection between this vision and the subsequent vision in chapter 6:1–8 as well as with John's vision of the four horsemen in Revelation 6:1–8.

1:8. I saw by night, and behold a man riding upon a red horse, and he stood among the myrtle trees that were in the bottom; and behind him were there red horses, speckled, and white.

The words "I saw" mean this is a vision, not a dream. A different word is used than is used for dreams, and visions were "seen" by people who were not asleep. Zechariah even had to be waked *before* the fifth vision (4:1). A vision is a revelation of God in which one sees things that cannot ordinarily be seen, whether they be spiritual realities or things God has prepared to symbolize those spiritual realities. So it is here.

Because Zechariah mentions the night, these visions are referred to as his "night visions." Some commentators suggest that the night symbolizes the "dimness of the restored condition,"[1] but it is, in my view, of no special significance other than that the night would ordinarily be the time for visions and dreams.

Zechariah's *seeing* also means that the visions are not to be interpreted literally. Very often the prophets saw the word of God (Isa. 6:1; Ezek. 1:1; Dan. 8:2; Amos 9:1; Rev. 1:11), and when they saw it, they saw it in pictures and symbols. What follows, then, is not to be taken literally but is a word of God given through figures and symbols and must be interpreted accordingly.

Most important are the four elements of the vision: the man on the red horse, the myrtle trees among which he stands, the bottom, and the other horses and riders of different colors that stand behind the man on the red horse. The interpretation that Zechariah receives focuses only on the group of riders and barely mentions the myrtle trees and the rider on the red horse. Nevertheless, those elements are an important part of the vision. Indeed, the riders on different colored horses are of significance only in relation to the other elements of the vision.

The riders' walking to and fro and the report they bring are under the direction of the rider on the red horse and are in his service as the one who stands among the myrtle trees. That report is necessary because both rider and myrtle trees are "in the bottom." But what does it all mean?

That the rider on the red horse is Christ is beyond doubt. In verses 10–11 the man is identified as the angel of Jehovah, the special Old Testament revelation of the promised Messiah. Always in the Old Testament he is identified with Jehovah as the savior of his people. Isaiah 63:7–9 is a good example of such passages:

---

1 Pusey, *The Minor Prophets*, 2:341.

7. I will mention the lovingkindnesses of the LORD, and the praises of the LORD, according to all that the LORD hath bestowed on us, and the great goodness toward the house of Israel, which he hath bestowed on them according to his mercies, and according to the multitude of his lovingkindnesses.

8. For he said, Surely they are my people, children that will not lie: so he was their Saviour.

9. In all their affliction he was afflicted, and the angel of his presence saved them: in his love and in his pity he redeemed them; and he bare them, and carried them all the days of old.

This passage not only identifies the Lord and the angel of his presence, but also says that through this angel God comes as the savior of his people. In him God himself is afflicted on behalf of his people, redeems them, and carries them throughout the Old Testament.

That the angel of Jehovah appears in Zechariah riding on a red horse reminds us of Revelation 19:11, where he appears riding on a white horse. While that is not the most important part of the vision, the difference has to do with his appearance in the Old Testament. Red being the color of war, his red horse symbolizes the battle yet to be fought, whereas in the New Testament, riding on a white horse, he appears as the victor in that battle.

Later on in the book of Zechariah Christ appears again, but riding on a donkey (Zech. 9:9). Together the two visions of Christ show him in his exaltation and humiliation, as both suffering and conquering king, lord and servant of his people. He in all his appearances in the book of Zechariah is the central figure.

The myrtles represent Judah and in Judah the church. Hengstenberg calls them "a striking image of the kingdom of God."[2] Since the myrtle is more of a shrub than a tree and bears fragrant flowers, it is possible that the myrtle is chosen here as a symbol of the church from the viewpoint of both its acceptableness with God and its lowly condition in the world. That it is symbolic of the church of God is evident from a comparison of Zechariah 1:8 with two passages in Isaiah:

---

2 Hengstenberg, *Christology*, 3:275.

I will plant in the wilderness the cedar, the shittah tree, and the myrtle, and the oil tree; I will set in the desert the fir tree, and the pine, and the box tree together. (Isa. 41:19)

Instead of the thorn shall come up the fir tree, and instead of the brier shall come up the myrtle tree: and it shall be to the LORD for a name, for an everlasting sign that shall not be cut off. (Isa. 55:13)

In these passages the return of the Jews from captivity is compared to the replanting of the wilderness, and the various trees mentioned must each be pictures of the nation, the church of the Old Testament. This language is not unusual in scripture. In both testaments the people of God individually and collectively are often compared to beautiful and fruitful trees (Ps. 1:3; Isa. 61:3; Jer. 17:8; Matt. 7:17–19; Luke 13:18–19).

There is also a connection between trees, the church, and the candlesticks that stood in the temple, which appear again in Revelation 1–3 and symbolize the church of God. We should remember that the candlestick was itself a kind of tree and deliberately modeled on a tree.

31. And thou shalt make a candlestick of pure gold: of beaten work shall the candlestick be made: his shaft, and his branches, his bowls, his knops, and his flowers, shall be of the same.
32. And six branches shall come out of the sides of it; three branches of the candlestick out of the one side, and three branches of the candlestick out of the other side:
33. Three bowls made like unto almonds, with a knop and a flower in one branch; and three bowls made like almonds in the other branch, with a knop and a flower: so in the six branches that come out of the candlestick.
34. And in the candlesticks shall be four bowls made like unto almonds, with their knops and their flowers.
35. And there shall be a knop under two branches of the same, and a knop under two branches of the same, and a knop under two branches of the same, according to the six branches that proceed out of the candlestick.

36. Their knops and their branches shall be of the same: all it shall be one beaten work of pure gold. (Ex. 25:31–36)

When one adds to this picture of the church as myrtle trees the figure of the man on the red horse, it is not difficult to see the similarity between this vision and the vision of Christ among the candlesticks in Revelation 1:10–20. The book of Zechariah opens with the same comforting vision as the book of Revelation, Christ in the midst of his church.

It must be emphasized, however, that Judah and Israel not only represent the church, but also *are* the church of the Old Testament. If this were not true, these prophecies would have little or no application to us as New Testament Christians. That Israel is the church we learn from Acts 7:38, where Israel is called "the church in the wilderness," using the ordinary New Testament word for the church, and from Hebrews 12:22–23, where Mount Zion and Jerusalem are identified with the "general assembly and church of the firstborn." This is the key to the whole Old Testament and especially to the prophets. Understanding the relation between Israel and the church, we receive the words of the prophets as of value for us and as being addressed to us. Not understanding this, many view the words of the prophets as being addressed to and applicable to a people living in another age, under another covenant, and whose connection with us is tenuous at best.

That the church is represented by myrtle trees may also be a reminder of the feast of tabernacles, for myrtles were one of the trees whose branches were used at that feast to build booths (Neh. 8:15). If so, the vision looks, as did the feast of tabernacles, to the final tabernacling of God's people in the heavenly kingdom (Rev. 21:1–3), to that day when the prophecy of Isaiah will be fulfilled:

12. For ye shall go out with joy, and be led forth with peace: the mountains and the hills shall break forth before you into singing, and all the trees of the field shall clap their hands.
13. Instead of the thorn shall come up the fir tree, and instead of the brier shall come up the myrtle tree: and it shall be to the Lord for a name, for an everlasting sign that shall not be cut off. (Isa. 55:12–13)

That leaves only the most difficult element of the vision, what is called in the KJV "the bottom." Many commentators and most of the modern versions attach no special significance to this word.[3] If it means anything to them, it is only a further symbol of the lowly condition of the people of God in those days.

Yet the word is not what one would expect if the word of God were only speaking of a piece of low-lying ground. It is a word that always in scripture refers to the depths of the sea (Ex. 15:5 "bottom"; Neh. 9:11 and Ps. 88:6 "deeps"; Job 41:31, Ps. 69:15, 107:24, and Jonah 2:3 "the deep"; Ps. 68:22, 130:1, Isa. 51:10, Ezek. 27:34, and Mic. 7:19 "depths"). Not only that, but it is a word used of the sea as a picture of the forces of evil at whose hands God's people suffer great affliction. It is even used of the powers of hell (Ps. 68:22; 88:6; 130:1). Although Isaiah does not use this word, he compares the wicked to the troubled waves of the sea that can never rest (Isa. 57:20). Out of that troubled sea persecution comes for God's people (Ps. 69:15; 88:6; 130:1). Ultimately, out of the depths of the sea the great enemy of God's people appears (Rev. 13:1). Out of the sea God's people are delivered (Ps. 68:22), and because those depths are closely associated with hell, into those depths the enemies of God's people are hurled in defeat by God. Pharaoh and his horsemen are cast into the depths of the sea. Sin itself is buried in the depths (Mic. 7:19), and ultimately all God's enemies are cast into the lake of fire (Rev. 19:20; 20:14–15).

In that light "bottom" cannot refer in Zechariah 1:8 to a piece of low-lying ground and cannot be merely an incidental part of the vision. Even the KJV with its translation "bottom" does not get the real idea across. The word must be a reference to the troubled sea of the nations of the world, the enemies of God's church, and to the abyss of hell itself, the source of all this enmity. Perhaps a better translation of the verse would be: "I saw by night, and behold a man riding upon a red horse, and he stood among the myrtle trees that were beside the deep." The vision, therefore, reveals Christ in the midst of his church that is itself in the world and exists side by side with that

3 The modern translations have "the glen" (English Standard Version (ESV) and RSV), "a ravine" (NIV and New American Standard Version (NASV), "the hollow" (NKJV), "a river" Today's English Version (TEV), none of which is any improvement over the KJV.

wicked world. The bottom is the place out of which all the troubles of the church arise.

No wonder, then, that the vision begins with "behold"! No wonder Zechariah was surprised, awed, and filled with appreciation by what he saw! What clearer picture could be drawn of the situation of God's church in the world and what greater comfort given?

1:9. Then said I, O my lord, what are these? And the angel that talked with me said unto me, I will shew thee what these be.

There are two angels in this vision. There is the ordinary angel who is identified as the "angel that talked with me" and who appears repeatedly in these visions as an intermediary between Zechariah and God, and there is the angel of Jehovah, who is not an ordinary angel but God himself as the savior of his people. He is, in one way or another, the main figure in these visions. The one angel is only a messenger, the other is Christ himself. The book of Zechariah, like the last book of the Bible, is the "revelation of Jesus Christ."

Zechariah is the one asking for an interpretation of these things, and his request is answered not by the first angel but by the man on the red horse, by Christ, though the first angel is the one who says, "I will shew thee." That interpretation focuses not on the other elements of the vision but on the other horsemen.

Literally we read that the angel who speaks with Zechariah speaks "in" him, an unusual expression. Numbers 12:6–9 and Habakkuk 2:1 are the only other passages where this expression is used in scripture. These are visions: not matters of the senses, but of revelation, in this case of direct revelation from God that transcends ordinary hearing and seeing.

1:10. And the man that stood among the myrtle trees answered and said, These are they whom the LORD hath sent to walk to and fro through the earth.

It must be assumed that the angel who speaks with Zechariah all through these visions relays Zechariah's request for an interpretation to the angel of the Lord, who interprets the vision focusing on the other horsemen. His answer is first troubling, then comforting.

Those other horsemen cannot be understood apart from the horsemen of Revelation 6:1–8, though the connection between Zechariah and Revelation is ignored or overlooked by most commentators. That they are under the authority of the rider on the red horse—they report to him—that they go to and fro through the earth, and that they are horses and riders of different colors make the similarity between the two passages unmistakable.

Some suggest that the different colors of the horses represent different nations or the glory of the divine presence. In light of Revelation 6:1–8, the differently colored horses can only represent the forces by which God directs and controls the course of history and turns it to his own ends. In Revelation the identity of these forces, the gospel (the white horse), war (the red horse), social inequality (the black horse), and death (the pale horse), are more easily understood. Perhaps they are exactly the same in Zechariah, but that is not so easily determined since the colors are not the same and there are only three colors mentioned—red, speckled, and white.

It has been suggested that the speckled horses are a kind of gray, bay, sorrel, or chestnut, similar to the pale horse of Revelation 6, and then the red and white horses would also represent the same forces as in Revelation 6. That would mean there is no horse and rider corresponding to the black horse and rider of Revelation. Later, in Zechariah 6:1–3, these horses appear again, though drawing chariots, and all four colors of Revelation are present. Why the color black is not present in Zechariah 1 we do not know, perhaps because the forces represented by the black horse were not active among the nations at the time of Zechariah's first vision. In any case the main thing is not the identity of these separate horsemen but the report they bring, a report that the earth is still and at rest.

These horses and their riders are under the control of the rider on the red horse. They are sent by him and report back to him. The verse says that they are sent by the Lord, but he is identified with the rider on the red horse in the following verses. Their riding and the report of their riding, therefore, can only be for the benefit of God's church. Whatever their mission, they act for the good of Zion and Jerusalem. They must, for they are under the direction of Zion's Redeemer. For that reason their report must also come through him. He will make sure that their report, disturbing as it is, is a message of peace and hope for God's people.

1:11. And they answered the angel of the LORD *that stood among the myrtle trees, and said, We have walked to and fro through the earth, and, behold, all the earth sitteth still, and is at rest.*

Note that this verse identifies the angel of Jehovah with the rider on the red horse. He has been referred to as a *man* standing among the myrtle trees in verse 10 and is now identified as the *angel of Jehovah* who stands among the myrtles. There can be no doubt that this is Christ himself who receives the report of the other riders and who makes intercession for his people.

The other riders bring their report to him because they are subject to him. He is the supreme ruler through whom God executes his will and to whom all power is given in heaven and on earth. In Revelation that is evident in his opening the book with seven seals by which the four horsemen run. Here it is evident in his authority over these other riders and in the mission on which he sends them, which encompasses the whole earth.

That the earth sits still and is at rest means that the heathen nations were for the most part at peace among themselves, prosperous and completely unconcerned about the presence of the kingdom of God among them in the nation of Judah. Judah had no king of its own, was of no account militarily or politically, was poor, defeated, and oppressed by these nations, and therefore was of no concern at all to them. Jerusalem was still in ruins and the temple only partially rebuilt.

This report, as it stood, was troubling. God had promised to bless Judah, and it appeared that his blessing rested instead upon the heathen nations. God had promised to deliver Judah from her enemies, and the heathen nations were prospering and at peace. The report of these riders raises the same troubling question as Asaph in Psalm 73, though Asaph speaks from a more personal viewpoint.

> 3. For I was envious at the foolish, when I saw the prosperity of the wicked.
> 4. For there are no bands in their death: but their strength is firm.
> 5. They are not in trouble as other men; neither are they plagued like other men.
> 6. Therefore pride compasseth them about as a chain; violence covereth them as a garment.

7. Their eyes stand out with fatness: they have more than heart could wish.

8. They are corrupt, and speak wickedly concerning oppression: they speak loftily.

9. They set their mouth against the heavens, and their tongue walketh through the earth.

10. Therefore his people return hither: and waters of a full cup are wrung out to them.

11. And they say, How doth God know? and is there knowledge in the most High?

12. Behold, these are the ungodly, who prosper in the world; they increase in riches.

13. Verily I have cleansed my heart in vain, and washed my hands in innocency.

14. For all the day long have I been plagued, and chastened every morning. (Ps. 73:3–14)

These troubling questions are answered in the verses that follow, but the very fact that the rider on the red horse is aware of these things through his agents is itself a comfort. God is not unaware of what is happening in the world and of the danger the world poses to his church. He knows what is going on and is the one who has brought the church's situation in the world to pass. The report of the three riders demonstrates his sovereignty over these nations.

1:12. Then the angel of the LORD answered and said, O LORD of hosts, how long wilt thou not have mercy on Jerusalem and on the cities of Judah, against which thou hast had indignation these threescore and ten years?

That the report of these riders, on the face of it, is not a good report is evident from the reaction of the angel of Jehovah in the next verse. It moves him to make intercession for Jerusalem and Judah and to pray for an end to God's anger.

His intercession is not just a prayer *for* the people of God. Through his intercession the prayers of God's people actually come to God as Christ's own prayers. So completely does he identify with them that their prayers become his own. In bringing those prayers to God he makes sure they are heard, coming as the one whose blood was shed for them and who cleanses their prayers by his Spirit. The words, "O Jehovah of hosts, how long wilt thou not have mercy on Jerusalem," are the cry of distressed Judah and of the afflicted people of God until the end of the ages brought by Christ himself into the presence of his Father.

He addresses God as Jehovah of hosts, reflecting the faith of God's people in God's sovereignty. Their questions are not a denial that all creatures, including the heathen nations, are God's great host by which and through which he accomplishes his purpose. In asking these questions, they are not falling into unbelief and denying his covenant with them. In their bewilderment and discouragement there is always deep down in the hearts of God's people the conviction that he is God and their God. There is even in their question the conviction that God would be merciful. The question is only, "How long?"

That question echoes through the ages and is heard in every age from God's people. It is heard in Psalm 6:3, 80:4, 90:13, and 94:3. Daniel had asked the question twenty or more years before (Dan. 12:8). It seemed since then that little progress had been made in the fulfillment of God's promises: things had declined and gone backward. And now, twenty-five hundred years later, God's people continue to ask the same question.

What is most striking of all, however, is that in Revelation 6:10 this cry is heard immediately following and in connection with the vision of the four horsemen, just as it is in Zechariah. It is a cry that rises from the hearts of God's people as their lives are touched by the forces God lets loose in his world for the accomplishment of his purpose. It arises because there always seems to be a delay in the realization of God's kingdom.

It expresses the bewilderment of God's people in the face of outward circumstances. They were bewildered by the peace and prosperity of the heathen nations and their own evil circumstances. It seemed to them, as it seemed to Asaph in Psalm 77, that God's mercy was "clean gone for ever," that "he in anger had shut up his tender mercies" (vv. 8–9). It seemed to them that though the seventy (three score and ten) years of the captivity were over and they had returned to Judea, the anger of God that had brought them into captivity had continued. He had prospered the heathen at their expense, or so it seemed, and was slow to bless his church.

God had his purpose in this delay. His people had to learn that they were only sojourners in the world and that the things of this world, even the earthly temple and the earthly city of Jerusalem, would perish. They had to learn to look for an abiding city and the heavenly country that God promised them and to look for the coming of Christ. All this is as true for us as for them. That they learned this only with difficulty is the reason for their cry.

That the angel of Jehovah makes their cry his own is a marvelous example of the teaching of Hebrews 4:15, that he is "touched with the feeling of our infirmities," for this prayer is in the best and highest sense his own, as he, under the wrath of God for the sins of his people, waits for mercy's dawn. It is the prayer that he prayed on the cross when in his hellish agonies he said, "My God, my God, why hast thou forsaken me?" It is the prayer that he brings continually to God as the one who shares our nature and our experiences.

1:13. And the LORD answered the angel that talked with me with good words and comfortable words.

Not only is the rider's intercession immediately answered, but the answer is "good words and comfortable." The idea is that they are good because they are comfortable; good in that they exactly suit the needs of God's people; good because they are full of comfortable reassurance in trying times.

Most striking, however, is that the angel of Jehovah is now simply identified with Jehovah. The Lord is not another figure in the vision who suddenly speaks out of nowhere, but the one previously identified as the angel of the Lord. We see that the angel and the Lord are the same in that the messenger angel addresses him and immediately receives an answer from him. Zechariah, then, sees him first as the man among the myrtles (vv. 8, 10), then as the angel of Jehovah (v. 11), and now as Jehovah himself. It is as though the longer Zechariah looks and listens, the clearer the identity of this important figure is to him.

What is even more striking is that the angel of the Lord is both the one who makes this intercession and the one who answers it. That is understandable only to those who believe that Christ, though like us in all things except sin, is also personally the second person of the Trinity, God almighty, and therefore not only the one who prays for his people and obtains an answer, but also the one from whom that answer comes.

That the answer comes from him is part of the comfort his words hold, for whatever he speaks he speaks as the redeemer and savior of his people, here as the conqueror and protector of his church, the one who stands among the myrtle trees. Standing where he does and appearing as he does, how could his words be anything but "good and comfortable"?

1:14. So the angel that communed with me said unto me, Cry thou, saying, Thus saith the LORD of hosts; I am jealous for Jerusalem and for Zion with a great jealousy.

1:15. And I am very sore displeased with the heathen that are at ease: for I was but a little displeased, and they helped forward the affliction.

The answer of the angel of the Lord, conveyed by the messenger angel to Zechariah and through him to Judah and to the church in every era of history, is that they must not judge God's attitude by observed outward circumstances. Though circumstances would seem to indicate that God is gracious to the heathen and full of anger toward his people, the opposite is true. His anger is against the heathen even in their prosperity, and his jealous love is toward his people even in their trials.

This is the very opposite of what the doctrine of common grace teaches. That doctrine says that the prosperity of the heathen is a mark of God's favor, grace, and blessing, and by implication that his anger is against his people when they are poor and suffering. Not all who hold to common grace will admit the latter, but there are those, especially in the charismatic movement, who are not afraid to draw the matter out to its logical conclusion and to insist that prosperity and health are the principle signs of God's blessing, and the lack of them a sign of God's disfavor.

This raises again the question whether outward earthly prosperity is ever a sign of God's favor and blessing. In the Old Testament it was under certain circumstances, but only for Israel as a nation and not for individual Israelites.

Material prosperity, according to scripture, can be an evidence of God's blessing. That would be impossible to deny. I believe that in the Old

Testament this was far more true than in the New Testament. God made it clear to Israel that prosperity in the land of Canaan was evidence of his good pleasure and that drought and enemies were signs of his displeasure. Even in the Old Testament, however, this was not true absolutely. The book of Job is a lengthy lesson otherwise and shows that prosperity does not equal blessing on a personal level.

In the Old Testament, therefore, prosperity was a sign of God's blessing *nationally* but not *individually*. Even then, however, times of national prosperity did not even mean that everyone in the nation was blessed by God. What is more, there were times when God sent enemies and other troubles for reasons of his own and not because the nation as a whole was living wickedly. Had Hezekiah and Judah been unfaithful when God sent Rabshakeh and the Assyrians against them?

There is no evidence that they had. The people of God therefore needed the prophets and the word of God to interpret their circumstances and to tell them that God was pleased or displeased with them.

What was true individually in the Old Testament continues to be true in the New. Prosperity or the lack of it cannot be interpreted as signs of God's favorable or unfavorable attitude. God can, as Psalm 73 so clearly teaches, send prosperity as a curse or send evil things for our good, so that all things work together for good to those who love God (Rom. 8:28). There is no common grace or favor or mercy of God in things, and those who think so have no explanation for the fact that God gives prosperity and earthly gifts to the ungodly whom he will send to hell, nor any explanation for the fact that he sends cancer and other ills to those he loves (see explanation of Haggai 1:5–6).

The jealousy of the Lord for Jerusalem and Judah, then, is not the cruel jealousy that suspects and hates those of whom it is jealous, but the jealousy of love that protects and desires only good for Jerusalem and Judah. It is a jealousy that is an expression of the jealousy he shows for his own glory (Ezek. 39:25), since the salvation of his people is eternally tied up with his glory. As he is jealous for his own name, so he must be, reverently speaking, jealous for Jerusalem, his people, and for Jerusalem, his church. Nor may the outward circumstances of the church cause his people to doubt his jealous love for them.

By the same token, the prosperous peace of the heathen may not ever be taken as a sign of God's favor toward them. That the heathen are at ease does not reflect God's approval of them. He is angry with the wicked every day (Ps. 7:11) and when he sends them prosperity he is setting them in slippery places that they may quickly be destroyed (Ps. 73:18). In fact, at the time of Zechariah he was very angry with the heathen nations because they were responsible for the lowly condition of his people: they helped forward the affliction.

When God speaks of being but a little angry, he is speaking of his anger toward Judah and the punishment he inflicted on them by bringing them into captivity. Though he sovereignly used the nations to accomplish this punishment of Judah, yet they are but the axe with which God hews and the saw with which he cuts and will themselves be destroyed for the hewing and cutting they have done (Isa. 10:15–16). That is the sovereignty of God over evil.

As Isaiah says, God holds them accountable and punishes them for their part in the chastising of his people because that heathen nation and its king "meaneth not so." Their purpose is not God's purpose but is only to "destroy and cut off nations not a few" (Isa. 10:7). They are used to work out God's decree and will, but what they do, they do always with wicked hands. Christ is delivered to the cross by the determinate counsel and foreknowledge of God, but the hands of those who crucified him are wicked and they are punished for their wickedness (Acts 2:23). The heathen nations, though used by God to chastise his people, take a malicious delight in the suffering inflicted on the saints (Ps. 137:7; Jer. 50:11).

This message Zechariah is commanded to cry to Judah and Jerusalem. They must know these things, for these things are their comfort and hope. Zechariah's cry, however, was not only heard by Judah and Jerusalem, but also rings down through the ages and speaks comfort to God's people always. God may be a little displeased with his people. That he redeems them and justifies them does not mean that he is pleased with their sin and foolishness. He even uses the ungodly to chastise and correct them, but his jealous love for his people never changes: it is eternal and immutable (Mal. 3:6). The ungodly persecute his people, and in persecuting his people are sovereignly used for their purification and salvation, but it is the ungodly who feel the weight of God's wrath. They feel it now and will feel it again when he comes to judge the nations in the great day of his wrath.

1:16. Therefore thus saith the LORD; *I am returned to Jerusalem with mercies: my house shall be built in it, saith the* LORD *of hosts, and a line shall be stretched forth upon Jerusalem.*

1:17. Cry yet, saying, Thus saith the LORD *of hosts; My cities through prosperity shall yet be spread abroad; and the* LORD *shall yet comfort Zion, and shall yet choose Jerusalem.*

God promises Judah prosperity and growth through his presence among them. His house, the temple, would be completed, the city of Jerusalem would be rebuilt, its boundaries would be marked again by the line of which Jehovah speaks, and the nation would not only be prosperous but would grow and spread abroad. Good words and comfortable indeed!

God speaks of having already returned to Jerusalem. He had never truly forsaken her but in wrath had hidden his face for a moment. He is *Jehovah* who changes not, and he reminds Israel of it four times in these two verses. He is Jehovah of hosts who governs all the hosts of heaven and earth and uses them for the good of his people.

That he promises to return is wonderful. Judah had returned from Babylon, but that meant nothing if God did not return. Then they might just as well have stayed in Babylon, for then the city of Jerusalem would have been no different from the city of Babylon, and the land no better than another foreign land. But God not only promises that he *would* return, he assures them that he already *had* returned. He had returned before they did! They were able to return only because he first returned to them. In his mercy and pity he had gone with them to Babylon and had preserved them there, unlike the ten tribes who disappeared. When the time came he had gone ahead of them, first to Cyrus the great king, to obtain from him a decree, then to Zerubbabel and Joshua and later to Ezra, to stir them up to lead the people. Then, as Ezra says, by his own good hand he had protected them, brought them back, and helped them in the building of their homes and of his house (Ezra 8:18, 31). The mercies of which he speaks were the mercies that brought him to Babylon and were the reason for their restoration, for they were the "sure mercies of David" (Isa. 55:3; Ps. 89:1–2, 24), mercy kept in Christ forevermore (Ps. 89:28).

He speaks too of choosing Jerusalem. The word is the ordinary word for God's election of his people, but it cannot mean that election is revocable and changeable. He is not promising to choose them again, having first chosen and then rejected them. Rather his promise to choose them is a promise that he will make them know and experience again his electing love. Election is eternal and unchangeable; our experience of it is not. It may seem to us, as it did to Judah, that God has cast off his people. He never does, but when we once again experience and enjoy God's electing grace and know that he has not cast us off, we see the fulfillment of God's word, "I will *yet* choose Jerusalem."

These promises are further developed in the third vision (Zech. 2:1–13), so a full explanation of them must wait until we come to that vision, but it is necessary to see that the fulfillment of these promises is spiritual and heavenly. Judah remained small and despised, a remnant people, but that did not mean the promises of God went unfulfilled. They were and are fulfilled in the blessed prosperity of the heavenly Canaan, in the new Jerusalem, and in that house of God made without hands eternal in the heavens. By the Spirit of God the faithful in Israel recognized this and looked for better things. They looked for a city that has foundations whose builder and maker is God, for a better country where there are no more tears or suffering and a home in heaven with God himself. So do we.

All this is true because of the man who stands among the myrtles. For his sake Jehovah returns to Jerusalem with mercies. Because of him the temple is built, for it must foreshadow him whose body is the true temple of God. For his sake a line is stretched upon Jerusalem and the city rebuilt, for it is after all his city, the city of the great king. He is the one who brings true prosperity to God's people and through whom they are truly spread abroad and inherit the new heavens and the new earth. This first vision, just like the book of Revelation, shows us Christ's presence in his church as the guarantee of God's richest blessings and continued favor.

Chapter 8

THE SECOND VISION:
ZECHARIAH 1:18–21

1:18   Then lifted I up mine eyes, and saw, and behold four horns.

1:19   And I said unto the angel that talked with me, What be these? And he answered me, These are the horns which have scattered Judah, Israel, and Jerusalem.

1:20   And the LORD shewed me four carpenters.

1:21   Then said I, What come these to do? And he spake, saying, These are the horns which have scattered Judah, so that no man did lift up his head: but these are come to fray them, to cast out the horns of the Gentiles, which lifted up their horn over the land of Judah to scatter it.

The second and third visions are a further development of the first. The third vision develops the promise that God would return to Jerusalem in mercy and that the temple would be finished, the city rebuilt, and prosperity restored in the nation. This second vision develops and displays God's great displeasure with the heathen and shows the destructive power of his displeasure.

1:18 Then lifted I up mine eyes, and saw, and behold four horns.

The references to seeing something usually mark the beginning of a new vision in the prophecies of Zechariah; that is the case here. This new vision is of four horns and four carpenters and portrays the destruction of the heathen nations who had scattered and oppressed Judah. If there is any doubt about this identification of the horns, verse 21 tells us that they are the "horns of the Gentiles."

Horns in scripture are often a symbol of power. God himself often appears with horns. Habakkuk 3:4 portrays him with horns coming out of his hand, and he is called the "horn of my salvation" in Psalm 18:2 and 2 Samuel 22:3. In Revelation Christ is pictured as a lamb with seven horns (Rev. 5:6). Even the power of the heathen is portrayed in this way (Ps. 75:5; Lam. 2:17), and so is the power of the dragon and the beast in Rev. 12:3 and 13:11. God, speaking of judgment on the heathen, speaks of breaking their horns (Jer. 48:25). In contrast, the exaltation of his people to dignity and power is described as lifting up their horn (Ps. 89:17; 92:10; 148:14) or causing their horn to bud and grow (Ezek. 29:21).

It is likely in view of these references that even the horns of the altars have the same significance. Both the great brazen altar of burnt offering and the golden altar of incense had hollow horns on the corners into which the blood of the sacrifices was poured. These horns must represent the power of the altars and the sacrifices that were offered on them, the power of the blood of atonement, of the thank offerings, and of the intercessory incense.

Here the four horns represent the power of the heathen nations that oppressed God's people. That there are four horns leads many to believe that they represent four different nations, perhaps Egypt, Assyria, Babylon, and Persia, the four nations that had been the principle oppressors of God's people in those times, but this is not stated and cannot be established with certainty.[1] They might with equal likelihood represent the four points of the compass and the fact that these nations surrounded Israel. However many they are, they represent the heathen nations as part of the antichristian world power.

Today the four horns of Zechariah are seen in the growing power of the antichristian kingdom that, represented again as a horned monster (Rev. 13:1), lifts up the horn against God and his kingdom by opening his mouth in blasphemy against God and by making war with the saints (vv. 6–7). His power, that is, his horned head, is really the power of the horned dragon (Rev. 12:3), for the dragon gives him his power, and his seat, and great authority (Rev. 13:2). Always in history Zechariah's vision of the four horns is being fulfilled, and the church must know about the four carpenters sent by God to deal with the horns.

It is worth noting as well, though not specifically mentioned here, that both in Revelation and in Daniel the horned beasts that represent the enemies of God's church arise out of the depths of the sea (Dan. 7:2–3; Rev. 13:1). That is not stated in this vision but can be assumed, since the "bottom," the depths, is such an important element in the previous vision. The four horns, then, are the powers of hell arrayed against the church of Christ.

1:19. And I said unto the angel that talked with me, What be these? And he answered me, These are the horns which have scattered Judah, Israel, and Jerusalem.

Again Zechariah asks for an interpretation. His asking is another feature of the visions and distinguishes them from the incidents in which Zechariah is an actual participant. In the reclothing of Joshua (Zech. 3:1–10), the crowning of Joshua (6:9–15), and the rejection of Zechariah himself as shepherd (11:1–17), Zechariah actually participates in the events that take place. This feature distinguishes those events as being of special importance and is one of the reasons they are viewed as key passages in the book of Zechariah. Here he only sees and asks.

---

1 "Babylonians, Medes and Persians, Macedonians and Romans," in Pusey, *The Minor Prophets*, 2:346. Such a correspondence is possible, but it forces one to interpret the four carpenters along the same lines, that is, by looking for specific historical figures or nations that they might represent.

In response to Zechariah's question, the angel tells him that the four horns represent the heathen nations, Judah's oppressors. That they are represented as horns testifies to what they did to Israel and Judah: they attacked God's people, scattered them, and destroyed them as a nation. In doing this they lifted up their horn not only against Judah and Israel, but also against God himself. In Psalm 75:5 the enemies of God's people are exhorted not to lift up their horn on high, that is, against heaven, and in Daniel 7 the little horn, representing Antiochus Epiphanes and in him the antichrist, lifts up himself against heaven in speaking great words against the Most High (v. 25). Psalm 2:1–3 speaks more plainly of the rebellion of the heathen against God: "Why do the heathen rage, and the people imagine a vain thing? The kings of the earth set themselves, and the rulers take counsel together, against the LORD, and against his anointed, saying, Let us break their bands asunder, and cast away their cords from us."

Here not only Judah and Jerusalem are mentioned as the objects of this persecuting power of the heathen nations, but also Israel. God never recognized the division of the nation, as he does not recognize the divisions into which the church has fallen today, but continues to speak of Israel as his people though as a nation they were scattered and gone. He must therefore be thinking and speaking of the remnant from the ten tribes that by this time had become part of the nation of Judah. God does not cast off his people.

1:20. And the LORD shewed me four carpenters.

Along with these horns God shows Zechariah four carpenters whose business it is to destroy the horns. Although the word "carpenters" is variously translated, the KJV is accurate enough. The word does not refer exclusively to those who build with wood or work in wood, but to any craftsman or builder. Thus the word is translated "artificer," "craftsman," "maker," "workman," "smith," even "engraver" or "plowman" (Ps. 129:3) and refers to any skilled worker who would be able to deal with these horns. The emphasis is not on their identity but on their skill. A form of the word used to describe these carpenters is found in Ezekiel 21:31, which speaks of those who are skillful to destroy.

The four carpenters are God's defense against the power of the horns and the means he uses to destroy them. What exactly they represent is difficult to say. Some would see in them other nations by which the power of Israel's oppressors would be destroyed. Others see them as men whom God used to bring down the heathen world powers at different times in history.[2] Still others refer to them as angels. Since they are not specifically identified, it is best to see in them all the means by which God executes his judgments on the heathen and takes away their power to oppress and afflict his people. That they are portrayed as carpenters, however, emphasizes the skill with which God will destroy the heathen. The heathen for all their power are little more than brute beasts, but God is wise and skillful and will always prevail against them.

Ultimately this vision is fulfilled in Christ, who casts down and destroys all the power of the heathen, and who in Revelation 19 appears as victor over the Beast and the kings of the earth and their armies. Through him the Beast is cast back into the depths from whence he came, that is, into the lake of fire, and his followers are left as a gruesome feast for the fowls of the air.

1:21. Then said I, What come these to do? And he spake, saying, These are the horns which have scattered Judah, so that no man did lift up his head: but these are come to fray them, to cast out the horns of the Gentiles, which lifted up their horn over the land of Judah to scatter it.

When Zechariah asks the meaning of the carpenters, he is told that they will be used by God to destroy the heathen nations. The word "fray" in the KJV means "to make afraid," and that is also the meaning of the Hebrew word used here. God not only makes them afraid, but also destroys them. In destroying them he also makes them know his power and majesty and causes them, though proud and boasting, to tremble before him. Even they in their destruction must acknowledge his sovereignty.

Twice God mentions their sin of scattering his people, both by way of showing the magnitude of their wickedness and by way of showing the strict justice of his dealings with them. Though used by God, their sin is their own, and they are always held accountable for what they do wickedly. He mentions the extent to which they had afflicted his people when he describes his

---

2 They are Zerubbabel, Joshua, Ezra, and Nehemiah according to Lightfoot as cited in Charles Henry Hamilton Wright, *Zechariah and His Prophecies* (London: Hodder and Stoughton, 1879), 31.

people as unable to lift their heads. They had lifted up their horns against his people, so that his people could not lift their heads anymore but were bowed down entirely under the burden of oppression. God would raise up against them his carpenters and bring them down, and thus raise up again the heads of his people.

This second vision therefore gives us the second word of the comfort from God to his people in every age. The first word, so vividly portrayed in the first vision, is that God remains among and with his people. The second, pictured here, is that he will always deliver them from their enemies and wreak judgment on those who oppressed his people. Thus he answers the cry of Judah, "How long?" and continues to answer the cry of the souls under the altar, "How long, O Lord, holy and true, dost thou not judge and avenge our blood on them that dwell on the earth?" (Rev. 6:10).

Chapter 9

THE THIRD VISION:
Zechariah 2:1–13

2:1   I lifted up mine eyes again, and looked, and behold a man with a measuring line in his hand.

2:2   Then said I, Whither goest thou? And he said unto me, To measure Jerusalem, to see what is the breadth thereof, and what is the length thereof.

2:3   And, behold, the angel that talked with me went forth, and another angel went out to meet him,

2:4   And said unto him, Run, speak to this young man, saying, Jerusalem shall be inhabited as towns without walls for the multitude of men and cattle therein:

2:5   For I, saith the Lord, will be unto her a wall of fire round about, and will be the glory in the midst of her.

2:6   Ho, ho, come forth, and flee from the land of the north, saith the Lord: for I have spread you abroad as the four winds of the heaven, saith the Lord.

2:7   Deliver thyself, O Zion, that dwellest with the daughter of Babylon.

2:8   For thus saith the Lord of hosts; After the glory hath he sent me unto the nations which spoiled you: for he that toucheth you toucheth the apple of his eye.

2:9   For, behold, I will shake mine hand upon them, and they shall be a spoil to their servants: and ye shall know that the Lord of hosts hath sent me.

2:10   Sing and rejoice, O daughter of Zion: for, lo, I come, and I will dwell in the midst of thee, saith the Lord.

2:11   And many nations shall be joined to the Lord in that day, and shall be my people: and I will dwell in the midst of thee, and thou shalt know that the Lord of hosts hath sent me unto thee.

2:12 And the Lord shall inherit Judah his portion in the holy land, and shall choose Jerusalem again.

2:13 Be silent, O all flesh, before the Lord: for he is raised up out of his holy habitation.

The third word of comfort is found in this third vision. Here God promises to build up Zion, to protect her, and to make her the place of his covenant, the place where he dwells as the God of his people. He answers here anew the old prayer of David, "Do good in thy good pleasure unto Zion; build thou the walls of Jerusalem" (Ps. 51:18).

This vision is similar to those of Revelation 11:1–2 and Revelation 21:9–27 as well as the visions of Ezekiel 40–42, not only because a measuring line is used in each case, but because the message of the visions is the same. Ezekiel, Zechariah, and Revelation all speak of the church as the place where God keeps covenant with his people, of his determination to build the church and make it beautiful, and of his marking out its boundaries in order to preserve it and keep it safe and undefiled.

This third vision is also closely connected with the first, a measuring line being an important part of both visions. The second vision was an elaboration on the first vision's theme of God's sore displeasure with the heathen who "helped forward the affliction" (1:15). This third vision is a further expansion of the first vision's promise: "My cities through prosperity shall yet be spread abroad; and the LORD shall yet comfort Zion, and shall yet choose Jerusalem" (1:17). Thus the first three visions form a triad of visions that complement each other.

2:1. I lifted up mine eyes again, and looked, and behold a man with a measuring line in his hand.
2:2. Then said I, Whither goest thou? And he said unto me, To measure Jerusalem, to see what is the breadth thereof, and what is the length thereof.

The new vision is introduced by the words, "I lifted up mine eyes again, and looked," and so Zechariah is once more given the privilege of seeing things that cannot be seen except by revelation from God. What catches his attention is a measuring line, the same line God spoke of in his first vision. There, however, he only heard tell of it; now he sees it being used. There, in the first vision, God spoke of stretching a line upon Jerusalem; now he sends a man to do what he had promised.

It is clear from the rest of the vision that the purpose of this measuring line is connected with Jerusalem's prosperity and blessedness. The same is true of the similar visions in Ezekiel 40–42 and Revelation 11:1, where the temple is measured, and in Revelation 21:9–27, where the new Jerusalem (which has no temple) is measured. In every case the measuring is done to show the glorious extent and prosperity of what is being measured.

The first purpose of this measuring in the different passages is to show God's care in building a place for himself and his people. It amounts therefore to a promise that God will dwell with his people in every age. In every similar passage the promise of God to be the God of his people and to live among them is recorded (Ezek. 43:1–6; Zech. 2:5; Rev. 21:3). The visions of Ezekiel are especially instructive, for after following the man who so carefully measures every part of the visionary temple, Ezekiel sees the glory of the Lord coming into the house by way of the gate whose prospect is to the east, that is, toward the rising of the sun. He sees the coming of the rising Sun of Righteousness through whom God lives among his people eternally in the new kingdom.

The second purpose of this measuring is to show that in dwelling among his people God separates and delivers them from their enemies. That idea is further developed in verse 5, where God promises to be a wall of fire around Jerusalem. It is also found in the visions of Ezekiel and John. In Ezekiel 44:9 God promises, "No stranger, uncircumcised in heart, nor uncircumcised in flesh, shall enter into my sanctuary, of any stranger that is among the children of Israel," and John is told, "There shall in no wise enter into it any thing that defileth, neither whatsoever worketh abomination, or maketh a lie: but they which are written in the Lamb's book of life" (Rev. 21:27). The measuring is also for the safety of God's people, therefore.

The measuring done in Zechariah must be compared to the measuring done in Revelation 11:1–2. In both cases, what is measured comes under God's protection and care, while that which is unmeasured is abandoned to judgment and ruin: "given unto the Gentiles…[to] tread under foot forty and two months" (Rev. 11:2).

Finally, the measuring is done to show the glories and wide extent of God's covenant with his people. Verses 4, 6, and 11 describe this wideness of God's covenant in beautiful terms. It includes Jew and Gentile, male and female, great and small, rich and poor, all whom God pleases to save. In

Ezekiel 40–42 this comes across in the size of the temple that is measured, far greater in extent than the temples of Solomon, Zerubbabel, and Herod. It was a temple that was never built in this world, whose fulfillment and building lie beyond this world in heavenly glory. John too, in measuring the new Jerusalem, measures a city that transcends imagination, a city that is a cube twelve hundred miles on every side, as high as its length and width, fabulously rich and fantastically beautiful (Rev. 21:9–27).

It is interesting that this man goes to measure the length and breadth of Jerusalem, while the new Jerusalem of Revelation is measured not only in length and breadth, but also in height. This is a reminder that the church represented by Jerusalem and having the same name (Heb. 12:22–23) is a living thing, which grows (Eph. 2:21) until it reaches its full glory in the new creation. To put it another way, this measuring continues until Christ comes and the church is perfected and no longer needs to be measured.

God sends this man to measure Jerusalem when Jerusalem had not yet been rebuilt, which may seem strange, but it shows the rebuilding to be God's purpose for Jerusalem. It would surely come to pass. Because "our God is in the heavens," because "he hath done whatsoever he hath pleased" (Ps. 115:3), it is as though Jerusalem is already built and able to be measured.

Who is the man with the measuring line? Most commentators believe he is the same man who was riding on the red horse in the first vision, the angel of Jehovah, Christ himself. Yet the man in John's vision of the new Jerusalem and its measuring is almost certainly not Christ (Rev. 21:9–27). Probably it makes no difference, since Christ is certainly a part of this vision, as we shall see in the next verses.

Zechariah does not ask who the man is, nor does he ask about the measuring line, but he does ask where the man is going. He must have known of Ezekiel's visions, given in the early years of Judah's captivity (Ezek. 1:1–2), and must have known the comforting message of Ezekiel's visions. Aware of the similarity between what he was seeing and what Ezekiel had seen, he takes a great deal of interest in the man's work, as anyone interested in God's covenant and church would do.

2:3. And, behold, the angel that talked with me went forth, and another angel went out to meet him,

2:4. And said unto him, Run, speak to this young man, saying, Jerusalem shall be inhabited as towns without walls for the multitude of men and cattle therein:

In response to Zechariah's question, the messenger angel of the first two visions does not himself answer but receives an answer for Zechariah from someone referred to as "another angel." It would seem therefore that there are five different persons active in this vision: Zechariah, the man with the measuring line, the messenger angel, the angel who speaks on God's behalf and relays God's word to Zechariah, and God who speaks through the angel.

It is clear from his answer that this other angel is once again the angel of Jehovah, God himself in Christ. He is not another relay in a chain of messengers, but the one from whom Zechariah's answer comes and one who speaks in God's name. That is clear from what follows in verses 5–13.

The angel messenger is told to run because the message is urgent. Zion and Jerusalem must know that God will fortify and glorify her. God does not just promise to deal with the heathen nations, her oppressors. Vengeance is something Zion prayed for (Ps. 137:7–9), and God's message in the second vision answered those prayers, but his answer is vital to all her interests. Zion's hope and glory and her only possible reason for being faithful in the work of rebuilding the house of God is God's promise of his blessing and presence.

It is likely that Zechariah is addressed as "this young man" because he had never seen Jerusalem inhabited—had never seen her prosperous and at peace. All he had experienced were the years of deprivation and struggle that followed the return, and what was true of him was true of most in Judah. It is a reminder, therefore, of the need for this hope-filled message.

God, then, not only promises complete deliverance from Jerusalem's enemies, but also promises her prosperity. At the time of this message the city was still in ruins and would not be rebuilt for a number of years. The building of the temple had to come first, and it was not finished. Yet God promises that the city too would be restored, a message of hope that is difficult for us to grasp who do not see clearly what that city meant to the people of God in the Old Testament.

The earthly city of Jerusalem, though only a type and shadow, was more than just a capital city, the center of their earthly life, and the focus of their nation. It was the place God had chosen, his city and the place of his covenant, a visible and tangible evidence of God's presence. It was the visible and tangible evidence also of the city that has foundations, whose builder and maker is God, the city for which Abraham had looked and hoped: Jerusalem was their hope of heaven.

That Jerusalem would be rebuilt as a city without walls is a promise of complete deliverance from all enemies. Though the ruin of Jerusalem's walls was a cause of sorrow to Nehemiah (Neh. 2:3) and the reproach of the nation (Neh. 1:3), a day would come when her lack of walls would be evidence of her glory: her walls would no longer be necessary. That did not happen and would not happen in the Old Testament, but it is fulfilled first of all in the church, which exists in the world as an unwalled city. Its final fulfillment is not in this world but in the world to come. Though described in Revelation 21 as a city with walls, she nevertheless exists as an unwalled city, for "the gates of it shall not be shut at all by day" (v. 25).

The multitudes of men and cattle are part of Jerusalem's future prosperity. There will be no need to assign people to live in Jerusalem because its inhabitants are so few and the people themselves but a remnant, as in the days of Nehemiah (Neh. 11:1–19). Those who have seen the urban sprawl and growing populations of modern unwalled cities can appreciate what Zechariah is told here, except that this promise looks beyond the filth and grime and crime of modern cities to a city that is unspoiled and heavenly.

There is here also a hint of the promise stated more plainly in verse 11, the promise that the future expansion of Jerusalem, as a city without walls, would be worldwide and would come to pass through the gathering of the Gentiles. Jerusalem, now the church of the New Testament (Gal. 4:26; Heb. 12:22), is that city without walls whose inhabitants are the elect out of all nations, gathered in by the gospel, and one spiritual nation in Christ (1 Pet. 2:9).

We should think as we read this promise of the word of God in Ephesians 2:14–22 concerning Christ's work:

14. For he is our peace, who hath made both one, and hath broken down the middle wall of partition between us;
15. Having abolished in his flesh the enmity, even the law of commandments contained in ordinances; for to make in himself of twain one new man, so making peace;

16. And that he might reconcile both unto God in one body by the cross, having slain the enmity thereby:

17. And came and preached peace to you which were afar off, and to them that were nigh.

18. For through him we both have access by one Spirit unto the Father.

19. Now therefore ye are no more strangers and foreigners, but fellowcitizens with the saints, and of the household of God;

20. And are built upon the foundation of the apostles and prophets, Jesus Christ himself being the chief corner stone;

21. In whom all the building fitly framed together groweth unto an holy temple in the Lord:

22. In whom ye also are builded together for an habitation of God through the Spirit.

2:5. For I, saith the LORD, will be unto her a wall of fire round about, and will be the glory in the midst of her.

Jerusalem would have no need of walls, for God himself would be an impenetrable wall of fire around her. This wall of fire harks back to the cherubim with flaming swords who guarded Eden, only then they kept fallen Adam and his descendants out of the garden. This wall keeps the enemies of God's redeemed people out of restored Jerusalem and guarantees the safety of his covenant people.

Even more beautiful is the comparison between this wall of fire and the pillar of fire that separated Israel from the Egyptians before the Red Sea crossing. Interesting too is that the pillar of cloud and fire is identified with the angel of Jehovah in Exodus:

19. And the angel of God, which went before the camp of Israel, removed and went behind them; and the pillar of the cloud went from before their face, and stood behind them:

20. And it came between the camp of the Egyptians and the camp of Israel; and it was a cloud and darkness to them, but it gave light by night to these: so that the one came not near the other all the night. (Ex. 14:19–20)

As at the Red Sea, so too here the Lord himself stands as a fiery wall between the citizens of Jerusalem and their enemies.

There can be no doubt that this promise in Zechariah includes the promise that God will do to Jerusalem's enemies in every age what he did to the Egyptians: "And it came to pass, that in the morning watch the LORD looked unto the host of the Egyptians through the pillar of fire and of the cloud, and troubled the host of the Egyptians" (Ex. 14:24). Though we might not make the connection between this promise and what God did for Israel in the days of Moses, no believing Israelite would have missed the reference. They would have understood that God was promising not only to protect his people, but also to destroy their enemies as he had done in the days of their fathers.

In the New Testament this promise is fulfilled in God's care for his church through the fiery judgments he sends on the ungodly that prevent them from marshaling their forces against the church until the very end of the age; also through the fire of church discipline and the preaching of the gospel, by which he continually purifies and preserves his church; and finally through the judgments of the last day, when the judgment fire consumes his and our enemies.

But God not only promises to be around Jerusalem as her protection, he also promises to be in the midst of her as the Lord, her covenant God. That is the central reality of the covenant, expressed in the oft-repeated formula of the covenant, "I will be your God, and ye shall be my people." That is the desire of God's people always. As Moses said at Mount Sinai, when God, still angry over Israel's sins, would only promise to send an angel with them to Canaan: "If thy presence go not with me, carry us not up hence," that is, "If you do not go with us, there is no point in going at all" (Ex. 33:1–2, 14–15).

When God promises to be the glory in the midst of his people, the reference is very specifically to the cloud of glory that accompanied Israel in the wilderness. The word "glory" is the same word used repeatedly to describe that cloud (Ex. 16:7, 10; 24:16–17; 40:34–35, etc.). That glory, revealed in the pillar of cloud and fire, is the fiery glory of God's holiness. What Moses saw at Sinai at the burning bush is promised once again. The church is not only surrounded by the fire of God's glory, but is filled with that fire and lives herself in the fire. She burns with the glory of God, whose holiness is as a consuming fire, and yet she is not consumed.[1]

---

1 For this reason many Presbyterian churches have taken the burning bush as their symbol.

God is the glory of his church. The church, whether in the Old or New Testament, has no glory, no blessedness, except in God. But that is not only true in this life. When finally the church is gathered to glory, then too God will be the glory in the midst of her. Then the promise will be fulfilled: "Behold, the tabernacle of God is with men, and he will dwell with them, and they shall be his people, and God himself shall be with them, and be their God" (Rev. 21:3). Then the church will have no need of a temple "for the Lord God Almighty and the Lamb are the temple of it" (v. 22). Then there will be no need of sun or moon, for the glory of God and the Lamb's light will be in that eternal city (v. 23). Then "there will be no more curse; but the throne of God and of the Lamb shall be in it" (Rev. 22:3). There "they shall see his face; and his name shall be in their foreheads" (v. 4). Heaven and the glory of the church in heaven are all about God:

> We learn here the true glory of the Church. It is not in any external pomp or power, of any kind; not in frowning battlements, either of temporal or spiritual pretensions; not in rites and ceremonies, however moss-grown and venerable; not in splendid cathedrals and gorgeous vestments, and the swell of music, and the glitter of elo-quence, but in the indwelling glory of the invisible God.[2]

2:6. Ho, ho, come forth, and flee from the land of the north, saith the LORD: for I have spread you abroad as the four winds of the heaven, saith the LORD.

2:7. Deliver thyself, O Zion, that dwellest with the daughter of Babylon.

Out of captivity and to heavenly glory God calls his people. The land of the north and Babylon are the same, and it is out of captivity in Babylon that God calls. The call is the powerful and effectual call of the Almighty that accomplishes what it requires and gives what it commands.[3] It is not a call, therefore, that depends on the will of the sinner: God does not merely

---

2 Moore, *Zechariah*, 60.

3 Augustine, *Confessions*, trans. J. G. Pilkington, in *The Nicene and Post-Nicene Fathers, First Series* (Grand Rapids, MI: Eerdmans, 1988), 1:153 (10.29): "Give what Thou commandest, and command what Thou wilt."

speak and leave it up to those who hear to decide whether or not they will obey, but by irresistible grace working through the call, he brings his people out of Babylon in every age.

> But that others who are called by the gospel obey the call and are converted, is not to be ascribed to the proper exercise of free-will, whereby one distinguishes himself above others equally furnished with grace sufficient for faith and conversion (as the proud heresy of Pelagius maintains); but it must be wholly ascribed to God, who, as he hath chosen his own from eternity in Christ, so he confers upon them faith and repentance, rescues them from the power of darkness, and translates them into the kingdom of his own Son, that they may show forth the praises of him who hath called them out of darkness into his marvelous light; and may glory not in themselves but in the Lord, according to the testimony of the Apostles in various places.[4]

Babylon (with Egypt) is always in scripture a figure of this world of sin, the place where God's people were also held captive and that now persecutes them. This is nowhere so evident as in Revelation 18, where God's people are also called out of Babylon. Babylon, the great whore, is the apostate church, become one with the world, interested only in earthly commerce, and drunken with the blood of the saints: "Come out of her, my people, that ye be not partakers of her sins, and that ye receive not of her plagues. For her sins have reached unto heaven, and God hath remembered her iniquities" (Rev. 18:4–5).

The call therefore is the call to conversion that accompanies the gospel in every age and that certifies the only way of enjoying God's blessings. That call was heard by Judah in the opening words of Zechariah's prophecies and is heard again here.

No doubt both God and the prophet have in mind those who were content to remain in Babylon, though they counted themselves the people of God. They were like people today who call themselves church but remain in and with the world. God reminds them of this when he describes them as

---

4   Canons of Dordt 3–4.10, in Schaff, *Creeds of Christendom*, 3:589–90.

"dwelling with the daughter of Babylon." Not only had they gone to Babylon for their sins, but they had sinned further by settling there and finding homes there. Babylon had become their home.

God's call is also for those who had already returned to their own land. They needed to hear that call, for though they had left Babylon, there was still much of Babylon left in them, evident in their neglect of God's house and unfaithfulness in other matters.[5]

Today there are also those who think that the call to conversion is only for those who are still in Babylon, who have not yet been called out and delivered, but they forget how much of Babylon remains in them; they forget that though they are dead to sin, sin is not yet dead in them. The call to conversion is to daily and continual conversion, not only to an initial turning from sin to God.

That call to conversion is also a call to spiritual separation, to what is sometimes called the antithesis.[6] Second Corinthians 6:17–18 comes to mind as one reads these verses from Zechariah: "Wherefore come out from among them, and be ye separate, saith the Lord, and touch not the unclean thing; and I will receive you. And will be a Father unto you, and ye shall be my sons and daughters, saith the Lord Almighty."

In calling his people to separate and return to himself, God not only speaks of their blessedness, but also hints at the gathering of the Gentiles and the enlarging of Shem's tents. Such is the meaning of the words, "I have spread you abroad as the four winds of heaven." God is not referring to the past scattering of Jerusalem through Assyria and Babylon but to the future increase, growth, and prosperity of Jerusalem, something that would not be fulfilled until the time of the Gentiles came and not entirely fulfilled until the end. The verse could more properly be translated, "I am spreading you abroad."

That future glory is the reason for returning. Those Jews who stayed in Babylon saw only the difficulties of returning to a land that was overrun with weeds and wild beasts, where the cities and houses had been destroyed and

---

5 See the prophecies of Haggai, Ezra, and at a later date, Malachi and Nehemiah.
6 The antithesis is the spiritual separation and opposition that exists by God's grace between Christ and Belial, between the church and the world, and between believer and unbeliever, and that must be maintained in the way of holiness.

the temple left in ruins, but they did not see the future glory and blessedness of the church. Many today are the same. They will make no sacrifice for the church, undergo no hardship on her behalf, because they see only her troubles and trials and not her future blessedness. They remain in Babylon because they do not see the church gathered out of all nations, soon to be spread abroad in the new earth and the new heavens!

What a reason for rejoicing! If the angels rejoice at the salvation of one lost sinner (Luke 15:10), then how much more cause is there for rejoicing when the Gentiles are made "fellowheirs, and of the same body, and partakers of his promise in Christ" (Eph. 3:6):

> O God, let people praise Thee,
> Let all the nations sing,
> For earth in rich abundance
> To us her fruit shall bring.
> The Lord our God shall bless us,
> Our God shall blessing send,
> And all the earth shall fear Him
> To its remotest end.[7]

And what rejoicing there will be when the glorified church is spread abroad for an eternity in heavenly glory!

2:8. For thus saith the LORD of hosts; After the glory hath he sent me unto the nations which spoiled you: for he that toucheth you toucheth the apple of his eye.
2:9. For, behold, I will shake mine hand upon them, and they shall be a spoil to their servants: and ye shall know that the LORD of hosts hath sent me.

Whenever God's people go out of the world—Lot out of Sodom, Israel out of Egypt, Judah out of Babylon, and God's people out of Babylon the great, the mother of harlots—there is no longer any reason for God to withhold his judgments, and the world in which his people once lived is

---

7 No. 176:3, in *The Psalter*.

completely destroyed. When God's glory is fully revealed in his church, he goes out to deal with the nations who insolently dared to touch his beloved.

This is what scripture refers to as God's forbearance. He bears with the wicked for a time, not because of any compassion for them—not out of grace or mercy—but for the sake of his people who live among them. Thus when Lot goes out of Sodom, Sodom is destroyed with fire and brimstone. When Israel is gone from Egypt, Pharaoh and his hosts are drowned in the Red Sea. When Israel leaves Babylon, God reveals his anger against Babylon for spoiling his people, even though they were the rod with which God chastised Judah.

"After the glory" may mean "after God becomes the glory in the midst of his people." Then he also becomes the scourge of the wicked nations. The phrase can, however, be translated "with the glory," that is, "with the glory" of the divine presence he will come to judge the nations. The glory that is the delight of his church, the glory of his own presence, is the terror of the heathen. So it is at Christ's return. The event for which we pray, "Come quickly, Lord Jesus," is the event that brings such terror to Christ's enemies that they pray for the mountains to fall on them and hide them from his face (Rev. 6:15–17).

Judah, God's church, was the apple of his eye, a phrase always used in scripture to describe something especially valuable and loved. Judah was the apple of his eye not for any value that she had in herself or because she was worthy of his love, but because he had loved her from eternity and because in that same love he would send his dearest possession to die for her.

As the eye is too sensitive to be touched and must always be guarded, so God guards his people. As even the smallest speck of dust in the eye is unendurably painful, so what the nations had done to Israel pained God. No wonder God was angry with the nations.

God's judgments on Babylon and the other heathen nations would require nothing more than the shaking of God's fist at them. With but a shake of the hand Babylon would be gone. Indeed, where is she now? With nothing more than a wave of God's hand, her glory would be forgotten forever and she who spoiled many would herself be spoiled. As Moses lifted his hand against Egypt at the Red Sea (Ex. 14:27), so God lifts his hand against Babylon, and then "[those] whom ye have seen today, ye shall see them again no more forever" (v. 13).

Revelation 18:6–8 demonstrates that this word of God applies not only to old Babylon, now gone forever, but also to Babylon as she always exists spiritually and is a figure of the wicked world in which God's people live:

> 6. Reward her even as she rewarded you, and double unto her double according to her works: in the cup which she hath filled fill to her double.
> 7. How much she hath glorified herself, and lived deliciously, so much torment and sorrow give her: for she saith in her heart, I sit a queen, and am no widow, and shall see no sorrow.
> 8. Therefore shall her plagues come in one day, death, and mourning, and famine; and she shall be utterly burned with fire: for strong is the Lord God who judgeth her.

Judah had been servant to Babylon, as Israel had been servant to Egypt in her early history, but by the judgments of God these nations were themselves reduced to servitude and their wealth became the inheritance of Israel. Israel spoiled the Egyptians when they left Egypt (Ex. 12:35–36), receiving in that spoil the wages for their long service, but Judah in Zechariah's day would never become wealthy and powerful. For her the fulfillment of this promise waits, as it does for us, until Christ comes to give the heavens and the earth, now under the domination of the ungodly, to his people as their inheritance.

Indeed, it is not only spiritual Babylon that is spoiled, but also her prince, the prince of darkness. Christ speaks of this in Matthew 12:29, when in connection with his casting out of demons he describes himself as the one who enters the strong man's house, binds him, and spoils his goods and his house. Revelation 20:1–3 describe that binding in more detail, not as a complete binding of Satan's power, but so that he is unable to deceive the nations for a time.

This binding, as Christ indicates in Matthew, is not future but has already happened. It took place when he came into the world, and the result of it has been the gathering of the nations into the kingdom and church of Christ. In Zechariah 2 this promised spoiling of Babylon, therefore, leads into the promise of the gathering of the Gentiles in verse 11.

When we see these things fulfilling, we know beyond doubt that the one who conveys this message to Zechariah was sent by God. What the Belgic Confession of Faith says of all scripture is true here also: "The Holy Ghost witnesseth in our hearts that they are from God, whereof they carry the evidence in themselves. For the very blind are able to perceive that the things foretold in them are fulfilling."[8]

In Zechariah 2:8–9 there seems to be confusion regarding who is speaking. The Lord of hosts himself says, "Ye shall know that the Lord of hosts hath sent me." As Calvin says, "Whose herald can God be? and by whose order or command could he promulgate what the Prophet here relates?"[9] Belief in the Trinity, however, clears this up. No doubt the person who is speaking, who is himself to be identified with the Lord of hosts, is also the one sent by the Lord of hosts. He is the angel of Jehovah, the man who is speaking to Zechariah: "We hence conclude that Christ is here introduced, who is Jehovah, and yet the Angel or the messenger of the Father."[10]

2:10. Sing and rejoice, O daughter of Zion: for, lo, I come, and I will dwell in the midst of thee, saith the LORD.

The promise of God's presence is repeated, both because of its importance and because the salvation of the Gentiles is about to be expressly prophesied. It is through the one whom the Lord of hosts has sent, the one who has just spoken, that this promise is fulfilled. He is the one in whom dwells all the fullness of the Godhead bodily and the one in whom we are complete. He is Immanuel, God with us, in his two natures as God and man the realization of God's covenant and the fulfillment of the covenantal promises. He is the true temple, the dwelling place of God among his people. He is the glory in the midst. To see him is to see the Father, and to be in him is to be partaker of the divine nature.

God's people are called here and elsewhere the daughter of Zion in light of their relationship to God. The daughter of Zion is the bride of Christ, as Revelation 21:9 shows so clearly. "Come hither," the angel says to John, "I will show thee the bride, the Lamb's wife," and then he shows John the

---

8 Belgic Confession 5, in Schaff, *Creeds of Christendom*, 3:386–87.
9 Calvin, *Commentaries on the Twelve Minor Prophets*, 5:67.
10 Ibid., 5:68.

holy city, new Jerusalem descending out of heaven from God, the same new Jerusalem described in verse 2 as "a bride adorned for her husband." As the bride of Christ she lives in unspeakably blessed fellowship with him and in that way knows and enjoys God himself.

God's presence among his people is always the cause of rejoicing and singing. Even in the Old Testament, when that promise was only fulfilled typically and partially, it was so: in Psalm 89, contemplating God's covenantal promises, David says he will sing of the mercies of the Lord forever. When the covenantal promise is fulfilled in the new heavens and earth, it will be so again and forever: "And they sing the song of Moses the servant of God, and the song of the Lamb, saying, Great and marvellous are thy works, Lord God Almighty; just and true are thy ways, thou King of saints" (Rev. 15:3).

2:11. And many nations shall be joined to the LORD in that day, and shall be my people: and I will dwell in the midst of thee, and thou shalt know that the LORD of hosts hath sent me unto thee.

The covenantal promise is not only for the Jews but also for all nations and is fulfilled in the gathering in of the Gentiles. They too are joined to the Lord in the day when Christ comes, and God's dwelling in the midst of his people includes them.

This joining of the nations to the Lord and his dwelling in the midst of them is not something separate from his dwelling in Israel, not a separate covenant from his covenant with the Jewish people, but together Jew and Gentile form the one people of God, the church of all ages. God is still speaking here to the daughter of Zion, and to her he says that when these nations are joined to him he will dwell in the midst of her. That cannot mean anything else but that Jew and Gentile dwell together as the one people of God with God in the midst.

The day of which God speaks to Zechariah is a day that began when Christ was born and does not end until he returns to make all things new. It is the day of the Lord, a day of which the prophets speak often. It is described as a day because the prophets from their Old Testament perspective did not see the different aspects of Christ's coming and did not realize that this day of the Lord would be stretched out over many calendar years. They could not distinguish between Christ's first and second comings but saw it all as one event.

The difference between their perspective and ours is like seeing the Rockies from the highway as one drives toward them and seeing them from a plane as one flies through them. Only from the plane can one see that they are formed of range after range and that they and their foothills stretch for miles so that it takes many hours to get through them. The saints of the Old Testament saw the New Testament from a distance and did not see its extent in terms of time and history. We see it more clearly now in the New Testament.

Yet the Old Testament believers were not wrong in their perspective either, for as the oft-used phrase "day of the Lord" reminds us, the whole New Testament, now reaching out over two thousand years of history, is from God's perspective a short time, the time in which he finishes his work and cuts it short in righteousness (Rom. 9:28). It is, from the time Christ first appeared until his return, the end of the ages (1 Cor. 10:11).

It is worth noticing that the gathering of the Gentiles is referred to in terms of nations. That does not mean that every person in these nations is saved. We know both from God's word and from our own experience that it is not so. Those who are saved are usually only a small minority out of the nations, a remnant according to the election of grace (Rom. 11:5). Nevertheless, just as with Israel, the elect out of that nation are in God's sight the whole of the nation. The true Israel, the only Israel God recognizes, is elect Israel: "For they are not all Israel, which are of Israel" (Rom. 9:6). The world that Christ comes to save does not include every person born in the world but is the world of God's elect in distinction from the world for which he neither prayed nor died (John 3:16; 17:9). All together the elect out of every nation are the melting pot of nations that becomes by God's grace the holy nation and peculiar people of which God speaks in 1 Peter 2:9.

Here again the angel of Jehovah speaks of himself as the one God sent. His coming is the proof that God's words do not fail: that Jehovah is faithful and true. But he is speaking not only of the fact that he is the living proof of God's faithfulness, but also of the fact that when he comes God's people will experience the truth of all God said to them. What were promises will become realities. What was only known through types and shadows will be known face-to-face. Thus we know now that the Lord of hosts sent him to us, and so we shall know forever.

2:12. And the LORD *shall inherit Judah his portion in the holy land, and shall choose Jerusalem again.*

God finishes his word of promise to Judah in a very unusual way, by speaking of them as his inheritance and re-electing Jerusalem. Nevertheless, the unusual character of his word serves to impress on his people his determination to bless them.

God speaks of inheriting Judah to emphasize his love for them and their value to him. If they are his inheritance, though, he receives that inheritance from himself, for no one but himself can give anything to him. A similar statement is found in Deuteronomy 32:9, "For the LORD's portion is his people; Jacob is the lot of his inheritance." God says in effect that in giving his people as an inheritance, he gives them to himself and so also receives an inheritance. That is the blessed reality of his covenant and the glory of his people.

The re-election of Jerusalem is not to be understood as something other than God's eternal election of his people, nor a denial of the eternal and unchangeable character of election. His choice of Jerusalem is eternal and irrevocable. God in choosing Jerusalem does not change his mind and change it again.

So too, Jerusalem is not finally an earthly city, but the heavenly Jerusalem of Hebrews 12:22, the Jerusalem of Revelation 21:9 that is also the bride, the Lamb's wife. This new election of Jerusalem, then, must be a new revelation of God's eternal love and electing purpose with respect to Jerusalem.

Some would argue that God's choice of Jerusalem is only of the earthly city and a choice that only brings earthly and temporal blessing to that city. This same argument is used to deny any eternal choice and rejection of Jacob and Esau in Romans 9. There is no choice that God makes, however, that is not grounded in his eternal will and purpose, for he is not many gods with many purposes and of many different minds, but the one true God. The choices he makes are eternal and unchangeable, and he who has chosen Jerusalem will choose her forever.

When these promises are fulfilled, the land in which Jerusalem is like a city without walls, surrounded by the fire of God's presence and itself afire, filled to every corner with those whom God has called out of the nations, will truly be the "holy land":

18. Violence shall no more be heard in thy land, wasting nor destruction within thy borders; but thou shalt call thy walls Salvation, and thy gates Praise.

19. The sun shall be no more thy light by day; neither for brightness shall the moon give light unto thee: but the LORD shall be unto thee an everlasting light, and thy God thy glory.

20. Thy sun shall no more go down; neither shall thy moon withdraw itself: for the LORD shall be thine everlasting light, and the days of thy mourning shall be ended.

21. Thy people also shall be all righteous: they shall inherit the land for ever, the branch of my planting, the work of my hands, that I may be glorified. (Isa. 60:18–21)

It will be Messiah's land.

2:13. Be silent, O all flesh, before the LORD: for he is raised up out of his holy habitation.

What other possible conclusion could there be to the revelations of this vision but awed silence—awed silence before God as he raises himself up in all his majesty and shows himself to his people.

That God raises himself up means that he has taken notice of the plight of his people and having taken notice will surely come to deliver them. When Stephen was being martyred, he saw something very much like what God promises here. He saw "the heavens opened, and the Son of man standing on the right hand of God" (Acts 7:56). God does not sit idly by when his people are threatened and suffering, but takes notice and having taken notice comes.

> God shall arise and by His might
> Put all His enemies to flight
> With shame and consternation.
> His haters, haughty though they be,
> Shall at His august presence flee
> In utter desolation;
> For when Jehovah shall appear,

He shall consume, afar and near,
All those that evil cherish.
As smoke before His dreadful ire,
As wax is molten by the fire,
So shall the wicked perish.

But let the righteous, blessed of yore,
Joy in their God as ne'er before,
Faith's victory achieving.
Their joy shall then unbounded be
Who see God's face eternally,
Their heart's desire receiving.
Exalt, exalt the Name of God;
Sing ye His royal fame abroad
With fervent exultation;
Cast up a highway smooth and wide
That through the deserts He may ride,
Jehovah, our salvation.

Ye kings and kingdoms of the earth,
Extol Jehovah's matchless worth
With psalms of adoration.
Praise Him whose glory rides on high,
Whose thunders roll through clouded sky
With mighty intonation.
Ascribe ye strength to God alone,
Whose worth in Israel is known,
For whom the heavens tremble.
O Lord, our strength, to Thee we bow,
For great and terrible art Thou
Out of Thy holy temple.[11]

God's holy habitation is heaven. He is not limited to heaven, for heaven and the heaven of heavens cannot contain him (1 Kings 8:27). Yet it is

---

11 No. 420:1–2, 6, in *The Psalter*.

from heaven that he comes in the person of his Son. In Christ he has come, continues to come, and will come again as the great deliverer of his people. Surely if he took notice of their affliction in those evil days, how much more will he today when his church is like a besieged city, a mere remnant according to the election of grace.

Chapter 10

THE FOURTH VISION AND THE FIRST STORY:
ZECHARIAH 3:1–10

3:1 And he shewed me Joshua the high priest standing before the angel of the Lord, and Satan standing at his right hand to resist him.

3:2 And the Lord said unto Satan, The Lord rebuke thee, O Satan; even the Lord that hath chosen Jerusalem rebuke thee: is not this a brand plucked out of the fire?

3:3 Now Joshua was clothed with filthy garments, and stood before the angel.

3:4 And he answered and spake unto those that stood before him, saying, Take away the filthy garments from him. And unto him he said, Behold, I have caused thine iniquity to pass from thee, and I will clothe thee with change of raiment.

3:5 And I said, Let them set a fair mitre upon his head. So they set a fair mitre upon his head, and clothed him with garments. And the angel of the Lord stood by.

3:6 And the angel of the Lord protested unto Joshua, saying,

3:7 Thus saith the Lord of hosts; If thou wilt walk in my ways, and if thou wilt keep my charge, then thou shalt also judge my house, and shalt also keep my courts, and I will give thee places to walk among these that stand by.

3:8 Hear now, O Joshua the high priest, thou, and thy fellows that sit before thee: for they are men wondered at: for, behold, I will bring forth my servant the BRANCH.

3:9 For behold the stone that I have laid before Joshua; upon one stone shall be seven eyes: behold, I will engrave the graving thereof, saith the LORD of hosts, and I will remove the iniquity of that land in one day.

3:10 In that day, saith the LORD of hosts, shall ye call every man his neighbour under the vine and under the fig tree.

This fourth vision is one of the story passages in Zechariah. Three things distinguish this section from those that precede and that follow. First, there are no "imaginary objects"[1] in the vision, though some elements are symbolic. Second, the focus of the vision is a real historical person, Joshua in this case. And third, Zechariah is not only a bystander who asks questions, but he also becomes a participant in the action.

These elements are found in all three story passages, also in Zechariah 6:9–15 and 11:1–17. In the other two story passages, Joshua again and then Zechariah are the persons around whom the action takes place. In the three story passages therefore, Zechariah is not only a participant in the action but also becomes more and more involved until in the third story passage (11:1–17) he is the center of the prophetic action. Here, in the first of these passages, he requests that a mitre be set on the head of Joshua. In the next (6:9–15), Zechariah obtains gold and silver, makes crowns, and puts them on the head of Joshua. In the third, Zechariah becomes the main figure in the prophetic action as the rejected shepherd.

In each of these story passages the main figure, Joshua in the first two and Zechariah in the third, is a very vivid type of Christ as the great priest. In this fourth vision and first story Christ appears as the priestly justifier of his people, the one who takes their sin on himself and so removes it from them, thus delivering them from the power of Satan. In the second story he is the crowned priest who unites in himself the kingly and priestly offices, thus empowering his priestly work, and in the third story he appears as the shepherd-priest who is rejected by those for whom he comes. In this way Christ is the central figure in Zechariah's visions.

There is progression therefore in the three story passages. In the first Christ shows himself to be the savior of all those who were given him by his father. In the second he shows us why he is *able* to save his people from their sins, for as priest he also has the power of a king, a power that was lacking in the Aaronitic priesthood. In the third he shows how he justifies his people in the way of his humiliation and suffering. The three together give us a complete picture of Christ's atoning priestly work.

---

1 Kline, *Glory in Our Midst*, 242.

3:1. And he shewed me Joshua the high priest standing before the angel of the LORD, and Satan standing at his right hand to resist him.

That chapter 3 is also a vision we learn from the words "he shewed me." Similar words introduce each of the visions. In this vision Zechariah is not only awake and able to see things that otherwise could not be seen, but also he actually participates in the visionary events.

He sees Joshua the high priest standing before the angel of the Lord. Of Joshua we know very little. Since the line of the priesthood was lost in obscurity during the years of the captivity, we learn of him only when the returned captives emerge once again from the dark years of the captivity under his leadership and that of Zerubbabel. The lack of information does serve, however, to remind us that his office, not his person, is the important thing.

As high priest he is the representative of all the people. What happens to him happens to all, and here, the judgment passed on Joshua is God's judgment of all the people. That Joshua is justified therefore reflects God's justifying sentence on the church of both the Old and New Testaments. In this capacity Joshua pictures our Savior, who is the priestly representative of all those the Father gave him, the representative who is justified on their behalf and they through him.

He is called Jeshua, a minor difference of spelling, in Ezra and Nehemiah. Both of those books as well as Haggai and Zechariah identify him as the son of Jozadak (Ezra and Nehemiah) or Josedech (Haggai and Zechariah), but of his father we know nothing. When Joshua became high priest we do not know, but other accounts tell us that he died the year after the temple was finished, in 515 BC, about twenty-two years after the return, at which time his son Joiakim became high priest (Neh. 12:10, 12, 26). He lived to see the temple rebuilt, therefore, but not the city walls.

He is the only one besides the son of Nun to have the name Joshua, the Hebrew Old Testament form of the name Jesus (see Heb. 4:8, where Joshua the son of Nun is called "Jesus"). He is, in name and office and in what happens to him in Zechariah's visions, a very special type of our Savior, and he proves symbolically and typically the meaning of his name and that of our Savior, "Jehovah saves."

He is described as standing before the angel of Jehovah, not merely as a matter of location, but in order to be judged by God through that angel.

He is on trial before him to whom the Father has committed all judgment (John 5:22). In the trial the angel of Jehovah acts as spokesman for the Judge (Zech. 3:4–7) and as the defense (vv. 1–2). He appears therefore as the mediator, representing both the accuser and the accused. So it is always in God's courtroom, the courtroom in which we are justified. The one who takes up our defense and is our advocate is also the representative of the Judge, his own Son, and that in spite of the fact that we offended against him. He is both God the Judge and the accused, the best of all mediators.

The Judge in this trial is not impartial, therefore, but determined to find Joshua and all whom he represents innocent, though without denying his own justice and righteousness. Thus the angel of his presence appears for the defense and successfully defends Joshua against the prosecution of Satan, rebuking Satan in the process.

That Satan appears as Joshua's accuser is no surprise. His name, Satan, means "accuser" or "adversary," and he is called in Revelation 12:10 "the accuser of our brethren...which accused them before our God day and night." He comes in that role in Job 1, accusing Job before God of serving God for his own advantage (vv. 8–11). In scripture we have only the examples of Job and Joshua, but there can be little doubt in light of Revelation 12:10 that this despicable activity of Satan never ceased until Christ entered heaven. There is even a play on words in Zechariah 3:1 in that the Hebrew word translated as "resist" is the word "satan." Literally, Satan stands at Joshua's right hand to "satan" him.

Satan's accusations, especially in the Old Testament, appeared to have validity, since the blood of atonement had not yet been shed and payment made for sins. He could argue that those whom God took to heaven had no right to be there, that they belonged to him. Jude 9 informs us that he fought with the archangel Michael over the body of Moses. That must have been when God, who buried Moses, raised him again from the dead in order that he might appear to Jesus on the mount of transfiguration with Elijah as the representative of the law, Elijah then representing the prophets.

Satan's struggle for the body of Moses could only have been on the grounds that Moses had no right to resurrection life and heavenly glory, but because of his sins was worthy of eternal damnation with both body and soul. "Moses's body belongs to me," must have been Satan's argument. "In that body he struck the rock, so that God himself forbad him to enter the earthly Canaan. How then can he enter the heavenly Canaan?" Nor did Michael dare bring against him a railing accusation, but he could only say, "The Lord rebuke thee" (Jude 9).

Standing at Joshua's right hand, he is the prosecutor here (Ps. 109:6). His position also indicates the power of his case against Joshua and against us. With the Lord at our right hand, we cannot be moved (Ps. 16:8), but here Satan is at Joshua's right hand. In what an unenviable position, then, Joshua stands! Yet that is the position in which we all stand apart from the justifying sentence of God: with Satan, not God, at our right hand, ready both as prosecutor and as executioner. What is more, Joshua's silence in the face of these accusations shows the truth of them.

This accusing activity of Satan was brought to an end first by the cross and then by the ascension of Christ to heaven. Before he died on the cross, Jesus, looking ahead, said, "I beheld Satan as lightning fall from heaven" (Luke 10:18). And in Revelation 12:5–11, when the man child is caught up to God and to his throne, there is no place for Satan in heaven anymore as accuser, and he and his angels are cast out. He is overcome "by the blood of the Lamb" (v. 11) now shed as an atonement for sin and brought into God's presence in heaven (Heb. 9:12), and the glorified church celebrates.

Here his presence is itself an accusation, but he is rebuked before he ever has a chance to speak, not because he was then yet silenced as the accuser but in hope of that day. Now he is silenced forever and Romans 8:33–34 is true: "Who shall lay any thing to the charge of God's elect? It is God that justifieth. Who is he that condemneth? It is Christ that died, yea rather, that is risen again, who is even at the right hand of God, who also maketh intercession for us."

3:2. And the LORD said unto Satan, The LORD rebuke thee, O Satan; even the LORD that hath chosen Jerusalem rebuke thee: is not this a brand plucked out of the fire?

Satan is rebuked by Jehovah himself, the only time he speaks directly in the trial of Joshua. Satan is rebuked on the basis of election and grace, but not on the basis of the blood of atonement. That had not yet been shed. Nevertheless, the Lord's rebuke is effective and Satan is silenced. God's choice of Jerusalem guaranteed that the blood of atonement would be shed, as did the grace of God that plucked Joshua from the fire. Election, God's choosing of Jerusalem, demanded the atonement, and because election is eternal and unchangeable, the fruits of the atonement were evident in the Old Testament, hundreds and thousands of years before the blood of atonement was actually poured out on the altar of God's justice.

This confrontation between God, in the person of Christ, and Satan is the central theme of the second half of the book of Revelation. Both halves of Revelation show us the battle of the ages, but from a different perspective. Chapters 1–11 show us that battle as a struggle between the church and the world, the battle as we experience it; but chapters 12–22 (or 20) show us the spiritual background of that battle, the long war between Christ and Satan, in which Christ is triumphant and Satan is rebuked by being cast into the lake of fire.

All this was prophesied at the very beginning, when God said to Satan, "And I will put enmity between thee and the woman, and between thy seed and her seed; it shall bruise thy head, and thou shalt bruise his heel" (Gen. 3:15). The fourth vision is one incident in the fulfillment of that prophecy. Satan was rebuked every time God delivered his people in the Old Testament and preserved in them the holy seed. Satan was rebuked in the temptations of Christ, in Jesus' own rebukes of Satan's servants the scribes and Pharisees, in the rebuking of Peter (Matt. 16:23), and above all at the cross, when Satan's power was completely taken away. At the cross God not only rebukes Satan but also laughs at him, for all his plotting and evil work is sovereignly used by God to finish the redemption of his people (Ps. 2:1–4; Acts 4:24–28). All this leads to the final terrible rebuking of Satan when the Lord roars out of Zion (Joel 3:16; Amos 3:2) and by the blast of the breath of his nostrils drives Satan forever away (Ps. 18:15–17).

God does not, however, tell Satan that he has chosen *Joshua*, but that he has chosen *Jerusalem*. Joshua is the representative of Jerusalem, and what happens to him is true not only for him but also for all who belong to Jerusalem. Jerusalem is not the earthly city, for that was not even built at this time. Jerusalem is the city that is above (Gal. 4:26), the church (Heb. 12:22–23). All of which is to say that election, though personal, is the election of the church, the body of Christ, and of each individual to a place in that body.

Some deny the personal character of election and speak of it only in terms of a number. God has chosen, so they say, a certain amount of people to be saved, but he does not know who are actually part of that number until they, of their own free will, choose to believe, and only when sufficient numbers have believed is election finished. The election of the church does not mean that. Rather it means that God in choosing certain persons to salvation and eternal life chooses them to be part of a unified whole, a body of believers, which in its unity as well as its diversity shows the glory of his grace (Eph. 1:10–12).

How little of that is seen today, when even in the church selfishness prevails and the body is neglected and despised, when individual gifts and their exercise are the only thing that matters, when unity and peace are sacrificed on the altar of personal advantage and feeling, and when the individual rather than the covenantal community is the focus. Does not anyone understand anymore that the Lord has chosen *Jerusalem*?

When Joshua is described as a brand plucked from the burning, a stick pulled out of the fire just as it begins to smolder and burn, the word of God is reminding us all that we are naturally dead in trespasses and sins, ready to be cremated in eternal fire. That is also our experience. Considering our sins and the curse due to us for them, we feel that we have escaped the fire of hell only by a hairsbreadth and know that we are saved by grace alone and by God alone: "It is not Jerusalem that chooses Jehovah, but Jehovah that chooses Jerusalem. It is not the burning brand that plucks the hand, but the hand that plucks it."[2]

This same figure is used in Amos 4:11: "I have overthrown some of you, as God overthrew Sodom and Gomorrah, and ye were as a firebrand plucked out of the burning: yet have ye not returned unto me, saith the Lord." Amos confirms that the fire is the fire of God's wrath and judgment by the reference to Sodom and Gomorrah, but Amos's purpose is a little different. He is reminding Judah of what God had done for them and of their ingratitude. In Zechariah's vision the angel of Jehovah is telling Satan what God has done for his people in order to silence Satan's accusations.

In Zechariah's days the people would also have remembered the word of Isaiah describing the captivity in Babylon as a "furnace of affliction" in which

---

2 Moore, *Zechariah*, 64.

God's just judgments had burned among the people (Isa. 48:10), but out of which they had been plucked by a faithful and merciful God. So too do we remember the fire out of which we were plucked when we read these words.

We are taught in this powerful metaphor, therefore, the power and miracle of God's grace, for in the person of his Son God stretches out his mighty arm, reaches into the fires of hell, and draws us out. Christ is not only the arm of God, but is also the brand, first cast into the fire and then snatched out again on behalf of those he represents. He is the one who says and we with him, "The sorrows of death compassed me, and the pains of hell gat hold upon me: I found trouble and sorrow. Then called I upon the name of the LORD; O LORD, I beseech thee, deliver my soul. Gracious is the Lord, and righteous; yea, our God is merciful. The LORD preserveth the simple: I was brought low, and he helped me" (Ps. 116:3–6).

3:3. Now Joshua was clothed with filthy garments, and stood before the angel.

What a way to appear at one's trial! Even the vilest of criminals puts on a suit and necktie when in court in order to make a good impression on the judge, but Joshua appears in the dirtiest and most ragged clothing. In real life that would be an insult to the judge and to the court, but in the figure that is all Joshua has. We can only imagine what this must have meant to Judah—the high priest appearing ragged and dirty and with nothing to wear into God's presence. How shocking!

Joshua's filthy garments are a picture of his sin and ours. The angel's statement in the next verse proves that, for when those garments are taken away, he says, "Behold, I have caused thine iniquity to pass from thee." Our righteousnesses, that is, our own works, which are our sins, are also described as filthy rags in Isaiah 64:6.[3] God sees man's depravity in Psalm 14:3 as filthiness. Sin is like grime and dirt in that it clings to everything and spoils everything, and it shows its filthiness in filthy speech, filthy thoughts, and filthy deeds, some of which are too vile and filthy even to be named among saints (Eph. 5:3). Sin is not something exciting and enjoyable: it is filth. Living in sin is like living in a pigsty or in the gutter. It is misery, not happiness, and the pleasures that sin promises are only an illusion, not reality.

---

3 The figure is slightly different in Isaiah in that the words "filthy rags" actually refer to menstruous cloths.

Joshua, clothed in these filthy garments and standing before the angel, represents us all in our sinful condition. Indeed, in verse 9 Joshua's sin is described as the sin of the land.

In the Old Testament, when the priests had to be scrupulously clean by constant washing, Joshua's filthy garments would have excluded him from the temple and its service. Thus the picture is not only of his sin, but also of his unfitness to appear before God, to serve him, to be in his house. Clothed also in such garments, we too are unfit to appear before God or to live in his house. Even if we would try, we would be like the man in the parable of the wedding feast, who without a proper garment was cast out into eternal fire.

Whether Joshua was guilty of specific gross sins, we do not know. Some of his sons were among those who married heathen wives during Ezra's time (Ezra 10:18), but that is not necessarily a reflection on Joshua himself. In the end it does not matter, for the least of his sins, and of ours, is sufficient to bring upon us the wrath of God and eternal condemnation.

Joshua's uncleanness gives support to Satan's accusations even though he never has opportunity to make them. Before Joshua's appearance is so much as mentioned, Satan is already rebuked. Yet Satan, it would seem, would be justified in claiming those garments as proof that their owner belonged to him.

Yet Joshua is described as standing before the angel, the first indication that he will be justified and declared innocent in this courtroom. Though clothed in filthy rags, he has nothing to fear. Standing is often in scripture a figure for being righteous and being assured of one's righteousness. Psalm 1:5 reminds us that the ungodly will "not stand in the judgment," and Revelation 6:17 asks in connection with Christ's coming as judge, "Who shall be able to stand?" Joshua, for all the filthiness of his garments, is able to stand before the angel. He appears in the passage as a sinner, but a justified sinner.

3:4. And he answered and spake unto those that stood before him, saying, Take away the filthy garments from him. And unto him he said, Behold, I have caused thine iniquity to pass from thee, and I will clothe thee with change of raiment.

Here the justification of the sinner is vividly pictured. The filthy rags of our own works, which can never gain us acceptance with God, are replaced with the clean garments of Christ's righteous works. The righteousness of Christ, ours by faith, is often described in scripture as clean or white linen: "Let us be glad and rejoice, and give honour to him: for the marriage of the Lamb is come, and his wife hath made herself ready. And to her was granted that she should be arrayed in fine linen, clean and white: for the fine linen is the righteousness of saints" (Rev. 19:7–8), our change of raiment.

The modern Bible versions are guilty of gross doctrinal error in their translations of this passage from Revelation. The NKJV, the RSV, NASV, and the ESV all say something like the NIV: "The fine linen stands for the righteous *acts* of the saints." If we must appear before God clothed in our own acts, there is no one who can appear before him and be justified. So serious is this mistranslation, and its denial of the doctrine of justification by faith alone, that it makes these versions worthless.

Justification is not something God works in the sinner, but something he says about the sinner. It is the divine sentence of the almighty Judge. Here God's justifying sentence is declared in the words "Behold, I have caused thine iniquity to pass from thee." The word "behold" reminds us that this is an amazing and wonderful thing, for it is the sinner who is justified and God the righteous Judge, the one who never lies, who justifies the sinner.

When Joshua's filthy garments are taken away, he has nothing left with which to cover himself. He is naked. What a way to stand in this court before the angels, before his fellows (Zech. 3:8), before the angel of Jehovah, and before God himself! He has nowhere to hide and nothing with which to cover himself. So scripture reminds us that we have nothing to bring to God, nothing with which to cover our spiritual nakedness, no righteousness before him. We are without one plea, and the labors of our hands cannot atone for sin. We are "naked and open before the eyes of him with whom we have to do" (Heb. 4:13), and so we will be in the last great day of judgment when we must appear before God as Joshua does here.

God's justifying sentence is executed by others who stand by. They are probably other angels, though they are not identified as such in the vision. There are other angels besides the messenger angel present in the first and second visions, so it should not surprise us that there are others waiting in the background here. They, the court officers, are commanded to execute

God's justifying sentence by reclothing Joshua in a change of raiment, symbolic of the "righteousness of saints," which is the righteousness of Christ given to the sinner through faith.

All this is beautifully expressed in the following poem, written from an experience of grace similar to what is pictured here:

With Satan, my accuser, near
My spirit trembled when I saw
The Lord in majesty appear,
And heard the language of his law.

In vain I wish'd and strove to hide
The tatter'd, filthy rags I wore;
While my fierce foe insulting cry'd
See what you trusted in before!

Struck dumb, and left without a plea,
I heard my gracious Saviour say,
Know, Satan, I this sinner free,
I died to take his sin away.

This is a brand which I, in love,
To save from wrath and sin design!
In vain thy accusations prove;
I answer all, and call him mine.

At his rebuke the tempter fled;
Then he remov'd my filthy dress;
Poor sinner, take this robe, he said,
It is thy Saviour's righteousness.

And see, a crown of life prepar'd!
That I might thus thy head adorn;
I thought no shame or suff'ring hard,
But wore for thee a crown of thorn.

O how I heard these gracious words!
They broke and heal'd my heart at once;
Constrained me to become the Lord's,
And all my idol-gods renounce.

Now, Satan, thou hast lost thy aim,
Against this brand thy threats are vain;
Jesus has pluck'd it from the flame,
And who shall put it in again?[4]

Our response? What else but "I will greatly rejoice in the LORD, my soul shall be joyful in my God; for he hath clothed me with the garments of salvation, he hath covered me with the robe of righteousness, as a bridegroom decketh himself with ornaments, and as a bride adorneth herself with her jewels" (Isa. 61:10).

3:5. And I said, Let them set a fair mitre upon his head. So they set a fair mitre upon his head, and clothed him with garments. And the angel of the LORD stood by.

Having witnessed Joshua's justification, Zechariah boldly tells the bystanders to add a priestly mitre to Joshua's new clothes. The word used for this head covering is at its root the same word used in Exodus and Leviticus for the priestly head covering (Ex. 28:4, 37, 39; 29:6; 39:28, 31; Lev. 8:9; 16:4). It is used in several other passages as well and translated as "diadem," but in those passages as well there is good evidence that it refers not to a royal crown but to the priestly mitre. Even Isaiah 3:23, which has the translation "hoods" in reference to the head coverings of the vain and wanton daughters of Israel, may refer to the priestly mitre, imitated in the head coverings of these foolish women.

Zechariah understands that Joshua must be exonerated and justified and restored to his priestly office. He must not be left with nothing to do and must be given the opportunity to show his gratitude to God for God's justifying sentence. Joshua is not fully restored to his place in God's covenant until

---

4 John Newton, *Olney Hymns*, 1779, vol. 1, hymn 77.

he is given back his old position of service and allowed back into the holy of holies, into God's presence. Sacrifice for sin must be offered and intercession made at the golden altar. The Aaronitic blessing must be pronounced on the people of God, and if Joshua the high priest is not fit to do these things, there is no one to do them.

Man was created to serve God, and only in service does he enjoy God and have fellowship with him. He is God's friend, but a friend-servant, who in his relationship to God must always acknowledge that God is God and he is but a creature of God. Such service is priestly in its nature. It is fulfilled in holy separation from sin and in consecration to God.

To that priestly service man was called when God put him in the garden of Eden to dress it and keep it (Gen. 2:15) and said to him, "Of every tree of the garden thou mayest freely eat: But of the tree of the knowledge of good and evil, thou shalt not eat of it: for in the day that thou eatest thereof thou shalt surely die" (vv. 16–17). To that priestly service Aaron and his sons were called on behalf of all Israel, and the nature of their priestly calling was stated on the crown of gold that Aaron wore on the mitre: "HOLINESS TO THE LORD" (Ex. 28:36–37). Doing that service, every Old Testament and New Testament priest comes into God's presence and has a place in his house.

To that priestly service we are restored through the justifying work of Christ, for he has made us kings and priests unto God and his father (Rev. 1:6). Sanctification follows justification, must follow, for Christ purchased not only forgiveness for all our disservice, but also the right to serve God once again. And so, without holiness, priestly holiness, "no man shall see the Lord" (Heb. 12:14).

As Joshua is symbolically restored to his priestly office, the angel of the Lord stands by, not because there is nothing for him to do but because he is deeply interested in what is happening. He is, after all, the great high priest in the house of God, under whose rule all other priests must serve. He is the one upon whose head the priestly mitre would be set forever, in order that he might offer himself as a sacrifice for sin at the great altar. Having offered that one sacrifice for sin, he goes with coals from the altar into the presence of God to make intercession behind the veil and to sprinkle his blood on the mercy seat, thus obtaining for his own the blessing of God. He is the one upon whom the responsibility for keeping God's courts and judging his house will fall (Zech. 3:7). Later, during his ministry on earth, he took that responsibility, twice cleansing the temple of those who made his Father's house a den of merchandise, but doing so as a picture of what he would do when he would build again the true temple of God in three days. As our great high priest, we would not expect to find him anywhere else on such an occasion as this.

He watches also to make sure all that happens prefigures his own priestly work on our behalf. Knowing from eternity the work the Father had given him to do as the high priest of his people, he makes sure the work is properly and profitably pictured in the reclothing of Joshua.

3:6. And the angel of the LORD protested unto Joshua, saying,

3:7. Thus saith the LORD of hosts; If thou wilt walk in my ways, and if thou wilt keep my charge, then thou shalt also judge my house, and shalt also keep my courts, and I will give thee places to walk among these that stand by.

Now the angel of Jehovah addresses Joshua on behalf of the Judge and tells him as one who is uncondemned to "go and sin no more." "Protested" is a term that implies the authority or sovereignty of the one who speaks. It is used here to describe the judge's charge to one who has been before the bar and who has been cleared of all charges. The prisoner has been cleared. He must not fall back again into old sins.

In Joshua's case this charge had to do with the work of the temple. Looking ahead to the completion of the temple building, God admonishes Joshua to be faithful personally and in his priestly office. He must not, through personal sin, show himself unworthy of his priestly office: he must walk in God's ways and keep his commandments. He must also take oversight of the temple service and make sure it is not again corrupted or allowed to fall into decay.

The need for this charge is seen in the accounts of Ezra and Nehemiah. Ezra had just arrived in Jerusalem when the princes reported to him: "The people of Israel, and priests, and the Levites, have not separated themselves from the people of the lands, doing according to their abominations" (Ezra 9:1). When Nehemiah returned to Jerusalem after his first term as governor, he found that Eliashib, the grandson of Joshua, had allied himself with Tobiah the Ammonite and made a special chamber in the temple for him (Neh. 13:4–7); that the portions of the Levites had not been given them, and as a result the house of God was forsaken (vv. 10–11); and that the priesthood and the covenant of the priesthood was defiled by intermarriages with the heathen (vv. 28–29). One of Joshua's great-great-grandsons had married a daughter of Sanballat, the enemy of God's people.

Thus the word of God shows the need for a better priest than Joshua, not a priest who would arise out of the line of Aaron but a priest after the order of Melchizedek, a priest who had the power of an endless life and an unchangeable priesthood, who is "holy, harmless, undefiled, separate from sinners, and made higher than the heavens" (Heb. 7:15–26). The charge to Joshua would be kept only by his namesake, and only through him would the promised blessings come to those who are called to be a holy priesthood in the house of God.

God promises Joshua that the priesthood would continue with him and his descendants. That is what God means when he says, "Then thou shalt also judge my house, and shalt also keep my courts," for both the judgment of the people and the care of God's house were given to the priesthood. But God promises as well a place in God's heavenly house, that greater and more perfect tabernacle, not made with hands (Heb. 9:11). Those who stand by are the angel hosts who stand ready to do God's bidding, among them those who had clothed Joshua and set the priestly mitre on his head. They already served in heavenly glory, and God promises to give Joshua a place to walk among them, a permanent and higher place.

The conditions God sets, however, must not make us think that anything depended on Joshua. Obedience and faithfulness are the way in which we enjoy God's blessings, but nothing can depend on us. It is Jesus, Joshua's great successor, who keeps God's charge perfectly and by his perfect service covers all the shortcomings and sins of other priests, earns for them the priesthood, preserves them in it, and obtains for them the promised glory.

3:8. Hear now, O Joshua the high priest, thou, and thy fellows that sit before thee: for they are men wondered at: for, behold, I will bring forth my servant the BRANCH.

As we have seen, all this applies not just to Joshua but to us. So the angel addresses also Joshua's fellows, whom we now learn were present. They in turn represent all of true Israel, including us. Made a royal priesthood by Christ, we are among Joshua's fellows.

Nevertheless, the reference is especially to the Old Testament priesthood. They especially were "men to be wondered at," literally "men of the sign." In their priestly offices they were a sign of things to come and of a better priesthood, that of the Branch. The word of God, then, is not talking about the amazing grace shown to that Old Testament priesthood, but about the picture it made of the priesthood of Christ.

"BRANCH" is used as a name for Christ here and in chapter 6:12 as well as in Isaiah 4:2, Isaiah 11:1 (where a different word, though a synonym, is used), Jeremiah 23:5, and Jeremiah 33:15 (see also Ps. 80:15 and Isa. 53:2). It refers to Christ as a descendant of David (Isa. 11:1) and therefore speaks of his kingly office.

Used of Christ, it refers to him not as the mighty branch of a great tree, but as the sprout or shoot of a tree that has been cut down. As son of David he is indeed king, but without the glory of the kingship in his beginnings. The name reminds us therefore of the sad estate to which the house of David had come and would come in the years ahead. As in Nebuchadnezzar's vision, it was like a great tree cut down with only its stump remaining. Out of that stump Christ comes, unexpected, lowly, and despised as something worthless.

Yet his kingly office was important even in the days of his humiliation, for it lent power to his priestly office. We will look at this more closely in the second story passage, which describes the crowning of Joshua, for without the power of the kingly office the priestly office was powerless. We see that in the days of godless kings who were able to shut the temple, shut down the worship of God, and prevent the priests from performing their duties, even if they wanted to do them.

This is what Jeremiah says in one of his references to the Branch: "Behold, the days come, saith the LORD, that I will raise unto David a righteous Branch, and a King shall reign and prosper, and shall execute judgment and justice in the earth. In his days Judah shall be saved, and Israel shall dwell safely: and this is his name whereby he shall be called, THE LORD OUR

Righteousness" (Jer. 23:5–6). He is a priest, a king from the line of David, and one who brings in everlasting righteousness.

Joshua and his fellows were indeed a sign therefore, not only of a better priesthood that would come, but also of the need for a better priesthood, a priesthood that also had the power and authority of the kingly office. Christ would have that priesthood as the Branch. "Behold," God says, in order to focus our attention on him, for he, not Joshua, is the main figure in this vision and in all of God's work.

3:9. For behold the stone that I have laid before Joshua; upon one stone shall be seven eyes: behold, I will engrave the graving thereof, saith the LORD of hosts, and I will remove the iniquity of that land in one day.

God promises not only the coming of Christ as the high priest of God's people, but also the Holy Spirit under this figure of a stone with seven eyes.[5] Revelation 5:6 is conclusive in interpreting this part of the vision: "And I beheld, and, lo, in the midst of the throne and of the four beasts, and in the midst of the elders, stood a Lamb as it had been slain, having seven horns and seven eyes, which are the seven Spirits of God sent forth into all the earth."

In Revelation the Spirit is described as seven not because there are seven Holy Spirits but because he lives in the seven churches of Asia Minor, which are a picture of the church in every age with its strengths and weaknesses:

> He is called "the seven Spirits," for the number seven denotes the fulness of God's covenant of grace, and the fulness of the church in which He dwells is also indicated by the same number. For there are seven churches in Asia, and there are seven candlesticks and seven stars, Revelation 1:11–12, 16, 20. And the Lamb, Whose Spirit He is, has seven eyes, which are the seven Spirits of God, Revelation 3:1...There can be no question, therefore, that "the seven Spirits which are before his throne" refer to the Holy Spirit as He is given to the exalted Christ and poured out into the church.[6]

---

5   The NIV in a note calls these seven "facets," but that is not the idea here. Zechariah 4:10 identifies them as the eyes of the Lord that see all things.

6   Herman Hoeksema, *Behold He Cometh: An Exposition of the Book of Revelation* (Grand Rapids, MI: Reformed Free Publishing Association, 1969), 20.

Revelation 5:6 shows us that the Spirit is Christ's Spirit, for there the seven eyes are the seven eyes of the Lamb. In Zechariah 4:10 they are "the eyes of the LORD, which run to and fro through the whole earth," because the Spirit is the one who searches all things, even the deep things of God (1 Cor. 2:10). The Spirit is given to Joshua and the priesthood that through him they may conduct themselves in their offices as faithful priests.

Here too he is represented by seven eyes to show his place in God's covenant, for seven is the number of the covenant. As the covenantal Spirit he is also the one who lived in the church of the Old Testament and who by his presence made the church, even in the Old Testament, the dwelling place of God. The Branch and the seven eyes, therefore, would accomplish what the Aaronitic priesthood had never been able to do.

The stone is more difficult. Some commentators refer it to the plummet that is mentioned in the next vision or the headstone also mentioned there. It may, according to others, have reference to the twelve precious stones that were on the high priest's breastplate or the two on his shoulders, only in this case there is only one, not two or twelve. Nor are these the only explanations.[7]

That this stone is engraved seems to indicate that the stones of the breastplate or of the shoulder straps are the reference here, or the golden plate, or all of them, since all were engraved, the onyx stones that Aaron wore on his shoulders and the stones of the breastplate with the names of the twelve tribes and the golden plate with the words "HOLINESS TO THE LORD." That this stone is set before Joshua, however, would seem to mean that it is not a part of Joshua's garments but is a larger stone.

In light of Revelation 5:6, where the seven eyes belong to the Lamb, and Zechariah 4:10, where they are referred to as the eyes of the Lord, it is difficult to see that the stone can be anything or anyone but Christ himself, who appears in the passage as both the Branch and the stone. As the stone, he is the foundation of the church and those seven eyes belong to the church,

---

7 The stone is the golden plate on the high priest's mitre (Kline), the breastplate stone, the headstone of the temple (Wright and Pusey), the altar (c. Von Orelli, *The Twelve Minor Prophets* (Minneapolis: Klock and Klock, 1977), the stone that according to tradition stood in the most holy place, one of the stones of the temple (Moore), or symbolically the church (Leupold and Bentley), Christ (Wright), or in connection with Isaiah 28:6, the kingdom of Christ (Keil).

just as the seven spirits live in the seven churches of Asia. As the Branch guarantees the regrowth of the church, so the stone represents a guarantee in Christ of the rebuilding of the church.

What is the engraving on this stone? Here again there are many suggestions. Some say that the eyes are engraven on the stone, others that the engraving is the names of the twelve tribes, since the stone in their opinion is one of the stones of the high priest's garments.

The last phrase of the verse is the key. By the engraving of the stone the iniquity of the land is removed. The word translated "engrave" or "graving" should be understood to refer not to writing something on the stone, but to carving and polishing the stone, by which it was prepared for its place as the cornerstone or headstone of the temple. It prefigures the coming and work of Christ, through which he becomes the chief cornerstone of the temple and by which the iniquity of the land is removed in one day.

In principle the removal of iniquity is already accomplished in the death of Christ. The day of his death is the "one day" referred to, though Joshua and Judah may have thought of the great Day of Atonement. It cannot be anything else. His death removes sin not only in the sense that the guilt of sin is taken away once for all, but also that the power of sin is destroyed and the possibility of holiness is established. Paul says, "For in that he died, he died unto sin once: but in that he liveth, he liveth unto God. Likewise reckon ye also yourselves to be dead indeed unto sin, but alive unto God through Jesus Christ our Lord" (Rom. 6:10–11). We must count ourselves dead unto sin (though it is not yet dead in us) and alive unto God, because Christ died and rose again. Nor does his work require many sacrifices: "Who needeth not daily, as those high priests, to offer up sacrifice, first for his own sins, and then for the people's: for this he did once, when he offered up himself" (Heb. 7:27).

3:10. In that day, saith the LORD of hosts, shall ye call every man his neighbour under the vine and under the fig tree.

The result of Joshua's reclothing, the result of Christ's work as priest and of the sanctifying work of the Spirit, will be peace and prosperity for God's people. The vine and the fig tree, because both needed much care and attention, are symbolic in scripture of peace and prosperity. The vine and fig flourished and were properly tended only when the land had peace. That peace would also make possible again the communion and fellowship of the people in the land. They would have opportunity to speak to one another and to live together in harmony.

In the days of Solomon, the high point of Israel's history, when God had fulfilled the promises made to them long before, when they were prosperous and at peace (the name Solomon even means "peace"), then "Judah and Israel dwelt safely, every man under his vine and under his fig tree, from Dan even to Beersheba, all the days of Solomon" (1 Kings 4:25).

Rabshakeh, the king of Assyria's top general, falsely promised these things to Judah in the days of Hezekiah:

16. Hearken not to Hezekiah: for thus saith the king of Assyria, Make an agreement with me by a present, and come out to me: and eat ye every one of his vine, and every one of his fig tree, and drink ye every one the waters of his own cistern;
17. Until I come and take you away to a land like your own land, a land of corn and wine, a land of bread and vineyards." (Isa. 36:16–17)

God not only promises peace and prosperity but also gives it and gives it exceedingly abundantly above all that we would ever ask or think, for he gives it to Judah and to us in the new heavens and the new earth. There we eat of the tree of life that bears twelve manners of fruit and yields its fruit every month, and whose leaves are for the healing of the nations (Rev. 22:2). There we have blessed communion with one another and with God himself and have it forever. There we enjoy paradise regained.

Chapter 11

THE FIFTH VISION:
ZECHARIAH 4:1-14

4:1   And the angel that talked with me came again, and waked me, as a man that is wakened out of his sleep,

4:2   And said unto me, What seest thou? And I said, I have looked, and behold a candlestick all of gold, with a bowl upon the top of it, and his seven lamps thereon, and seven pipes to the seven lamps, which are upon the top thereof:

4:3   And two olive trees by it, one upon the right side of the bowl, and the other upon the left side thereof.

4:4   So I answered and spake to the angel that talked with me, saying, What are these, my lord?

4:5   Then the angel that talked with me answered and said unto me, Knowest thou not what these be? And I said, No, my lord.

4:6   Then he answered and spake unto me, saying, This is the word of the LORD unto Zerubbabel, saying, Not by might, nor by power, but by my spirit, saith the LORD of hosts.

4:7   Who art thou, O great mountain? before Zerubbabel thou shalt become a plain: and he shall bring forth the headstone thereof with shoutings, crying, Grace, grace unto it.

4:8   Moreover the word of the LORD came unto me, saying,

4:9   The hands of Zerubbabel have laid the foundation of this house; his hands shall also finish it; and thou shalt know that the LORD of hosts hath sent me unto you.

4:10   For who hath despised the day of small things? for they shall rejoice, and shall see the plummet in the hand of Zerubbabel with those seven; they are the eyes of the LORD, which run to and fro through the whole earth.

4:11 Then answered I, and said unto him, What are these two olive trees upon the right side of the candlestick and upon the left side thereof?

4:12 And I answered again, and said unto him, What be these two olive branches which through the two golden pipes empty the golden oil out of themselves?

4:13 And he answered me and said, Knowest thou not what these be? And I said, No, my lord.

4:14 Then said he, These are the two anointed ones, that stand by the Lord of the whole earth.

The symbolism of the fifth vision is the most complicated, yet the symbolism is not only crucial to the development that takes place in Zechariah's visions, but also is part of the vision of Revelation 11, the concluding and decisive chapter in the first half of that book. Zechariah 4 cannot be understood apart from Revelation 11, nor Revelation 11 apart from Zechariah.

In the fourth vision Zechariah saw the Spirit of God symbolized by the seven eyes that are upon the one stone. That brief reference to the Spirit is developed in more detail in the fifth vision, and the Spirit becomes the main figure, symbolized not only by seven eyes but also by the golden oil that pours from the olive tree into the seven lamps of the golden candlestick. The theme of this vision is found therefore in the words of verse 6, "Not by might, nor by power, but by my spirit, saith the LORD of hosts."

Just as Christ mounted on the red horse was the important figure in the first three visions, so now the Spirit poured into the church like oil is the central figure in the last three visions. The sequence of visions thus far is: Christ in the midst of his church (vision 1), bringing judgment on the church's enemies (vision 2) and rich blessing to his church (vision 3), and doing that as the justified one (vision 4). Now the word shows how he does his work in the church, by his Spirit (vision 5), for the Spirit always works in the church as the Spirit of Christ.

There is a beautiful progression in the visions therefore, for the focus moves not only from Christ to the Spirit of Christ, but also from the removal of sin and guilt to the overcoming of other obstacles and enemies. By every means God would ensure that his house was built and his covenant fulfilled.

4:1. And the angel that talked with me came again, and waked me, as a man that is wakened out of his sleep.

Here is clear proof that a vision is not the same as a dream, for Zechariah has to be wakened by the angel before he is able to receive this vision. That he was wakened does not mean, however, that he was asleep in the usual sense. The language suggests that this was not so. "Waked me as a man that is wakened out of his sleep" only compares Zechariah's state to sleep:

A pause seems to have occurred after the preceding vision, and the prophet, for a time, to have relapsed into his ordinary and normal state. This state compared with the prophetic ecstasy, was as sleep to waking; the ordinary state of the soul being so insensible to those impressions that were made upon it in the prophetic condition.[1]

Why this reference to the prophet's condition? It may serve to show the greatness of the visions he received. Twice in the middle of his visions, Daniel also fell asleep, apparently overwhelmed by what he saw (Dan. 8:18; 10:9).

Calvin makes a nice application of the matter:

As the Prophet says that he was awakened by the Angel, let us learn, that except God awakens us by his Spirit, torpor will so prevail over us, that we cannot raise our minds above. Since God then sees that we are so much tied down to the earth, he rouses us as it were from our lethargy. For if the Prophet had need of such help, how much more have we, who are far below him in faith?[2]

Once again the messenger angel wakes Zechariah and calls him to receive this vision, reminding us of the deep interest the angels have in the work of redemption (Heb. 1:14; 1 Pet. 1:12). The angel is not an interested bystander or mere agent of God but an active participant in the prophetic visions. That interest is the fruit of the universality of Christ's work. He reconciles all things, even the things in heaven, in the body of his flesh through death (Col. 1:20).

That is not to say that the fallen angels are reconciled or the unfallen angels are guilty of any sin, but it does show that through the fall of Satan and of man, all things were affected in their relation to God and must be put right by Christ. The participation of angels in Zechariah's visions reflects on Christ's work as priest and reminds us of the greatness of his work.

The emphasis on angels also parallels the book of Revelation. There is no book in the Old Testament in which angels appear as often and are as

---

1 Moore, *Zechariah*, 71–72.
2 Calvin, *Commentaries on the Twelve Minor Prophets*, 5:106.

busy as in the book of Zechariah. The same is true of Revelation in the New Testament.

4:2. And said unto me, What seest thou? And I said, I have looked, and behold a candlestick all of gold, with a bowl upon the top of it, and his seven lamps thereon, and seven pipes to the seven lamps, which are upon the top thereof:

4:3. And two olive trees by it, one upon the right side of the bowl, and the other upon the left side thereof.

The apparatus of the vision is quite complicated. Zechariah sees a candlestick of gold with a bowl on the top of it and seven lamps, apparently arranged around the bowl. The candlestick therefore is very much like the candlesticks in the tabernacle and temple, though no mention is made of a bowl at the top of those candlesticks. Pipes run from the bowl to the seven lamps. Literally the Hebrew speaks of "seven and seven pourers," perhaps referring to the fact that each of the two golden pipes mentioned in verse 12 are divided at the bowl into seven pipes, so that each lamp had two pipes running to it through which it received oil from each of the trees. Some commentators believe that the reference is to seven pipes running to each of the lamps, forty-nine in all, emphasizing again both the number seven and the abundant supply of oil.

Situated on either side of the candlestick are two olive trees that empty their oil directly into the bowl of the candlestick through golden pipes, thus providing it with a continuous source of fuel and keeping it burning perpetually. If there were any doubt about the arrangement, verse 12 confirms that this is what Zechariah sees. The two olive trees are there described as emptying the golden oil out of themselves through the golden pipes.

We must remember that this is a vision and that the symbolism of the different elements and the number seven, rather than the exact physical arrangement of things, is important. So too, the different elements are all important and symbolic. We should note also that the symbolism of the two olive trees is explained by the angel only after he has given the application of the vision to Zechariah, first in verses 6–7 and then in verses 9–10. That is scripture's way of showing us that the interpretation is far more important than the various elements of the message. They are only the vehicle by which the message comes.

The candlestick represents the church. In Revelation 1 the seven churches of Asia are represented by similar candlesticks, and any other interpretation of the candlesticks here would be arbitrary and a rejection of the unity of scripture as the word of God. In Revelation a number of candlesticks are used to represent the seven churches of Asia, thus showing the church in all her strengths and weaknesses. Here there is one candlestick because the church of the Old Testament was formed from one nation and one people, the Jews.

The number seven is always intimately associated with God's covenant. Most understand it to be a combination of three, the number of the Trinity, and four, a number associated with man and his world. Scripture often speaks of the four corners of the earth or the four winds (Isa. 11:12; Jer. 49:36; Ezek. 7:2; Matt. 24:31), meaning the whole expanse of the earth, man's home. The number seven then "symbolizes the perfected communion of God (three) and the cosmos (four), the perfected covenant of God's friendship in Christ, God's dwelling with men."[3]

If the candlestick is the church, the church existed in the Old Testament in the nation of Israel. That should be no surprise in light of Stephen's words in Acts 7:38, which identify Israel as the church in the wilderness, using the ordinary New Testament word for the church.

Indeed, Israel was exactly the same as the church of the New Testament from every point of view except that she was not gathered yet out of every nation. She was chosen of God (Deut. 7:6; Eph. 1:4), she was the object of God's grace (Ex. 34:6; Eph. 2:8), and God was pleased to dwell with her (Ex. 29:45–46; John 1:14) as his bride (Hos. 2:19; Eph. 5:32). She was justified by faith alone (Hab. 2:4; Rom. 4:23–25; Gal. 3:11), had the gospel preached to her (Heb. 4:2), and had the hope of eternal life (Heb. 11:13–16). Even the fact that not all who were called Israel were truly Israel (Rom. 2:28–29; 9:6) makes her like the church, for not all who have the name church are part of the body of Christ and among the elect.

That church is beautifully pictured by a candlestick, for as a candlestick

---

3 Hoeksema, *Behold He Cometh*, 43.

gives light, so the church is the light of the world, shining with the glory of God's holiness and being a witness through the gospel of God's saving grace. "Ye are the light of the world," Jesus says. "A city that is set on an hill cannot be hid. Neither do men light a candle, and put it under a bushel, but on a candlestick; and it giveth light unto all that are in the house. Let your light so shine before men, that they may see your good works, and glorify your Father which is in heaven" (Matt. 5:14–16). Paul speaks of "holding forth the word of life" and so shining "as lights in the world" (Phil. 2:15–16). Revelation 21:11 describes the heavenly glory of the church in the same terms: "Having the glory of God: and her light was like unto a stone most precious, even like a jasper stone, clear as crystal."

The church is that light, not because she has any light in herself, but because she is indwelt by the Spirit of God, who is represented in the vision by the olive oil that continually pours into the candlestick through the golden bowl. Not only is the Spirit often represented by oil, whether anointing oil or oil for light, but he is also specifically referred to in this vision in verse 6. The only thing that could possibly represent the Spirit in the vision is the oil. The fact that the message of God is "by my Spirit" makes it even clearer that the oil pictures the Spirit and his work, for just as the lamp shines "by" the oil that is poured into it, so the church shines as light in the world "by" the Spirit of God. Even the "pouring out" of the Spirit helps us see the comparison.

The candlestick was placed in the holy place of the tabernacle and temple to represent Israel and to show that she had a place in the very presence of God. There, symbolically, she not only had her place but served her God-given purpose as well, showing forth the praises of him who had called her out of darkness into his marvelous light (1 Pet. 2:9). So finally will the church, glorified and made pure and holy, be forever for the praise of the glory of his grace (Eph. 1:14).

This picture of the church is not an aside from the previous emphasis on the rebuilding of the temple, as the candlestick suggests. God is assuring his people that by the Spirit the temple will be built and in that temple the church's candlestick will shine in his presence. In the symbol of the glowing candlestick God's purpose to dwell in and with his church is realized, and the temple truly becomes the house of God, the one roof under which God and his people live together forever. The figure has changed slightly, but the message is the same.

4:4. So I answered and spake to the angel that talked with me, saying, What are these, my lord?

4:5. Then the angel that talked with me answered and said unto me, Knowest thou not what these be? And I said, No, my lord.

Once again Zechariah is back in his role as a passive observer. Only in the three story passages does he become an active participant in the visionary action. It is his question that gives the messenger angel opportunity to bring what is even today one of the most comforting messages that has ever been given to God's church, the assurance that all that is necessary will be done by the Spirit of God and that nothing depends on man and his efforts. We must work and be diligent, but it is nevertheless always true that what is accomplished is "not by might, nor by power, but by my Spirit."

Zechariah is especially puzzled by what he sees in this vision. He asks twice the meaning of the vision without being prompted, and when asked whether he knows what the two olive trees represent, he shows not the slightest comprehension of what he has seen. Yet his questions show that even without understanding he could see the vital importance of these things.

Surely that must have been true because of the candlestick. That would have made Zechariah think of the temple and of its purpose. It would have reminded him that the temple would soon be built and furnished and once again serve its purpose. He could not possibly have seen the vision without thinking of Solomon's temple and of the tabernacle in the wilderness and of the promise of God to dwell among his people there. Without understanding the vision, he knew that what he was seeing had to do with the temple and with God's presence.

4:6. Then he answered and spake unto me, saying, This is the word of the LORD unto Zerubbabel, saying, Not by might, nor by power, but by my spirit, saith the LORD of hosts.

The answer to Zechariah's question comes this time from the messenger angel, who does not immediately interpret the symbolic elements of the vision. Instead he brings the gospel message of the vision and focuses on its main emphasis, that is, the work of God's Spirit, who is also the Spirit of

Christ, in the work of building God's house. The message is the same as that of Haggai 2:5, "So my spirit remaineth among you: fear ye not."

This word of God is addressed to Zerubbabel, who is mentioned here for the first time in Zechariah. The word is addressed to him as the one who was responsible for the work. Zerubbabel was a descendant of David and in the royal line of David. He would have been Judah's king had they not been under the domination of Persia, and he represents the kingly office as it was perpetuated in the line of David and ended in Christ.

The emphasis of the book of Zechariah is on Joshua and his priestly office, but Zerubbabel is important too. As subsequent visions show, Joshua's priestly office had to be combined with the kingly office of Zerubbabel to ensure that the work of building God's house would be done and would prosper when finished.

Though the work of building the temple is not specifically mentioned in this word of God to Zerubbabel, it is clear from Zechariah 4:9 that it was the temple that would be built, not by might, nor by power, but by the Spirit of God. Verse 7 mentions the headstone, which can only be the head or cornerstone of the temple that was being built.

On its cornerstone the temple would be built not by man but by God, that is, not by human might or human power, but by the Spirit of God. "Not by might, nor by power" did not mean, however, that Zerubbabel and the others who were engaged in the work of rebuilding could abandon what they were doing and leave everything to the Spirit of God. God had called them to the work of rebuilding, as the book of Haggai shows so clearly, and made plain to the builders that his blessing was only in the way of their obedience. Neglecting the house of God, they could not prosper.

God is saying that the Spirit would work through them in such a way that when the temple was built, the credit for the work would all be given to his Spirit. It would be the Spirit who called them to the work, who moved them to obedience, who gave them the wisdom and skill they needed for the work, and who protected and helped them in the work.

Zerubbabel may have but few visible resources, but the work was one that after all was to be completed by God, and not by man, and however feeble the Church might seem to be, there was more for her than against her. Hence, as the Jew gazed on this ceaseless flow of strength and grace, he could forget the feebleness of man in the unfailing supply of the power of God.[4]

Thus it is always. God works through his people and uses their efforts to build his kingdom, but nothing depends on them. The work is really the work of his Spirit in them and through them, done in such a way that all the glory of the work is God's. The builder's sign that stands in front of the work only ever says, "Built by the Holy Spirit." It never gives any credit, even as assistants, to us; it never adds, "Assisted by Saints."

That is especially true of the spiritual temple of God in the New Testament, the church. God's word concerning his church in the New Testament is always, "I will build my church" (Matt. 16:18), not, "You and I together will build my church." Ephesians 2:19–22 says this:

> 19. Now therefore ye are no more strangers and foreigners, but fellowcitizens with the saints, and of the household of God;
> 20. And are built upon the foundation of the apostles and prophets, Jesus Christ himself being the chief corner stone;
> 21. In whom all the building fitly framed together groweth unto an holy temple in the Lord:
> 22. In whom ye also are builded together for an habitation of God *through the Spirit* (emphasis added).

The work of building God's house, the church, is done in many different ways. It is done by the preaching of the gospel. It is done by all the means we use to edify and build up one another. It is done in evangelism and missions, when the call of the gospel goes out to the nations. It is done in the work of the elders and deacons in the church. It is done when parents bring into the world and train covenantal children, the future generations of the church. It is done by prayer and the study of the word of God, by being "built up" ourselves in every good word and work. Yet nothing depends on these efforts, else it would be wasted effort and fruitless endeavor.

---

4 Moore, *Zechariah*, 73.

Our confidence, therefore, in doing the work God gives us is still the same as it was for Zechariah and the Jews: "Not by might, nor by power, but by my Spirit, saith the LORD of hosts." If we thought that anything depended on us, we would despair of the work as soon as it was begun and would very quickly become unfaithful. If we did not know that the Spirit works in us and through us, the work would look as impossible to us as it did to the Jews, who were poor, oppressed, and few in number.

Nothing can depend on our efforts because we are still sinners and all we do, even the best, is tainted by our sinfulness. We do nothing perfectly, and the house in which God dwells must be perfect. Nothing less will suit his majesty. Only the sovereign power of the Spirit can overcome our sinfulness and make straight that which would otherwise always be crooked. The house, when fully and finally built, will be a monument to the power and skill of the Holy Spirit, not to any man. No man's name will be over the door, no bronze plaque with a list of subscribers and volunteers will be inside the entrance, there will be no ribbon-cutting ceremony at which men like Paul and Peter and Luther and Calvin will have front seats and be commended for their work. There will only be the words of God himself, written into every stone of that spiritual temple, "Not by might...but by my Spirit, saith the LORD of hosts."

O sing ye Hallelujah!

'Tis good our God to praise;
'Tis pleasant and becoming
To Him our songs to raise;
He builds the walls of Zion,
He seeks her wand'ring sons,
He binds their wounds and comforts
The brokenhearted ones.

No human pow'r delights Him,
No earthly pomp or pride;
He loves the meek who fear Him
And in His love confide;

Then praise Thy God, O Zion,
His gracious aid confess;
He gives thee peace and plenty,
His gifts thy children bless.[5]

God names himself here the Lord of hosts because he through the Spirit uses all things, the hosts of heaven and hell, the vast multitude that no man can number, even the ungodly and every created thing, to do what his hand and his counsel had determined before to be done (Acts 4:28). None can stay his hand or say to him, "What doest thou?" (Dan. 4:35). He is the sole architect and builder of his church. He alone does wondrous things (Ps. 136:4).

4:7. Who art thou, O great mountain? before Zerubbabel thou shalt become a plain: and he shall bring forth the headstone thereof with shoutings, crying, Grace, grace unto it.

God shows that he would use Zerubbabel and the Jews in the work of building his house by describing Zerubbabel as the one who would bring forth the cornerstone or headstone of the house. Since the cornerstone was the most important stone in a building, it is evident that under his leadership the Jews' work was important. God does not give them insignificant work and minor tasks to do but calls them to the most important work of all.

Whether headstone is the same as cornerstone is open to debate. Some take it as a reference to the topstone of the building, others as a reference to a stone from the temple of Solomon that occupied a prominent place in this second temple, but it really makes no difference. In any case it refers to the most important or most prominent stone in the building. Pusey says:

Two images appear to be used in Holy Scripture, both of which meet in Christ: the one, in which the stone spoken of is the foundation-stone; the other, in which it is the head corner-stone binding the two walls together, which it connects. Both were cornerstones; the one at the base, the other at the summit...Both images together express, how Christ is the Beginning and the End, the First and

---

5 No. 402:1, 4, in *The Psalter.*

the Last; the Foundation of the spiritual building, the Church, and its summit and completion; the unseen Foundation which was laid deep in Calvary, and the Summit to which it grows and which holds it firm together.[6]

The cornerstone or headstone was not in those days a mere decoration as it is today, but more on the order of a modern building's foundation. Upon it the whole building rested, and its shape and strength determined the shape and strength of the whole building. That is emphasized by the word "headstone," used also in other passages (Ps. 118:22; Matt. 21:42; Mark 12:10; Luke 20:17; 1 Pet. 2:7). The word does not so much mean "uppermost stone" as "chief stone," that is, the stone without which the rest of the house could not be built.

In this case it may also refer to something like the capstone of an arch, the stone that gives an arch its strength and stability, for the foundations of the temple had already been laid (Ezra 3:10–13) but the work remained unfinished. God is saying, then, that as Zerubbabel had been instrumental in the beginning of the work, he would also be instrumental in its completion, something expressly stated in Zechariah 4:9. Indeed, the shouts of which the passage speak remind us of the shouting that was heard when the foundation was laid (Ezra 3:12). That same kind of shouting would be heard again.

There is much more to the passage, however, than just a reference to the historical event of completing the second temple. The promise is that Zerubbabel would be the ancestor of Christ (Matt. 1:13–16); that Christ would come of the royal seed of David as God had always promised, though that royal seed had come upon hard times. He would be the true headstone brought forth by Zerubbabel.

First Peter 2:6–7 cannot possibly be overlooked in interpreting the word of God here:

6. Wherefore also it is contained in the scripture, Behold, I lay in Sion a chief corner stone, elect, precious: and he that believeth on him shall not be confounded.

---

6 Pusey, *The Minor Prophets*, 2:361–62.

7. Unto you therefore which believe he is precious: but unto them which be disobedient, the stone which the builders disallowed, the same is made the head of the corner.

However, Christ is not only the headstone, but pictured in Zerubbabel, he is also the one who brings it forth and sets it in its place.

That is always the amazing thing about the work of our Lord. He shows himself in all his work to be the one upon whom everything depends. In the offering he made for sin, he is both priest and sacrifice. In his resurrection, he is both the one who is raised and the one who raises. In the covenant, he is both the God of the covenant and the representative of his people, like them in all things except sin. In the building of God's house, he is both builder and headstone.

The shouting that accompanies the bringing forth of the headstone is heard not only in the shouting of the Jews at the completion of their work, but also in the song of the angels at the birth of Christ, in the rejoicing of the shepherds, in the praise of the church down through the ages, in the song of Moses and the Lamb when it is sung forever in heaven. It is, according to Leupold, "crashing bursts of applause."[7] It is always about the grace of God, "Grace, grace, unto it," because in Christ dwells all the fullness of God's grace, given to him by God to be given in turn to his people.

We should never forget that the word "thanks" in scripture is really the word "grace." Thanksgiving is the ascription of all grace to God, the giving of grace to him in the acknowledging of his sovereign saving grace. Indeed, it is in the praise of his people that grace is given to him and returns to him, for it is grace that produces and motivates the thanks of his people. For unending ages, then, the church will be shouting and singing, "Grace, grace, unto it," that is, "All praise and thanks be unto him, through Jesus Christ our Lord, world without end."

It is significant that the people attribute the work to God, crying, "Grace! Grace!" to the stone. They do not celebrate their own abilities or national might, for they had little of that.[8]

---

7 Leupold, *Zechariah*, 90.
8 McComiskey, *Zechariah*, 3:1088.

In accomplishing this God also overcomes and destroys the enemies of his people. The mountain, representing the looming power of those enemies, would be leveled. There is a great deal of disagreement about the meaning of the mountain. One interpretation, for example, sees in that mountain the pile of ruins that had to be cleared away before the temple could be built. Even if there is a reference to that difficulty and others, it still refers to the removal of all opposition to the kingdom of Christ.

Kingdoms are often portrayed as mountains in scripture, even the king-dom of Christ, as in Daniel 2:35, where the stone cut out without hands becomes a great mountain that fills the whole earth. It should not be strange then that the enemies of the church are often portrayed as a mountain that stands as the opposite of the mountain of the Lord's house. Edom, one of the Old Testament enemies of God's people, is described as "mount Seir" (Ezek. 35:2–3, 7, 15; Obad. 19). Other enemies, especially Babylon, are described as coming from the mountains (Joel 2:1–5), and God's judgments are often described in the prophets as judgment upon the mountains. Isaiah 41:15 is a good example: "Behold, I will make thee a new sharp threshing instrument having teeth: thou shalt thresh the mountains, and beat them small, and shalt make the hills as chaff." Even the fact that waters of the flood covered the highest mountains may hint at this.

The earth, especially the mountains, are seen by the ungodly as evidence that this world will last forever and that their opposition to God and efforts to make this world their own kingdom will be successful. Those mountains, claimed by the ungodly as their own, are the symbol of their opposition to God and their utter lack of fear of his judgments. They are even a perceived refuge from the judgments that God threatens:

15. And the kings of the earth, and the great men, and the rich men, and the chief captains, and the mighty men, and every bondman, and every free man, hid themselves in the dens and in the rocks of the mountains;
16. And said to the mountains and rocks, Fall on us, and hide us from the face of him that sitteth on the throne, and from the wrath of the Lamb. (Rev. 6:15–16)

Those mountains will be overthrown and melted when God comes in judgment, and his enemies will be deprived of all that in which they trusted. They will be left unprotected and exposed to the destroying wrath of God in the day when he brings forth the headstone. That began to be true when the headstone was brought forth and given to the builders, it was further accomplished when his enemies rejected and despised that headstone to their own condemnation, and it will be completed when God brings forth the headstone once again in the final coming of Christ and the judgments that follow. "He stood, and measured the earth: he beheld, and drove asunder the nations; and the everlasting mountains were scattered, the perpetual hills did bow: his ways are everlasting" (Hab. 3:6).

We ought to think as we read these verses of Luke 14:11, "For whosoever exalteth himself shall be abased; and he that humbleth himself shall be exalted," and of 2 Corinthians 10:4–5, "(For the weapons of our warfare are not carnal, but mighty through God to the pulling down of strong holds;) Casting down imaginations, and every high thing that exalteth itself against the knowledge of God, and bringing into captivity every thought to the obedience of Christ." The question, "Who art thou, O great mountain?" is ironic, something on the order of the question, "Who do you think you are?" and when asked by Almighty God is frightening.

When all is finished the headstone will not only be the head of the corner, the stone upon which the church is built as a kingdom that cannot be moved, but it will also be the stone upon which the enemies of the church stumble and are broken and ground to powder. "And he beheld them, and said, What is this then that is written, The stone which the builders rejected, the same is become the head of the corner? Whosoever shall fall upon that stone shall be broken; but on whomsoever it shall fall, it will grind him to powder" (Luke 20:17–18).

4:8. Moreover the word of the LORD came unto me, saying,

4:9. The hands of Zerubbabel have laid the foundation of this house; his hands shall also finish it; and thou shalt know that the LORD of hosts hath sent me unto you.

Not only would all enemies and obstacles be taken out of the way, but also the house of God would be built and Zerubbabel would be used by God to do God's work. What a comfort for Judah in trying times! God would use them and the work they were doing, no matter how difficult and discouraging the work might be. That promise is for us also. It is a promise that God's spiritual house will be built and that God will use us to do his work. Our labors are not in vain in the Lord (1 Cor. 15:58). Our enemies will not triumph. The opposition we face and the suffering we endure will have its good fruit in the end.

It would appear that this word of God comes directly to Zechariah and not through the angel intermediary. If that is the case, it emphasizes the importance of this message and the personal comfort it carried for Zerubbabel. There is nothing so disheartening as the thought that our work and efforts will be in vain; that they will be forever unfinished and therefore fruitless. God promises that it will not be so for his people as far as the work of building his kingdom is concerned.

So it is always. Whatever is beyond our ability, whatever is still not perfected in our brief lifetimes and by our strength, is completed in Christ. For that reason our works are never our righteousness before God, but his works are. We need never think that anything at all depends on us, but we may trust him to build and preserve his church, to gather his elect, to fulfill the promises of the covenant to our children, and to make us acceptable to God, that the Lord God may dwell among us. That does not make our labors needless but gives us confidence to work as long as it pleases the Lord to use us.

Christ is at the center of this promise also, for even though Zerubbabel would live to see the completion of the second temple, the work would really not be finished. The house that he was building was only an earthly type and not the eternal reality. Nevertheless, Christ would come and would finish the work by building a temple most glorious, a house not made with hands, eternal in the heavens, and so he would complete with his own hands and on their behalf what God's people have worked for in every age. This promise is really the promise of Christ in Matthew 16:18: "I will build my church; and the gates of hell shall not prevail against it."

4:10. For who hath despised the day of small things? for they shall rejoice, and shall see the plummet in the hand of Zerubbabel with those seven; they are the eyes of the LORD, which run to and fro through the whole earth.

Now God gives the reason these promises were needed, and why it was necessary for Zerubbabel and Judah to know that their enemies, portrayed as a great mountain, would be destroyed by God. The church then appeared only a small thing in the world, powerless and of no account in relation to her enemies. What was true then is often true in the history of the church. One of the Reformation creeds, the Belgic Confession of Faith, says:

> And this holy Church is preserved or supported by God against the rage of the whole world; though she sometimes (for a while) appear very small, and, in the eyes of men, to be reduced to nothing: as during the perilous reign of Ahab, when nevertheless *the Lord reserved unto him seven thousand men, who had not bowed their knees to Baal.*[9]

The question of verse 10, placed side-by-side with the question of verse 7, "Who art thou, O great mountain?" shows clearly that those who despise the small things of the kingdom of God are those represented by the great mountain, the enemies of God's church. The great mountain, representing the might of the world and its opposition to the kingdom of God, despises the church and boasts of having destroyed the church.

From a spiritual point of view and in God's sight, the church is never a small thing. She may be insignificant and of no account in the sight of the ungodly, but as we saw in chapter 2:8, she is the apple of God's eye. Numerically she may be very small in one place or at a particular time, but gathered out of every nation and in every age she is nevertheless a multitude that no man can number (Rev. 7:9). Men may think her worthless and powerless, but she is chosen of God and will triumph finally over her enemies and inherit heaven and earth.

Nevertheless, there are times in her history when she is so small that she does appear to be reduced to nothing. In the days of Noah, there were only eight souls left who entered the ark, and not all of them proved to be the true church. Elijah thought he was the only one left. Isaiah speaks of a tenth (Isa. 6:13) and Paul in Romans 11:5 of a remnant according to the election

---

9 Belgic Confession 27, in Schaff, *Creeds of Christendom*, 3:417.

of grace. Before the Reformation the true church was hardly to be found, and today it appears that the faithful church is once again very small.

In Zechariah's day there were few who wanted to go back to Jerusalem, and those who did were poor and powerless, the remains of a few tribes. The throne of David had fallen into obscurity. The temple was still unbuilt and even when finished would have but a shadow of the glory of Solomon's temple, lacking even the ark of the covenant and the mercy seat. Nor would things improve in the years that lay ahead. The temple would be beautified outwardly but would come under the authority of the self-righteous Pharisees and doubting Sadducees. The office of high priest would become a commodity to be sold to the highest bidder at the pleasure of the Romans. The royal seed of David would be reduced to one poor virgin fiancée of a Galilean carpenter.

In these last times the great work of God in the Reformation is forgotten and the churches of the Reformation become apostate. Faithful churches cannot even be found in many places, and those churches and denominations that are faithful are so small that they are almost unnoticed even in the church world. The still small witness of the gospel is drowned out, so it seems, by the voices of those who preach a health and wealth Christ and a God who is subject to every whim of his creatures. True worship is a lost art and faithful church membership almost unknown.

There has been many a day of small things in the history of Christ's church, and today is another in which it seems there is little hope of seeing again the kind of work God did in his church in the days of Moses or the apostles or the Reformation, when he delivered her from spiritual captivity, made her vigorous and fruitful, and caused even the wicked world to take notice of her. Indeed, if the history of Zerubbabel and Zechariah is a pattern for the New Testament, it seems an inescapable conclusion that the closer we come to the return of Christ and the end of all things, the more we must expect "the day of small things." In Matthew 24, when Jesus describes his return, he speaks of the love of many waxing cold (v. 12) and of God's shortening the days lest there be no one saved (v. 22).

In the eyes of many this is pessimism of the worst kind, but it is nevertheless the testimony of scripture. Jesus asks whether he will even find faith on the earth when he comes again (Luke 18:8). Nor is this expectation really pessimism, for the day of small things is a sign that Jesus is coming again soon. It is therefore the greatest reason for optimism the church has ever had, for it speaks of the fact that the church will soon be gathered in one in him. "And when these things begin to come to pass, then look up, and lift up your heads; for your redemption draweth nigh" (Luke 21:28).

This day of small things is really the day of Christ's coming and work. He came "as a tender plant, and as a root out of a dry ground," without form or comeliness (Isa. 53:2). He was born in little Bethlehem, unnoticed even by the majority of the Jews. In his work he was despised and rejected of men for his humble origins and lack of kingly glory, and his work ended in an ignominious death at the hands of the Romans, rejected by his own people.

So his cause and kingdom are always small in their beginnings, as Jesus teaches in the parable of the mustard seed: "The kingdom of heaven is like to a grain of mustard seed, which a man took, and sowed in his field: Which indeed is the least of all seeds: but when it is grown, it is the greatest among herbs, and becometh a tree, so that the birds of the air come and lodge in the branches thereof" (Matt. 13:31–32). What belongs to the kingdom is also small, insignificant, and humble in its beginnings. The gospel is a still, small voice (1 Kings 19:11–12). The church is a remnant according to election (Rom. 11:5). The people of God are for the most part the poor and weak and despised of this world (1 Cor. 1:26–29). It must be so lest we glory in ourselves or in man's wisdom and ability.

As it did in Zechariah's day, the smallness of God's cause can lead to unfaithfulness on the part of church members. Like those who remained in Babylon, they sometimes despise the faithful church because she is so small. Desiring numbers and size, the church often loses the truth and the presence and blessing of Christ. Many church members judge a congregation or denomination solely on the basis of the number of members. A church that is small cannot be, in their eyes, "successful." It is not a blessing merely to be small, but when it pleases God to keep the church small, the church must not trade her treasures for numbers; must not sell her heritage for a mess of ecclesiastical pottage that will enable her to become great in the world.

God tells us not to despise the day of small things. This can only mean that he does not despise it—that it is his good pleasure for the church in such days that she be few and insignificant:

The day of small things is especially God's day, Whose strength is made perfect in weakness; Who raised Joseph from the prison, David from the sheepfold, Daniel from slavery, and converted the world by the fishermen and the tentmaker, having Himself first become the Carpenter.[10]

Her smallness is not reason for despair, for she has two helps, the plummet in the hand of Zerubbabel and the eyes of the Lord that run to and fro through the whole earth.

The word "plummet" is literally "stone of tin," and the stone must be the same as the stone that is laid before Joshua in Zechariah 3:9, since the word of God also refers there and here to seven eyes in connection with that stone. The stone is Christ, the cornerstone of the church and the one who guarantees her safety and well-being: "Upon this rock I will build my church; and the gates of hell shall not prevail against it" (Matt. 16:18).

Although this stone of tin is usually understood as a reference to a plummet or plumb line, the phrase "stone of tin" is not the usual way that tool is referred to in the Hebrew Old Testament. If it does indeed refer to something like a plumb line, then the reference is not to a line used to keep things square or level, but to a line that is drawn to separate good from bad, useful from useless. It could better be translated "stone of separation," more of a boundary stone than a plummet.

The word used to describe this stone often refers to dross, to something that must be separated out, and the root of the word means "to separate." The idea must be that though the church as represented by the returned remnant and the new temple is in itself small and despised, God keeps her separate and safe by building her on Christ. This is also the function of the seven eyes, which are a symbolic representation of the Spirit of God. The stone is the foundation of the church, and the Spirit who searches all things watches over that stone and what is built on it. The church, therefore, will always be safe.

What God says here is almost word for word what the prophet Hanani said to King Asa when faced with numerous enemies: "For the eyes of the

10 Pusey, *The Minor Prophets*, 2:363.

LORD run to and fro throughout the whole earth, to shew himself strong in the behalf of them whose heart is perfect toward him" (2 Chron. 16:9). The function of both stone and eyes is the safety of the church, though she is small. She is safe now and safe forever, through the work of Christ and his Spirit. The stone, whether foundation stone or boundary stone, is her safety.

4:11. Then answered I, and said unto him, What are these two olive trees upon the right side of the candlestick and upon the left side thereof?

4:12. And I answered again, and said unto him, What be these two olive branches which through the two golden pipes empty the golden oil out of themselves?

4:13. And he answered me and said, Knowest thou not what these be? And I said, No, my lord.

4:14. Then said he, These are the two anointed ones, that stand by the LORD of the whole earth.

Having heard this message, Zechariah focuses on the main symbolic objects in the vision, the two olive trees with the candlestick between them. That he asks twice shows their importance to him, and the further question of the angel shows that he was not wrong in focusing on those figures. The question of the angel in verse 13 is the angel's way of saying that the two olive trees are indeed the main thing in the vision and that Zechariah was correct in fixing his attention on them. That these are the main things in the vision is also clear from Revelation, which speaks of them again, though ignoring the other elements of the vision. Indeed, Revelation 11:3–19 is essential to the interpretation of Zechariah and should be quoted in full:

> 3. And I will give power unto my two witnesses, and they shall prophesy a thousand two hundred and threescore days, clothed in sackcloth.
> 4. These are the two olive trees, and the two candlesticks standing before the God of the earth.
> 5. And if any man will hurt them, fire proceedeth out of their mouth, and devoureth their enemies: and if any man will hurt them, he must in this manner be killed.

6. These have power to shut heaven, that it rain not in the days of their prophecy: and have power over waters to turn them to blood, and to smite the earth with all plagues, as often as they will.

7. And when they shall have finished their testimony, the beast that ascendeth out of the bottomless pit shall make war against them, and shall overcome them, and kill them.

8. And their dead bodies shall lie in the street of the great city, which spiritually is called Sodom and Egypt, where also our Lord was crucified.

9. And they of the people and kindreds and tongues and nations shall see their dead bodies three days and an half, and shall not suffer their dead bodies to be put in graves.

10. And they that dwell upon the earth shall rejoice over them, and make merry, and shall send gifts one to another; because these two prophets tormented them that dwelt on the earth.

11. And after three days and an half the spirit of life from God entered into them, and they stood upon their feet; and great fear fell upon them which saw them.

12. And they heard a great voice from heaven saying unto them, Come up hither. And they ascended up to heaven in a cloud; and their enemies beheld them.

13. And the same hour was there a great earthquake, and the tenth part of the city fell, and in the earthquake were slain of men seven thousand: and the remnant were affrighted, and gave glory to the God of heaven.

14. The second woe is past; and, behold, the third woe cometh quickly.

15. And the seventh angel sounded; and there were great voices in heaven, saying, The kingdoms of this world are become the kingdoms of our Lord, and of his Christ; and he shall reign for ever and ever.

16. And the four and twenty elders, which sat before God on their seats, fell upon their faces, and worshipped God,

17. Saying, We give thee thanks, O Lord God Almighty, which art, and wast, and art to come; because thou hast taken to thee thy great power, and hast reigned.

18. And the nations were angry, and thy wrath is come, and the time of the dead, that they should be judged, and that thou should-est give reward unto thy servants the prophets, and to the saints, and them that fear thy name, small and great; and shouldest destroy them which destroy the earth.

19. And the temple of God was opened in heaven, and there was seen in his temple the ark of his testament: and there were lightnings, and voices, and thunderings, and an earthquake, and great hail.

The main difference between Zechariah and Revelation is that Revelation speaks of two candlesticks, a minor difference in light of the fact that the olive trees and candlesticks are so closely associated with each other. Revelation identifies the olive trees and candlesticks, and Zechariah in speaking of the two golden pipes that join the one candlestick to the two olive trees also in effect speaks of two candlesticks and associates them very closely with the olive trees.

Zechariah also speaks here of two golden pipes where he had previously spoken of seven. What he saw was probably two golden pipes leading from the two trees and emptying the golden oil into the bowl at the top of the candlestick, each dividing into two at the bowl, with fourteen pipes carrying the oil from the bowl to the seven branches of the candlestick. (See the explanation of Zecharaiah 4:2–3.)

We have already seen that the candlestick or candlesticks are the church, of both the Old and New Testaments, as the church is filled with the oil of the Spirit and called to be a light in the world. The olive trees therefore must also represent the church, since the olive trees and the candlesticks are the same in Revelation 11:4 and are joined together in Zechariah by the system of pipes and bowl. Simply to say the olive trees are the church, however, is not enough, for they are further identified in Zechariah as two anointed ones and in Revelation 11 as two witnesses.

In Zechariah the two anointed ones are Zerubbabel and Joshua, the two anointed leaders of God's Old Testament people, the priest and the king. Through them and their offices the golden oil representing the Spirit of God flowed into the church of the Old Testament. The picture then is of the church as a light in the world through her God-appointed leaders. The offices of priest

THE COMING OF ZION'S REDEEMER

and king were the means by which the Spirit of Christ lived in the church and made her a bright and shining light, glowing with the glory of God.

In Revelation the two anointed ones are the two witnesses and also the two olive trees and two candlesticks, all representing the offices through which the Spirit of Christ is present in the church, so that the church becomes a witness to the whole world, a light that cannot be hid.[11] What appears at first reading to be strange, that candlesticks, olive trees, witnesses, and anointed ones should all be fundamentally the same thing, is not so strange when the symbolism is understood. As anointing with oil in the Old Testament symbolized the gift of the Spirit, so these two anointed ones of the Old Testament, two witnesses in the New Testament, have the Spirit of God, and through them the Spirit works in the church. That they stand before the Lord of the whole earth reminds us that the Spirit is the Spirit of God, who is in the church only as a gift of God.

I agree, therefore, with Hoeksema:

But who are the two olive trees? In Zechariah 4:14 we read that they were the two anointed ones, standing before the Lord of the whole earth. From this we learn...first...that they are servants of God. They stand before the Lord of the whole earth. They are, therefore, ready to serve. And that they stand before the Lord of the whole earth also implies that they are especially the ones who are ready to serve the Lord before the whole world with their testimony in word and deed...Second...we learn that they are *anointed* servants of the Lord. They are therefore officially called and ordained for service. They are divine media through which the people of God receive the blessings of God's grace, especially the blessing of the knowledge of God, so that they may let their light shine. In the Old Testament there were but two who were thus officially anointed to be servants in the theocracy, namely, the king and the priest. And there is for that reason no question among interpreters generally but that by the two olive trees...first...Zerubbabel the prince and Joshua the high priest are meant...Second...a general reference is made to the

---

11 For a good discussion of the various interpretations of the two witnesses, see Hoeksema, *Behold He Cometh*, 374–84.

royal and priestly office in Israel. And in the word of our text [Rev. 11:3–4], therefore, the olive trees are evidently none other but the divinely ordained and called true ministers of the Word, who must serve as media to supply the church with light.[12]

These two offices of king and priest were never combined in the Old Testament except in Melchizedek, and they pointed to the need for one in whom they would be again joined. Zechariah 6:9–15 prophesies of their union, but that would not be fulfilled until Christ, the great priest-king of his people, came in the fullness of time:

> They existed once in Melchisedek, but were ever afterwards divided, as in Moses and Aaron, Joshua and Zerubbabel, &c., &c., until the time of the Messiah, who again combined them in his own person, and who by his work, made his people kings and priest unto God.[13]

The name Christ means "anointed one" and reminds us that he is the fulfillment of this vision. As the priest and king of the church, he pours out his Spirit on the church, providing in the church an inexhaustible supply of grace and blessing through the offices that reflect his own. He is the true "son of oil" through whom God's Spirit dwells in the church. The word translated as "branches" in verse 12 is actually the word used in Hebrew for ears of grain, and it is used here to show the fruitfulness of these two olive trees.

If the two witnesses are indeed the church as she functions through her offices and brings the light of the gospel to every nation, the death of the two witnesses represents the silencing of the church's witness just prior to the end of the world, something that would indeed be a cause of rejoicing to all who hate the church of Christ. Then the raising of the two witnesses represents the resurrection of the righteous dead and the glorification of the church, which becomes the occasion for God's final judgments on the world, described so vividly in Revelation 11:13–19.

Then the fire that comes out of their mouth is not literal fire, but the judgment of God as it comes through the preaching of the gospel. Nor is

---

12 Ibid, 381.
13 Moore, *Zechariah*, 75–76.

their power to shut heaven and bring plagues on the earth some magical power, but is a symbolic representation of the fact that through the work of preaching the gospel and praying for the coming of Christ's kingdom, the judgment of God does come upon the world.

There is a warning here, as Hoeksema points out in his interpretation of Revelation 11:

Many have been the false prophets of all times. Many are the false prophets today. Fearful wrath and condemnation, no doubt, there will be in store for those who have pretended to preach the truth of God and have filled the pipes of the bowl with the darkness of hell.[14]

Taken as a whole, the vision serves to teach the people of God to whom Zechariah was speaking, as well as the New Testament church, that however small and despised the church may be in the eyes of the world, she through the offices that God has ordained has the Spirit of God and shines with the splendor of the glory of God, a light in the world and an inextinguishable testimony to God's love and grace. The message is one of comfort such as we sing in Psalm 132:

Thy Zion Thou hast chosen, Lord,
And Thou hast said, I love her well,
This is my constant restingplace,
And here will I delight to dwell.

I will abundantly provide
For Zion's good, the Lord hath said;
I will supply her daily need
And satisfy her poor with bread.

Salvation shall adorn her priests,
Her saints shall shout with joy divine,
Messiah's pow'r shall be revealed,
His glory in His Church shall shine.[15]

---

14 Hoeksema, *Behold He Cometh*, 384.
15 No. 368:3–5, in *The Psalter*.

Chapter 12

THE SIXTH VISION:
Zechariah 5:1–11

5:1   Then I turned, and lifted up mine eyes, and looked, and behold a flying roll.

5:2   And he said unto me, What seest thou? And I answered, I see a flying roll; the length thereof is twenty cubits, and the breadth thereof ten cubits.

5:3   Then said he unto me, This is the curse that goeth forth over the face of the whole earth: for every one that stealeth shall be cut off as on this side according to it; and every one that sweareth shall be cut off as on that side according to it.

5:4   I will bring it forth, saith the LORD of hosts, and it shall enter into the house of the thief, and into the house of him that sweareth falsely by my name: and it shall remain in the midst of his house, and shall consume it with the timber thereof and the stones thereof.

5:5   Then the angel that talked with me went forth, and said unto me, Lift up now thine eyes, and see what is this that goeth forth.

5:6   And I said, What is it? And he said, This is an ephah that goeth forth. He said moreover, This is their resemblance through all the earth.

5:7   And, behold, there was lifted up a talent of lead: and this is a woman that sitteth in the midst of the ephah.

5:8   And he said, This is wickedness. And he cast it into the midst of the ephah; and he cast the weight of lead upon the mouth thereof.

5:9   Then lifted I up mine eyes, and looked, and, behold, there came out two women, and the wind was in their wings; for they had wings like the wings of a stork: and they lifted up the ephah between the earth and the heaven.

5:10   Then said I to the angel that talked with me, Whither do these bear the ephah?

5:11   And he said unto me, To build it an house in the land of Shinar: and it shall be established, and set there upon her own base.

There is some disagreement as to whether chapter 5 constitutes one or two visions.[1] Some commentators believe that the flying scroll and the woman in the basket are different visions, referring to the words "Lift up now thine eyes, and see what is this that goeth forth" in verse 5 as evidence that a new vision begins there. Such references to seeing do introduce all the visions, but not every reference to seeing does so. More important is the fact that the word *behold* is not found in verse 5. That word, with one exception, is always found at the beginning of a new vision, and its omission in verse 5 shows that the flying roll and the woman in the basket are one vision.

We should see chapter 5, therefore, as one vision and one message with two closely related parts. The message is of God's judgment on the apostate and wicked element in the nation of Judah. God's judgment will come, the vision says, in the way of another exile, so that these Jews who had only recently returned from Babylon would be brought there once again.

The two parts of the vision describe the two parts of this judgment, the first part describing the ruin of their homes in the land of Israel and the second part their being carried away to Babylon. In that way the same thing would happen to them as happened to their fathers, who would not hear the word of God and would not turn from their wicked ways (see Zech. 1:1–6). God would deliver his people not only from the heathen but also from the apostate and carnal element in the nation of Israel, which was as great a threat to their spiritual well-being as the oppression and persecution of the heathen.

This judgment was not literally executed in history. The Jews were not actually brought again to Babylon, but in fulfillment of this vision the nation was once again scattered and lost its place as a favored people after rejecting their Messiah. It is fulfilled whenever God sends the church into spiritual exile for her sins and disobedience, and it will be finally and forever fulfilled when the ungodly, both those within the church and those outside, come under Babylon's judgment and are destroyed together with Babylon at the end of the ages.

---

1 "The vision of the flying roll and that of the woman in the ephah are so closely connected, as to form properly but one vision, though some scholars have regarded them as being two...The two visions together form a striking picture of the result of sin, and the end of transgression" (Wright, *Zechariah and His Prophecies*, 105).

This threat of judgment on the apostate element in Israel constitutes a further development in the visions and parallels the first set of three visions. Just as the first vision is of Christ in the midst of his church, so the fourth vision is of the Spirit working in the church. And just as the first vision is followed with a vision of judgment on the heathen nations, so the fourth is followed with a vision of judgment on apostate Israel.

5:1. Then I turned, and lifted up mine eyes, and looked, and behold a flying roll.

5:2. And he said unto me, What seest thou? And I answered, I see a flying roll; the length thereof is twenty cubits, and the breadth thereof ten cubits.

In his sixth vision Zechariah sees an enormous flying scroll, thirty feet long and thus unrolled, and fifteen feet from the top to the bottom. Rolled up, the scroll would be taller than long, so it is clear that this scroll is open. Verse 3 confirms this by suggesting that both sides of the scroll were visible and readable.[2] In the vision the scroll turns out to be a curse scroll.

The angel's question not only focuses Zechariah's attention on the scroll, but is also used to introduce the messenger angel's explanation, which immediately follows. That explanation is not, as such, difficult to understand, but its application is less clear.

How Zechariah is able to estimate or know the size of the scroll is unimportant, but the dimensions are an important element of the vision. Indeed, the fact that the dimensions are given so precisely indicates that it is not just the huge size of the scroll that is being emphasized. It ought not to be missed that fifteen by thirty feet, or ten by twenty cubits, are the dimensions of the porch of the temple (1 Kings 6:3), the area just outside the sanctuary. The curse scroll exactly covers that area, which is simply to say that the curse itself lies upon that area, "the spot from which God was supposed to hold intercourse with his people."[3]

---

2 "In ancient times books were written on long sheets or rolls made of papyrus, a sort of paper made of the pith of the papyrus plant, the paper reed. The pith was cut into strips, several layers of which were laid crosswise and pressed or glued together to form the writing paper of the ancients. Sometimes both sides were used (Ezek. 2:9ff.; Rev. 5:1)" (Laetsch, *The Minor Prophets*, 431).

3 Hengstenberg, *Christology*, 3:305.

The vision is similar to that of Revelation 11:1–2 and must be interpreted together with that passage. There the temple is measured, but not what lies outside of the temple proper. That which lies outside, called the "court" in Revelation, is given to the Gentiles for a period of forty-two months to be defiled and "trodden under foot" by them, essentially the same as being placed under God's curse. Here the outside of the temple is measured, and the result of the measurement is that the area measured comes under the curse of God, for the curse exactly covers the area just outside the door of the sanctuary.

The measurements, even though different areas are measured in Zechariah and in Revelation, serve to distinguish the two areas. In Revelation, the temple itself is measured to mark off the area as being under God's protection. In Zechariah, the area measured is under God's curse. By implication or by direct statement that means that in Revelation the area not measured is not under God's protection and in Zechariah the area not measured is not under the curse. In somewhat different ways the two passages clearly distinguish the two areas.

Both in Zechariah and in Revelation the word of God is showing that there is a difference even in the church between clean and unclean, between that which is holy and that which is accursed, between believer and unbeliever. Wickedness and opposition to God's kingdom is not only to be found in the great mountain of Zechariah 4:7, that is, in the world of the heathen nations, but is also to be found in the covenant nation itself.

All too often in the history of the covenant people it was an ungodly element that brought on the whole nation the anger of God. That element introduced idolatry, intermarried with the heathen, closed the temple, invited in the heathen nations to help Israel, persecuted the faithful, and refused to hear the prophets' warnings. Of this element various Psalms complain, notably Psalms 73 and 106.

Leupold introduces a discussion of this vision thus:

One important problem in the life of Israel has not yet been touched upon: How shall the sinners and the ungodly be dealt with? Outwardly they belong to the nation but inwardly are not of Israel. They were the Israelites who prospered in their sins and were the cause of much suffering on Israel's part. They seemed to be having their day. It may have seemed that by their oppression of the poor and the helpless they were able to undo more than godly, constructive effort was able over a period of years to build up.[4]

This does not mean that the faithful in Israel were without fault. The fact that all had gone into captivity shows it was not so: there was a communal responsibility for the sins of the nation. Often by their silence the faithful encouraged the ungodly element. They could be weak, turning a blind eye to what was happening in the nation. That was true of both the people and their rulers. The number of God-fearing kings was small, but the number of those who valiantly tried to reform the nation was much smaller. The faithful, though blessed of God, are represented in the previous vision by Joshua and his filthy garments. There was no one righteous in himself and by his own works.

Nevertheless, when God saves and justifies his people, he makes a difference between them and the rest. The rest come under the curse of God and come under it always, for "the curse of the LORD is in the house of the wicked" (Prov. 3:33), but those who are justified are "redeemed from the curse" (Gal. 3:13) and their habitation is blessed (Prov. 3:33).

That is the message of this vision, especially regarding the curse of God upon the ungodly and unrepentant in Judah. It is therefore a promise that he would deliver his church not only from the heathen, but also from those who had the name of being God's people but were not, that is, from the carnal and ungodly who were of Israel but who were not the true Israel of God at all, who were children of Abraham but not children of God (Rom. 9:6–7), who were circumcised outwardly and not in heart, and who were therefore not true Jews. The word "cut off" in the next verse has the root meaning of "cleanse" or "purge." That God would do for his justified people by ridding the nation of this ungodly element.

That the curse scroll is represented as flying must indicate the speed with which God's curse would come upon the ungodly in Judah. It also suggests the story of Israel's deliverance from Egypt, when the angel of judgment

---

4 Leupold, *Zechariah*, 97.

passed over the houses of the Israelites but entered the houses of the Egyptians and visited the firstborn with death. In this case, however, it is the houses of many in Israel that are so visited. Flying is also a reminder that God in heaven is the source of the curse. In either case it shows the horror of that curse. Moore says:

> There is something most vivid and appalling in this image of the hovering curse. It flies viewless, and resistless, poising like a falcon over her prey, breathing a ruin the most dire and desolating, and when the blind and hardened offender opens his door to his ill-gotten gains, this mystic roll, with its fire-tracery of wrath, enters into his habitation, and fastening upon his cherished idols, begins its dread work of retribution, and ceases not until the fabric of his guilty life has been totally and irremediably consumed.[5]

5:3. Then said he unto me, This is the curse that goeth forth over the face of the whole earth: for every one that stealeth shall be cut off as on this side according to it; and every one that sweareth shall be cut off as on that side according to it.

God's curse is the word of wrath and judgment that he speaks against his enemies, the wicked. Our curses are merely wishes that harm or evil will come to those we curse, but God's curse is the word of the almighty and everywhere-present God that always finds its object and that drives the person who is under God's curse out of his sight and into eternal damnation. As a result of God's curse, Christ upon whom our curse came "descended into hell" not literally but in suffering the torments of the outpouring of God's anger against sin.

In Zechariah 5 the curse is on those in the covenant nation who were wicked and unfaithful. Verse 3 seems to suggest that it is against all the wicked, heathen or otherwise, but the next verse shows that it is against those who knew the name of God and swore by his name, but falsely. That the curse goes forth over the whole earth (literally "land"), therefore, does

---

5 Moore, *Zechariah*, 80.

not mean that it is spoken against every inhabitant of the earth, but that it is spoken against carnal and unfaithful Israel. It goes through the whole earth seeking them out and destroying them. In those days already it would have gone beyond the borders of Canaan to find these thieves and false swearers. Now, when the church is spread through every land, this curse still goes forth through all the earth.

The scroll is like the two stone tables of the law given to Moses, written on both sides and written in two tables because the law has two parts, love God and love your neighbor for God's sake. The curse is therefore also that of the law, "I the LORD thy God am a jealous God, visiting the iniquity of the fathers upon the children unto the third and fourth generation of them that hate me" (Ex. 20:5). Though the actual execution of that curse is not described until the next verse, it is clearly a matter of God's visiting sin by visiting the houses of sinners and leaving those houses desolate. Just as their sins were within the boundaries of God's covenant, so his curse is also covenantal, pronounced against their houses.

Later Jesus pronounced the same curse against unbelieving Jerusalem: "O Jerusalem, Jerusalem, thou that killest the prophets, and stonest them which are sent unto thee, how often would I have gathered thy children together, even as a hen gathereth her chickens under her wings, and ye would not! Behold, your house is left unto you desolate" (Matt. 23:37–38).

Those who are destroyed by this curse are the thieves and false swearers, not because these were the only sins of which they were guilty, or even because these two sins were particularly heinous or common in apostate Israel, but to show that God upholds both tables of the law. The curse comes not only on those who are guilty of idolatry, false worship, Sabbath breaking, and blasphemy, but also against those who kill and commit adultery and steal and rebel and covet.

That they are referred to as false swearers suggests, however, that under a cloak of piety and devotion to God they were guilty of this sin more than others. The words they spoke, whether in worship or in their daily business, though professing a love for God, were really lies. Under a mask of religiosity they were only interested in gain, as are so many in the church today who use the word of God and a profession of faith to fill their pockets.

The emphasis is on the sins that were troubling Judah at this time. They

THE COMING OF ZION'S REDEEMER

had been cured of the sins of open idolatry by the seventy years in Babylon, but that form of idolatry had been replaced by another, the love of mammon. Nehemiah during his two terms as governor had to deal with this (Neh. 5:1–13; 10:31–39; 13:10–22), in that the people were oppressing their poorer brethren, exacting usury of them, not bringing their tithes, and buying and selling on the Sabbath, evidence of covetousness and materialism that were only a different form of idolatry. Malachi complains of these same sins.

The language of this vision emphasizes this not only by speaking of the thief and false swearer, but also by using many commercial terms: cubit, ephah, and talent. The curse, then, is against those who are unfaithful in the unrighteous mammon (Luke 16:11) and who, having through false weights and measures filled their own pockets, will experience the truth of Luke 6:38, "With what measure ye mete, it shall be measured to you again." They would be cut off just as they had cut short by weights and measures.

In Israel's history, the cutting off involved either the execution of the evildoer or his exile, execution in the case of individuals or families, exile in the case of the nation. In 1 Kings 9:7 God threatens to cut off the nation by captivity: "Then will I cut off Israel out of the land which I have given them; and this house, which I have hallowed for my name, will I cast out of my sight; and Israel shall be a proverb and a byword among all people." In 2 Kings 9:8 God threatens to cut off the family of Ahab for their wickedness, a threat fulfilled in the execution of Ahab's family by Jehu: "For the whole house of Ahab shall perish: and I will cut off from Ahab him that pisseth against the wall, and him that is shut up and left in Israel." In either case, the person's relation to the covenant people and to God is severed and that person banished by either death or exile from the presence of God.

This cutting off was very much like excommunication in the New Testament church and signified the same thing, as Jesus reminds us in Matthew 18:16–18:

16. But if he will not hear thee, then take with thee one or two more, that in the mouth of two or three witnesses every word may be established.
17. And if he shall neglect to hear them, tell it unto the church: but if he neglect to hear the church, let him be unto thee as an heathen man and a publican.

18. Verily I say unto you, Whatsoever ye shall bind on earth shall be bound in heaven: and whatsoever ye shall loose on earth shall be loosed in heaven.

It is, from the viewpoint of God's covenant, the worst that can happen.

The repeated phrase "according to it" is a sharp reminder that God's judgments always come according to his word. His judgments never come unannounced. He always first warns and then sends judgment. Thus the sinner is always left without excuse and shows himself worthy of those judgments by ignoring them, excusing himself, and pretending they do not apply to him. In this case, the leveling of the houses of the wicked was explicitly threatened in Deuteronomy 28:30, "Thou shalt build an house, and shalt not dwell therein."

5:4. I will bring it forth, saith the LORD of hosts, and it shall enter into the house of the thief, and into the house of him that sweareth falsely by my name: and it shall remain in the midst of his house, and shall consume it with the timber thereof and the stones thereof.

Here we are reminded that the curse is God's curse, and that he as the Lord of hosts is able to execute that curse through every means, for all things are at his disposal as the Lord of hosts. He executes that curse through everything he gives the ungodly. His gifts, though in themselves good gifts, are given for their destruction. "Surely thou didst set them in slippery places: thou castedst them down into destruction," Asaph says in Psalm 73:18, as he considers their prosperity and seeming safety from every kind of evil. That curse is at their tables and in their cupboards. It follows them to their beds and is with them in their work. It is in their houses and is visited on them in everything they do.

The curse is described very graphically as being permanently in their houses (Prov. 3:33). It not only enters their houses but literally "stays the night" there, remaining in their houses until even the houses are ruined and destroyed. That happened when God sent Judah into exile in Babylon and will happen again when everything the accursed have is destroyed in the great judgment day by the judgment fires. Nothing will be left to them when the curse of God has done its work.

This curse is fulfilled throughout history, therefore, against all apostates. It had been fulfilled when God sent Judah into captivity:

8. And in the fifth month, on the seventh day of the month, which is the nineteenth year of king Nebuchadnezzar king of Babylon, came Nebuzaradan, captain of the guard, a servant of the king of Babylon, unto Jerusalem:
9. And he burnt the house of the LORD, and the king's house, and all the houses of Jerusalem, and every great man's house burnt he with fire. (2 Kings 25:8–9)

It would be fulfilled again when, in the words of Jesus, not only the individual houses of the Jews but also the earthly temple was destroyed by the Romans: "Behold, your house is left unto you desolate" (Matt. 23:38). It is fulfilled whenever New Testament churches are left spiritually desolate and their place among the candlesticks is taken away. It is fulfilled in the judgment day when the ungodly and apostate lose everything.

That God brings the curse forth suggests that it is always there waiting to be released, and it is released when the wicked fill up their iniquity, as the Canaanites had done when Israel entered the land and took everything away from them. That curse, then, has never been brought forth as it will be in the last day, when God leaves them neither root nor branch but cuts them off by consigning them forever to eternal fire.

Nor can any against whom God speaks his curse escape:

The covenant breakers will discover that the fiery doom of the curse cannot be averted. The arrogant Jehoiakim tried. He took the scroll on which God's prophet had transcribed the covenantal curses, cut it in pieces, and cast them into the fire until all the scroll was incinerated (Jer. 36:1–26). But he was not done with it. The curse-scroll rose from the ashes, rewritten, with many like curses added to it (Jer. 36:27–32). And...it flew over the land, incinerating the houses of all who despised its warning, people and king alike (cf. Jer. 39:8).[6]

---

6 Kline, *Glory in Our Midst*, 182.

Truly, "the curse of the LORD is in the house of the wicked" (Prov. 3:33)!

5:5. Then the angel that talked with me went forth, and said unto me, Lift up now thine eyes, and see what is this that goeth forth.
5:6. And I said, What is it? And he said, This is an ephah that goeth forth. He said moreover, This is their resemblance through all the earth.

As we have seen, there are a number of commentators who believe that verses 5–11 constitute a separate vision, but there are several reasons for seeing this as one vision, not two. The word *behold* is not found at the beginning of this section, and with the exception of the very special fourth vision of Joshua in his filthy garments, that word always marks a new vision. Also, the subject matter of these two sections is really the same, the removal of iniquity from the land.

The words "this is their resemblance through all the earth," that is, "this is what one sees through all the land," also connect these two parts of this sixth vision. The reference is to the thieves and false swearers who were everywhere, but who always appeared spiritually in the form of this woman in a basket. Indeed, the same phrase "in all the land" ("through all the earth") is used in both sections, in verses 3 and 6, further uniting the two sections and showing that they have to do with the same things. Those words remind us of the flight of the scroll over all the land, for wickedness was to be found in every corner of the land. Yet God would remove it by his just judgments and would deliver his people. What a terrible thing, though, that the word of God depicts a part of the covenant nation, the church, in this manner and that God so sees them.

The thieves and false swearers are represented in this second part of the vision under a new form therefore, and what will happen to them is further shown. The two sections are related in that they both show the results of God's curse upon the ungodly element in the nation of Judah. The curse will bring upon them captivity once again, though they had only just returned from Babylon. In the first part of the vision therefore, God tells them that once again their houses will be destroyed. In this second part he tells them that they will once again be carried away to a foreign land.

What we see here is the opposite of what we saw in vision three. There the true people of God were summoned and brought out of Babylon. Here the wicked are sent away to Babylon. The result is a complete separation of righteous and wicked, something that will not be finished until the judgment day, but which sorting-out process goes on throughout history under the preaching of the gospel and through all God's work in the church.

Zechariah initially sees an ephah, a basket estimated to hold somewhat less than a bushel. The ephah that Zechariah sees must have been considerably larger, for it holds a woman, though its contents are not immediately visible to Zechariah. Zechariah is told, however, that it is a resemblance or likeness of the evildoers just mentioned, something that must have puzzled him until the basket was opened. The messenger angel who directs Zechariah's attention to the basket tells him what he is seeing and connects what he sees with the previous part of the vision. Perhaps that was necessary because of the striking character of the first part. The suggestion is that he was so wrapped up in the vision of the flying scroll that he had to be reminded that there was more to see.

5:7. And, behold, there was lifted up a talent of lead: and this is a woman that sitteth in the midst of the ephah.

5:8. And he said, This is wickedness. And he cast it into the midst of the ephah; and he cast the weight of lead upon the mouth thereof.

Once Zechariah's attention is directed to the basket, he sees that it has a very heavy covering of lead that is lifted momentarily before being dropped down on the mouth of the basket, to reveal a woman sitting in the basket. The English translation is a little confusing, especially in verse 8. It is the woman who is described as being cast into the basket and the talent of lead that is cast upon the mouth of the basket.[7] It is obvious therefore that the lead covering is for the purpose of keeping the woman in the basket and making sure she does not escape. That the weight of the lead is given, a talent being the equivalent of about seventy-five to one hundred pounds, cannot be of any significance other than to emphasize that it is very heavy and that escape is impossible for the woman.

---

7 "And he pushed her back into the basket and pushed the lead cover down over its mouth" (NIV).

The weights and measures, ephah and talent, are a reminder of the sins for which this woman, "wickedness," is being taken away. Representing the apostate element in the covenant nation, she is taken away for the sins of covetousness, materialism, and worldliness—the service of mammon. What a warning to those in the church today who are guilty of these same sins and pride themselves on their worldly success and their place among God's covenant people, who often use their worldly success to push their own agendas in the church and to obtain for themselves positions of influence and leadership. They have no part among God's people, and God will deliver his people from them!

The woman is the main element in this part of the vision and is identified as "wickedness" in verse 8. She is not wickedness in general but, as the following verses show, the wicked and carnal and unbelieving element in Judah. Verse 4 describes them as those who swear falsely by God's name.

The model for *this* woman is probably wicked Queen Athaliah, who killed her own grandchildren, appropriated the temple treasures for her own use, and introduced into Judah the heathen practices of her mother, Jezebel (2 Chron. 22:10; 24:7). She is actually called "wickedness" in 2 Chronicles 24:7, and the same word is used there as here. Zechariah did not intend his readers to think only of her, however.

Scripture seems to use a woman as a picture of sin or symbol of wickedness because of the "alluring, captivating, deceptive power of sin."[8] Numerous passages in the prophets, notably Ezekiel 16 and Hosea 2, represent apostate Israel, the false church of the Old Testament, as an adulterous woman. Revelation 17 gives the same picture of the apostate church in the New Testament. There too the false church is represented as a woman riding on the Beast. Her name is "Mystery, Babylon the Great, The Mother of Harlots and Abominations of the Earth" (v. 5). There can be no doubt that these women are the same and that Revelation 17 and Zechariah 5 are similar visions.

This woman is the counterpart of the woman who is portrayed in Revelation 12 as the mother of Christ, the church of both the Old and New Testaments. Revelation's portrayal, however, is nothing new, for Israel is often pictured in the Old Testament as the wife of God.

---

8 Laetsch, *The Minor Prophets*, 434.

Here, as in Revelation, the opposite of the wife of God is pictured and used to represent the hypocrites, the ungodly, the worldly in the church. That carnal element is often a graver danger to the church than the heathen, for it is found within the church. It is the enemy in the camp who will always lead the church astray in doctrine and in practice. It is like the mixed multitude who went with Israel out of Egypt, among whom most of the complaining and rebellion originated. Those who are part of this element are those who try to serve God and mammon, who commit spiritual idolatry, who intermarry with and make friends of the ungodly, and who are really no different from the wicked world.

This identification of the woman of Zechariah, the great harlot of Revelation 17, and the apostate church is confirmed in Revelation 11:8. There the great city Babylon is identified not only with Sodom and Egypt, but also with apostate and wicked Jerusalem "where our Lord was crucified." She is Jerusalem in name but Babylon in her rebellion against God, Sodom in her toleration of every form of wickedness, Egypt in her oppression of God's people, and the place where Christ is always crucified. One does not have to look far to find her today. She is found in every denomination and church.

An ephah is used because it was not only a container but also a measure, thus serving as a reminder that the wickedness of carnal Israel had been measured by God, that she had filled or soon would fill up her measure of wickedness, and that God, who had measured her wickedness, had also adequate means to deal with her wickedness. Jesus said to the unbelieving Jews of his day, "Fill ye up then the measure of your fathers" (Matt. 23:32), something they would soon do in crucifying him. These Jews had already done that.

When the woman, representing wicked Israel, is thrown into the basket, we see that God himself was executing judgment on her. He had put her in the basket; he would keep her there; and he would deal with her wickedness as so vividly portrayed in the verses that follow. In dealing with her wickedness, he would deliver his people from her. Sitting in the basket, she represents all those who are comfortable in their wickedness, who "sit in the seat of the scornful" (Ps. 1:1) and are not afraid of God's judgments.

5:9. Then lifted I up mine eyes, and looked, and, behold, there came out two women, and the wind was in their wings; for they had wings like the wings of a stork: and they lifted up the ephah between the earth and the heaven.

While Zechariah is watching, two winged women come and lift up the ephah basket and carry it away above the earth. Zechariah soon learns that these women have come to take the basket away to the land of Shinar. These women have wings like the wings of a stork, an unclean animal to the Jews (Lev. 11:13, 19; Deut. 14:12, 18). The wings show that these women have come for no good purpose, but in the anger of God and as judgment of God. That they come to execute God's judgment is also suggested by the wind in their wings. The wind is both itself a symbol of God's judgment and the quick coming of judgment.

When these unclean bird-women carry the woman in the basket away, we learn that the wickedness of the wicked is their own undoing. In their pride and rebellion, they act as though God does not see and is helpless to act, but they find finally that it is not so. Whether these other women actually represent evil spirits is difficult to say, but if they do the point is the same. The ungodly are carried away by their own wickedness and fall into the snare their own hands have made and into the pit their own hands have dug.

The idea of judgment is further taught when this basket, before being carried away, is lifted up between earth and heaven. That is in scripture a sign of God's curse, as is evident from the Jewish practice of hanging the dead bodies of executed criminals on a tree (Deut. 21:22–23). Hanging on a tree, they hung between heaven and earth, symbolizing that there was room for them neither in God's creation nor in his heaven. Thus Christ too in hanging on a tree became a curse for us.

Here that curse comes on those who were not in Christ by faith, not redeemed by his blood from the curse, though it comes symbolically and before his death. They showed that they were under God's curse by their continued, unrepentant wickedness.

5:10. Then said I to the angel that talked with me, Whither do these bear the ephah?

5:11. And he said unto me, To build it an house in the land of Shinar: and it shall be established, and set there upon her own base.

It is obvious to Zechariah that these bird-women are carrying the basket away, and so he asks the messenger angel, "Whither do these bear the ephah?" The angel informs him that the women are carrying the basket to the land of Shinar, that is, the land of Babylon, and that there a house will be built for the woman in the basket and she and the basket set upon a base in that house.

The mention of Babylon further identifies this woman with the mystery woman of Revelation 17. Babylon is really her name as well as the place where she belongs. Outwardly her name may be Jerusalem or Zion or Israel, but her real name is Babylon, the mother of harlots and abominations. She is the false church and has the name church but is really one with the world. She has, as John says in Revelation, a name that she lives, but is dead.

In the Old Testament the people she represents are Israelites in name only. Though they make a pretense of worshiping God, their hearts are the hearts of idolaters. Though they live in Israel, their real home is Babylon. They are the Jews who intermarried with the heathen, who worshiped the gold and silver gods of the nations, who loved the reward of unrighteousness, who sacrificed the covenantal seed on the altar of their own ambitions, who closed the temple and desecrated the worship of God. They are the leaders who made a pious pretense of serving God but persecuted the true worshipers of God and ultimately crucified the Lord of glory. They are the self-righteous Pharisees and the unbelieving Sadducees. They are the mixed multitude who followed Israel out of Egypt but were forever complaining and rebelling.

They are those who said, "The people of God, the people of God, are we," while taking their ease in Zion. They are those who killed the prophets and then laid flowers on their graves. They are those who also looked for help from the heathen and their gods and not from the Lord who made heaven and earth. They are those who, when in need, sought help from gods of Ekron and who, when they came under the judgments of God through the heathen, said that they would worship the gods as did King Ahaz (2 Kings 16:5–16).

In the New Testament they are in the church but do not really belong. They are the enemy in the camp, those who are allied with Satan and the world. They are the brazenly wicked Nicolaitans, the lukewarm Laodiceans, the followers of Jezebel who thought they should continue in sin in order to test the depths of Satan. They are those described in Hebrews 6:1–6, those who make a profession of faith in Christ but whose lives never match their profession, who love the world much more than they love the kingdom of God, who are so busy laying up treasure on earth that they have no time for the kingdom. They are not and never will be anything else than Babylon, for that is where their hearts are, and with Babylon they perish.

Having destroyed and taken away their place among his covenant people, symbolized by the destruction of their houses, God builds them a house in the land of Babylon where they belong. It is possible, as some commentators suggest, that this house is really a temple, so that the picture is of covetousness and materialism being enshrined as the gods of Babylon and the gods of those who are carried there. There the woman has her place "where idolatry, oppression, and cruelty already abide."[9] There she is "adored and worshiped and served with an eagerness and devotion which puts to shame many a one claiming membership in God's Church."[10]

Shinar is also the place of man's first great attempt to set up the kingdom of antichrist. It was in Shinar (Gen. 11:2) that the attempt to build the tower of Babel was made, and so Shinar and Babylon, whose name is derived from Babel, are always pictures of that great kingdom and of every attempt to establish an antichristian kingdom. Thus the setting of the ephah on a base represents the attitude of this woman: "For she saith in her heart, I sit a queen, and am no widow, and shall see no sorrow" (Rev. 18:7).

God promises then to deliver his people of these enemies as well as from the heathen. That he speaks of transporting this woman in her covered basket to Shinar and building her a house there and setting her upon a base means that he would separate his people from her, bring her to her own place, and establish her there permanently. This has the same force as the word of God in Revelation 18:4–8:

4. Come out of her, my people, that ye be not partakers of her sins, and that ye receive not of her plagues.

---

9 McComiskey, *Zechariah*, 1103.
10 Laetsch, *The Minor Prophets*, 434.

5. For her sins have reached unto heaven, and God hath remembered her iniquities.

6. Reward her even as she rewarded you, and double unto her double according to her works: in the cup which she hath filled fill to her double.

7. How much she hath glorified herself, and lived deliciously, so much torment and sorrow give her: for she saith in her heart, I sit a queen, and am no widow, and shall see no sorrow.

8. Therefore shall her plagues come in one day, death, and mourning, and famine; and she shall be utterly burned with fire: for strong is the Lord God who judgeth her.

This is the complete deliverance of God's church from all her enemies. This deliverance is accomplished in principle in the cross and resurrection of Jesus, but it continues to be accomplished through church reformation and purification throughout the New Testament. It will be finished when the church is glorified with Christ, for "there shall in no wise enter into it any thing that defileth, neither whatsoever worketh abomination, or maketh a lie: but they which are written in the Lamb's book of life" (Rev. 21:27). When those who are not of us go out from us, Zechariah's vision is fulfilled. When those who are "sensual, having not the Spirit" (Jude 19) separate themselves, we see again the woman in the basket carried away to Shinar. When finally the chaff is separated from the wheat and cast into the fire, Zechariah's vision will have reached its conclusion.

The kingdom of antichrist is established when the woman of Revelation 17 rides the beast and is drunken with the blood of the martyrs. Then this vision is fulfilled. Carried away to Babylon, she is enthroned there and considers herself a queen, allies herself with the wicked world, and establishes a kingdom that she claims is the fulfillment of prophecy and the everlasting kingdom of Christ. But it is the kingdom in which man is worshiped as God, the man of sin claiming to be God and sitting in the temple of God as though he were God. Thus he does what Babylon has always done, in setting up its tower that reaches to heaven and in claiming the worship of men as Nebuchadnezzar did when he made his golden image.

That this will be a time of deliverance for the true people of God is shown in the next vision and again in Zechariah 13:8–9. God speaks of a remnant that will be saved from these judgments:

> 8. And it shall come to pass, that in all the land, saith the LORD, two parts therein shall be cut off and die; but the third shall be left therein.
> 9. And I will bring the third part through the fire, and will refine them as silver is refined, and will try them as gold is tried: they shall call on my name, and I will hear them: I will say, It is my people: and they shall say, The LORD is my God.

Chapter 13

THE SEVENTH VISION:
ZECHARIAH 6:1-8

6:1 And I turned, and lifted up mine eyes, and looked, and, behold, there came four chariots out from between two mountains; and the mountains were mountains of brass.

6:2 In the first chariot were red horses; and in the second chariot black horses;

6:3 And in the third chariot white horses; and in the fourth chariot grisled and bay horses.

6:4 Then I answered and said unto the angel that talked with me, What are these, my lord?

6:5 And the angel answered and said unto me, These are the four spirits of the heavens, which go forth from standing before the LORD of all the earth.

6:6 The black horses which are therein go forth into the north country; and the white go forth after them; and the grisled go forth toward the south country.

6:7 And the bay went forth, and sought to go that they might walk to and fro through the earth: and he said, Get you hence, walk to and fro through the earth. So they walked to and fro through the earth.

6:8 Then cried he upon me, and spake unto me, saying, Behold, these that go toward the north country have quieted my spirit in the north country.

The seventh and last vision is similar in both symbolism and intent to John's vision of the four horsemen in Revelation 6:1–8. It is also the climax of Zechariah's visions. These visions begin with the assurance that Christ is in the midst of his church (the rider on the red horse among the myrtles) and continue with the assurance that God delivers his church in her struggle against the world (the four horns and four carpenters) and that God will prosper his people and build up his church (the man with the measuring line). Central to all of this is God's justification of his people (the reclothing of Joshua), which leads to further revelations of the work of God's Spirit in the church (the olive trees and candlestick) and of his delivering his church from the carnal element that is always found within her (the flying scroll and the woman in the basket).

To these revelations this final vision forms a conclusion in that it points to the second coming of Christ, the final judgment, and the new heavens and the new earth, though an actual look at the glories of the new creation waits until the second half of the book, especially chapter 14. To the horsemen of this vision we have been introduced in the first vision, and now we see them accomplishing their purpose in the service of the rider on the red horse and bringing in the everlasting kingdom of God.

6:1. And I turned, and lifted up mine eyes, and looked, and, behold, there came four chariots out from between two mountains; and the mountains were mountains of brass.

6:2. In the first chariot were red horses; and in the second chariot black horses;

6:3. And in the third chariot white horses; and in the fourth chariot grisled and bay horses.

Zechariah now sees not just four horsemen, but four chariots drawn by different colored horses and appearing from between two mountains of brass. There are therefore differences between this vision and that of Revelation 6:1–8, for neither the chariots nor the mountains are found in Revelation. Nevertheless, it would be irresponsible not to take Revelation 6 into account when interpreting Zechariah 6, and the same is true of Zechariah 1.

There too there are differences, notably the lack of black horses in Zechariah. Because the other three are found in Revelation, however, the two visions must be interpreted together.

There is not any real difference between the horses of Revelation and the horse-drawn chariots of Zechariah. Both are instruments of battle and both are directed and controlled in their course of battle, either by their riders or by their drivers. The same is true of the mountains. Though they are not mentioned in Revelation, what they signify is found there. In both cases these horses ride for the sake of the kingdom of God and under the control of Christ. From the first vision we know Christ controls them, for they report to him and therefore are under his sovereign sway.

The English translation does not show that the colors of the horses Zechariah sees are really the same as the colors of the horses John sees five hundred years later. The black, red, and white are clearly the same, but Zechariah (in the KJV) speaks of grisled and bay horses, while John speaks of a pale horse. "Pale" in Revelation 6:8 actually means "green" or "yellow," though the KJV certainly catches the intent of the word in that the horse and its rider represent death. In Zechariah the word translated as "grisled" is the word used to describe a color and is somewhat difficult to interpret. "Grisled" probably means "spotted" and is used also in Genesis 31:10, 12.

The word translated as "bay" is not a color and does not refer only to the last group of horses, but to them all. The word translated as "bay" means "active" or "powerful." A literal translation of the passage is, "With the first chariot were red horses, and with the second chariot black horses, and with the third chariot white horses, and with the fourth chariot spotted horses, [all] powerful ones."

The four horses of Revelation represent the powers by which God controls and directs the course of history, and the same is true here. War, famine and social inequality and unrest, death in all its forms, and the triumphant progress of the gospel are the means God uses to bring down one kingdom and to set up another, to cut lives short, to make division among the nations, and to prevent the premature development of the kingdom of antichrist—to do what he did at Babel through the confusion of tongues.

As long as the world's problems are not solved, the nations cannot unite to form a world kingdom and unite against the church. Thus God controls and directs them and gives opportunity to the church to preach the gospel and to fulfill her mission in the world, and only then can the end come. History must run in the channel that God has prepared for it, and by the power and work of these riders God makes sure that it does.

They are called therefore, in Zechariah 1:10, "they whom the LORD hath sent to walk to and fro through the earth." God directs them, and that these are not horses running wild, but hitched to chariots and driven with a purpose, reminds us of that. Their mission is through "all the earth" (v. 11). There they fulfill God's eternal and unchangeable will and bring about what he has eternally purposed for the glory of his name, for the salvation of his church, and for the execution of his just judgments.

That these horses are drawing chariots is a further indication of their mission, for chariots are instruments of war, in this case of God's war against his enemies. Psalm 68 tells of God's coming with his chariots "thousand thousand fold." God comes as a God of war to take vengeance on his enemies and to deliver his people. The battle here is the same battle we read of in Revelation, described first in chapters 1–11 as a battle between the church and the world and in chapters 12–22 as the battle between Christ and Satan. In that battle God always triumphs on behalf of his church.

That there are four chariots symbolizes their universal mission.

> The number four has the same significance here as in the four winds of Daniel, the four cherubs of Ezekiel, the four angels at the four corners of the earth in the Apocalypse, and the four horns and four artificers of the second vision. Alluding to the four points of the compass, it is the symbol of universality, a judgment that goes in every direction.[1]

The two mountains of brass are the place from which these chariots come. Zechariah 6:5 explains the mountains by saying they (the chariots) "go forth from standing before the Lord of all the earth." Between these two mountains or in the midst of them God dwells in his glory. That these mountains are of brass reminds us of the glory of the Lord, for shining brass

---

1 Moore, *Zechariah*, 87.

is often associated with God's glory and especially with his glory as he comes for judgment and for salvation. The cherubim who carry the throne of God in Ezekiel 1 have legs of brass (v. 7), as does the one like the son of man who appears to Daniel (Dan. 10:5–6), and this same person appearing again in Revelation 1 has "feet like unto fine brass, as if they burned in a furnace" (v. 15). Brass and iron were the metals of war.

There seems to be a correspondence between the two mountains and the two legs of the man in Daniel and Revelation. In coming out from between the two mountains, the chariots come, as it were, from between Christ's feet, feet that are firmly planted on the earth, for he is always present here on earth by his power and providence, directing and controlling all things.

Alternatively, the two mountains are Zion and the Mount of Olives, between which runs the Valley of Jehoshaphat, the scene of God's judgment of the nations: "I will also gather all nations, and will bring them down into the valley of Jehoshaphat, and will plead with them there for my people and for my heritage Israel, whom they have scattered among the nations, and parted my land" (Joel 3:2). In either case the meaning is the same: out of Zion God comes for judgment and for the salvation of his people.

Yet the mountains also represent God's kingdom and church. The church is often described as a mountain and appears here as two (perhaps a reference to Zion and Moriah, the fortress and temple mountains of the Old Testament). The church was a mountain in the Old Testament and continues to be so described in scripture because of her lofty glory as the city and dwelling place of God. Thus the symbolism of the two mountains is along these lines: the mountains are the almighty feet of God as he visits the earth and comes in judgment, sending out his agents to perform his will, and are in turn also the church and kingdom of God, the place where his feet are planted and where he dwells as the God of his people.

This part of the seventh vision corresponds to Zechariah 14:4–5:

4. And his feet shall stand in that day upon the mount of Olives, which is before Jerusalem on the east, and the mount of Olives shall cleave in the midst thereof toward the east and toward the west, and there shall be a very great valley; and half of the mountain shall remove toward the north, and half of it toward the south.

5. And ye shall flee to the valley of the mountains; for the valley
of the mountains shall reach unto Azal: yea, ye shall flee, like as ye
fled from before the earthquake in the days of Uzziah king of Judah:
and the LORD my God shall come, and all the saints with thee.

In Zechariah 14:4–5 we see the two mountains connected with the presence of God, for his feet stand upon them. Out from between those two mountains God comes with his saints. The language is unmistakably the language of judgment. Zechariah 6:1–8 uses the same language but does not mention the saints as being involved in the judgment. The picture is the same.

The picture of the vision is of God's sovereign rule over the nations and his coming for judgment, not just at the end of the world but throughout history, for the chariots are always going out. Thus the ungodly are destroyed, the prayer of the man on the red horse answered (1:12), and the kingdom of God brought in. This Isaiah prophesied in chapter 2:2–4:

2. And it shall come to pass in the last days, that the mountain of the
LORD's house shall be established in the top of the mountains, and
shall be exalted above the hills; and all nations shall flow unto it.
3. And many people shall go and say, Come ye, and let us go up to
the mountain of the LORD, to the house of the God of Jacob; and
he will teach us of his ways, and we will walk in his paths: for out of
Zion shall go forth the law, and the word of the LORD from Jerusalem.
4. And he shall judge among the nations, and shall rebuke many
people: and they shall beat their swords into plowshares, and their
spears into pruninghooks: nation shall not lift up sword against
nation, neither shall they learn war any more.

6:4. *Then I answered and said unto the angel that talked with me, What are these, my lord?*
6:5. *And the angel answered and said unto me, These are the four spirits of the heavens, which go forth from standing before the Lord of all the earth.*

When Zechariah asks about these chariots and their horses, he is told that they are "four spirits of the heavens." This is grammatically the most difficult part of the passage, and various translations have been suggested. The translation of the KJV suggests that the spirits are angels who are involved in the work of directing and controlling history and bringing all things under the judgment of God.

Another translation, however, is "these are the four winds of heaven." The words "spirit" and "wind" are the same word in Hebrew and only the context can determine which way the word ought to be translated, so that translation is indeed a possibility here. If that translation is followed, the emphasis is on the judgment mission of these charioteers, for the winds represent God's judgment in scripture. That the word here refers to the winds and not to the Holy Spirit is confirmed by Revelation 7:1, where four angels stand at the four corners of the earth holding the four winds of the earth.

Using the translation "winds" there is still a third possible translation, "these go forth *to the four winds of heaven* from standing before the LORD of all the earth." In that case the verse is teaching the truth that the judgments and work of God executed through these chariots encompass the whole earth. It seems in light of verses 6–7 that this translation is preferable, since those verses continue the thought of verse 5 and speak of the different directions to which these chariots go.

This translation and interpretation makes the passage similar to Ezekiel's vision of the wheeled vehicle that bears God's presence and goes in all directions (Ezek. 1–2, 10): "When they went, they went upon their four sides; they turned not as they went, but to the place whither the head looked they followed it; they turned not as they went" (Ezek. 10:11). There the vehicle represents the same thing as the four chariots of Zechariah: the providential presence of God as the God of judgment and salvation, the God who is always near and who goes forth for the salvation of his people.

God's providential direction of all things is the message of the passage therefore, just as in Ezekiel. This is a message of great hope and comfort for God's church, for he sovereignly directs all things through Jesus Christ and therefore controls them for the good of his church so that all things work together for good to those who love God (Rom. 8:28). That message was sorely needed in the difficult times of Zechariah's prophecies. It is sorely needed today as the end of the ages approaches and the great conflict of the last days looms.

That these chariots go out from the Lord ought to remind us of the many scriptural passages that speak of God's coming for judgment *from his church.* Psalm 68:7–8 describe him as going forth from his holy habitation. 1 Peter 4:17 reminds us that judgment always begins at the house of God, and Zechariah 2:13, a similar passage, says, "Be silent, O all flesh, before the Lord: for he is raised up out of his holy habitation." Not against the church but from the church he comes. What comfort!

6:6. The black horses which are therein go forth into the north country; and the white go forth after them; and the grisled go forth toward the south country.

6:7. And the bay went forth, and sought to go that they might walk to and fro through the earth: and he said, Get you hence, walk to and fro through the earth. So they walked to and fro through the earth.

That these chariots are described as going in different directions has caused commentators no end of trouble. Numerous efforts have been made to identify each chariot with a specific judgment of God upon a specific nation.[2] It seems, however, that the interpretation is more general, for the red horses are not mentioned, nor east and west. It is better to see in this God's word concerning his sovereign sending of these judgment chariots. He sends them as he wills, where he wills, and when he wills to accomplish his purpose.

It may be that the black horses and chariot and what they represent were riding in a northerly direction at the time of Zechariah's prophecy, but that is certainly not the only direction in which they ride as history goes on, and the same is true of the others. The white horses, representing the triumphant progress of the gospel, may have ridden first to the north, but in the end they too make their journey through all the earth.

This is stated in verse 7. The word translated in the KJV as "bay" does not refer to a color, but means "powerful ones" and refers to all the horses. Thus, though verse 6 describes specific missions and directions, verse 7 is

---

2 The NIV, without any textual support whatever, says "the one with the white horses toward the west," typical of the arbitrary and careless method of translation that characterizes the NIV from beginning to end.

more general and describes these powerful horses going into the whole world. This is also the teaching of chapter 1, where the horses first appear. There too they are described as going "to and fro through the earth." The mission of these chariots is worldwide, and that is only to say that God's providence is all-comprehensive, including all things, controlling all events, and directing all things to their appointed end and for the good of the church.

6:8. Then cried he upon me, and spake unto me, saying, Behold, these that go toward the north country have quieted my spirit in the north country.

The land of the north is Babylon and all she represents. The north is mentioned because to the north in those days lay Judah's chief enemy, the Babylon world power that had destroyed temple and city and held the covenant nation in bondage. The other nations are not outside God's control or safe from his judgments. They are not in view only because it was Babylon and not they who were in the minds of God's people. Babylon, the northern power, as a representation of wickedness and rebellion against God, Babylon as the persecutor and oppressor of God's church, includes the other nations and other directions.

The north country is in Ezekiel 38 and 39 the place from which Gog and Magog come to make their war against Zion. Revelation 20, describing the same war, shows us that Gog and Magog represent the antichristian world power as it makes war against the people of God. Daniel too identifies the little horn with the "king of the north" (Dan. 11:36–45), who is further identified in Matthew 24:15, 2 Thessalonians 2:4, and Revelation 13 with the antichrist. The north country therefore represents the kingdom of antichrist in all its different manifestations throughout history and in its final apparent triumph over the church, in its rebellion against God and in its gross idolatry, "the world's final satanic insurrection."[3]

That God's Spirit is quieted looks to the goal of the work of these chariots. The result of their going will be that God's justice is satisfied, his judgments fully worked out, his purpose accomplished, and the final glory of his kingdom brought in. Literally the passage says, "Behold, those that go toward the north country have given my spirit rest in the north country."

---

3 Kline, *Glory in Our Midst*, 213.

Babylon is destroyed, the church is delivered from her oppression, and all that God has planned for his church comes to pass.

Just as in the beginning he rested when he had finished his work of creation, so he now rests when his work of redemption through judgment is finished. He "finishes the work and cuts it short in righteousness" (Rom. 9:28), and so the eternal Sabbath comes, the Sabbath rest that still remains for the people of God (Heb. 4:9). This glorious rest is more fully described in chapters 8 and 14 of Zechariah, but the visions he saw would not have been complete without a glimpse of what is ahead, for that is the goal of God's work, the hope of God's people, and the eternal blessedness of his church.

Here is a vista of the world to come. The holy war is over. At the great battle of Har Magedon the Lord has triumphed; he has eliminated the hostile forces. The final trumpet has sounded and there is "delay no longer;" the mystery of God has been finished as he announced to and through his servants the prophets (Rev. 10:6, 7). Sabbath time has come.[4]

---

4 Ibid., 214.

Chapter 14

THE SECOND STORY:
ZECHARIAH 6:9–15

6:9   And the word of the LORD came unto me, saying,

6:10 Take of them of the captivity, even of Heldai, of Tobijah, and of Jedaiah, which are come from Babylon, and come thou the same day, and go into the house of Josiah the son of Zephaniah;

6:11 Then take silver and gold, and make crowns, and set them upon the head of Joshua the son of Josedech, the high priest;

6:12 And speak unto him, saying, Thus speaketh the LORD of hosts, saying, Behold the man whose name is The BRANCH; and he shall grow up out of his place, and he shall build the temple of the LORD:

6:13 Even he shall build the temple of the LORD; and he shall bear the glory, and shall sit and rule upon his throne; and he shall be a priest upon his throne: and the counsel of peace shall be between them both.

6:14 And the crowns shall be to Helem, and to Tobijah, and to Jedaiah, and to Hen the son of Zephaniah, for a memorial in the temple of the LORD.

6:15 And they that are far off shall come and build in the temple of the LORD, and ye shall know that the LORD of hosts hath sent me unto you. And this shall come to pass, if ye will diligently obey the voice of the LORD your God.

N ow follows, not another vision, but the second story passage and the most important part of Zechariah's prophecy. This is the principle message. This, focusing on Christ the great priest-king, gives meaning to everything else Zechariah says:

> Yet this portion has a very direct connection with the eight preceding visions.[1] It follows them so closely that it appears as a practical continuation of them. But there is also a deeper inner connection... In pointing prominently to the Messiah as a personage who is furnished with unique and unheard-of authority as King our portion indicates that it shall in reality be He who achieves these mighty works, both in building His kingdom and in judging sinners.[2]

In this section Zechariah becomes once again a participant in the action and enters more deeply into the prophetic action. Having only made a suggestion in the previous story passage, he is now the one who sets crowns of gold on the head of Joshua the high priest, making him one of the great Old Testament portraits of Christ the redeemer of his people.

There are several parts to this section. There is first the symbolic action in verses 9–11. Then follows an interpretation of this symbolic action in verses 12–13, concluding with a reference to the fact that the material for the crowns Zechariah is commanded to make and use came from a far land.

6:9. And the word of the LORD came unto me, saying,

6:10. Take of them of the captivity, even of Heldai, of Tobijah, and of Jedaiah, which are come from Babylon, and come thou the same day, and go into the house of Josiah the son of Zephaniah;

6:11. Then take silver and gold, and make crowns, and set them upon the head of Joshua the son of Josedech, the high priest;

---

1 Leupold divides chapter 5 into two visions and thus finds a total of eight visions in the first part of Zechariah.

2 Leupold, *Zechariah*, 119.

Zechariah 6:9–15 is the climax and conclusion of all the preceding visions, particularly the vision of chapter 4 (the candlestick and olive trees). These verses are not another vision, therefore, but record an incident that sheds light on the other visions of the first six chapters. This is a word from the Lord and a historical record of the resulting prophetic action that accomplishes God's word to Zechariah.

Three men, Jews of the captivity, had recently come from Babylon to Jerusalem with gifts of gold and silver for the temple. Zechariah is commanded to go and meet the men before they have the opportunity to present these gifts in the temple. Zechariah must take the gifts, make from them crowns, and put the crowns on the head of Joshua the high priest. This action would be a sign to Joshua and all Israel concerning the building of the temple (vv. 12–13).

That plural crowns are spoken of should not cause confusion, since Christ, who is pictured here, is described in Revelation 19:12 as wearing many crowns. "Crown him with many crowns, the Lamb upon his throne": so we sing in the well-known hymn.

This command must have seemed very strange to Zechariah and to the people who witnessed the sign. Never before in all their history had the high priest worn the crown of the king, or the king the robes of the priest. The one man who had tried to assume both offices, King Uzziah of Judah, had been punished by God for his presumption with a terrible plague of leprosy. God had always insisted that the two offices of priest and king remain separate in Israel. The only one the Jews could remember who had borne both offices had been Melchizedek, the king of Jerusalem in the days of Abraham, but he was connected with their history only through his meeting of Abraham when Abraham returned from his victory over the armies of the five kings (Gen. 14:17–24).

Nevertheless, strange though the sign may have seemed to the people, it pointed to the necessity of the union of these two offices for the building of the temple of God. In the case of Zerubbabel and Joshua, this union was not complete but was seen only very dimly in the cooperation that existed between them in the work of building the temple. This union did not mean that either of them had to give his rightful office to the other. Rather it meant that they must be one in zeal and purpose in rebuilding and maintaining God's house.

This cooperation was necessary first because only Zerubbabel as ruler had the authority and power to cause the work to continue. Second, it was necessary because only through the work of Joshua as priest could the Lord dwell in the house as the God of his people. Thus we find in Zechariah 3 a special word of God to Joshua as the one through whom the Lord will remove the iniquity of the land (vv. 7–8), and in chapter 4 to Zerubbabel as the one whose hand had laid the foundation and who would also bring forth the headstone and finish the work (vv. 7–10).

Through their cooperation therefore, the promises revealed and illustrated in the visions of chapters 1–5 would be fulfilled. The house would be built (Zech. 1:16). God himself would dwell in that house (Zech. 2:10–11), and his presence would be the glory of that new-built house (v. 5), though it was small and despised in the eyes of others (Zech. 4:10). Thus also the fruit of God's presence would be peace and prosperity for his people (Zech. 3:9–10). The unity and cooperation of Joshua and Zerubbabel in their respective offices are therefore the typical, Old Testament fulfillment of the counsel of peace prophesied in Zechariah 6:13.

This was something that the people could understand. Their own history showed how the inevitable result of a lack of cooperation between priest and king was the neglect of the worship of God and the ruin of the temple. When the king was wicked, no matter who was priest, the doors of the temple were shut, its treasures were sold, and the building fell into disrepair (2 Chron. 28:24; 33:4–5). When the priests did not fear God, all the authority and wealth of the rulers was not sufficient to maintain the true worship of God among the people, and the temple was abandoned and ruined (Mal. 2:1–8). The "counsel of peace," (Zech. 6:13) therefore, was absolutely necessary for the spiritual well-being of the nation.

All of this, though, was only the typical fulfillment of this sign of the crowning of Joshua. That was immediately evident from the fact that the two offices were not personally united in one man, but remained separate and distinct. Joshua did not replace Zerubbabel as ruler when he was crowned, nor did he even continue to wear the crown. Rather, the crown, as a sign of a future and better unity between the offices of priest and king, was placed in the temple for a memorial (Zech. 6:14). And as long as these two offices were not united in one man, the possibility of disharmony and disunity always remained as a threat to the spiritual life of God's Old Testament people.

6:12. And speak unto him, saying, Thus speaketh the LORD of hosts, saying, Behold the man whose name is The BRANCH; and he shall grow up out of his place, and he shall build the temple of the LORD:

Zechariah is also commanded, in connection with this sign, to call the attention of Joshua and the people to one man who would be a priest upon the throne, who would both rule and bear the glory, whose name would be the Branch. In him the counsel of peace would be fully revealed and the offices of priest and king united forever. Because he would be a priest upon the throne, he also would be able to build a better temple than Joshua and Zerubbabel could ever build.

This man, the Branch, is our Lord Jesus Christ, of whom we read in Hebrews 8:1: "We have such an high priest, who is set on the right hand of the throne of the Majesty in the heavens." He is a high priest forever after the order of Melchizedek, for he is both king of peace and priest of the most high God (Heb. 7:1–3). By the union of the priestly and kingly offices in him, both the glory of his kingly office and the power of his priestly office are increased, the significance of his coming and work are revealed, and the full wonder of our salvation is made known for our comfort and for the glory of God.

Christ had already been promised as the Branch in Zechariah 3:8. He has this name, the Branch, also in the prophecies of Isaiah (4:2; 11:1) and Jeremiah (23:5; 33:15). In other places, similarly, he is called "a rod out of the stem of Jesse" (Isa. 11:1) and "a tender plant and…a root out of a dry ground' (Isa. 53:2). That these names all refer to Christ is clear from Revelation 5:5 and 22:16, where Christ is called the root and offspring of David.

There are several different words used in Hebrew in these passages, but all have the idea of something small and unlooked for. These names emphasize Christ's coming suddenly, unexpectedly, and gloriously out of the ruined line of David. Christ is the Branch both as the one whose coming was all but forgotten in the fullness of time and as the one whose coming was so insignificant from a human viewpoint as to go unnoticed.

When he was born, the majority of the Jews were no longer interested or had begun to look elsewhere. The Herodians even looked to bloody Herod and his family as the fulfillment of the Messianic promises (Matt. 22:16; Mark 3:6; 12:13). When the wise men inquired in Jerusalem about the birth of Christ, no one seemed interested, and the leaders who piously informed Herod that Christ was to be born in Bethlehem did not bother to go to find out if the tidings of the wise men were true.

The circumstances of his birth, the stable, the manger and the swaddling clothes, the announcement of his birth to a few shepherds, his parents' flight into Egypt, all show him to be the Branch of whom God speaks through Zechariah. His humble origins, his poverty, his choosing fishermen and tax collectors to be his disciples, his refusal to establish an earthly kingdom, his shameful death on the cross, all made him of no account among the wise and mighty. These things should have identified him as the one long promised, but to most they did not, for most were looking for someone to lead them against the Romans, to fill their bellies, and to heal their bodies. They were like so many today who are interested in him only as long as he gives them what they want.

Mary's question in Luke 1:34 reflects back on this prophecy. When Mary said, "How shall this be, seeing I know not a man?" she could not have been referring to her unmarried state, for she was betrothed to Joseph. Rather she was puzzled about the words of the angel, which had identified the son she would bear as the great king who would rule on the throne of David forever. Her question must mean that there was no man to be the father of such a king; no one left in the house of David who could carry on David's royal line, for even Joseph, though himself of the family of David (Luke 3:23–38), was not of the royal line. The kingly line of David would have ended with Mary, and Christ's birth from that ruined line is very much on the order of a sprout springing out of a tree cut down, or a root out of dry ground.

That he would grow up does not mean that he would grow from child to adult, but that he would become much more than a sprout or stem out of the stump of David's tree. He would become the greatest of all David's royal line and would so surpass his father David that David himself would call him Lord (Matt. 22:43–45). His throne would be forever (2 Sam. 7:13), and he would be higher than the kings of the earth (Ps. 89:27). He would be the King of kings and Lord of lords.

THE COMING OF ZION'S REDEEMER

As king he would have the authority and power to build the temple of God and to see to the offering in that temple of a sacrifice that would take away sin forever. He would build that temple by being himself the temple of God, the one in whom God would dwell with his people perfectly and unendingly. He would be Immanuel, God with us as the one born in our flesh, yet remaining God's only begotten Son. He would build that temple by allowing the Jews to tear down the temple of his body that he might build it again in three days by his resurrection from the dead. He would build that temple by becoming the one through whom we come to God, so that in the new Jerusalem there is no need of any temple but himself. He builds the temple by building his church as the place where God dwells in us and walks in us (2 Cor. 6:16). Temple builder indeed!

What an encouragement that must have been to Zerubbabel and the Jews, who were struggling to build a temple that would not begin to compare with Solomon's! Though this word of God meant that the temple they were building was not the true temple, it did mean that their efforts were not in vain and that the outward poverty of the temple they were working on did not matter, for one greater than Solomon was coming and he would build a temple that would eclipse the glory of Solomon's.

What an encouragement to New Testament believers, who in the face of endless difficulties are building the church as the temple of God (1 Cor. 3:10–14; Jude 20). They do not work alone, nor is their work in vain in the Lord (1 Cor. 15:58). God's house will be built by the master builder himself and will stand for all eternity.

6:13. Even he shall build the temple of the LORD; and he shall bear the glory, and shall sit and rule upon his throne; and he shall be a priest upon his throne: and the counsel of peace shall be between them both.

The promise that Christ would build the house of God is repeated since that was the great matter of concern to Zechariah and his contemporaries. The temple was at the heart of their existence as a nation, and without it nothing they did was of any value. There the sacrifices were offered, and there God fulfilled his promise to live among them. That temple, not now a temple made with hands but the church as the body of Christ, is of equal importance to us, and the promise that it will be built eternal in the heavens remains for us.

Verse 13 is a word of explanation. Christ is the temple builder because he bears the glory and sits and rules on his throne as a priest on the throne. It is only because the counsel of peace is established between the priestly and kingly offices that the temple is built to stand forever. This verse is the most important verse in Zechariah's prophecy, both in its identification of Christ as priest-king and in its mention of the counsel of peace.

When Zechariah says that he will bear the glory, he means that Christ as priest will also have the glory of the kingly office, the glory of which God spoke to David:

22. The enemy shall not exact upon him; nor the son of wickedness afflict him.

23. And I will beat down his foes before his face, and plague them that hate him.

24. But my faithfulness and my mercy shall be with him: and in my name shall his horn be exalted.

25. I will set his hand also in the sea, and his right hand in the rivers.

26. He shall cry unto me, Thou art my father, my God, and the rock of my salvation.

27. Also I will make him my firstborn, higher than the kings of the earth.

28. My mercy will I keep for him for evermore, and my covenant shall stand fast with him.

29. His seed also will I make to endure for ever, and his throne as the days of heaven. (Ps. 89:22–29)

When Zechariah prophesies of Christ's sitting and ruling on his throne, he means that he will rule as a priest: "He shall be a priest upon his throne." When he speaks of the counsel of peace, he means that in Christ there will be peace and reconciliation between the offices of priest and king.

That Christ is both priest and king means that he is unique in the whole history of God's church. The only ones at all like him in this respect were Moses and Samuel, who were both of the priestly family while at the same time serving as leaders of Israel. Nevertheless, neither Moses nor Samuel were the high priest, and in each case one or the other of their offices is all but obscured. In Moses's case it is the priestly office. So much does his position as leader of God's people take prominence that most of the time we do not even remember that he was also a priest. The opposite is true of Samuel. His priestly office and duties are so much on the foreground in his history that we often do not remember that he was one of Israel's judges and thus the civil ruler of Israel in the days prior to the kingdom.

The book of Hebrews emphasizes this uniqueness of Christ, first by reminding us several times that he is a priest, not after the order of Aaron and the Levitical priesthood but after the order of Melchizedek, who was not only priest of the most high God, but also king of the City of Peace. This Melchizedek, a strange, shadowy figure, is a type of Christ (more than anyone else in the Old Testament), so much so that even today many commentators make the mistake of actually identifying him with Christ. Yet it seems that Melchizedek himself is all but forgotten in the Old Testament and left in the shadows, exactly because he was almost too clear a picture of Christ who was to come. It is as though he had to be mentioned, so that the saints in later ages would have a point of reference in respect to Christ's offices and work, but at the same time next to nothing is said about him so we might not forget that not he but Christ was the one promised.

The book of Hebrews also reveals Christ's uniqueness as a priest by telling us that he came out of the tribe of Judah rather than out of the tribe of Levi, something for which the law made no provision and by which the weakness of the law as a means of salvation is revealed (Heb. 7:11–19). Thus we are able to see that Christ is the better hope by whom perfection comes and we draw nigh to God (v. 19).

What especially concerns us, however, is the significance of this union of the priestly and kingly offices in Christ. That Zechariah and other writers in the Old Testament (notably David in Psalm 110) as well as the book of Hebrews emphasize this union shows its great significance for the salvation of God's church and for the work of redemption.

This union is significant for the offices. Each of the two offices needs the other to complement and complete it. The kingly office gives power and authority to the office of priest, and the priestly office tempers the authority and power of the kingly office by its own unique gifts. Without the power and authority of the kingly office, therefore, the priestly office was weak.

That was its great lack in the Old Testament too. Hebrews 10:18 speaks of this when it mentions the weakness and unprofitableness of the commandment. This passage is not talking about the law in general, but about the specific commandment concerning the priesthood. Because the commandment that generated the priesthood was weak, the priesthood itself was weak; and because the priesthood was weak, its work was also weak and could not save. This is all explained in Hebrews 7:21–28, where the word of God tells us three things about the Levitical priesthood: first, that priesthood had no oath of God to guarantee its work and continuation; therefore each priest died and his work was discontinued; and because each priest's work was discontinued, atonement was never made for the sins of the people.

The priests' weakness was finally this: they were sinners and unworthy of their office, so that in their work they first had to make sacrifice for their own sins before offering for the people. The result of this was not only that the people were left still waiting for a better priest, but also that they were reminded of their sins by those very sacrifices the priests offered and they continued to be plagued with a conscience of sin (Heb. 10:2–3).

The weakness of the Old Testament priesthood was critical as far as the spiritual life of Israel was concerned. This was evident in the many times in the Old Testament when the temple was shut up so that the whole worship of God ceased. How often did not that happen when ungodly and idol-worshiping kings sat on the throne of David? The priest did not have the authority or power to maintain the worship of God during such times. He did not have the power to keep the temple open or to collect the taxes necessary for the maintenance of the temple and its service. That power belonged to the king; and when the king was wicked, the priest was helpless.

All the authority and power that the priesthood needed was found in the office of king, for that office had as its support the oath of God, by which its continuation was guaranteed (Heb. 7:21–22; see also 2 Sam. 7:16; Ps. 89:35–37; 110:4). This kind of a powerful priesthood is revealed in Melchizedek, who as priest-king had the authority and power to claim from Abraham the spoils of Abraham's victory over the five kings of Mesopotamia, a claim that Abraham himself recognized.

All this concerns the building of the temple. It was not the priesthood but the line of David that received the command and thus the authority to build and later restore the temple (2 Sam. 7; 2 Chron. 24:4–14; 29:3–36; 34:3–13). There was implicit in the history of Israel in the Old Testament, therefore, the need for a better priesthood that would be always and intimately supported by the power of the kingly office. Only in that way could the temple of God be built and the worship of God maintained.

The kingly office, however, also needed the office of the priest. The priestly office tempered the authority and power of the kingly office by constantly bringing to bear upon it the word of God. Apart from that word of God the office of king always degenerated into tyranny and wickedness, so that rather than being a blessing to God's people, it became to them a curse. The priestly office was a constant reminder to the king that he was a servant of God, called to rule the kingdom of God. The priestly office was such a reminder because in its very nature it was an office of complete consecration and service to God. But the priests also had the duty of anointing the king to his office as a reminder of these things and of instructing him and teaching him "the manner of the kingdom," as Samuel did with Saul (1 Sam. 9:25–27; 10:25).

For this reason many of the priests were also prophets, not just to Israel as a nation but especially to the royal house (Samuel, Elijah, Jeremiah, Ezekiel, Zechariah, etc.). Israel's kings could not even know "the manner of the kingdom" without the priests. The authority of kings of David's line to build, restore, and rebuild the temple was useless without the priesthood, for without the priesthood there could never be any temple worship, since even the king was forbidden to enter the temple or to offer sacrifices (see the examples of King Saul and King Uzziah). Only the priests had the gifts and consecration necessary for those duties. Thus Israel needed not only a better priesthood, a royal priesthood, but she also needed a better government, and that priestly.

Zechariah in his prophecy sees the coming of these better things. He lived at a time when not only the offices had lost much of their splendor, but when also the temple had been rebuilt but without its former glory. The decline of the offices went hand in hand with the decline of the temple itself. But all that was necessary according to the purpose of God, for it was time for a better king and a better priest to come who would build the better

242

temple. It was Zechariah's great duty to remind the people that they must not cling to the Old Testament pictures but begin to look for the reality to which those pictures pointed and for the glory and salvation that would be revealed in that great priest-king and in the house that he would build.

Zechariah's prophecy, then, looks far beyond these two men, Zerubbabel and Joshua, and their work, for Zechariah prophesies concerning one man, whom he calls the Branch, who would be both priest-king and temple builder of the highest order. That man, the Branch, is our Lord Jesus Christ.

The "counsel of peace" in Zechariah 6:13 refers to the union of the two offices of priest and king in Christ, typically represented in the cooperation of Zerubbabel the governor and Joshua the high priest in the days of the restoration of the temple. This union is significant for the offices, in that the two offices complement and complete each other. The kingly office adds power and authority to the priestly office, and the priestly office tempers the authority of the royal office with its own peculiar gifts.

Nevertheless, there is a far deeper significance to the union of these two offices in Christ. That union lies at the very heart of the work of redemption, it shows that the work of grace is a miracle work of God, and it uncovers the significance of Christ's offices in their relation to the work of redemption.

In order to see all this, we must first understand the meaning of the offices, that is, that the kingly office is a revelation of God's righteousness, and the priestly office a revelation of God's mercy. To this could be added that the prophetic office is a revelation of God's wisdom and knowledge. The prophetic office, however, is not of firsthand importance in our discussion, as it is an office that belongs to both priest and king, and the proof and significance of that would be the subject of another study.

That the kingly office is a revelation of God's righteousness or justice is clear from many passages of scripture. Especially prominent is Psalm 45:4–7, where righteousness is mentioned no fewer than four times (once as truth) in connection with the kingly office. Especially significant is verse 6 of this chapter, which states that the scepter of the king's kingdom, the symbol of all his authority and power, is a *right* scepter. Hebrews 1:8 is even clearer when it quotes this passage in reference to Christ: "A scepter of righteousness is the scepter of thy kingdom," that is, it is a scepter characterized especially by righteousness and wielded in righteousness.

This points us to the chief duty of the king: to uphold and reveal true righteousness, the righteousness of God, in all the king's work. His work, therefore, was that of maintaining the law of God as the standard of all righteousness and judging the people righteously and justly in accordance with the demands of that law. Israel's judges, for example, who were the forerunners of the kings, had as their primary task the restoration of the people of God through instruction in God's law (see Judges 4:5; 6:25–27; 12:8–15, etc.). It was the solemn duty of the king to rule the people righteously by rewarding and protecting the good and by punishing and destroying all evil as the law demanded (2 Sam. 15:1–3; 1 Kings 3:16–28, etc.).

This righteousness was the real power of the kingly office. God's own power as king is maintained and supported not by brute strength but by his righteousness. In other words, he is justified in his works not merely because he is all powerful and can do as he pleases, but also because he always acts righteously. This is the usual answer of scripture to all the objections of wicked men against God's rule (Gen. 18:25; Rom. 3:5–6). As it is with God, so also it is with all who bear rule in his name.

The priestly office has God's mercy as its foundation and chief gift. This is not so easy to see, unless we remember that it was the priests who had not only the work of sacrifice, but also such duties as the cleansing of lepers and the maintenance of the cities of refuge. Especially the latter reveals this aspect of the priestly office, since the cities of refuge were places where certain types of criminals could find mercy and safety from the demands of the law as executed by the revenger of blood (Num. 35).

When we understand the meaning of the two offices, we can also see that there is a certain conflict between them. Already in the Old Testament it was the duty of the king to see that all who broke the law were dealt with according to the demands of the law and punished for their evil. The priest's duty as keeper of the cities of refuge often conflicted with that duty of the king.

The judgment of the man who killed someone "without malice aforethought" is a case in point. The scriptures hold such a man guilty, as is clear from the fact that the revenger of blood was justified in killing such a man if he did not seek the safety of the cities of refuge. If the king's duty was the maintenance of justice, certainly the revenger of blood was at least to be supported by the king, if he was not in actual fact to be considered an agent of the king. And yet it was the priest's duty to show mercy to such a man and protect him from the demands of justice by giving him a home in the cities of refuge.

Even in this case there was a certain justice mixed with the mercy of the priest, but even then the demands of justice and the offices of mercy conflicted at least in this, that neither was entirely fulfilled in trying to meet both. Even the mercy of the priest, exactly because it was mixed with justice, was not entire. The man who had come under the protection of the priest had to live in the city of refuge away from his home until the death of the priest, at best a very severe mercy.

The same conflict can be seen in the life of David. More than any other of Israel's kings he represented the ideal of a righteous ruler, and he is thus the clearest picture of Christ as king in the whole Old Testament. As a righteous king, it was he who delivered Israel from her enemies and executed God's law against the heathen and idolatrous nations around Israel. He also restored Israel to righteousness, by upholding the law of God in the nation. Thus it was that he followed and stood in contrast to Saul. Nevertheless, exactly because he had bloodied his hands in the execution of God's righteous judgments in Israel and among the nations, David was forbidden by God to have any part in the work of building the temple, the great place of God's mercy.

This conflict is the main reason the offices of priest and king could never be combined in the Old Testament. The separation points to the truth that righteousness (justice) and mercy are forever irreconcilable through any human effort or wisdom. We see that even today. In any judicial system it is simply a fact that the judge, in executing the law, has mercy and justice as two options, but he can never really be just and show mercy at the same time. Either he maintains the demands of the law and punishes the criminal to the full extent of the law (and that is really his only duty), or he shows "mercy" by setting the criminal free or by lessening his punishment. But even when he tries to temper justice with mercy, he really ends with neither, as is so evident in our judicial system. The attempt to be merciful by mitigating the punishment the law demands (or ought to demand) always has as the end result that justice is not really done.

However, for salvation reconciliation of justice and mercy must take place. Because God is a righteous judge above all others, the demands of his law must be met and fully satisfied. If God is not just and righteous, he is not God (Ps. 11:5). Yet at the same time he has determined to reveal himself also as a God of mercy and he promises mercy to the sinner.

Such reconciliation is forever beyond man's reach. If he seeks the glory of God (as he ought) in insisting upon justice for himself, he rules out all possibility of mercy, in that the punishment of sin is everlasting. If he seeks mercy, he can seek it only at the expense of justice. The separation of the priestly and kingly offices underlines this inadequacy of every human effort. We could even say that the priestly and kingly offices in the Old Testament had to remain separate, because those who served in those offices were only men and the union of all that those offices represented was too great a task even for the best and greatest of them.

In Christ God performs a notable and necessary miracle when he bestows on Christ the gifts of both offices and in Christ reconciles the duties of those offices. In Christ God satisfies all the demands of his justice while clearing the way for the full revelation of his tender mercy. As the sinless Son of God in our flesh, Christ the king is able to bear not only the responsibility of upholding and executing the law of God, but also the responsibility of standing in the place of those over whom he rules when the wrath of God's righteous anger against sin is uncovered. Thus he can be not only the king of his people but also the great high priest who provides for the people of God a place of refuge and shelter from the destroying power of God's wrath. Indeed, he is not only the one who provides the place of refuge, but he is also that place of refuge that we by the grace of God now seek.

This is the miracle celebrated in Psalm 85:10: "Mercy and truth are met together; righteousness and peace have kissed each other." The psalm sings of Christ as our great priest-king and about the miracle of redemption in him. This is the counsel of peace that Zechariah prophesied and that Israel saw so dimly in the cooperation of Zerubbabel and Joshua in the work of rebuilding the temple. It is that union of the two offices of priest and king in Christ by which the true temple of God is built as the place where God's people find everlasting peace in the fellowship of God. As the great temple builder, he is now and shall forever be a priest upon his throne. Thus John saw him in the visions of Revelation (5:6; 19:11–13), and thus we shall see him when the tabernacle of God that he has built is revealed from God out of heaven. Then the counsel of peace shall be fulfilled.

The idea that the covenant of God is an agreement or contract, first between God and Adam, now between God and his people in Christ, has prevailed in Reformed theology for many years. At the heart of this view of the covenant lies the teaching that there are always two parties who contract with one another in the establishment of the covenant. Until very recently, Zechariah 6:13 has been a key passage in defense of this view.

Most of those who teach a two-party covenant have rightly understood that whatever the covenant may be, it must have an eternal pattern in God himself. This is true of all God's works, including the covenant. God is never different in his revelation of himself to us from what he is in himself. All his works have both their source and pattern in the being and life of God.

Those who believe that the covenant is an agreement or contract look for some kind of agreement in God himself and in his own life that can be the eternal pattern of the covenantal agreement he makes with his people. This agreement, so they say, would have demands, promises, and penalties, as any agreement or contract should have, and would have as its purpose the salvation of God's people. At one time, proof for such an eternal agreement within the Godhead was found in Zechariah 6:13, which speaks of "the counsel of peace" that "shall be between them both." This "counsel of peace" therefore was interpreted as referring to an eternal agreement between the first and second persons of the Trinity, the Father and the Son, and it demanded, with appropriate penalties, the incarnation and obedience of the Son, promising salvation to God's people.

In these studies it is not my purpose to discuss or defend one view of the covenant over against another, or to repeat all the arguments that have been raised against this interpretation of Zechariah 6:13. Even a superficial reading of the passage will show that this interpretation has been "read into" the text, and that Zechariah 6:13 has nothing at all to do with the doctrine of the covenant. In recent years this has been conceded even by those who still teach the idea of a two-party covenant. Prof. Louis Berkhof, an ardent defender of this view of the covenant, says for example, "Coccejus and others found in this passage a reference to an agreement between the Father and the Son. This was clearly a mistake."[3]

---

3 Louis Berkhof, *Systematic Theology*, 4th ed. (Edinburgh, UK: Banner of Truth Trust, 1958), 266.

THE COMING OF ZION'S REDEEMER

Nevertheless, because this passage has been so long misused and mis-interpreted, almost all discussion of the passage has centered in either a defense or rejection of that older interpretation, and the positive teaching of the passage has been forgotten or neglected. This is not surprising but is often the result of controversy over a passage of scripture. It is to be espe-cially regretted here, however, since the passage is the key first of all to a proper interpretation of the first six chapters of Zechariah's prophecy, and second to a clear understanding of the offices of Christ in relation to his work as mediator. To that positive teaching we wish to give our attention.

We have seen that the counsel of peace referred to in Zechariah 6:13 does not refer to the intra-trinitarian covenant of friendship but to the union of the priestly and kingly offices in Christ. This is evident from the passage itself. Verse 13 is an example of Hebrew parallelism, where two thoughts, expressing the same thing though in different ways, are used to explain and interpret each other. Here the parallel thoughts are "he shall be a priest upon his throne" and "the counsel of peace shall be between them both." The counsel of peace, therefore, is realized between priest and throne.

We have shown that the union of these two offices was foreshadowed in the cooperation of Joshua, the high priest, and Zerubbabel, the governor, who was of the royal seed of David, during the years following the return of the Jews from Babylon. This cooperation was necessary in the work of rebuilding the temple.

The cooperation between these two men was only a very dim figure and type. That is clear from the fact that although their cooperation was very close, it did not result in the actual union of the two offices of priest and king in one man. It was also evident from the decline of both offices. In the days of Zechariah's prophecy, neither the office of priest nor the office of king retained its former splendor. Especially is this true in the case of Zerub-babel, who was not really king, but only a regional governor under the king of Persia. Christ is the fulfillment of the counsel of peace as the priest and king of saints.

6:14. And the crowns shall be to Helem, and to Tobijah, and to Jedaiah, and to Hen the son of Zephaniah, for a memorial in the temple of the LORD.

Here the four men of verse 10 are mentioned once again. Heldai and Helem are the same man, as are Josiah and Hen, who is identified in both verses as the son of Zephaniah. The first three were the men lately come from Babylon from whom Zechariah took the gold and silver for Joshua's crowns. Josiah or Hen the son of Zephaniah was either a goldsmith or a temple official to whom the crowns were given to be kept as a memorial in the temple of God.

I agree wholeheartedly with what Leupold says about the names of these men:

> It so happens that all the men involved have names whose meaning can readily be deciphered, like Tobijah, "Good-is-Jahweh." But to try to work these names into the scene is unsatisfactory, for all combinations that are made turn out to be more or less artificial. Besides, practically all Hebrew names had a definite meaning and were for the most part compounded with the name of Jahweh or of God.[4]

Not the names of these men but what they did with the crowns is important. The memorial is not a receipt for the gold and silver, as Kline suggests, but the crowns themselves. Stored in the temple, they would be a memorial to all Israel of the union of the kingly and priestly offices until Messiah came. They would be, as long as they were in the temple, a pledge that he would come and that the "counsel of peace would be between them both," as well as a reminder to Zerubbabel and Joshua of the needed cooperation between them if the house of God was to be finished.

That the crowns are described as a memorial to these men does not change the fact that they pointed to Christ the great priest-king, but only means that the crowns would be kept as a memorial in their names as the donors of the precious materials from which they had been made. They would stand, therefore, as representatives of all who had contributed their gifts in the hope of Messiah's merciful and just rule.

---

4 Leupold, *Zechariah*, 122.

6:15. And they that are far off shall come and build in the temple of the LORD, and ye shall know that the LORD of hosts hath sent me unto you. And this shall come to pass, if ye will diligently obey the voice of the LORD your God.

The closing assurance once again concerns the house of God, the temple of the Old Testament and the church of the New Testament. God's house would be built through the coming of the great priest-king. Indeed, it would be built as never before, for the Gentiles also would come and build the house and be built as part of it.

They are those far off, as Paul reminds us in Ephesians 2:12–13. Speaking to the Gentiles, he says: "That at that time ye were without Christ, being aliens from the commonwealth of Israel, and strangers from the covenants of promise, having no hope, and without God in the world: But now in Christ Jesus ye who sometimes were far off are made nigh by the blood of Christ." Gathered out of all nations, God's spiritual house is built upon the foundation of the apostles and prophets, Jesus Christ himself being both the chief builder and the cornerstone. Built on such foundations, built by Messiah himself of living stones, it is a house that cannot be destroyed, that stands for eternity, and that grows to be a holy temple to the Lord, a temple in which God is pleased to dwell forever.

The building of that house would be the proof that Zechariah had been sent by God and that his wonderful words of encouragement, hope, and promise were God's own word to his people. The rebuilding of the temple would be that to the Jews, the church of the Old Testament, and the building of God's spiritual house the proof of that through the long years of the New Testament. And when built finally and forever in the new heavens and the new earth, that house will stand as an everlasting testimony to the faithfulness of God and to the power and mercy of Christ.

That the gold and silver came from far off as an offering for the temple was itself a reminder that "they that are afar off shall come and build in the temple of the Lord." Christ would bring the glory and honor of the nations into the kingdom of God. They would contribute willingly their hands and their gifts to the house of God for his sake. He is the one all nations worship and serve. He is King of kings and Lord of lords.

The passage closes with a solemn reminder of what was said in the opening words of the prophecy and what will be repeated again, that these comforts and promises belong only to those who heed God's word, not to the careless, the unconverted, and the disobedient. Those who diligently obey the voice of God do so only by grace, but the command of God establishes the responsibility of all to hear and obey.

Chapter 15

THE INTRODUCTORY
EXHORTATION AND
INSTRUCTION:
ZECHARIAH 7:1–8:23

7:1   And it came to pass in the fourth year of king Darius, that the word of the LORD came unto Zechariah in the fourth day of the ninth month, even in Chisleu;

7:2   When they had sent unto the house of God Sherezer and Regem-melech, and their men, to pray before the LORD,

7:3   And to speak unto the priests which were in the house of the LORD of hosts, and to the prophets, saying, Should I weep in the fifth month, separating myself, as I have done these so many years?

7:4   Then came the word of the LORD of hosts unto me, saying,

7:5   Speak unto all the people of the land, and to the priests, saying, When ye fasted and mourned in the fifth and seventh month, even those seventy years, did ye at all fast unto me, even to me?

7:6   And when ye did eat, and when ye did drink, did not ye eat for yourselves, and drink for yourselves?

7:7   Should ye not hear the words which the LORD hath cried by the former prophets, when Jerusalem was inhabited and in prosperity, and the cities thereof round about her, when men inhabited the south and the plain?

7:8   And the word of the LORD came unto Zechariah, saying,

7:9   Thus speaketh the LORD of hosts, saying, Execute true judgment, and shew mercy and compassions every man to his brother:

7:10   And oppress not the widow, nor the fatherless, the stranger, nor the poor; and let none of you imagine evil against his brother in your heart.

7:11   But they refused to hearken, and pulled away the shoulder, and stopped their ears, that they should not hear.

7:12   Yea, they made their hearts as an adamant stone, lest they should hear the law, and the words which the Lord of hosts hath sent in his spirit by the former prophets: therefore came a great wrath from the Lord of hosts.

7:13   Therefore it is come to pass, that as he cried, and they would not hear; so they cried, and I would not hear, saith the Lord of hosts:

7:14   But I scattered them with a whirlwind among all the nations whom they knew not. Thus the land was desolate after them, that no man passed through nor returned: for they laid the pleasant land desolate.

8:1   Again the word of the Lord of hosts came to me, saying,

8:2   Thus saith the Lord of hosts; I was jealous for Zion with great jealousy, and I was jealous for her with great fury.

8:3   Thus saith the Lord; I am returned unto Zion, and will dwell in the midst of Jerusalem: and Jerusalem shall be called a city of truth; and the mountain of the Lord of hosts the holy mountain.

8:4   Thus saith the Lord of hosts; There shall yet old men and old women dwell in the streets of Jerusalem, and every man with his staff in his hand for very age.

8:5   And the streets of the city shall be full of boys and girls playing in the streets thereof.

8:6   Thus saith the Lord of hosts; If it be marvellous in the eyes of the remnant of this people in these days, should it also be marvellous in mine eyes? saith the Lord of hosts.

8:7   Thus saith the Lord of hosts; Behold, I will save my people from the east country, and from the west country;

8:8   And I will bring them, and they shall dwell in the midst of Jerusalem: and they shall be my people, and I will be their God, in truth and in righteousness.

8:9   Thus saith the Lord of hosts; Let your hands be strong, ye that hear in these days these words by the mouth of the prophets, which were in the day that the foundation of the house of the Lord of hosts was laid, that the temple might be built.

8:10   For before these days there was no hire for man, nor any hire for beast; neither was there any peace to him that went out or came in because of the affliction: for I set all men every one against his neighbour.

8:11   But now I will not be unto the residue of this people as in the former days, saith the Lord of hosts.

8:12 For the seed shall be prosperous; the vine shall give her fruit, and the ground shall give her increase, and the heavens shall give their dew; and I will cause the remnant of this people to possess all these things.

8:13 And it shall come to pass, that as ye were a curse among the heathen, O house of Judah, and house of Israel; so will I save you, and ye shall be a blessing: fear not, but let your hands be strong.

8:14 For thus saith the LORD of hosts; As I thought to punish you, when your fathers provoked me to wrath, saith the LORD of hosts, and I repented not:

8:15 So again have I thought in these days to do well unto Jerusalem and to the house of Judah: fear ye not.

8:16 These are the things that ye shall do; Speak ye every man the truth to his neighbour; execute the judgment of truth and peace in your gates:

8:17 And let none of you imagine evil in your hearts against his neighbour; and love no false oath: for all these are things that I hate, saith the LORD.

8:18 And the word of the LORD of hosts came unto me, saying,

8:19 Thus saith the LORD of hosts; The fast of the fourth month, and the fast of the fifth, and the fast of the seventh, and the fast of the tenth, shall be to the house of Judah joy and gladness, and cheerful feasts; therefore love the truth and peace.

8:20 Thus saith the LORD of hosts; It shall yet come to pass, that there shall come people, and the inhabitants of many cities:

8:21 And the inhabitants of one city shall go to another, saying, Let us go speedily to pray before the LORD, and to seek the LORD of hosts: I will go also.

8:22 Yea, many people and strong nations shall come to seek the LORD of hosts in Jerusalem, and to pray before the LORD.

8:23 Thus saith the LORD of hosts; In those days it shall come to pass, that ten men shall take hold out of all languages of the nations, even shall take hold of the skirt of him that is a Jew, saying, We will go with you: for we have heard that God is with you.

This opening section of the second half of Zechariah's prophecy, though lengthy, is all one piece. It begins with a question about the law and about fasting in chapter 7:3. That question ties together material that appears to be very diverse. There are in chapters 7 and 8 reminders of God's past dealings with Judah, a call to new obedience, and wonderful promises that reach to the end of time: promises of renewed prosperity, of a rebuilt temple and city, and of the gathering of the Gentiles. All these are God's answer to the question about fasting. Chapter 7 is the negative answer and chapter 8 the positive answer.

There is material in these chapters, especially chapter 8, that is reminiscent of Haggai's prophecy. Especially the section of chapter 8 that speaks of the poverty and famine the people had suffered (vv. 9–15) reminds us of Haggai 1:5–11 and 2:15–19. But that is only to say that the message in both cases is from God and was sufficiently important to bear repetition. It is a message that needs repeating often in the church of Christ in every age.

Chapters 7 and 8 are also similar in language and thought to the first introductory section in chapter 1:1–6, and they serve as an introduction to the burdens that follow in chapters 9–14. Each introductory section begins with a date (1:1; 7:1, 4) and continues with a call to conversion. Included in these calls to conversion are lessons from past history, including a reminder of what the former prophets had said (1:4–6; 7:7), a further reminder of the failure of the former generations to listen to those prophets (1:4; 7:11–12; 8:16–17), and a solemn reminder of what God had done to punish them for their disobedience and hardheartedness (1:6; 7:13–14). These reminders from past history are the basis for an exhortation to new obedience (1:3–4; 8:16–17), with promises of God's blessing to encourage such obedience (1:3; 8:2–15, 18–23).

This is to say that the two halves of Zechariah's prophecy, chapters 1–6 and 7–14, are parallel. Both open with similar introductions and a study of the two parts shows that they follow the same pattern and teach the same lessons. Thus this second part of the prophecy is a reiteration and expansion of the first part. We never learn our lessons easily but must be continually retaught. We are so slow of heart to hear and believe that God must repeat his word over and over. In this we are no different from the Jews to whom

Zechariah was speaking and show ourselves to be one with them. Yet it is God's mercy and goodness that he does not give up on us, but does bring his word again and again.

The parallelism of the two sections is easy to see. Not only are the two introductions parallel in language and thought, but so is what follows. Just as the promises of the first introductory section, chapter 1:1–6, are expanded in the first, third, fifth, and seventh visions, so the promises of the second introductory section, chapters 7 and 8, are expanded on in the second burden. Likewise with the threats: mentioned in the first introductory section (1:1–6) and expanded in the second and fourth visions (1:18–21; 5:1–11), they are mentioned again in the second introductory section and expanded in the first burden (see the parallelism chart on page 92).

This new material was given to Zechariah two years after his visions (1:7; 7:1, 4) and two years before the completion of the temple. God knew that his people needed further admonition and further encouragement, so he sent Zechariah to them once again, bringing what was essentially the same message though expanded and with some additional material. This is a powerful reminder to us of our constant need for the word of God. We must hear the same message as these Jews and hear it repeatedly. Especially we must hear because the promises are only for those who heed God's warnings. That is the message of this opening section of both halves of Zechariah's prophecy. There is no comfort, no peace for those who do not turn from evil and to the Lord. There is no blessing for the unconverted.

7:1. And it came to pass in the fourth year of king Darius, that the word of the LORD came unto Zechariah in the fourth day of the ninth month, even in Chisleu;

7:2. When they had sent unto the house of God Sherezer and Regemmelech, and their men, to pray before the LORD,

7:3. And to speak unto the priests which were in the house of the LORD of hosts, and to the prophets, saying, Should I weep in the fifth month, separating myself, as I have done these so many years?

The date reminds us that we are in the second half of the book and also that it is now nearly two years later. The visions had been received in the second year of Darius and the eleventh month. Now it is the fourth year of Darius and the ninth month. During the interval Haggai had finished his prophecies, but the temple was not yet completed. The difficulties of the work remained. The people were still wavering and sinful, so God sends his word to them once more.

It is not the temple that is referred to in verse 2 as the "house of God," but the town of Bethel. The Hebrew word for house of God is *beth-el*, but never in scripture does the Hebrew word *beth-el* refer to the temple. It always refers to the town of that name. When the temple is called "the house of God," a different word is used. A clearer translation of verse 2 would be "when they had sent unto Bethel Sherezer and Regemmelech, and their men, to pray before the Lord."

It is even possible to translate verse 2 thus: "When Bethel sent Sherezer and Regemmelech and their men to pray before the Lord." Then the town of Bethel is the source of the question about fasting, not the place where the question was answered. That is, in fact, the best translation of the verse. Then, though the temple is not referred to as the house of God, it may nevertheless have been to the unfinished temple that this question came.

Why the question came from Bethel is not stated, but it may have been that Bethel was one of the places where the tabernacle resided in Israel's early history and the people of that town would have pondered such questions in light of their history. It was also one of the places that had been desecrated by Jeroboam's golden calves (1 Kings 12:25–33), another reason the men of the city would have been very concerned to do what was right in the worship of God. "Should *I* weep" is then used collectively, that is, this question comes from all the citizens of Bethel but concerns them personally.

We know nothing about Sherezer and Regemmelech, except that they must have been important men to have been sent on this errand. That they were sent to pray and to ask a question must mean they were recognized as men of piety and wisdom, but beyond that we can say nothing about them, except that their names are Babylonian. It is even possible that they had come recently from Babylon, but it is the question, not the men, on which the word of God focuses.

The word translated as "pray" means "to stroke someone's face" and refers to these men's seeking an answer from God to their questions. They were

assigned through supplication and entreaty, through the priests and prophets, to come into God's presence and seek from him an answer. But what a
beautiful reminder of the love that exists between God and his people that
allows them to come so near to him as to stroke his face in prayer, as it were.

The priests, whose duty it was to interpret and apply the law, were the
ones who had the responsibility to answer the question. That they were
unable to do so is clear from verse 5. Not only does God answer the question, but he also addresses both the priests and the people with his answer.
He had something to say about this matter of fasting that the priests would
not have been able to say:

> Shall I weep? It was not a question for the priests to answer. They were
> doubtless bound by tradition and, therefore, would have said: Weep,
> surely yes. The fast must be observed. The fathers have so ordained.
> And so it was. The fast as an institution, this weeping at stated times,
> in the fifth month or in any other month, in commemoration of
> calamities in the history of the nation, was not of God but of man.
> No mention is made of it in the law. It was a human institution. As to
> the question of the deputies, it was one for the Lord to answer. And
> He hastened to reply (vers 4–7) through Zechariah as His organ.[1]

The men's question concerns the fast that was customarily held in the
fifth month, even though the word *fasting* is not used here. The word is used
in Zechariah's answer and shows that the weeping and separating were associated with fasting. There was one fast stipulated in the law of God, the great
day of atonement, but this was not it. During the fifth month the temple
was destroyed by Nebuchadnezzar, and the date of the temple's destruction
was kept as a fast day all during the captivity. There were four such fasts,
all mentioned in Zechariah 8:19: the seventeenth day of the fourth month
(Thammuz), the anniversary of the capture of Jerusalem by Nebuchadnezzar;
the ninth day of the fifth month (Ab), commemorating the burning of the city
by Nebuchadnezzar; the third day of the seventh month (Tishri), in memory
of the massacre of Gedaliah and others by Ishmael as recorded in Jeremiah

---

1 George M. Ophoff, "The Prophecy of Zechariah," *Standard Bearer* 32, no. 18 (July 1, 1956): 443.

41:1–10, also mentioned in Zechariah 7:5; and the tenth day of the tenth month (Tebeth), the date Jerusalem was first besieged by Nebuchadnezzar.[2]

All these fasts were matters of tradition, not commandment, but the question concerns especially the fast of the fifth month. It seemed as though there was no longer any reason to keep that fast, since the temple was being rebuilt and the Jews were back in their own land. Since the *city* was not yet rebuilt, there was some reason, or so it seemed, to keep the other three fasts.

On the face of it, the question could easily be answered. Since the fast of the fifth month was not commanded in the law of Moses, it could be dropped just as it had been adopted, without a word from God. No doubt that was the case, but the question runs deeper. The question is really that of the angel in Zechariah 1:12, "O LORD of hosts, how long wilt thou not have mercy on Jerusalem and on the cities of Judah, against which thou hast had indignation these threescore and ten years?" The Jews, both in Babylon and in Canaan, needed to know that the anger of the Lord for past sins was now appeased and the reason for fasting truly taken away. The temple was being rebuilt, but there was evidence, in the troubles the Jews had endured, in the famine that had come, in the messages of Haggai and Zechariah, and in the opposition of enemies, to suggest that the reason for fasting had not been taken away. Thus the question.

Weeping and separation were part of fasting in the Old Testament and remind us that even in the New Testament fasting is not an end in itself, but a very personal and private matter that involves repentance and humbling oneself before God. In chapter 12:12–14, Zechariah speaks of the separation of each individual and family to mourn for their sins, the very essence of fasting:

> 12. And the land shall mourn, every family apart; the family of the house of David apart, and their wives apart; the family of the house of Nathan apart, and their wives apart;
> 13. The family of the house of Levi apart, and their wives apart; the family of Shimei apart, and their wives apart;
> 14. All the families that remain, every family apart, and their wives apart.

---

2 Moore, *Zechariah*, 121.

Weeping and fasting are the outward signs of the repentance for sin and self-denial that are the main things in fasting. Mere abstinence from food is in itself of no value.

Fasting is not in itself bad. It is recommended by Jesus in Matthew 6:16–18 and is therefore something that may and ought to be used by New Testament Christians. Though there are no set fasts in the New Testament, fasting can be used as need requires and is profitable when used for self-denial, for repentance, for turning to God with all one's heart, but only when so used. It is of no value as a mere rite. So it is with all the outward observances that are commanded by God or used by God's people. They are not in themselves bad but can become mere ritual without spiritual profit.

Before the question of this delegation could be answered therefore, there was a great deal that needed to be said, so the question is not finally answered until Zechariah 8:18–19. The people had to be reminded that fasting must be sincere and from the heart. They had to be reminded of the stubbornness of their fathers and of what God had promised them in the way of obedience and faithfulness. Only then did the question of fasting mean anything. Apart from true spiritual obedience, fasting was nothing but an external rite devoid of any spiritual profit. So it is always with the rituals and outward observances that are part of the worship and service of God. Singing, praying, preaching, church attendance, attendance on the sacraments, bowing the head, memorizing God's word, Bible study, and every other religious observance are of no value in themselves. They must be done out of a true heart and for God's glory.

7:4. Then came the word of the LORD of hosts unto me, saying,

7:5. Speak unto all the people of the land, and to the priests, saying, When ye fasted and mourned in the fifth and seventh month, even those seventy years, did ye at all fast unto me, even to me?

7:6. And when ye did eat, and when ye did drink, did not ye eat for yourselves, and drink for yourselves?

7:7. Should ye not hear the words which the LORD hath cried by the former prophets, when Jerusalem was inhabited and in prosperity, and the cities thereof round about her, when men inhabited the south and the plain?

God in verses 5–7 reminds the people that these outward observances are in themselves of no value. He addresses both the people and the priests because both were guilty of turning the true worship and service of God into mere formalism. Malachi deals with that problem in the first chapter of his prophecy.

It is so easy in the different parts of the worship of God to fall into a meaningless formalism—to sing without a thought for the words we sing, to pray over and over the same words without pouring out our hearts to God, to sit under the preaching of the gospel without really hearing and without any intention of obeying, and to assume that God is pleased with such mere outward observances. The danger is the wrong thinking that God must bless us if we carefully observe the outward rites he has appointed.

The word of God reminds us that it is not so. All that is involved in the worship and service of God must be in truth and in spirit. It must be done according to his word and from the heart. It is easy in the service of God to do the things that are required not out of any love of God or with any thought of him, but merely because it is expected of us or because we expect to gain from it. This is the problem in formalism, legalism, and dead orthodoxy.

The tendency toward formalism was the sin into which the Jews had already begun to fall and that would plague them into the New Testament. They had been cured of their idolatry by the seventy years of exile in Babylon, but those sins had now been replaced by others equally heinous to God. The sins of coldheartedness and formalism would trouble them through the rest of the Old Testament and into the time of Jesus and the apostles. They are still the sins of Judaism today. The rebuke of the prophet indicates that in Zechariah's times this was no abstract matter or just a possibility. Nor is it today. The sin continues to plague the church.

"Did ye at all fast unto me?" God says. To fast or perform any other religious rite "unto God" means that we do it with him in mind and in his presence; that we do it not out of habit but in the fear of God; that we do it for his glory and not for our own profit or honor in the sight of others. That is the opposite of doing such things, fasting included, as empty, profitless rituals, which is the same as doing it for ourselves. God is not saying that it was wrong to fast on the anniversary of the day the temple was destroyed. It still is not wrong to fast when we think it appropriate. We must, however, do all things for his honor, that is, "unto him."

All things, not only religious rites, must be done for God's glory. There is no activity nor any way of life that is especially holy in itself. There are many who think so. Roman Catholicism teaches that a solitary, celibate life is more holy, and many Protestants seem to have similar ideas. They seem to think that one is not really serving God unless one is involved in some church ministry, some kind of Christian service, or some sort of missionary activity.

Any activity when done "unto God" is holy, pleases him, and is used by him for the coming of his kingdom. There is a real sense, therefore, in which the work that a trash collector does is just as holy and pleasing to God as the work of a minister of the gospel or some other Christian worker. Understanding this is essential to contentment and faithfulness in whatever calling God has placed us.

Doing ordinary things for the glory of God does not mean that we somehow try to think of him the whole time we are involved in some activity, but that we do whatever is set before us cheerfully, honestly, diligently, faithfully, and because it is required of us by God or given to us by him. Many of our everyday activities require us to keep our attention on things we have to do. The truck driver who tries to glorify God by thinking of him the whole time he is driving will probably be involved in a wreck. The mother who tries to do the dishes for the glory of God by thinking about him the whole time she is washing and drying the dishes will probably not get them clean.

We do all things "unto God" when our hearts are right with him, when we are living by faith, when we love him, and when it is the deepest desire of our hearts to please him. Anything else he hates. Anything else is not even counted as obedience, not even civil obedience.

People do these things for themselves when they do them for the praise of men, to look good in the eyes of others, or for financial gain. There is no doubt that much of what passes for religion today is done for these reasons. God is hardly mentioned in most religious observances, hardly thought of, and when he is mentioned it is as though he exists only to satisfy every desire of men's hearts, to confirm what they have already decided in their hearts, and to give his seal of approval on whatever it is they have set their hearts on doing.

All this God had told Israel through the "former prophets." A good example is found in Isaiah 66:2–3, where God chastises the people for bringing their sacrifices without being "poor and of a contrite spirit" and without trembling at his word. There is no difference in such a case between the sacrifice of a calf or of a dog, between sacrifice and murder, God says:

2. For all those things hath mine hand made, and all those things have been, saith the LORD: but to this man will I look, even to him that is poor and of a contrite spirit, and trembleth at my word.
3. He that killeth an ox is as if he slew a man; he that sacrificeth a lamb, as if he cut off a dog's neck; he that offereth an oblation, as if he offered swine's blood; he that burneth incense, as if he blessed an idol. Yea, they have chosen their own ways, and their soul delighteth in their abominations.

Amos says something very similar about God's dislike of mere outward observance of his commands:

21. I hate, I despise your feast days, and I will not smell in your solemn assemblies.
22. Though ye offer me burnt offerings and your meat offerings, I will not accept them: neither will I regard the peace offerings of your fat beasts.
23. Take thou away from me the noise of thy songs; for I will not hear the melody of thy viols.
24. But let judgment run down as waters, and righteousness as a mighty stream. (Amos 5:21–24)

God is not pleased with formalism, for all that is not of faith is sin (Rom. 14:23).

He is not pleased with coldheartedness, with indifference and thoughtlessness, but says always, "My son, give me thine heart" (Prov. 23:26). Only with the weeping and separation and fasting that is from the heart is he pleased. Then he turns weeping to joy, draws near to those who have separated themselves, and feeds the fasting soul with every good thing.

7:8. And the word of the LORD came unto Zechariah, saying,

7:9. Thus speaketh the LORD of hosts, saying, Execute true judgment, and shew mercy and compassions every man to his brother:

7:10. And oppress not the widow, nor the fatherless, the stranger, nor the poor; and let none of you imagine evil against his brother in your heart.

The proofs that what is done in worship and in daily life is done for God are true judgment, mercy, compassion, and a heart free of enmity. This is just another way of saying what the apostle John says repeatedly in his first epistle: that the love of the neighbor, love in deed as well as in word, is the proof of our love for God. John says plainly, "If a man say, I love God, and hateth his brother, he is a liar: for he that loveth not his brother whom he hath seen, how can he love God whom he hath not seen?" (1 John 4:20). Nor may that love be merely a matter of words, for he also says, "My little children, let us not love in word, neither in tongue; but in deed and in truth. And hereby we know that we are of the truth, and shall assure our hearts before him" (1 John 3:18–19). Obedience to God and his word is part of true fasting, that is, of true repentance.

James says the same:

14. What doth it profit, my brethren, though a man say he hath faith, and have not works? can faith save him?
15. If a brother or sister be naked, and destitute of daily food,
16. And one of you say unto them, Depart in peace, be ye warmed and filled; notwithstanding ye give them not those things which are needful to the body; what doth it profit?
17. Even so faith, if it hath not works, is dead, being alone. (James 2:14–17)

It has always been so. Those whose hearts are not right with God show it by neglecting and taking advantage of those who are helpless. They put on a good front before others and even make a great show of mercy and true judgment, but because they are servants of mammon and not of God they will always seek themselves when they have opportunity to do so. Few notice what they are doing, though God always sees, but of him they take no thought.

If confronted, they will always have a pious excuse. Their covetousness will always be excused as "good stewardship," their lack of compassion by the faults of those whom they will not help, their refusal to seek and execute true judgment by extenuating circumstances. They are always on the side of the rich and famous. They are always more concerned about their own reputations than about truth and justice. Position and popularity mean more to them than right.

Their professions of friendship and brotherly love cover a slanderous tongue. Their offers to help are false. They conveniently forget the promises they made and deny the evil they have privately spoken. They accuse those whom they oppress of evildoing and do the evil they themselves condemn. The helpless they oppress are not only the widows and the poor, but also those who have no opportunity to defend themselves, who have no one to witness on their behalf for the truth. By brow-beating, by false accusations, by slander, all covered with a show of piety, they make sure they have their own way.

They are like the leaders of the Jews, so scrupulous about the law when others were watching, but perfectly willing when they were in the majority and when it suited their interests to set aside every principle of justice and righteousness in the condemnation and crucifixion of our Lord. They are like whitewashed sepulchers; like cups that have been washed only on the outside and are unfit for use.

This is true not only of the ordinary members of the church but all too often of ministers and elders and other leaders in the church as well. They can talk very piously, but when it comes to matters of truth and right, the only thing that matters is their advantage. Under a show of religion they work evil, and many of those who are unhappy with the church are that way because they have suffered such evildoing at the hands of those they trusted and who ought to have known better.

7:11. But they refused to hearken, and pulled away the shoulder, and stopped their ears, that they should not hear.

7:12. Yea, they made their hearts as an adamant stone, lest they should hear the law, and the words which the LORD of hosts hath sent in his spirit by the former prophets: therefore came a great wrath from the LORD of hosts.

Such sin is not only against those they oppress and treat without mercy, but also against God. Their lack of love for their neighbor whom they can see proves that their protestations of love for God are false. God vividly describes here their stubbornness and wickedness. They are like a disobedient child who pulls away from the hand that seeks to correct him and who pretends not to hear and claims he never did hear. God speaks literally of a "backsliding shoulder" (Hos. 4:16; Neh. 9:29) in reference to the beast that pulls away from the yoke that is laid on it. The problem, however, is not the shoulder but the heart, which is hard as stone and untouched by the grace of God. A heart as hard as an adamant stone is an unregenerated heart, for a regenerated heart is renewed and softened by God's saving grace. God, who sees and knows the heart, condemns them.

This hardening is often spoken of in scripture, and the great example is that of Pharaoh in the days of the exodus. From his example we learn the same thing that is emphasized here: this hardening is both something that God does in anger and something that a person does to himself. Repeatedly, Exodus says that Pharaoh hardened his heart. That is the reason everyone who is hardened is responsible before God for his hardened heart.

But we also learn that this hardening is an act of God. Indeed, Exodus speaks more often of God's hardening Pharaoh than of Pharaoh's hardening himself. Hardening displays the sovereignty of God in the case of Pharaoh and in the case of the hard-hearted Jews.

This hardening takes place, as the verse shows, under the proclamation of God's word. The word is the means God uses to harden hearts as well as to save them. That word is the savor of life and death, not an attempt of God to save all who hear or a well-meaning offer of salvation to all who hear.

There is a reference here to the work of the Spirit, the Spirit who is mentioned so often in Zechariah's prophecies. God sent the words "in his Spirit." The Spirit inspired the prophets and their words, and Israel sinned against the Spirit by refusing to hear. It is one thing to refuse to hear the words of a man. It is quite another thing to refuse to hear and heed the words of the living God.

Both the law and the prophets are mentioned as a reminder of Israel's sin in rejecting the whole word of God. We cannot pick and choose what we will hear and obey. It is all or nothing, as James reminds us: "For whosoever shall keep the whole law, and yet offend in one point, he is guilty of all" (James 2:10). Partial obedience is no obedience at all.

Such partial, outward, formal obedience is the cause of "great wrath from the LORD of hosts" since it is a sin committed by those to whom much is given. There are many who have never heard the word of God and perish in unbelief, but how much greater is the sin of those who remain in unbelief under the preaching of the gospel, who have heard of God's wonderful works of redemption and despised them! The words of Jesus continue to be true for all those who have the privileges that belong to church members and children of the covenant and who are hardhearted nevertheless:

> 21. Woe unto thee, Chorazin! woe unto thee, Bethsaida! for if the mighty works, which were done in you, had been done in Tyre and Sidon, they would have repented long ago in sackcloth and ashes.
> 22. But I say unto you, It shall be more tolerable for Tyre and Sidon at the day of judgment, than for you.
> 23. And thou, Capernaum, which art exalted unto heaven, shalt be brought down to hell: for if the mighty works, which have been done in thee, had been done in Sodom, it would have remained until this day.
> 24. But I say unto you, That it shall be more tolerable for the land of Sodom in the day of judgment, than for thee. (Matt. 11:21–24)

What a warning to those who have these privileges!

7:13. Therefore it is come to pass, that as he cried, and they would not hear; so they cried, and I would not hear, saith the LORD of hosts:

7:14. But I scattered them with a whirlwind among all the nations whom they knew not. Thus the land was desolate after them, that no man passed through nor returned: for they laid the pleasant land desolate.

The punishment always fits the crime when a just God judges and punishes, as he always will do. For fifteen hundred years he spoke to his Old Testament people and they were deaf to every threat, every promise, every plea. Now God tells them that when they cry he will not hear them. The reference is to the days prior to the captivity, but they are referred to by way of warning to those who lived in the days of Zechariah and to us today.

Reading God's threats, one thinks of those who fill the churches and pray fervently when disaster of some kind strikes, but who never darken the doors of a church or utter the name of God otherwise, except to blaspheme. Such are found in the church also. They are those who under the word of God remain hardhearted, who never really hear the word of God. His threats do not turn them from their wickedness. His pleas fall on deaf ears. Even his sweet promises leave them unmoved. When they, for whatever reason, cry to God, he remains deaf to them.

Worse, he also sends them into captivity and scatters them, leaving their land desolate, no empty threat; not then, not now. What God did he could and would do again, and do not only by sending the Jews out of their land into bondage, but also by delivering his New Testament people into spiritual bondage, by giving them over to Satan (1 Cor. 5:5), and by taking away from them the many privileges he gives. Let us then heed his word and not be hardhearted.

8:1. Again the word of the LORD of hosts came to me, saying,
8:2. Thus saith the LORD of hosts; I was jealous for Zion with great jealousy, and I was jealous for her with great fury.

Chapter 8 is a continuation of chapter 7 and part of Zechariah's introduction to the burdens of chapters 9–14. The chapter division is helpful, however, since the introduction falls naturally into the two parts. Chapter 7 records the warnings and threats of judgment that introduce the burdens, and chapter 8 the promises and blessings.

The opening words of this chapter, "Again the word of the LORD of hosts came to me," suggest that the word of God in this introduction came to Zechariah in several parts. Nevertheless, it is still one revelation with chapter 7. Indeed, it is only in chapter 8 that the question about fasts, raised in chapter 7, is fully answered. That answer is found among ten promises of future blessing, promises that belong to those who heed God's call to conversion in chapter 7.

Each of these ten promises of blessing is introduced with the words "thus saith the LORD of hosts." As the sovereign ruler of all and the one who by his providence directs and controls all things, he promises his blessing to his people, though he also reminds them of their duty to obey him (8:16–17). No blessing except in the way of obedience, but the fullness of blessing to all those who do obey—that is God's word in these verses:

> The chapter contains a decalogue of divine words, which by their very number (10) aim to demonstrate the completeness of God's program. The frequency with which the words; "Thus saith the Lord of hosts"…recur…serves to set forth emphatically, as Jerome already discerned, that the prophet was not promising these great facts of the future upon his own authority, but that every last one of them was separately guaranteed by the omnipotence of the Lord, and so faith in these divine promises was to be stimulated.[3]

These promises include protection (v. 2), God's presence among his people (v. 3), peace (vv. 4–5), grace (v. 6), the restoration of and gathering of his people (vv. 7–8), spiritual prosperity (vv. 9–12), forgiveness (vv. 13–15), joy (vv. 18–19), the gathering of the Gentiles (vv. 20–22), and the uniting of Jews and Gentiles into one eternally blessed church of God (v. 23): ten promises of blessing to parallel the ten commandments. Keeping the ten commandments would bring these ten blessings.

The promises of blessing found in this chapter are very similar to and parallel to the promises first published in Zechariah 1:1–6 and further laid out in 1:12–17 and 2:6–13. Indeed, these first three verses of Zechariah 8 are almost identical in content and language to chapter 1:14 and 16. What is more important, however, is that they are promises of *covenantal* renewal and blessing, promises that have as their heart the fellowship and friendship of God and his people.

The first promise is of Zion's protection and safety. God's jealousy insures that she will be forever safe from her enemies—that no harm can possibly come to her. This promise parallels chapter 1:14–15, where God's jealousy is the other side of his sore displeasure with the heathen who assisted so

---

3   Leupold, *Zechariah*, 141.

willingly in Zion's troubles. When compared to chapter 2:5, it is clear that his jealousy will be the wall of fire that will make walls of stone and timber unnecessary.

His jealousy for Zion, the church, is *holy*. It is not for earthly Zion that he was jealous, not for the nation of Israel as a nation, but for the true Israel and for the Zion of Hebrews 13, the elect from among the Jews and now also from among the Gentiles. Earthly Zion would be destroyed again and never restored, for though the mountain and the city are still there, they no longer have any significance or any special place with God.

Earthly Zion today is no different in the eyes of God than San Francisco or Amsterdam or Calcutta. If anything she is now remembered only as the city where our Lord was crucified (Rev. 11:8), the city that rejected Messiah and is now herself rejected of God and as much under God's judgment as Sodom or Egypt. Never again will he dwell in the earthly Jerusalem, but he does dwell and will forever dwell in the Jerusalem that is above, which is the mother of believers (Gal. 4:26).

> 2. And I John saw the holy city, new Jerusalem, coming down from
> God out of heaven, prepared as a bride adorned for her husband.
> 3. And I heard a great voice out of heaven saying, Behold, the
> tabernacle of God is with men, and he will dwell with them, and
> they shall be his people, and God himself shall be with them, and
> be their God. (Rev. 21:2–3)

That jealousy for Zion and Jerusalem is an expression of his love for his people, a love that protects them and delivers them from their enemies. Since that love is eternal and unchangeable as God is eternal and unchangeable, it must be understood that his jealousy is the working out of his eternal decree of election. Zion is elect Zion and Jerusalem elect Jerusalem, and those citizens whom God has in mind here are those who were chosen from eternity in Christ. So we sing:

> Zion, founded on the mountains,
> God, thy Maker, loves thee well;
> He has chosen thee, most precious,

He delights in thee to dwell;
God's own city,
Who can all thy glory tell?

Heathen lands and hostile peoples
Soon shall come the Lord to know;
Nations born again in Zion
Shall the Lord's salvation show;
God Almighty
Shall on Zion strength bestow.

When the Lord shall count the nations,
Sons and daughters He shall see,
Born to endless life in Zion,
And their joyful song shall be,
"Blessed Zion,
All our fountains are in thee."[4]

8:3. Thus saith the LORD; I am returned unto Zion, and will dwell in the midst of Jerusalem: and Jerusalem shall be called a city of truth; and the mountain of the LORD of hosts the holy mountain.

The most important promise of the ten is this second, in which God promises again to live among his people and to be "the glory in the midst of her" (Zech. 2:5). That this covenantal promise is found five times in chapters 2 and 8 (2:5, 10–11; 8:3, 8) shows the importance of the promise and demonstrates the parallelism between the two chapters.

God speaks again of having returned with the returning captives and, though no one was yet living in Jerusalem since the city was still in ruins, of his living there. The promise, then, includes that the city would be rebuilt and that it would once again be the "city of God." Nevertheless, the main thing is God's presence, for without his gracious and glorious presence the city would be no different from Babylon or Nineveh.

---

4 No. 237:1–3, in *The Psalter*.

That Jerusalem would be a city of truth and Mount Zion a holy mountain is God's guarantee that his presence would sanctify and cleanse the city and make it holy. No lies would be told there ever again, and no evil would enter. The word of God is similar therefore to Revelation 21:27, "And there shall in no wise enter into it any thing that defileth, neither whatsoever worketh abomination, or maketh a lie: but they which are written in the Lamb's book of life." Indeed, Revelation 21:27 is the final fulfillment of this word of God in Zechariah, for the earthly Jerusalem never became a city of truth and never will, but the heavenly Jerusalem will be the place where truth incarnate dwells forevermore.

That the mountain of the Lord's house will be called the mountain of holiness is a promise that God's church in Christ is a holy catholic church and that in the new Jerusalem she will be sinless and perfect.

The mountain referred to is first of all the earthly mountain on which the city was built, but one must think here also of that mountain that is exalted above every earthly mountain, higher than Everest and higher even than the heavens. It is that living mountain that is the eternal foundation of the church and her exaltation, the rock Jesus Christ, upon which the church is built as a city with foundations by God himself.

Only in this second of the ten promises does God call himself the Lord rather than the Lord of hosts. As Leupold suggests, "This is, perhaps, done so that 'Lord' stands alone and thus stresses the faithfulness which this name connotes, as it is manifested by this undeserved return to Israel."[5]

Some believe this promise is long ago fulfilled and finished. Wright says of this promise (and of the others): "Though Keil is inclined to view this passage as a promise of Messianic days, no evidence can be adducted in support of this opinion." He goes on to say:

We agree with Köhler, Kliefoth and others, in maintaining every promise contained in the seventh and eighth chapters has been fulfilled in the period which elapsed between the days of Zerubbabel and Christ. It has always seemed to us to be making sport of the prophecies to seek in all cases, in which an absolutely literal

---

5 Leupold, *Zechariah*, 145.

fulfilment cannot be pointed out, to apply such prophecies to some future, that keeps gradually receding from us.[6]

Having then mentioned especially the prophecies of the next verses, he says:

The actual fulfilment of these very promises has been beautifully recorded as one of the results of the victories of the Maccabee period. "Then did they till their ground in peace, and the earth gave her increase, and the trees of the field their fruit. The ancient men sat in all the streets, communing together of good things, and the young men put on glorious and warlike apparel.... He (Simon) made peace in the land, and Israel rejoiced with great joy. For every man sat under his vine and his fig-tree, and there was none to fray them" (1 Macc. 14:8–9, 11–12).[7]

This view of prophecy is entirely inadequate. If prophecy is fulfilled in only one literal instance either in the past or in the future, those passages of scripture that contain such prophecies are of no relevance or value to God's people today, but only matters of curiosity.

In this case, though the days of the Maccabees may have been a partial fulfillment of these prophecies, those days were so unimportant in God's plan and history of redemption that they are not even recorded or mentioned in scripture. Nor did those days last, nor the peace and prosperity of those days. They were so short lived that the period of the Maccabees is hardly an interlude in the history of the Jews.

To find no fulfillment of these prophecies in Messiah and his days is to be blind to what the book of Zechariah teaches. The three story passages in the book of Zechariah all focus our attention on the Messiah in the most notable terms, and to find no reference to the days of Messiah is inexcusable. The fulfillment of these prophecies not only includes the days of Messiah, both also those past and those to come, but the days of Messiah are the

---

6 Wright, *Zechariah and His Prophecies*, 178–81.
7 Ibid., 181.

principle fulfillment of such prophecies. It is Messiah who matters, not the Maccabees.

8:4. Thus saith the LORD of hosts; There shall yet old men and old women dwell in the streets of Jerusalem, and every man with his staff in his hand for very age.
8:5. And the streets of the city shall be full of boys and girls playing in the streets thereof.

The third promise is of endless peace, a picture drawn in the most beautiful terms imaginable. To understand this promise, it must be remembered that in times of war it would be the lives of the elderly and the children that would be first and most affected by the terrors of war. It is so even today: the helpless are those who suffer most. The elderly are not cared for and, exposed to the troubles that war brings—enemies, hunger, disease, and social chaos—they are the first to die. The little children are left orphans and homeless if they are not also killed, and all that belongs to family life is troubled. At the very least the streets would be unsafe at such times, and neither young nor old would be seen in the streets, only the warriors going about their grim business:

> Old age and childhood not only grace a community, the one by
> its venerableness, and the other by its beauty, but they also prove
> its peace and prosperity. When war, famine, pestilence or anarchy,
> have been raging, there are but few of either class, for their feeble-
> ness makes them the earliest victims.[8]

Jeremiah spoke of such things when he lamented the destruction of Jerusalem:

> 11. Mine eyes do fail with tears, my bowels are troubled, my liver
> is poured upon the earth, for the destruction of the daughter of my
> people; because the children and the sucklings swoon in the streets
> of the city.

---

8 Moore, *Zechariah*, 112.

12. They say to their mothers, Where is corn and wine? when they swooned as the wounded in the streets of the city, when their soul was poured out into their mothers' bosom. (Lam. 2:11–12)

God promises that the peace of Jerusalem will be restored and that the children and elderly will once again be seen in the streets of Jerusalem, the children playing there without fear and the elderly enjoying peace and quiet for their remaining days. Ultimately this promise too is fulfilled in the new heavens and the new earth, for there alone is perfect and lasting peace to be found, though the words of Isaiah must be remembered: "There shall be no more thence an infant of days, nor an old man that hath not filled his days: for the child shall die an hundred years old; but the sinner being an hundred years old shall be accursed" (Isa. 65:20).

Those who do not understand God's covenant have difficulty with this passage of Zechariah, for its fulfillment is in the church, and the passage suggests that children have as much a place in the church of Christ as the elderly or any other. The language is covenantal language. The peace promised is family peace. The blessings are those of the promise, "I will be thy God and the God of thy children after thee." The language is of the Old Testament, as are the figures, but the blessedness is that of the church and stretches into eternity, something to hope and wait for.

These covenantal blessings of peaceful old age and happy children are two of the premier blessings of the old covenant, and they are fulfilled in the eternal life and spiritual seed given to God's people in the new covenant.

8:6. Thus saith the LORD of hosts; If it be marvellous in the eyes of the remnant of this people in these days, should it also be marvellous in mine eyes? saith the LORD of hosts.

Verse 6 does not appear at first to be a separate promise but seems either to be the conclusion to the promise of verses 4–5 or a part of the promise of verses 7–8. Nevertheless, the words "thus saith the LORD of hosts" show that God has something new to say to his people here. It is a separate promise, however, not in that it promises something different from the preceding promise or any of the others, but because God promises to perform a miracle of grace for his people in order to bring all these promises to pass.

The idea of the passage is that the people, hearing the promises, would say, "It would take a miracle to bring all that to pass." God says in response, "Indeed it would, but I am able and willing to do such a miracle on behalf of those I love and choose to bless." God is saying, "Nothing is too hard for the Lord."

The passage is very important, for in speaking of the miracle of God's grace that he performed in the restoration of his covenant people, it points to the greatest miracle of all: the miracle of grace and redemption worked through the coming, sacrifice, and resurrection of our Lord Jesus Christ. He is the wonder, the miracle, to which every other miracle pointed and which every other foretold.

The reference to the sovereign and miraculous grace of God is of unspeakable value today. When there are troubles in the church; when it seems that we are tested beyond our limits; and when it seems as though the promises of God cannot possibly be fulfilled, then God says to us also: "If it be marvellous in the eyes of the remnant of this people in these days, should it also be marvellous in mine eyes?" This he says as the Lord of hosts, the one whom all things in heaven and on earth and in hell serve.

8:7. Thus saith the LORD of hosts; Behold, I will save my people from the east country, and from the west country;

8:8. And I will bring them, and they shall dwell in the midst of Jerusalem: and they shall be my people, and I will be their God, in truth and in righteousness.

This promise, the fifth, would have meant a great deal to the returned captives, because they were so few in number. Only a handful had returned from Babylon, and not all of them had proved faithful. Their smallness had been a source of much discouragement and hardship. Any New Testament believer who has been part of a small congregation knows the difficulties this brings and the sacrifice it requires.

That this was an issue is evident from the fact that it is explicitly addressed in Zechariah 4, where God admonishes the people not to despise the day of small things. The numbers given in Ezra and Nehemiah prove the case as well, and so does the story of the return under Ezra. After listing those who returned with him, Ezra speaks of his desire mixed with unwillingness to ask the king for an escort (Ezra 8:21–23), something he wanted to do fearing what lay ahead, but was afraid to do lest it give reason to question his trust in God.

When God speaks not of Babylon but of the east country and the west country, that must have sounded very strange. No one lived in the areas to the east and to the west. To the east lay the desert lands of Arabia and to the west the Great Sea, but God prophesies the gathering of the Gentiles. In bringing back his people, he would gather the believing Jews from Babylon and the places to which they had been scattered, and he would gather his people from unknown lands to the west and to the east—those who were Gentiles but also his people. The return of the Jews is the immediate fulfillment of the prophecy, therefore, but it looks ahead to the New Testament and the gathering of his saints out of this world and out of all nations into the glories of Christ's heavenly kingdom.

8:9. Thus saith the LORD of hosts; Let your hands be strong, ye that hear in these days these words by the mouth of the prophets, which were in the day that the foundation of the house of the LORD of hosts was laid, that the temple might be built.

8:10. For before these days there was no hire for man, nor any hire for beast; neither was there any peace to him that went out or came in because of the affliction: for I set all men every one against his neighbour.

8:11. But now I will not be unto the residue of this people as in the former days, saith the LORD of hosts.

8:12. For the seed shall be prosperous; the vine shall give her fruit, and the ground shall give her increase, and the heavens shall give their dew; and I will cause the remnant of this people to possess all these things.

The sixth promise is of renewed prosperity. Here Zechariah, as well as Haggai and Malachi, makes reference to drought and famine suffered by the Jews. Nehemiah 5:3 makes reference, though at a later date, to another dearth. Apparently the land, once a land flowing with milk and honey, had already then begun to resemble the land as it exists today: a semi-arid land from which a living can be drawn only with great effort.

There was no peace in those former days. The people, few in number, were surrounded by enemies. The people were so poor they had to sell houses and lands, even their children, to pay the usury required by their fellow Jews as well as the king's taxes (Neh. 5:1–13).

Just as with the temple, which never regained its former glory, this was God's way of teaching his people to look for a different kind of prosperity and blessedness, for earthly prosperity and material blessings are never what matter. They had to begin to look for a land that would be prosperous beyond imagination, that would never suffer drought or famine, and that would be filled from end to end with the blessing of God, the land that Abraham received through death, the "better country" of Hebrews 11:16.

That is not to say that the promise given to the Jews through Zechariah did not include a promise that God would lift the drought and famine they had suffered and give them fruitful fields, groves, and vineyards. In the Old Testament earthly prosperity was an important indication of God's favor, and famine an indication of his disfavor. Even then, however, as we have seen in our study of Haggai, it was such only on a national scale and not on a personal level.

That prosperity, even in the Old Testament, pointed to something better, for earthly prosperity is not in itself the blessing of God: it is not his grace or favor. The promise of prosperity pointed to the day the people of God would possess the new heavens and earth as their inheritance and be forever prosperous there with the blessings of grace and salvation.

8:13. And it shall come to pass, that as ye were a curse among the heathen, O house of Judah, and house of Israel; so will I save you, and ye shall be a blessing: fear not, but let your hands be strong.

8:14. For thus saith the LORD of hosts; As I thought to punish you, when your fathers provoked me to wrath, saith the LORD of hosts, and I repented not:

8:15. So again have I thought in these days to do well unto Jerusalem and to the house of Judah: fear ye not.

The emphasis is on spiritual things and not on earthly advantage, for this seventh promise is a promise of forgiveness, though that word is not used. God had forgiven them the sins that had brought them into captivity; he would continue to forgive them the sins that had brought upon them various troubles.

God's repentance is the same as his forgiveness. Instead of being angry, he repents and shows favor. Only from the viewpoint of our experience, though, does he repent, for God does not change and is not a man that he can repent. But in our experience it seems, when we have felt his anger and disfavor, that we bask once again in the sunshine of his love and grace.

The proof of forgiveness would be God's making them a blessing among the heathen. He would not bless the nations, but he would bless his people so abundantly that even the heathen would notice, just as they had noticed those occasions when his curse rested upon the nation. The word of God here parallels the word of God in Deuteronomy 28:10, "And all people of the earth shall see that thou art called by the name of the LORD; and they shall be afraid of thee." It is the opposite of Deuteronomy 29:24–25:

24. Even all nations shall say, Wherefore hath the LORD done thus unto this land? what meaneth the heat of this great anger?
25. Then men shall say, Because they have forsaken the covenant of the LORD God of their fathers, which he made with them when he brought them forth out of the land of Egypt.

Further proof of God's forgiveness would be his lifting of the punishment they had suffered. That he had thought to punish their fathers means he had done exactly that. History had proved it so, but now those who had been punished would be blessed and thus God would take away all cause of fear, for his judgments are fearsome indeed.

Christ is the one, finally, who would take away all cause of fear and all possibility of judgment. Through the Son of his love, God would do all he promised and more. In Christ's coming and finished work is the certainty of forgiveness. That work is prophesied and pictured in the story passages of Zechariah, and a promise such as this cannot be read apart from those important passages.

Interesting, though, is the exhortation to be strong and work. That is the goal and purpose of forgiveness. Pardon for sin and the promise of righteousness are not an end in themselves, but a motive to gratitude that works itself out in obedience to God's commands:

Neither does renewed confidence of persevering produce licentiousness or a disregard to piety in those who are recovered from backsliding; but it renders them much more careful and solicitous to continue in the ways of the Lord, which he hath ordained, that they who walk therein may maintain an assurance of persevering; lest by abusing his fatherly kindness, God should turn away his gracious countenance from them (to behold which is to the godly dearer than life, the withdrawing whereof is more bitter than death), and they in consequence thereof should fall into more grievous torments of conscience.[9]

8:16. These are the things that ye shall do; Speak ye every man the truth to his neighbour; execute the judgment of truth and peace in your gates:

8:17. And let none of you imagine evil in your hearts against his neighbour; and love no false oath: for all these are things that I hate, saith the LORD.

The promises of this chapter are interrupted by another reminder of the necessity of true piety and godliness. Never may it be assumed that the promises are for everyone. They are only for those who keep God's commandments and walk in his ways. Those who do so, however, do so only by grace. The commands that are given here are not conditions to be fulfilled, upon which God's grace and mercy depend.

That is true because no one can do what is required except by grace. The doctrine of total depravity means that it is impossible to please God except by a miracle of grace through which the dead are made alive. The command is here, however, because it is through the command that God gives the grace to obey. As Augustine says, "The command is the grace," and it is so because it is the almighty and effectual word of God, which always produces what it demands.

The requirement in verse 17 is the same as in verse 16: truth and justice. The two verses require the same things. Speaking truth to the neighbor and not imagining evil against him are really the same thing, as are executing judgment and not loving false oaths. In each case, however, both the inward

---

9 Canons 5.13, in Schaff, *Creeds of Christendom*, 3:595.

and outward expression of sin is forbidden. Speaking truth to the neighbor is the outward manifestation of loving the neighbor. Executing the judgment of truth is the outward expression of hating falsity.

That God forbids both the inward and outward manifestations of sin is an important reminder that it is not enough to live a life that is outwardly beyond reproach. Mere outward conformity is not obedience to God, nor is it pleasing to him. There are those who think that the ungodly are able to do good simply because they do things that are outwardly in conformity with God's law, but God requires also the heart. Those whose obedience pleases God are those who serve him in love and who love him with heart and soul and mind and strength.

That is the point of the tenth commandment. It is a reminder to all who hear the commandments that sin is also a matter of the heart, and that what man cannot see or judge God sees and judges. Covetousness is not counted evil by the ungodly, nor can it be seen when it is present, but it is hateful to God.

8:18. And the word of the LORD of hosts came unto me, saying,

8:19. Thus saith the LORD of hosts; The fast of the fourth month, and the fast of the fifth, and the fast of the seventh, and the fast of the tenth, shall be to the house of Judah joy and gladness, and cheerful feasts; therefore love the truth and peace.

Here, finally, God answers the question that gave rise to the revelations of Zechariah 7 and 8. He tells the Jews that the fasts they were keeping were not in themselves displeasing to him. He even indicates, at least indirectly, that they should continue to keep those fasts, all four of them, though the occasions for those fasts were no longer present. The temple was being rebuilt and the city would be rebuilt also, but there was still reason for the people to humble themselves before God in repentance and self-denial. There is always reason for such humiliation. It needs no external occasion, though such can usually be found in one's own life or in the life of the church. When kept for proper reasons, fasting and the spiritual exercises that accompany it are valuable and have God's blessing.

God even promises that the repentance and sorrow for sin and humiliation expressed in true fasting will be turned by him to joy and assurance. Humble yourselves in the sight of God, Peter says, and he will lift you up (1 Pet. 5:6). The joy of salvation and assurance of God's favor are always ours in the way of repentance. This promise, the eighth, is of joy in the Lord, assurance of salvation, and peace with God: "When God makes the sun shine, the teardrops should be dried; and when his blessing comes upon us, the memory of our sorrows should be used only to enhance our present joy."[10]

8:20. Thus saith the LORD of hosts; It shall yet come to pass, that there shall come people, and the inhabitants of many cities:

8:21. And the inhabitants of one city shall go to another, saying, Let us go speedily to pray before the LORD, and to seek the LORD of hosts: I will go also.

8:22. Yea, many people and strong nations shall come to seek the LORD of hosts in Jerusalem, and to pray before the LORD.

The ninth promise again assures the expansion of Israel through the ingathering of the Gentiles, something already promised symbolically in the third vision in chapter 2. The many cities, the peoples, and the strong nations do not include just the Jewish cities and people, but the people of the surrounding nations and finally of the whole earth.

Zechariah would have been thinking of Egypt and Babylon, Persia and Macedonia, but as with all the promises of God, this promise reaches far beyond anything Zechariah could have imagined and includes lands and peoples still unknown in his days.

That these nations would be gathered in as part of Israel is implied in their going with the Jews to the house of God to worship, something forbidden in the Old Testament except in the case of those who actually became Jews by undergoing circumcision and being adopted into the nation. Here again, therefore, the emphasis is on the spiritual and heavenly.

The fulfillment of this promise so often prophesied had to wait until the time of the apostles and their work, and it continues today as the gospel is preached to the farthest reaches of the earth. Indeed, the preaching of the

---

10 Moore, *Zechariah*, 121.

gospel to all nations has become one of the most important signs of the return of our Savior, for "this gospel of the kingdom shall be preached in all the world for a witness unto all nations; and then shall the end come" (Matt. 24:14).

> He [Zechariah] describes vividly the eagerness and mutual impulse, with which not only many but mighty nations should throng to the Gospel, and every fresh conversion should win others also, till the great tide should sweep through the world.[11]

Before the end of the second century one of the church fathers would write:

> We are but of yesterday, and we have filled every place among you, cities, islands, fortresses, towns, market-places, the very camp, tribes, companies, palace, senate, forum, - we have left nothing to you but the temples of your gods.[12]

So it shall be until that multitude that no man can number is gathered into God's blessed presence in heaven.

8:23. Thus saith the LORD of hosts; In those days it shall come to pass, that ten men shall take hold out of all languages of the nations, even shall take hold of the skirt of him that is a Jew, saying, We will go with you: for we have heard that God is with you.

The tenth and last promise is closely related to the ninth but adds to that promise of the gathering of the Gentiles the promise that Jew and Gentile would be one in Christ. The middle wall of partition would be broken down (Eph. 2:14), Christ reconciling both unto God in one body by the cross (v. 16).

We see the beginning fulfillment of this on Pentecost, when "Parthians, and Medes, and Elamites, and the dwellers in Mesopotamia, and in Judaea, and Cappadocia, in Pontus, and Asia, Phrygia, and Pamphylia, in Egypt,

---

11 Pusey, *The Minor Prophets*, 2:391.
12 Tertullian, *Apology*, 37, trans. S. Thelwall, in *The Ante-Nicene Fathers* (Grand Rapids, MI: Eerdmans, 1980), 3:45.

and in the parts of Libya about Cyrene, and strangers of Rome, Jews and proselytes, Cretes and Arabians" (Acts 2:9–11) came to Jerusalem to seek Jehovah. They heard in their own languages "the wonderful works of God" and were assured in the way of repentance that "the promise is unto you, and to your children, and to all that are afar off, even as many as the Lord our God shall call" (v. 39).

To take hold of someone's skirts is to seek unity and peace with them, in this case not only outward peace but also peace in the worship of God. The picture is of the Jew, preparing for a pilgrimage to Jerusalem and the temple, and the Gentile, insisting on going along by catching hold of the Jew's garment and refusing to let go. The Gentile confesses, as did Ruth and a few other Gentiles in the Old Testament, that God is with Israel.

To seize someone's skirts is an expression of humility and yet of faith. The woman who touched the skirts of Jesus in order to be healed of an issue of blood is an example. Though she did not hold on to his garment, her act expressed the same humility and faith that is expressed by these Gentiles in coming to Christ.

The text speaks of ten Gentiles not to say that the Gentiles would outnumber the Jews, but to teach what Paul teaches in Romans 11:25 concerning the fullness of the Gentiles coming in. Ten is the number of completeness and fullness. The promise is couched, as always, in Old Testament terms, but its fulfillment would involve a worship of God that no longer included the old earthly temple at Jerusalem. It would come in the way of the Jews being cut out of their own olive tree as a nation and the Gentiles being grafted in their place, though a remnant of the Jews would continue to be saved. In the end "all Israel" would be saved (Rom. 11:26).

The one whose skirts would lead the Gentiles to the house of God is not any Jew, but Christ. By faith in him the elect of every nation lay hold of the skirts of his garments and come to God's house and to the new Jerusalem.

In him one olive tree, one spiritual nation (1 Pet. 2:9), one true Israel of God, one church, worshiping God in spirit and in truth, would be the fulfillment of this prophecy. And finally Jew and Gentile, no longer even distinguishable from one another, would go to the heavenly house of God to worship him there, for they would have heard that God is with his people there forever and in eternal blessedness.

Chapter 16

THE BURDENS:
Zechariah 9:1–14:21

The remainder of the book of Zechariah is taken up by two burdens interrupted by the third story passage, chapter 11, the story of the rejected shepherd. Each burden is divided into three parts paralleling the visions of the first half of the prophecy.

The burdens are words of judgment and promise from God. The judgments are against the heathen nations that surrounded Israel and against the apostate element in Israel. The judgments are certainly a burden that all who are called to carry find heavy indeed. Those who bring that word of judgment often feel its weight. "Who is sufficient for these things," Paul says in 2 Corinthians 2:16, after describing the word of God as a savor both of life unto life and of death unto death.

But the blessings are also weighty and a burden. They are full of Christ and of eternal life. Even the judgments are not an end in themselves but part of God's care for his people and his protection of them. Thus each burden includes wonderful promises of help and blessing for the faithful. In presenting these burdens, intermingled with promises of divine help and blessing, the second half of the book closely follows the pattern of the first half, which also speaks first of God's judgments on the nations and then on apostate and unrepentant Israel, accompanied by wonderful promises of help and deliverance. The difference is that now the word of God speaks more plainly and in more detail, interpreting the visions.

In the first burden, Christ, now mounted on the foal of an ass, is the central figure, the one who is in the midst of his church and who with sovereign power oversees and judges the nations, who were represented in the first three visions by the deep and the four horns. In this way the first burden parallels the first three visions, where we see Christ mounted on a red horse, the governor of the nations and the deliverer of his people.

In the second burden, the Spirit of Christ is the central figure just as in the last three visions, and he is the one who ensures the sanctity of the covenant people, both by delivering them from the apostates who lived among them and by delivering them from their own sinfulness. "Not by might, nor by power, but by my Spirit" (4:6) is the theme also of the second burden.[1]

These burdens are interrupted, just as the first three and second three visions are divided, by a vision of Christ as the savior of his people. In the middle of the visions he was pictured in Joshua, clothed first in filthy garments and then reclothed in clean garments. In chapter 11, the chapter separating the two burdens, he is pictured in Zechariah as the rejected shepherd.

The book is arranged very neatly: two groups of three visions linked by the first story passage, the vision of Joshua in his filthy garments; then two burdens, each divided into three parts, again linked by the third story passage, the story of Zechariah as the rejected shepherd. These two halves of the book are in turn linked by the second story passage, the story of the crowning of Joshua.

In this last part of the book of Zechariah, God speaks of judgment, but he finishes that word of judgment by pointing to Christ as the reason for such judgments in that he is rejected and despised of men and yet is the one through whom those judgments pass over and are gone for God's own people. Christ's humiliation is Zion's exaltation, and his rejection is our acceptance. Having pointed us to Christ as the rejected shepherd, the word of God goes on in the closing chapters of Zechariah to thrill our hearts with a description of the blessings that are in Christ, in order to draw us in faith to those blessings and to him in whom they are found.

---

1 A further discussion of the parallelism that distinguishes Zechariah's prophecy can be found in the introduction to this commentary on pages 91–92.

Chapter 17

THE FIRST BURDEN:
ZECHARIAH 9:1–10:12

The first burden is divided into three parts: 9:1–8, which speaks of judgment on the heathen nations; 9:9–10, a prophecy of Christ mounted on the colt of an ass; and 9:11–10:12, which tells of the restoration of God's people. These three parts parallel the first three visions, though in a different order. The visions begin with Christ mounted on a red horse. Christ now mounted on the colt of an ass is the second part of this burden. The second vision of the four horns and four carpenters, representing judgment on the heathen nations, is paralleled in part one of this burden, and both the first set of three visions and the first burden end with a promise of Judah's restoration.

The first burden begins by focusing on the heathen nations that oppressed the Jews and held them in subjection, a figure of the unbelieving world that in every age is the enemy of God's church. The burden speaks of God's judgment on the nations and of deliverance for his church from these wicked oppressing nations.

The burden continues in the second part by focusing on the presence of Christ, who appears, as he does in the first vision, as a mounted warrior, but now mounted on the colt of an ass rather than on a red horse. He is still the king coming to his own, but in the way of humiliation and suffering. The first and third parts, judgment on the heathen nations and the restoration of the church, show the result of Christ's work as rider.

Wright describes the historical need for this word of God as follows:

The glorious prospects presented to the view of the restored exiles in the earlier visions of Zechariah were not soon realized. Notwithstanding the exhortations of Zechariah and Haggai, a very large number of Israelites preferred to remain as voluntary exiles in the land of their captivity, while many of those who had returned to the Holy Land, forgetful of their peculiar position, intermarried with the Gentile nations who inhabited the land, and thus recognised the equal right of those aliens to possess the land, which had been granted by the Divine decree to the posterity of Jacob. In place of gifts from all nations being poured into the treasuries of the temple, as had been promised by Haggai (2:7), and the holy city thereby becoming rich and powerful, its Jewish inhabitants still felt bitterly that they were but servants of the Persian kings (Neh. 9:36–37), to whom they had to pay tribute, while at the same time they were harassed on all sides by the Gentile nations among whom they dwelt (Neh. 4:7). They also, no doubt, suffered considerably during the campaigns carried on by Cambyses against Egypt (525 BC), and still later during that of Xerxes (484 BC), for in their march to Egypt the Persian hosts harassed the land of Judea, and caused much inconvenience to the Jewish settlers. The house of David, round which the hopes of the Jewish nation centered, seems to have fallen into political insignificance after the death of Zerubbabel, while on the other hand the political importance of the Phoenicians rose considerably, owing to their maritime power; and while there was no king in Israel, Phoenician kings were permitted to retain their regal dignity (Herod. 8:67), a privilege which seems to have been granted also to the cities of Philistia (Zech. 9:5). Damascus, too, the ancient capital of Syria, was at this period the residence of a high Persian official, whose authority was superior to that of the Jewish governor.[1]

These concerns are addressed in the first burden. God pronounces doom on the heathen nations and encourages his people with every possible promise of blessing and salvation.

---

1 Wright, *Zechariah and His Prophecies*, 199–200.

Chapter 18

THE FIRST BURDEN, PART 1:
ZECHARIAH 9:1–8

9:1 The burden of the word of the LORD in the land of Hadrach, and Damascus shall be the rest thereof: when the eyes of man, as of all the tribes of Israel, shall be toward the LORD.

9:2 And Hamath also shall border thereby; Tyrus, and Zidon, though it be very wise.

9:3 And Tyrus did build herself a strong hold, and heaped up silver as the dust, and fine gold as the mire of the streets.

9:4 Behold, the LORD will cast her out, and he will smite her power in the sea; and she shall be devoured with fire.

9:5 Ashkelon shall see it, and fear; Gaza also shall see it, and be very sorrowful, and Ekron; for her expectation shall be ashamed; and the king shall perish from Gaza, and Ashkelon shall not be inhabited.

9:6 And a bastard shall dwell in Ashdod, and I will cut off the pride of the Philistines.

9:7 And I will take away his blood out of his mouth, and his abominations from between his teeth: but he that remaineth, even he, shall be for our God, and he shall be as a governor in Judah, and Ekron as a Jebusite.

9:8 And I will encamp about mine house because of the army, because of him that passeth by, and because of him that returneth: and no oppressor shall pass through them any more: for now have I seen with mine eyes.

The two burdens each have three parts, paralleling the two groups of three visions, visions 1–3 and 5–7. This section of the first burden has the same message as the second vision of the four horns and four carpenters: judgment on Judah's enemies. This is followed by a prophecy of Christ now mounted on a donkey's colt instead of a red horse, humiliated rather than exalted. It is he, in his humiliation, who brings judgment on the heathen.

9:1. The burden of the word of the LORD in the land of Hadrach, and Damascus shall be the rest thereof: when the eyes of man, as of all the tribes of Israel, shall be toward the LORD.

9:2. And Hamath also shall border thereby; Tyrus, and Zidon, though it be very wise.

The word "burden" is usually used in scripture in connection with words of warning or threat and is so used here, as it is also in Malachi 1:1. God's angry words are a burden, both to prophets who carry those words to others and to those against whom God's anger is directed. Those who bring God's word find it a burden because of their compassion for those who are the objects of God's anger, and those against whom his anger is directed find it a burden because it crushes and destroys them. It is their doom.

In the first burden God mentions the nations that would soon come under his judgments: Syria (identified by its chief cities, Damascus and Hamath, and by the reference to the land of Hadrach), Tyre and Sidon, and the Philistines (including Ashkelon, Gaza, Ekron, and Ashdod). These were the nations that surrounded Israel and had proved to be Israel's enemies. They are mentioned too because they all lived in and claimed the territory that God had promised to the Jews (Gen. 15:8; Ex. 23:31). The Jebusites are mentioned as well, but not as an enemy that still threatened. They, Canaanites who lived in the land in the days of Israel's possessing the land, are an example of what God would do to these other nations: he would completely destroy them and cut them off.

There are differences of opinion about the reference to Hadrach. It has been understood to be a name for the Medes and Persians, a kind of revelation name, something like the name Ariel, used for Jerusalem in Isaiah

THE FIRST BURDEN, PART 1

29:1–2, 7. I understand it to be a city or territory in Syria, but the reference does not matter all that much. It is clear to anyone who reads the passage that it refers in one way or another to the nations that would experience God's wrathful judgment.

These are the nations pictured in the first three visions of Zechariah as the troubled deep and as the four horns. They represent all the enemies of the church, the enemies pictured in Revelation by the beast from the sea who persecutes and kills the people of God. Always God executes judgment on them and saves his church and his people from them.

These judgments are expressed in terms that are not the easiest to understand. When Zechariah says, "The burden of the word of the Lord in the land of Hadrach, and Damascus shall be the rest thereof," he means that the heavy burden of God's wrath would rest upon these countries. God's anger would find rest by being a burden to the nations! They would find his judgments to be a burden indeed! Hamath, Tyre, and Sidon would also be near enough to come under those judgments: they bordered this land of judgment and would not escape unscathed. Though they were proud and boasted in their wealth, they would also feel the weight of God's anger against them.

These judgments were executed in due time upon these nations, so completely that little evidence is left of their existence. The historical reference is generally understood to be to Alexander the Great and his conquests in the area, and indeed the order of the cities mentioned is exactly the order of his victories—first Damascus and Syria, then Tyre and Sidon, and finally the Philistines or Phoenicians. But the prophecy reaches beyond the destruction of these nations to the destruction, final and complete, of all God's enemies.

All of this would fix the eyes of men in general and of Israel especially on the Lord. That is the idea in verse 1. For the most part men live with little thought of the Almighty, but when he sends his judgments on the earth, they remember him either as their merciful God and Savior or as the one from whose face they wish to hide. Disasters and war awaken even the most hardened consciences to a sense of God's great anger.

9:3. And Tyrus did build herself a strong hold, and heaped up silver as the dust, and fine gold as the mire of the streets.

9:4. Behold, the LORD will cast her out, and he will smite her power in the sea; and she shall be devoured with fire.

Tyre is singled out for special attention because she was one of the richest and most powerful cities of ancient times. Her commerce reached as far as the British Isles, where Tyrian miners worked the tin mines of Cornwall. The city, whose stronghold is mentioned here, was built on a rocky island off the coast and was considered to be unconquerable. Yet Alexander took the city and so completely destroyed it that in the words of another prophet, the rock on which it was built became a place for the fishermen to spread their nets (Ezek. 26:4–5). Her power was smitten in the sea and she was devoured with fire as Zechariah prophesies. No doubt the tidings of Tyre's fall brought about the very reaction described in verse 5 among the Philistines: Ashkelon saw and was afraid, Gaza saw and sorrowed, Ekron with all her trust in Tyre's strength was ashamed, for they were next on Alexander's list of conquests.

Nevertheless, though Tyre is singled out for special attention because of her pride, she is representative of all the ungodly, of their wealth, and of their pride. She is what Augustine called "the city of men,"[1] the spiritual counterpart of the city of God. Tyre is described here and in Ezekiel 26–28 in similar terms to great Babylon of Revelation 18, which is also Sodom and Egypt and the city where our Lord was crucified (Rev. 11:8). Like Babylon and Assyria and all the great kingdoms of history, Tyre is portrayed in Ezekiel 28 as the persecutor of God's people and as the great enemy of God, in terms that remind us of the power and dominion of Satan and of antichrist, of whose kingdom all these others, including Tyre, were predecessors.

The destruction of Tyre foreshadows the destruction of all the kingdoms of this world in the great day of the Lord, but that must not be taken to mean that their destruction is postponed. The fire that will completely devour Tyre and all she represents, the fire of God's great anger, is already burning.

---

1 Augustine, *The City of God*, trans. Marcus Dods, in *The Nicene and Post-Nicene Fathers*, ed. Philip Schaff, First Series (Grand Rapids, MI: Eerdmans, 1988), 2:284. Augustine says, "This race [the human race] we have distributed into two parts, the one consisting of those who live according to man, the other of those who live according to God. And these we also mystically call the two cities, or the two communities of men, of which the one is predestined to reign eternally with God, and the other to suffer eternal punishment with the devil" (book 15, chapter 1).

Satan already falls as lightning from heaven (Luke 10:18), and the kingdoms of this world are already the kingdoms of our Lord and of his Christ (Rev. 11:15). Already the sound of Christ's footsteps is heard as he comes to judge the nations, his signs are seen on every hand, and the foundations of the kingdom and city of man, always rotten, are crumbling under his judgment. The world and all that is in it is already perishing, and very soon there will be nothing left—not one stone left upon another.

9:5. *Ashkelon shall see it, and fear; Gaza also shall see it, and be very sorrowful, and Ekron; for her expectation shall be ashamed; and the king shall perish from Gaza, and Ashkelon shall not be inhabited.*

9:6. *And a bastard shall dwell in Ashdod, and I will cut off the pride of the Philistines.*

9:7. *And I will take away his blood out of his mouth, and his abominations from between his teeth: but he that remaineth, even he, shall be for our God, and he shall be as a governor in Judah, and Ekron as a Jebusite.*

Philistines, though living on the very borders of Israel, would also feel God's wrath. Every phrase in verses 5 and 6 speaks of judgment. That Ashkelon and Gaza would see God's judgments on Babylon, Assyria, and Tyre and be afraid certainly indicates that they had no hope of escaping those judgments themselves. That Ekron's expectation would be ashamed refers to her every earthly hope. None would be fulfilled, as it is always with the ungodly. No king in Gaza, Ashkelon an uninhabited wasteland, and a bastard dwelling in Ashdod (that is, a stranger dwelling where the native people had once lived) are all indications of God's determination to destroy these nations. Thus the pride of the Philistines would be brought down and ruined.

In verse 7 God gives the reason for these judgments: the idolatry of Philistia and of the other nations. The blood is from the sacrificial animals whose flesh was eaten by the heathen with the blood, something forbidden in the law of God because of its connection with idolatry (Acts 11). The abominations referred to are the unclean meats offered to these same idols. That God threatens to take the blood and the abominations away out of their mouths and from between their teeth does not mean that he would save them from these abominations, but that he would destroy them and their idolatry—he would destroy them in the middle of their idolatrous practices.

Yet the execution of these judgments did not end with the destruction of these nations, but continues in the work of the conquering Christ as he saves and delivers his church and brings the judgment of God upon a wicked world. This is suggested by a comparison of this word of God with Ezekiel 28, where the king of Tyre is identified with Satan, the one who stood behind him in all his pride and rebellion against God. Obviously, these words have a wider application.

All of this is a warning that God *will* come in judgment, though it seems to the ungodly that he will not and that they are secure in their wickedness. "Where is the promise of his coming," they say, "all things continue as they were from the beginning of the creation" (2 Pet. 3:4) and, "Where is the God of judgment?" (Mal. 2:17), but judgment comes inexorably and in fury:

> However secure nations or men may think themselves in sin, their sin will be sure to find them out. Never has sin more proudly entrenched herself than in godless, but magnificent Tyre. Never has every element of earthly prosperity seemed more completely under control than in her case. And yet they were all swept like chaff before the whirlwind of the wrath of God, when the time for the fulfilment of his threatenings had come. Hence though nations now trample on law and right, and seem long to flourish in their sin, let not the child of God be impatient. Let him remember that two hundred years passed away after the utterance of these threatenings against Tyre, and she seemed stronger than ever, and yet when the day of doom had dawned, the galleys that left her on their stated voyages the peerless queen of the seas, when they returned found her but a bare and blackened rock, a lonely monument of the truth, that our God is a consuming fire. If, then, God thus executes his threats even on a mighty commonwealth, in spite of his delay, let not the fact that judgment against an evil work is not executed speedily cause the hearts of the sons of men to be fully set in them to do evil. Let men remember that it is a falsehood to violate a

threatening as much as to violate a promise, and that God will not make himself a liar to save man in his sins.[2]

9:8. *And I will encamp about mine house because of the army, because of him that passeth by, and because of him that returneth: and no oppressor shall pass through them any more: for now have I seen with mine eyes.*

Here is the assurance God gives to his people that, living among these nations, they will always be safe when his judgments are executed. The message is the same as the sealing of God's 144,000 servants in Revelation 7 who stand with the Lamb on Mount Zion in Revelation 14 and are blessed with him forever.

When Alexander conquered Damascus, Tyre, and Philistia, then Jerusalem and the temple were spared:

Whilst Damascus and Hamth are overtaken by the judgment of God and fall into the hands of the conqueror; whilst all the wealth of Tyre, its bulwarks and its insular position, fail to secure its safety, and it is taken and given up to the flames; whilst the neighboring Philistia is despoiled of its ancient splendour, and its leading cities, Askelon, Gaza, Ekron, and Ashdod, fall into the deepest obscurity; Jerusalem is still saved from destruction by the protecting hand of the Lord.[3]

Josephus, a Jewish historian from the time of the apostles, tells how a procession of priests and people went out to meet Alexander, who had determined to sack the city for its allegiance to his enemies but, on seeing the procession with the high priest at its head, not only spared the city and the temple but granted every request the Jews made. This literal and historical fulfillment, however, has a wider application, for that earthly house that Alexander spared was but a shadow and type of a better house, the church as the body of Christ:

---

2 Moore, *Zechariah*, 144–45.
3 Hengstenberg, *Christology*, 3:329.

But as the temple was only a symbol of the Church, the promise must have its widest fulfilment only in the glorious antitype, that Church that is kept as the apple of God's eye, and against which the gates of hell shall never prevail.[4]

Or as Leupold writes it: "The future developments and victories of the church are related in terms of Old Testament experience."[5]

The house of God here is the temple of the Old Testament and the church of the New. First Timothy 3:15 refers to her as the "house of God, which is the church of the living God, the pillar and ground of the truth." Her safety is guaranteed, for her everywhere-present God will camp all around her with his sovereign grace and mercy.

Not only is the safety of the church in both the Old and New Testaments promised here, but her future expansion is also hinted at in verse 7: "But he that remaineth, even he, shall be for our God, and he shall be as a governor in Judah, and Ekron as a Jebusite." This parallels chapter 2:11, "And many nations shall be joined to the Lord in that day, and shall be my people." It is a promise of the gathering of the Gentiles and uniting of Jew and Gentile in the New Testament church.

There would be a remnant saved out of these nations who would be God's people. Those who were part of that remnant would have a place of honor among the people of God like that of the governor, Zerubbabel. Out of Ekron, a traditional enemy of Israel, there would be those who, like Araunah the Jebusite, became part of the covenant nation (2 Sam. 24:18–25).

Never again does the church of God come under the heel of the oppressor! The word "oppressor" is the same word translated as "taskmasters" in Exodus (3:7; 5:6, 10, 13). Nothing like what happened in Egypt would ever again happen to the church of God. Even the gates of hell cannot prevail against her as a result of what God does for his church through Christ in delivering her from her greatest enemies, sin and death (Matt. 16:18). He who gave his own dear Son for her sins, will he not do all things for her and deliver her finally and forever from her enemies?

---

4 Moore, *Zechariah*, 144.
5 Leupold, *Zechariah*, 162.

Chapter 19

THE FIRST BURDEN, PART 2:
ZECHARIAH 9:9–10

9:9 Rejoice greatly, O daughter of Zion; shout, O daughter of Jerusalem: behold, thy King cometh unto thee: he is just, and having salvation; lowly, and riding upon an ass, and upon a colt the foal of an ass.[1]

9:10 And I will cut off the chariot from Ephraim, and the horse from Jerusalem, and the battle bow shall be cut off: and he shall speak peace unto the heathen: and his dominion shall be from sea even to sea, and from the river even to the ends of the earth.

---

1 "Upon an ass, and upon a colt the foal of an ass" does not refer to two beasts but is a double description of the one beast upon which Christ rode into Jerusalem, though some commentators like Leupold insist that he rode two different beasts, each part of the way into Jerusalem.

The second part of the first burden is parallel to the first vision. In both Christ appears as a mounted warrior, in the vision mounted on a red horse and now on the colt of a donkey; in the vision as our exalted king and here in his humiliation. Together the two give us a complete picture of his work as our savior. This important passage is quoted in Matthew 21:4–5, and the quotation shows, if there were any doubt about it, that the passage refers to Christ and his triumphal entry into Jerusalem. This is the main difference between the first and second parts of the book. Though parallel, the first part centers in Christ glorified and triumphant and the second in Christ lowly, humiliated, and rejected.

That raises the question, why is Christ shown as sovereign and triumphant first and as humiliated second? Why is the order of prophecy the opposite of the historical order? The answer must be, this is the Old Testament when the humiliation of Christ was so little understood and all was still future. Only in due time would his disciples and his church understand his coming so meek and lowly, his refusal to establish an earthly kingdom, and the necessity of his death. The travelers to Emmaus after the resurrection had to be told, "Ought not Christ to have suffered these things, and to enter into his glory?" (Luke 24:26). The glory was the only part of the message the church would understand until all was fulfilled, and so it is put first. Until the suffering of Messiah was finished and the Spirit poured out, they could not understand the rest.

What a revelation this is! The passage was literally fulfilled in Christ's triumphal entry, but that was only the climax of its fulfillment. He came as Zion's meek and lowly king already when he came into the world, born of the virgin Mary, born in Bethlehem. In all of his work he revealed himself to be humble and lowly. This humiliation, reaching its climax in his triumphal entry, is ultimately fulfilled when he in the way of humbling himself even to death enters his everlasting and heavenly kingdom. The passage shows us how he triumphs over sin and death not by sword and spear but by giving himself willingly and obediently into the hands of his enemies and so defeating them.

What a contrast this king is to Alexander: riding on an ass, without an army to follow him, headed for the cross and apparent defeat, and yet more powerful than Alexander, whose conquests are mentioned in the first eight verses of this chapter. Christ is king of a kingdom that will endure when Alexander's conquests are no longer remembered. Alexander died at the height of his power and his kingdom was immediately dismembered, but Christ, who had no visible kingdom, through death obtains the heavens and the earth as his own. Alexander, called "the Great," will be judged by him who rode into his own city on an ass.

This is one of those Old Testament prophecies of Christ (Isaiah 53 is another) where the literal truth breaks through the dark sayings of prophecy and is expressed in language that any New Testament believer can understand with little effort. We read of him here as the just one, the one who by his obedience and suffering is made righteous on behalf of his people and who therefore comes bringing salvation. We read of his lowliness and are reminded of the gospel accounts of his life and of those many other New Testament passages that speak of his humiliation, notably Philippians 2:5–8.

That he is himself righteous and has salvation means that by his work he becomes the righteous one—earns righteousness—though not needing it himself. To him also salvation is given (literally, he is endowed with it) that he may give it and the righteousness he earned to his own.

He is righteous as God's only begotten Son, but it is especially his righteousness as the king of his people that is in view here. On our behalf he is righteous by placing himself under the law (Gal. 4:4), taking our sins upon himself, and suffering the full penalty for sin, while at the same time rendering to God a perfect obedience that is a substitute for all our disobedience. In this way he also has salvation to give to his people.

Mounted upon the colt of an ass, he must have cut a ridiculous figure riding into Jerusalem, and indeed in all his life he was the scorn of his enemies. The early Christians were reminded that the Jesus they worshiped had ridden into Jerusalem on an ass and were even sometimes called *asini* (asses) for that reason. Nevertheless, he is the fulfillment of prophecy and the one for whom we look and in whom our hopes rest. He is now mounted on a great white horse and is the one who rides conquering and to conquer, the terror of his enemies, until such a time as all things are made subject to him, his enemies cast into outer darkness, and the kingdom delivered up to his Father.

As McComiskey says:

The lowly scene verse 9 creates encapsulates the nature of the kingdom that Christ established. The suffering, humiliation, and death that unfolded on the palm-strewn road he traveled would eventuate in the conquest of countless human hearts and in his ultimate rule over new heavens and a new earth.[2]

What a reason for rejoicing! Though little understood in the days of this prophecy or in the days of his ministry, we now have the Spirit to teach us both the need for and the wonder of his coming in the flesh, his suffering and death, his cross and grave. And, ironic as it may seem to those who still do not understand, we glory in his humiliation and agree with Paul, "God forbid that I should glory, save in the cross of our Lord Jesus Christ, by whom the world is crucified unto me, and I unto the world" (Gal. 6:14), and we sing, "My sinful self my only shame, my glory all—the cross."

When in connection with Messiah's humiliation God speaks of cutting off the chariot, the horse, and the battle bow, he is referring to the battle Christ fought against sin and death, a battle in which these earthly weapons would be of no avail, a battle that was fought in the way of suffering God's wrath against sin, of descending into hell, and of obedience unto death. Horse and chariot had been forbidden to Israel in the law as a picture of this battle, that is, of the battle Jehovah would fight for them and by which he would deliver them. The battle bow would be unnecessary in that titanic struggle. It would be fought by surrendering, by patient bearing of humiliation, by suffering reproach and shame, and by being obedient unto death. It would make the chariot, the horse, and the battle bow forever useless and would be the defeat of all who trust in earthly power. And so again the message is, "Not by might, nor by power" (Zech. 4:6).

That these would be unnecessary and the lack of them no lack at all we see in the last words of verse 10, which describe the results of his humiliation. Through humiliation would come Christ's universal, eternal, and peaceful reign. He would be humbled but in that way would receive glory and honor above all:

---

2 McComiskey, *Zechariah*, 1167.

6. Who, being in the form of God, thought it not robbery to be equal with God:

7. But made himself of no reputation, and took upon him the form of a servant, and was made in the likeness of men:

8. And being found in fashion as a man, he humbled himself, and became obedient unto death, even the death of the cross.

9. Wherefore God also hath highly exalted him, and given him a name which is above every name:

10. That at the name of Jesus every knee should bow, of things in heaven, and things in earth, and things under the earth;

11. And that every tongue should confess that Jesus Christ is Lord, to the glory of God the Father. (Phil. 2:6–11)

Zechariah 10:10 is in part a quote from Psalm 72:8, thus tying together the Psalms, the prophets, and the gospels and giving further insight into the nature of Christ's everlasting and peaceable kingdom. All leads to the wonderful doxology with which that Psalm closes:

17. His name shall endure for ever: his name shall be continued as long as the sun: and men shall be blessed in him: all nations shall call him blessed.

18. Blessed be the Lord God, the God of Israel, who only doeth wondrous things.

19. And blessed be his glorious name for ever: and let the whole earth be filled with his glory; Amen, and Amen. (Ps. 72:17–19)

These blessings are not for all, however, not even conditionally, for the daughter of Zion is addressed here as "the believing members of the covenant nation."[3] The daughter of Zion is the same as the children of Jerusalem of whom Jesus speaks in Matthew 23:37. Jerusalem would be left desolate, but her children would be saved, a remnant according to the election of grace. They are always those to whom Christ is not merely a king but "thy King," the one long expected and long waited for, the one whom they remember

---

3   Carl Friedrich Keil, *The Twelve Minor Prophets*, trans. James Martin, in C. F. Keil and F. Delitzsch, *Biblical Commentary on the Old Testament* (Grand Rapids, MI: Eerdmans, 1954), 2:333.

even when the whole nation forgets. They are those like old Anna and old Simeon, who had no other hope but Christ and who could say, "Lord, now lettest thou thy servant depart in peace, according to thy word: For mine eyes have seen thy salvation, Which thou hast prepared before the face of all people; A light to lighten the Gentiles, and the glory of thy people Israel" (Luke 2:29–32).

Chapter 20

THE FIRST BURDEN, PART 3:
Zechariah 9:11–10:12

9:11   As for thee also, by the blood of thy covenant I have sent forth thy prisoners out of the pit wherein is no water.

9:12   Turn you to the strong hold, ye prisoners of hope: even to day do I declare that I will render double unto thee;

9:13   When I have bent Judah for me, filled the bow with Ephraim, and raised up thy sons, O Zion, against thy sons, O Greece, and made thee as the sword of a mighty man.

9:14   And the LORD shall be seen over them, and his arrow shall go forth as the lightning: and the LORD God shall blow the trumpet, and shall go with whirlwinds of the south.

9:15   The LORD of hosts shall defend them; and they shall devour, and subdue with sling stones; and they shall drink, and make a noise as through wine; and they shall be filled like bowls, and as the corners of the altar.

9:16   And the LORD their God shall save them in that day as the flock of his people: for they shall be as the stones of a crown, lifted up as an ensign upon his land.

9:17   For how great is his goodness, and how great is his beauty! corn shall make the young men cheerful, and new wine the maids.

10:1   Ask ye of the LORD rain in the time of the latter rain; so the LORD shall make bright clouds, and give them showers of rain, to every one grass in the field.

10:2   For the idols have spoken vanity, and the diviners have seen a lie, and have told false dreams; they comfort in vain: therefore they went their way as a flock, they were troubled, because there was no shepherd.

10:3   Mine anger was kindled against the shepherds, and I punished the goats: for the LORD of hosts hath visited his flock the house of Judah, and hath made them as his goodly horse in the battle.

10:4   Out of him came forth the corner, out of him the nail, out of him the battle bow, out of him every oppressor together.

10:5   And they shall be as mighty men, which tread down their enemies in the mire of the streets in the battle: and they shall fight, because the LORD is with them, and the riders on horses shall be confounded.

10:6   And I will strengthen the house of Judah, and I will save the house of Joseph, and I will bring them again to place them; for I have mercy upon them: and they shall be as though I had not cast them off: for I am the LORD their God, and will hear them.

10:7   And they of Ephraim shall be like a mighty man, and their heart shall rejoice as through wine: yea, their children shall see it, and be glad; their heart shall rejoice in the LORD.

10:8   I will hiss for them, and gather them; for I have redeemed them: and they shall increase as they have increased.

10:9   And I will sow them among the people: and they shall remember me in far countries; and they shall live with their children, and turn again.

10:10   I will bring them again also out of the land of Egypt, and gather them out of Assyria; and I will bring them into the land of Gilead and Lebanon; and place shall not be found for them.

10:11   And he shall pass through the sea with affliction, and shall smite the waves in the sea, and all the deeps of the river shall dry up: and the pride of Assyria shall be brought down, and the sceptre of Egypt shall depart away.

10:12   And I will strengthen them in the LORD; and they shall walk up and down in his name, saith the LORD.

9:11. As for thee also, by the blood of thy covenant I have sent forth thy prisoners out of the pit wherein is no water.

9:12. Turn you to the strong hold, ye prisoners of hope: even to day do I declare that I will render double unto thee;

Just as the vision of Christ as the rider on the red horse ends with promises of blessing for Judah, so here the prophecy of Christ on the colt of an ass ends the same way. He will deliver the prisoners, give victory to his people, and visit them with unheard-of prosperity and blessing. This part of chapter 9 along with chapter 10 is very much parallel to Zechariah's third vision, the vision of the measuring of Jerusalem. The call to flee Babylon that is part of the third vision is paralleled by the promise of deliverance for the prisoners, and the measuring of Jerusalem, the main thing in the third vision, is paralleled by the promises of victory and prosperity.

There is reference in this section back to the first part of chapter 9. The similarity between these sections is highlighted by the use of similar terms, some of which are not found elsewhere in the book of Zechariah: "mighty man" (9:13; 10:5, 7), "oppressor" (9:8; 10:4), "battle bow" (9:10; 10:4), "mire of the streets" (9:3; 10:5); the "sea" (9:10; 10:11), and "joy" (9:9; 10:7). These terms link this third part of the burden with the previous two. This part is different, though, in that the emphasis is on the restoration of God's covenant people[1]

Verses 11–12 speak of the deliverance of Zion's prisoners, for though the Jews had been allowed to return from Babylon, there were many who were still in Babylon. They are viewed here as prisoners: if in fact no longer prisoners of the Babylonians, then of their own unwillingness and disinterest. God promises that he will bring them back, just as he had called them out of Babylon in chapter 2:6–7. He would do that by making them willing.

There is some interesting language in these verses, however, suggesting that the matter went deeper than just a return from Babylon: that it was a

---

1 I am indebted for these insights to Kline, *Glory in Our Midst*, 241–58, an appendix where Kline discusses in detail the structure of the book of Zechariah. Though very technical and somewhat difficult to follow, his arguments for the parallelism of the two parts of the book are compelling and his analysis of the structure of the book is thorough.

deeply spiritual matter. God speaks of delivering them from the pit, a synonym throughout scripture for hell. Indeed, the word used here is identified
in Isaiah 14:15 with hell: "Yet thou shalt be brought down to hell, to the
sides of the pit," and this in a passage where the king of Babylon is identified
with Satan or Lucifer, son of the morning. This was not because the king of
Babylon was personally the devil incarnate, but because he was an agent and
servant of Satan in his pride and opposition to the kingdom of God.

To be in Babylon, therefore, is to be in hell and under the power of
Satan, and it is from thence that God promises to deliver his people. Even
the reference to no water in the pit reminds us of the parable of the rich man
and Lazarus and the rich man's request for a drop of water to cool his tongue.
That the blood of the covenant is needed to deliver these captives is further
evidence that God has the spiritual bondage of his people and their salvation in mind, for though they could be delivered from earthly captivity by a
king's decree, only the blood of Christ could deliver them from the spiritual
captivity that kept them in Babylon when they had opportunity to return,
and from all Babylon symbolized.

Who does not think, as they read of God's delivering his people from the
pit, of the words of Psalm 40:1–2: "I waited patiently for the LORD; and he
inclined unto me, and heard my cry. He brought me up also out of an horrible pit, out of the miry clay, and set my feet upon a rock, and established
my goings"; or of the words of Hezekiah: "Thou hast in love to my soul delivered it from the pit of corruption" (Isa. 38:17)?

That the captives are described as prisoners of hope does not mean that
hope kept them captive, but that they are prisoners who have not been
left without hope. Their hope is in God, who promises to deliver them and
who calls them to the stronghold, that is, to himself, for he is our rock and
fortress. He declares that he will render them double, that is, not only give
them freedom and peace, but also repay them for the long years they spent
in captivity. He would restore the years that the grasshopper and caterpillar
had eaten (Joel 2:25). He would give not only what they lost through sin but
much more besides.

The deliverance promised, therefore, is the deliverance that every child
of God has in Christ. Every one of them has been delivered from the pit
where there is no water, that is, no refreshment and blessing for the soul.

Every one knows what it is to be a prisoner of hope, who instead of being without hope has the sure hope of full and complete deliverance even when that deliverance is still being worked out. Every one experiences what it is to receive double from the Lord when God gives "exceeding abundantly above all that we ask or think" (Eph. 3:20). Every one receives not only deliverance but the blessings of heavenly glory, of the adoption of sons, and of eternal life. Each one of God's children knows what it means to find in God a refuge in times of trouble, a fortress and a defense.

The blood of Christ by which all such prisoners are delivered is called the blood of the covenant because by that blood God's covenant with his people is ratified, so that the covenant is forever unbreakable. By that blood they are brought into the covenantal fellowship of God, receive the promises of the covenant, and are kept in the covenant. The blood of the everlasting covenant makes them "perfect in every good work to do his will" (Heb. 13:21). The blood is everything.

9:13. *When I have bent Judah for me, filled the bow with Ephraim, and raised up thy sons, O Zion, against thy sons, O Greece, and made thee as the sword of a mighty man.*

9:14. *And the LORD shall be seen over them, and his arrow shall go forth as the lightning: and the LORD God shall blow the trumpet, and shall go with whirlwinds of the south.*

God promises not only to deliver the captives but also to destroy those who held his people in bondage, along with all their enemies (vv. 13–15). That Judah is the bow, Ephraim the arrow, and Zion the sword only means that he will use them to destroy and pass judgment on the ungodly. They will be the instruments of vengeance in God's hand, a promise fulfilled when they are used by God to fight the battle of faith, to put Satan to flight, and to judge the world. Even then, however, Judah and Ephraim and Zion are such instruments because of Christ's presence in and among them. He is the one who as the captain of their salvation wins the battle and war and conquers every enemy.

Ephraim is mentioned because God never recognized the division of Israel into two nations and because he purposed to save a remnant out of apostate Ephraim and the other tribes represented by her. Jeroboam, from Ephraim, had led them away from the temple, from the throne of David, and from God, but God would bring them back! That theme, only suggested here, is further developed in chapter 10:5–17.

That Greece is mentioned is interesting, for it was in these days that war was begun between Darius, as he is known in the book of Zechariah, and the Greeks. The battle of Marathon, for example, was fought about twenty-five years after these prophecies, during the days of Nehemiah and Malachi. Though at this time only a distant and little-known land, Greece would nevertheless become one of the chief enemies of the Jews under generals who succeeded Alexander, especially Antiochus and his descendants, one of whom would be the little horn of Daniel and the great type of antichrist in Daniel's prophecies.

The Greeks were the enemies of the Jews not only through the persecution instituted by Antiochus IV, but also by their introduction of Greek culture into Judea and the surrounding areas. That culture was a mix of idolatry, sexual promiscuity including homosexuality, love of sports and entertainment, and worldliness and sensuality, not unlike the culture in which we live. It represented an enormous spiritual threat to holiness and godliness, from which only the Spirit of God could deliver his people. These threats to the well-being of the covenant people were still in the future, but God is already looking ahead to those days and promising help and protection.

It is probably for this reason that many find the fulfillment of these prophecies in the victories of the Maccabees who fought against and delivered Judah from Antiochus IV. Those victories, however, were at best only a shadow of the victories that Messiah would win, and it is his victories that Zechariah has in view, as the previous verses so clearly show with their references to the pit and to the blood of the covenant.

Verse 14, then, not only carries these victories forward into the New Testament and to the work of Christ in conquering sin, death, and Satan for the true Israel, but carries them forward to the end of all things. The lightning, the whirlwind, the trumpet, and the arrow are all associated in scripture with the final coming of Christ and the great day of judgment. Psalm 18 is a good example. It describes God's coming in judgment in virtually the same terms as does Zechariah:

7. Then the earth shook and trembled; the foundations also of the hills moved and were shaken, because he was wroth.

8. There went up a smoke out of his nostrils, and fire out of his mouth devoured: coals were kindled by it.

9. He bowed the heavens also, and came down: and darkness was under his feet.

10. And he rode upon a cherub, and did fly: yea, he did fly upon the wings of the wind.

11. He made darkness his secret place; his pavilion round about him were dark waters and thick clouds of the skies.

12. At the brightness that was before him his thick clouds passed, hail stones and coals of fire.

13. The LORD also thundered in the heavens, and the Highest gave his voice; hail stones and coals of fire.

14. Yea, he sent out his arrows, and scattered them; and he shot out lightnings, and discomfited them.

15. Then the channels of waters were seen, and the foundations of the world were discovered at thy rebuke, O LORD, at the blast of the breath of thy nostrils.

16. He sent from above, he took me, he drew me out of many waters. (Ps. 18:7–16)

As part of that description God is described as being seen over them, a reference to the cloud of glory that followed them through the wilderness and was their shade by day and their protection by night. Thus the word of God promises protection and grounds the promise in what he had done for his people in the past.

9:15. The LORD of hosts shall defend them; and they shall devour, and subdue with sling stones; and they shall drink, and make a noise as through wine; and they shall be filled like bowls, and as the corners of the altar.

This verse continues the thought though in more obscure language. The idea of the passage is: "The LORD of hosts shall defend his people [them], and they shall devour their enemies and subdue their enemies with sling stones; and they [the LORD's people] shall drink and make a noise as through wine [in rejoicing and giving thanks for their victory]; and thus his people will be filled like bowls, and as the corners of the altar." The promise is once again of victory with an obvious reference to David's victory of faith over Goliath with sling stones, but like David their victory will really be God's victory over his enemies.

Their drinking and making a noise as through wine is the celebration and feasting that follows their victory, described in Revelation as the wedding feast of the Lamb, also a victory feast (Rev. 19:9). The noise is the noise of rejoicing and feasting, for they will be filled with the wine of joy as bowls and as the corners of the altar through what God has done for them in Christ. Freed from the pit in which there is no water, they will be filled with every good and desirable thing.

The reference to the corners of the altar is to a part of the sacrificial ritual when the wine of the drink offerings was poured into the hollow horns at the four corners of the altar. That pouring of wine was symbolic of covenantal communion between God and his people and of their consecration to him, only now his people would be the ones filled with wine, enjoying not only symbolically but also in reality the communion so pictured.

The altar is viewed, then, as a table at which God and his people meet in covenantal communion, and the horns of the altar as the cups out of which they drink. Only the figure is carried a step further in that not only the horns but also the celebrants would be filled.

The horns also connect this passage with the second vision. There the four horns are symbolic of the power of Israel's oppressors, but removed by the four carpenters, they are now the vessels out of which God's people drink.

9:16. *And the* LORD *their God shall save them in that day as the flock of his people: for they shall be as the stones of a crown, lifted up as an ensign upon his land.*

9:17. *For how great is his goodness, and how great is his beauty! corn shall make the young men cheerful, and new wine the maids.*

The three figures of verse 16—the flock, the stones of a crown, and the ensign or banner—picture the exalted glory and honor that God would give his people through these victories. The reference to them as his flock emphasizes his love and care for them, the stones of the crown emphasize their value, and the ensign pictures their victorious glory. Though expressed in symbolic terms, the figures show the unspeakable glory God has prepared for his own people. That they will be not only his own flock, loved by him as a shepherd loves his sheep, but also his own crown of glory and the banner representing his name and kingdom is beyond imagination. All this depends on him who comes to Zion riding on the colt of an ass. Nothing without him!

So the chapter ends by breaking out into a doxology of praise and worship. It is all his goodness and beauty. The corn and wine that cheer both young man and maiden are his and their blessedness from him and from no other. Their beauty is his gift. He alone is the overflowing fountain of good and the source of every good and perfect gift, and therefore to him belong glory and honor and praise forever.

What a wonderful picture of what God has done, does, and will do for us in Christ:

> All the facts of the Jewish history are looked at in their relation to the Messianic blessings, and have their value mainly in this connection, and hence as objects seen in the same plane and parallel, their outlines and lights are often blended...We, too, are prisoners of hope, who are to go forth by the blood of the everlasting covenant; and we, too, have an enemy more terrible by far than the gigantic Epiphanes, and are menaced with a storm of ruin more fearful than that which swept over widowed Judea. Hence the call to turn and flee to the strong hold, is one that may still be sounded to man, and the promised blessings of this passage shall but prefigure those greater blessings that shall be bestowed upon those who are the flock of the good shepherd, and who are among the jewels that glitter in his diadem of many crowns.[2]

10:1. Ask ye of the LORD rain in the time of the latter rain; so the LORD shall make bright clouds, and give them showers of rain, to every one grass in the field.

---

2 Moore, *Zechariah*, 157.

10:2. For the idols have spoken vanity, and the diviners have seen a lie, and have told false dreams; they comfort in vain: therefore they went their way as a flock, they were troubled, because there was no shepherd.

Chapter 10 continues the promises of the restoration. The chapter begins with a further word of judgment on Israel's enemies. Like Zechariah's second vision of the four horns and four carpenters, and like chapter 9:1–8, these first verses of chapter 10 describe the scattering of God's people and the judgments that would come on the nations who scattered them. In chapter 1:18–21, those nations are pictured as four horns. Here they are pictured as those who left Israel as a flock without shepherds. In chapter 1, their military power against Israel is emphasized. Here their spiritual opposition through their idolatry is shown as a further cause of Israel's ruin.

Verse 1 is not so much a command to the people to ask for rain in a time of drought but a reminder to them that the Lord is the one who sends the rain. The idols, in contrast, only speak vanity and lies. They promise rain and other blessings but cannot give what they promise. The Lord is the giver of every good and perfect gift. The truth of these first verses is the same as Jeremiah 14:22, "Are there any among the vanities of the Gentiles that can cause rain? or can the heavens give showers? art not thou he, O LORD our God? therefore we will wait upon thee: for thou hast made all these things."

The emphasis on rain also fits the figure of flock and shepherd that follows. The result of Israel's idolatry was not only physical drought, but also that she was left spiritually as a flock without pasture. There was no shepherd to lead her to the green pastures of God's word and to the still waters of his grace. When Israel was restored and delivered from her enemies, the Lord would give his blessing, spiritual health, and prosperity.

The words of Moses ought to be remembered: "My doctrine shall drop as the rain, my speech shall distil as the dew, as the small rain upon the tender herb, and as the showers upon the grass: Because I will publish the name of the LORD: ascribe ye greatness unto our God" (Deut. 32:2–3). The charismatics are not wrong when they describe the coming and work of the Spirit as the "latter rain." Their error is the belief that this is some second blessing of the Spirit. Zechariah "describes under this common figure," Calvin says, "the kingdom of Christ—even that God will fill his elect with all good things, so that they shall not thirst, nor labour under any want."[3]

Verse 2 describes what happened in Israel as she fell deeper and deeper into idolatry and away from God. She was left to the mercy of her idols and their diviners and thus was subject to lies and vanity. In that way Israel was like a shepherdless flock, without comfort, without direction, without hope. This is what happens whenever the church turns away from God and serves idols, whether gods of wood and stone or the false gods of her false teachings and evil imaginations.

Idolatry is as prevalent among so-called Christians today as it was among the Jews in the pre-captivity years. The only difference is that today the idolatry is slightly more sophisticated and not immediately recognizable as idolatry. Some do worship gods of wood and stone, gold and silver, in that their affections and lives are ruled by a crass materialism. Their gods are their bellies, that is, their own physical well-being and prosperity. Others with their false ideas of God really worship an idol that has no resemblance to the true God. Theirs is a god who can do nothing unless man allows it, a god who, it seems, exists only to give people whatever they want, or a god who is nothing but a healer.

The word "idol" here is "teraphim" or household gods, the kind of idols Rachel stole from her father Laban (Gen. 31:19). These were personal idols on the order of the crosses, religious trinkets, amulets, and good-luck charms that people carry with them to supposedly help them. The emphasis, therefore, is on the personal nature of idolatry and on the fact that the sin of idolatry can be committed privately as well as publicly. Whatever we love, trust, and "idolize" next to God are "teraphim." Whatever desires, motives, and values control our lives apart from God are household idols.

The passage refers also to diviners and dreamers, and that includes for us not only horoscopes and other such foolish means by which people seek to know the future and direct their lives, but also every means by which Christians try to direct their lives and know the will of God apart from his word. "God told me," "God wants me to do this or that," and all such statements, when made apart from what God commands in his word, are idolatry.

---

3 Calvin, *Commentaries on the Twelve Minor Prophets*, 5:281.

The spread of idolatry was another way in which the heathen nations "helped forward the affliction" (Zech. 1:15). They encouraged and assisted the idolatry of the covenant nation and at times, through people like Jezebel and Athaliah, brought in and even imposed their idolatry on the nation, so that the nation came under the judgment and wrath of God. They were enemies not only through political pressure but spiritually as well. Indeed, the spiritual pressures brought to bear on the covenant nation were the greater threat, as the history of the nation proved again and again.

Beginning with Solomon's wives, the long list of heathen idolaters who infiltrated Judah and Israel and were the immediate cause of spiritual decline and apostasy is a list that explains the Lord's anger against his people. Nor were the people without blame. Both the shepherds and the goats mentioned in verse 3 were Israelite idolaters, but the heathen were the ones from whom the idolatry originated and who assisted it, knowingly or unknowingly.

No doubt the drought Judah suffered was real. Nehemiah makes reference to it in Nehemiah 5:3. Drought, even in the Old Testament, however, was a sign of spiritual dearth, as Jeremiah reminds them and us: "For my people have committed two evils; they have forsaken me the fountain of living waters, and hewed them out cisterns, broken cisterns, that can hold no water" (Jer. 2:13). Forsaking the Lord and turning to idols, they asked rain neither for their crops nor for their souls from God.

10:3. *Mine anger was kindled against the shepherds, and I punished the goats: for the LORD of hosts hath visited his flock the house of Judah, and hath made them as his goodly horse in the battle.*

God would redeem and deliver his people and use them to punish and destroy the heathen as he had used the heathen to chastise them. In his punishing the heathen, the shepherds and goats would also be punished. Some identify these shepherds as the heathen rulers, others with Israel's priests and prophets. The latter is more likely; the shepherds are Israel's leaders and the goats those in Israel who were not part of God's flock, not part of the true Israel, but goats among the sheep. In the end it makes little difference, for though the idolatry originated among the heathen, all who were guilty would be punished. The idolatrous Jews would be punished along with the heathen among whom they really belonged.

Thus in verse 3 is a reference to the Lord as the shepherd of his people and to his use of them to scourge the nations. He would come in the place of the shepherds who had led them astray and deliver them from their enemies. The reference certainly is to Christ, the great shepherd of the sheep and the one who delivers God's flock from thieves, robbers, and hirelings (John 10:1–18). This prophecy began to be fulfilled by Christ at his first coming when he paid for the sins of his people and became, under the oppression of his enemies, the cause of their judgment. Its fulfillment is complete when he comes again and brings his sheep into the heavenly fold, leaving only destruction for their enemies.

God promises to come to his flock and change his sheep into mighty war-horses through which he will visit destruction on their enemies, on those who scattered and destroyed his flock. In this way he shows in further detail the skill and wisdom he has to deliver them, the skill hinted at in the vision of the four horns and four carpenters. In fact, the reference to he-goats reminds us of Zechariah 1:18–21 and the four horns that scattered God's flock. That skill is displayed in Christ and his work, as the following verses show. In him God does the unimaginable and performs a miracle of grace and redemption for their deliverance.

10:4. Out of him came forth the corner, out of him the nail, out of him the battle bow, out of him every oppressor together.

10:5. And they shall be as mighty men, which tread down their enemies in the mire of the streets in the battle: and they shall fight, because the LORD is with them, and the riders on horses shall be confounded.

The first part of chapter 10 closes in verse 4 with a statement of God's sovereignty over the nations: from him, that is, from God Almighty, who in Christ is the true shepherd, are all things—the corner, the nail, the battle bow, even the oppressors of Israel are from him. He uses them to accomplish his purpose, to perform his will, first in the oppression and death of his own Son, and then in the chastisement and salvation of his people.

The passage is explicitly messianic. It is out of Judah that the corner, the nail, the battle bow, and the oppressor come. It is Christ who comes from Judah, meek and lowly and riding on the colt of an ass, but nevertheless the king of his people and the one who is everything to them. The corner is the cornerstone, the nail the tent peg or clothes hook or stake, and the oppressor everyone who is called to execute justice.

Christ is the cornerstone. He is repeatedly called the cornerstone of the church in the New Testament (Matt. 21:42–44; Acts 4:11; 1 Pet. 2:4–8). He is the nail, the one on whom everything depends, upon which everything hangs. He is the stake that holds up God's tabernacle with his people, the peg upon which hangs all the glory of God's holy place. In Isaiah 22:23–24, Eliakim, a figure of Christ, is described as a nail:

> 23. And I will fasten him as a nail in a sure place; and he shall be for
> a glorious throne to his father's house.
> 24. And they shall hang upon him all the glory of his father's
> house, the offspring and the issue, all vessels of small quantity, from
> the vessels of cups, even to all the vessels of flagons.

That Christ is the battle bow means that he is the one through whom God executes vengeance on the enemies of his church. That every oppressor comes from Judah refers to the line of kings that began with David and reached its highest point in Christ. The word "oppressor" can be used in a negative sense, but here it appears to be used in the positive sense of one who executes the justice of God, both against the apostate in Israel and against the heathen. Christ is the oppressor of all enemies.

Also possible is the interpretation of the oppressors in light of Isaiah 49:17, "Thy children shall make haste; thy destroyers and they that made thee waste shall go forth of thee." Then God is promising that those who oppressed his people would go away, never to return. The other interpretation, however, seems the better in that it parallels the other three and refers to Christ the king of his people. The promise is of deliverance through the sovereignty of God and the work of Christ.

The emphasis, as in Zechariah 9:9–10, is on Christ the *king*. Even the reference in Isaiah 22 to Christ as the nail includes reference to his kingly office, as do all the others. Though meek and lowly, he is nevertheless all that a king ought to be. Indeed, he is the great priest-king of his people, for as king he is also the cornerstone of the house of God and the nail that is found in the holy place. The people of God share in his kingly glory, for it is not only he but also they who are like mighty men, who tread down their enemies. In Christ they are more than conquerors.

10:6. And I will strengthen the house of Judah, and I will save the house of Joseph, and I will bring them again to place them; for I have mercy upon them: and they shall be as though I had not cast them off: for I am the LORD their God, and will hear them.

10:7. And they of Ephraim shall be like a mighty man, and their heart shall rejoice as through wine: yea, their children shall see it, and be glad; their heart shall rejoice in the LORD.

These verses are very much like the third vision of the man with the measuring line in their message and even in their language. God promises not only to bless and prosper his people who had been under the heel of their enemies, but also to enlarge them by bringing in their former enemies. Like the vision of the man with the measuring line, therefore, the promise is of the gathering of the Gentiles. But this promise stands side by side, as it does in the third vision, with the promise that God will also gather a remnant of exiled Israel, the lost ten tribes: thus the mention of Ephraim and Joseph.

Israel, once divided and scattered, would be made whole and be one again. Of special note is the repeated mention of the ten tribes. God had not forgotten them, and they too would be gathered again and brought from exile. The ten tribes are implied not only in the mention of Joseph, the ancestor of Ephraim, the leader of those tribes, and in the mention of Ephraim, but also in the reference to Assyria, Lebanon, and Gilead in verse 10.

Assyria had taken the ten tribes captive and scattered them among the nations. Gilead was the land across the Jordan from which many of them had been taken, and Lebanon the northernmost territory of the northern kingdom. So God is promising to restore not only those of Judah who were still in Babylon, but those of the ten tribes also. In verse 6 he says, "I will bring them again to place them." Their place was in the land of Canaan, united with the other tribes and welded together as one nation.

This would be in the mercy of God, for in their wickedness and apostasy

317

they had shown themselves unworthy of his goodness. Yet in his goodness he promises not only restoration but full restoration. It would be for them as though the captivity had never taken place.

There is evidence in the prophets that God never recognized the division of the kingdom in the days of Rehoboam and Jeroboam. That is seen even more clearly when we remember that the nation of Israel was the church of the Old Testament. There is in God's eyes only one church, one bride of Christ, one people of God. We confess that in the Apostles' Creed: I believe *one* holy catholic church. The divisions that have fragmented the visible church, though often unavoidable, are the result of sin. God does not recognize them.

That one church is now united in faith and will be one in every sense when Christ returns and takes the church to the place he has prepared for her. God implicitly promises to restore that unity in the promise to restore both Judah and Israel. This he has begun to do and will continue to do until there is again one holy catholic church. That is always a reminder to us to seek to the utmost of our power the unity of the church within the congregations to which we belong, in forming and maintaining the broader unity of denominational and federational ties, and in seeking that unity across the oceans and with those whom the Lord gathers by his word and Spirit out of other nations and peoples.

Just as the true Israel united in faith was found in those two nations in the Old Testament, so that one true church is found in many different denominations and churches. That true church God promises to restore and unite. The promise is not for all, but for the elect remnant of which the apostle Paul speaks in Romans 11. There he shows us that even though Israel as a nation has been cast off, God has not forsaken his people. There is, even to this present time, a remnant according to election. That remnant God always brings again and blesses, not for its own sake but for Christ's sake.

He also promises to enlarge his church and make her forever blessed. Ephraim will once again be like a mighty man instead of being like an impoverished and dying beggar. Joy would be their portion and that of their children, after the dreadful years in which those of their children who were not killed became slaves of their oppressors. They would increase once again and be a mighty nation as in the days when they came out from Egypt.

10:8. I will hiss for them, and gather them; for I have redeemed them: and they shall increase as they have increased.

10:9. And I will sow them among the people: and they shall remember me in far countries; and they shall live with their children, and turn again.

God promises several things here. He promises to reunite his divided church and to bring back those who were scattered or who had not returned from Babylon. Only Judah had returned, and many of them by choice or of necessity had stayed behind, but God promises to restore them also. He did this in the Old Testament and does so in the New Testament when he sends reformation and renewal in his church. His hissing for his people was heard in the days of the apostles and at the time of the Reformation, and it continues to be heard wherever the gospel gathers and restores God's church. It brings them out of spiritual bondage and involves the smiting of their enemies.

When God promises to sow his saints among the people, he does not mean that they would live in foreign lands, but that they would remember their God and come back to their place in the promised land. There they would live with their children, for God's covenant is also unchangeable and unbreakable. All that would happen in the way of their conversion from idolatry and wickedness to God. They would turn again not only physically in coming back to their own land, but also spiritually.

The word "hiss" is apparently used in reference to the management of bees. Though this is not a modern practice, beekeepers in ancient times would gather the swarm by making a sound that imitated the buzzing of bees. Isaiah 7:18 uses a similar figure to describe the Lord's calling the nations against Judah for judgment: "And it shall come to pass in that day, that the LORD shall hiss for the fly that is in the uttermost part of the rivers of Egypt, and for the bee that is in the land of Assyria." In Zechariah the figure is used to describe the Lord's gathering his people from the nations by the gospel. The gospel is described as hissing because it is a still small voice that is persistent and even annoying to those who do not believe it.

God says this all would happen because he had redeemed them. The reference is to what he did in Egypt, but that as a picture of the redemptive work of Jesus. Promised and sure, these people too were redeemed by the blood of the Lamb, justified and forgiven in him, and with a place in heaven.

319

God promises to gather them and to increase them. The reference to sowing explains how he will make of them a great nation and a multitude of people. Just as the seed sown increases miraculously, so will God increase his people, a wonderful promise for a church that is always a remnant and for the "day of small things" when the people of God are few and struggling. It will not always be so, for someday, gathered to glory, the church will be a multitude that no man can number. Israel had once been a great nation. It is estimated that around two million people came out of Egypt.[4] They had been reduced to a handful, but God would increase them once again.

10:10. I will bring them again also out of the land of Egypt, and gather them out of Assyria; and I will bring them into the land of Gilead and Lebanon; and place shall not be found for them.

10:11. And he shall pass through the sea with affliction, and shall smite the waves in the sea, and all the deeps of the river shall dry up: and the pride of Assyria shall be brought down, and the sceptre of Egypt shall depart away.

The sea and her waves represent the wicked world. They are the troubled waves of the sea (Isa. 57:20) out of which the great enemy of the church appears in Revelation 13. In dividing the sea and sending his people through as on dry land, God shows how he makes the enemies of his church powerless, stills their raging for the sake of his church, and overthrows them. The sea out of which the wicked enemies of God's people appeared and that represents their restless wickedness is finally also their grave.

This is couched in language that would have reminded the Jews of what God did for them when he brought them out of Egypt. He speaks not only of bringing them out of Egypt and Assyria, but also of bringing them through the sea, of smiting the waves in the sea, of the drying up of rivers, and of the pride of Assyria and the scepter of Egypt being humbled. No one who is acquainted with the Old Testament can think of anything else but of Israel's departure from Egypt, when he dried the Red Sea to give them passage and then also the River Jordan in order to place them in Canaan.

---

4 Homer C. Hoeksema, *Unfolding Covenant History: An Exposition of the Old Testament, Volume 3, From Jacob to the Exodus* (Grandville, MI: Reformed Free Publishing Association, 2003), 315.

The smiting of the sea is a reference to what Moses did at the Red Sea, but it was and is here a symbolic act. Zechariah 1:8 with its reference to the "deep" reminds us that the sea pictures the nations in their restless opposition to the kingdom of God. Indeed, the sea symbolizes the abyss out of which the opposition of the nations has its source. The deep, symbolizing hell and death and sin, must be smitten in order that God's people may pass over to the other side and be saved. The old Reformation creed the Belgic Confession of Faith says in the article on baptism: "Not that this is effected by the external water, but by the sprinkling of the precious blood of the Son of God; who is our Red Sea, through which we must pass to escape the tyranny of Pharaoh, that is, the devil, and to enter into the spiritual land of Canaan."[5]

The Nile, the river, is mentioned not because it was dried up at the time of Israel's departure from Egypt, but because it represented all the prosperity and power of Egypt. It *was* Egypt, and in smiting the Nile and delivering his people God smote and destroyed Egypt. God smote the river when he turned its waters to blood and brought frogs out of it. Every obstacle to the redemption of his people is removed, every enemy destroyed, and so they come to the land God promised them.

Gilead and Lebanon are mentioned as the farthest corners of the nation and areas that were especially fruitful. Gilead was the area on the east side of Jordan inherited by two and a half tribes, but that quickly fell under the domination of enemy nations. Except for several notices in the book of Judges, this area is never mentioned again in the Old Testament, nor are the tribes who settled there. Lebanon, though the northernmost territory promised to Israel, was never except in the days of Solomon under the direct control of the nation, but it is more closely associated with Tyre and Sidon. These farthest reaches of the land would be inherited once again.

God therefore renews the old land promise made to Abraham, a promise that is fulfilled only in the new heavens and new earth. If the earthly land was the real object of these promises, then neither Abraham nor Moses ever received what was promised, for Abraham remained a stranger and pilgrim in the land all his life and Moses had only one view of it before he died. But

---

5 Belgic Confession 34, in Schaff, *Creeds of Christendom*, 3:426.

Abraham knew that it was not the earthly land that God promised him, for he, with Isaac and Jacob, "desire[d] a better country, that is, an heavenly" country (Heb. 11:16). That heavenly land is the inheritance of all the true children of Abraham, both Jews and Gentiles.

Thus also, the gathering again of God's people looks forward to the day when God will gather them out of nations among whom they are dispersed through the whole New Testament period, living in those nations as strangers and pilgrims, and will take them to their own heavenly land and to the new Jerusalem.

Combined with the promise that God will humble Egypt and Assyria, the word of God in these verses is essentially the promise of Jesus in Matthew 16:18, "I will build my church; and the gates of hell shall not prevail against it." As Luther wrote:

A mighty fortress is our God, a bulwark never failing;
Our helper He, amid the flood of mortal ills prevailing:
For still our ancient foe doth seek to work us woe;
His craft and power are great, and, armed with cruel hate,
On earth is not his equal.

Did we in our own strength confide, our striving would be losing;
Were not the right Man on our side, the Man of God's own
    choosing:
Dost ask who that may be? Christ Jesus, it is He;
Lord Sabaoth, His Name, from age to age the same,
And He must win the battle.

And though this world, with devils filled, should threaten to
    undo us,
We will not fear, for God hath willed His truth to triumph
    through us:
The Prince of Darkness grim, we tremble not for him;
His rage we can endure, for lo, his doom is sure,
One little word shall fell him.[6]

---

6 Martin Luther, "A Mighty Fortress is Our God," 1–3, 1529, trans. Frederic H. Hedge.

10:12. And I will strengthen them in the LORD; and they shall walk up and down in his name, saith the LORD.

In this passage Jehovah is both the speaker and the one spoken of, indicating that "there are either two Gods, which leads us to polytheism, or two persons of the same Godhead, which leads us to the doctrine of the New Testament, that Christ, in whom all the redeemed are at last to be saved, is Jehovah, God over all, blessed forever."[7]

The things promised here never happened to the Jewish nation but are fulfilled in the church, in her spiritual prosperity and blessedness, in the realization of God's covenant with her, in her present joy, and in her eternal joy at the wedding feast of the Lamb, where she will indeed rejoice as through wine. They are a multitude that no man can number, and walking up and down in the name of the Lord now, they have the hope of doing so forever in glory.

That they walk up and down in God's name reminds us of those who are described as the friends of God, who walked with him, Enoch, Noah, and Abraham. What was true of them as God's covenant friends shall be true of every one when these promises are fulfilled. Then they will enjoy the everlasting blessedness described in Revelation 3:12, "Him that overcometh will I make a pillar in the temple of my God, and he shall go no more out: and I will write upon him the name of my God, and the name of the city of my God, which is new Jerusalem, which cometh down out of heaven from my God: and I will write upon him my new name," and Revelation 3:4, "They shall walk with me in white, for they are worthy." Even more like Zechariah is Revelation 21:24, "And the nations of them which are saved shall walk in the light of it: and the kings of the earth do bring their glory and honour into it." Here the light is the light of God himself and of the Lamb.

Revelation shows us, therefore, that the fulfillment of Zechariah's prophecies is not an earthly fulfillment and the glory of which he speaks is something that transcends our present experience. Made strong through the resurrection of the dead in the last day, unwearying and delivered from all weakness of the flesh and spirit, the redeemed shall walk up and down in the new Jerusalem, serving him whose name is written on them, never again sinning against his name, and enjoying the blessedness of him whose name is Jesus for eternity.

---

7 Moore, *Zechariah*, 168.

Chapter 21

THE THIRD STORY:
ZECHARIAH 11:1–17

11:1 Open thy doors, O Lebanon, that the fire may devour thy cedars.

11:2 Howl, fir tree; for the cedar is fallen; because the mighty are spoiled: howl, O ye oaks of Bashan; for the forest of the vintage is come down.

11:3 There is a voice of the howling of the shepherds; for their glory is spoiled: a voice of the roaring of young lions; for the pride of Jordan is spoiled.

11:4 Thus saith the LORD my God; Feed the flock of the slaughter;

11:5 Whose possessors slay them, and hold themselves not guilty: and they that sell them say, Blessed be the LORD; for I am rich: and their own shepherds pity them not.

11:6 For I will no more pity the inhabitants of the land, saith the LORD: but, lo, I will deliver the men every one into his neighbour's hand, and into the hand of his king: and they shall smite the land, and out of their hand I will not deliver them.

11:7 And I will feed the flock of slaughter, even you, O poor of the flock. And I took unto me two staves; the one I called Beauty, and the other I called Bands; and I fed the flock.

11:8 Three shepherds also I cut off in one month; and my soul loathed them, and their soul also abhorred me.

11:9 Then said I, I will not feed you: that that dieth, let it die; and that that is to be cut off, let it be cut off; and let the rest eat every one the flesh of another.

11:10 And I took my staff, even Beauty, and cut it asunder, that I might break my covenant which I had made with all the people.

11:11 And it was broken in that day: and so the poor of the flock that waited upon me knew that it was the word of the LORD.

11:12 And I said unto them, If ye think good, give me my price; and if not, forbear. So they weighed for my price thirty pieces of silver.

11:13 And the LORD said unto me, Cast it unto the potter: a goodly price that I was prised at of them. And I took the thirty pieces of silver, and cast them to the potter in the house of the LORD.

11:14 Then I cut asunder mine other staff, even Bands, that I might break the brotherhood between Judah and Israel.

11:15 And the LORD said unto me, Take unto thee yet the instruments of a foolish shepherd.

11:16 For, lo, I will raise up a shepherd in the land, which shall not visit those that be cut off, neither shall seek the young one, nor heal that that is broken, nor feed that that standeth still: but he shall eat the flesh of the fat, and tear their claws in pieces.

11:17 Woe to the idol shepherd that leaveth the flock! the sword shall be upon his arm, and upon his right eye: his arm shall be clean dried up, and his right eye shall be utterly darkened.

This third and last story passage is in some ways the most important. The other two lead up to and build up to this. As in the other two, this passage presents Christ and his saving work and shows once again that all the promises and comfort of the book depend on him and on his work as savior. It is no wonder that Zechariah 11:11–12 is quoted in Matthew as being fulfilled in the passion of our Lord.

There is development in the passage from the other two story passages. In each case Zechariah enters more and more into the prophetic action, only making a suggestion in the first story passage, setting crowns on Joshua's head in the second, but here becoming the main figure in the action that takes place. There is development also in that this passage shows, through what happens to Zechariah, the heart of Christ's saving work: his rejection and betrayal through which he became the sacrificial lamb who by his suffering and death made atonement for the sins of his people.

The first story passage had showed us Christ symbolically clothed in filthy garments as the one who takes the sins of his people upon himself. In his change of garments he appears as the one who justifies his own. The second story passage showed symbolically his power to deal with sin and to make sacrifice in portraying him as the great priest-king. Now we see him, again symbolically, as the one who justifies and offers sacrifice in the way of deepest humiliation and suffering. He came to his own and was not received, but his rejection became their acceptance.

This third story is also necessary to show the exceeding sinfulness of sin (Rom. 7:13). We cannot see the need for Christ's justifying work as portrayed in the first story passage, or the need for his power and glory as priest-king portrayed in the second story passage, until we also see how we have sinned against him—until we see in this third story passage the truth of Isaiah 53:6, "All we like sheep have gone astray; we have turned every one to his own way; and the LORD hath laid on him the iniquity of us all."

Zechariah 11 has three sections. In the first, verses 1–3, God speaks of impending judgment against his flock. In verses 4–14 God shows the reasons for these judgments: his care for the flock and their rejection of his kindness and love. And then in a vivid description of the giving over of the flock to worthless shepherds (vv. 15–17)—to those whom Jesus refers to in John 10 as hirelings—God shows how these judgments will come.

Yet the amazing thing is that this word of God is fulfilled in Christ in such a way that the end result is the rescue and salvation of the flock. Having heard the word of God in this chapter, one would expect that the rest of the book would be only gloom and judgment, but it is not. The remaining chapters of Zechariah picture in a remarkable and vivid way the future glory of God's flock. The end result of the judgments pictured here will be that the spirit of grace and supplication is poured on the people (12:10), that a fountain is opened to the house of David and to the inhabitants of Jerusalem for sin and for uncleanness (13:1), that a third part of the flock is brought through fire and refined and, calling upon God's name, is assured that they are God's people (13:8–9), and finally that even the horse bridles and the cooking pots are holiness to the Lord (14:20–21).

11:1. Open thy doors, O Lebanon, that the fire may devour thy cedars.

11:2. Howl, fir tree; for the cedar is fallen; because the mighty are spoiled: howl, O ye oaks of Bashan; for the forest of the vintage is come down.

11:3. There is a voice of the howling of the shepherds; for their glory is spoiled: a voice of the roaring of young lions; for the pride of Jordan is spoiled.

The chapter begins with an abrupt change of tone. Suddenly the promises of chapter 10 turn to threats and comfort turns to fear. These threats and judgments are directed at Judah and not the heathen. The story of the rejected shepherd that follows and the mention of Bashan and Lebanon show that God is speaking to Judah. So also in verses 4–6 God speaks not only against the shepherds but also against the sheep, clearly a reference to his people.

This change in tone is noticed by some commentators:

In the utterances of God to his people, the voice of Ebal is always set over against that of Gerizim, and the blessing to faithfulness is enforced by the curse against unfaithfulness. This is necessary, owing to our proneness to sever the blessing from that obedience which is its condition, and expect the one whilst we neglect the other. It is therefore necessary for God to show us that in the same cloud where the rain is treasured there also sleeps the thunderbolt. Hence after promising (chapter 10:1) the refreshing showers, on the condition of fidelity, the prophet now turns to the stormy rush of evils that would come in their place, if they were unfaithful. These evils are described in a highly dramatic form in ch. 11.[1]

This abrupt change of tone that is found all through the prophets is difficult to understand unless one remembers that there are always two groups in the church, as well in the New Testament as in the Old. To the one group, different only by election and grace, belong the promises, and to them the promises are surely fulfilled. Upon the other group the judgments are visited and consummated, so that both the promises and the threats are fully and completely realized.

Bashan and Lebanon are the same as Gilead and Lebanon in chapter 10:10. They represent the farthest corners of the territory of Israel and the richest and most fruitful areas. Lebanon is the might and Bashan is the pride of Israel. The forests of Lebanon and the pastures of Bashan would both be destroyed. As in the days of the kingdom, these areas came first under the judgment of God, though the rest of the land did not escape. The judgments reach beyond Lebanon and Bashan, for the pride of Jordan is also spoiled. The "pride" is the thicket-and tree-lined valley of the Jordan, the river that watered the land of Canaan. The judgment of God would be on everything beautiful, fruitful, and good in Israel.

These judgments come especially through the destruction of the trees, which are often symbolic in scripture of mighty leaders or of the pride and glory of a land. In every case, therefore, God destroys the glory and prosperity of these areas. So complete are these judgments that even the young lions are distressed for lack of prey and left without shelter.

God is not, however, threatening only the land. The cedars of Lebanon and fruitful pastures of Bashan represent also the prosperity and glory of their inhabitants. Both the shepherds and the trees are the leaders of

---

1 Ibid., 169.

Israel who "bemoan the loss of their glory, not the loss of their sheep."[2] The judgment of God comes first upon them and through them upon the whole flock. In Jeremiah 22:6–7 God says to the king of Judah, "Thou art Gilead unto me, and the head of Lebanon: yet surely I will make thee a wilderness, and cities which are not inhabited. And I will prepare destroyers against thee, every one with his weapons: and they shall cut down thy choice cedars, and cast them into the fire." It is even possible, as some commentators suggest, that the lions are the same as the shepherds and describe them as those who prey on the flock rather than feeding it. Shepherds who are also lions would be very much like wolves in sheep's clothing and worthy of God's judgment.

Nor are these judgments, when carried out, merely a destruction of earthly prosperity and glory. They are a picture of what God does spiritually when he executes his just judgments. He then sends spiritual famine (Amos 8:11) and diseases of the soul (Ps. 103:3). Instead of assurance and hope he sends despair and an evil conscience and makes the inner life of the sinner a spiritual wasteland. He humbles all their pride and scatters all possibility of blessing.

The figure is of a storm:

The prophet looks to the north, and sees sweeping down a terrific tempest, that bursts through the rocky ramparts of Lebanon, consumes with its lightnings the lordly cedars, lays waste the lofty monarchs of the forest, and spreads terror and ruin along its track. The cypress is called to tremble, because the mightier cedar has been unable to withstand the shock, and the oaks of Bashan to fear because the dense and firmly knit forest has been prostrated by its rush.[3]

Those judgments, however, are also addressed to the elect remnant, for they are also sinful and in themselves no different from the rest. The word of judgment warns them to turn from their sins to God, and it makes a difference between them and the others. When the elect remnant hear the word of judgment they repent of their sins. The difference is all of grace, but the

2 McComiskey, *Zechariah*, 1188.
3 Moore, *Zechariah*, 170.

THE COMING OF ZION'S REDEEMER

word of judgment is still important and needs to be brought to the church as a body. Leupold says it well: "Promises of future greatness need to be offset by words of judgment against sin lest the gracious words breed carnal pride and a false sense of security."[4]

The promises and comfort of the word also need to be preached in the ears of those who are perishing, for only in that way they become worthy of God's judgment for rejecting his love and mercy. The promises of the word are not for them, as their unbelief and rebellion always proves, but must nevertheless be preached to them so they crucify to themselves the Son of God afresh and put him to an open shame.

The word of God draws a line between these groups and separates them from one another as the wheat from the chaff. Preachers and leaders in the church often think it is their business to make this separation, and so they are constantly addressing one or the other group and suggesting that a particular word applies only to some in the congregation. The whole word must be preached to all alike, and no attempt need be made to separate the sheep from the goats, the remnant from the rest. God will do that part of the work. We cannot do it anyway, for the heart is unknown to us and many of those whom we judge to be elect prove themselves to be otherwise, while many of whom we despair are brought to repentance and faith by God.

The judgments of God threatened in these verses are so sure that Lebanon is summoned to open its gates to them. Resistance is useless!

Most commentators suggest that the reference is to the coming of the Roman legions at the close of the Maccabean era. That may very well be, but to limit the prophecy to those events is to make the prophecy irrelevant to us and to miss the broader scope of the prophecy and its application. It has to do not only with the coming of the Romans, but also with God's judgments as they come on the apostate church in every age. The word of God is a warning against all covenantal unfaithfulness. It threatens the Jews who lived just prior to the birth of Jesus and during the days of his ministry and all those who claim to be God's people and to have a place in his house but will not hear his word and despise those who bring the word.

---

4 Leupold, *Zechariah*, 203.

11:4. Thus saith the LORD my God; Feed the flock of the slaughter;

11:5. Whose possessors slay them, and hold themselves not guilty: and they that sell them say, Blessed be the LORD; for I am rich: and their own shepherds pity them not.

11:6. For I will no more pity the inhabitants of the land, saith the LORD: but, lo, I will deliver the men every one into his neighbour's hand, and into the hand of his king: and they shall smite the land, and out of their hand I will not deliver them.

Here begins the second part of the chapter, Zechariah's commission as shepherd of God's people. Commentators argue about whether the events of this passage really happened or not, but in the end that makes little difference. Whether Zechariah received a special commission as shepherd of Judah and whether his work as prophetic shepherd was actually rejected by the Jews of his day we do not know. Not all prophetic actions were carried out, Jeremiah 25:15 being a good example.

What evidence there is suggests a story completely symbolic. There is no record of such unfaithfulness in the books of Ezra and Nehemiah, nor anywhere else in the book of Zechariah. Rather the sacred record would seem to indicate that at least at this point in history the people had responded to the word of God and were busy with the work of rebuilding the temple. Haggai, Zechariah's contemporary, makes reference to their repentance and renewed faithfulness.

What matters is that the story of Zechariah's rejection as the shepherd of God's people reveals their sinfulness and need of redemption and reveals further the miracle of God's grace in turning their sins and evil deeds to good—in his sovereign majesty using even their evil deeds to work out the redemption of his people. He uses their wicked hands to do what his hand and counsel had determined before to be done (Acts 2:23; 4:27–28). In the way of their rejecting and despising their shepherd, God lays their iniquity on the shepherd and takes it all away (Isa. 53:4–6).

Zechariah as prophet had a commission from God from the very beginning of his prophetic career. The repeated statement in the prophecy, "and ye shall know that the LORD of hosts hath sent me unto you" (2:9, 11; 4:9; 6:15) refers to his commission. Whether he had at some point a special commission to feed the flock makes no real difference. It is in the role of prophetic shepherd that he is rejected and makes another picture of Christ, and it is what happened to Christ, not to Zechariah, that really matters.

He is called to feed "the flock of the slaughter." God calls his flock by that name, a name that refers to judgments that will come on the flock. It is destined for slaughter and so destined because it is worthless. God receives neither meat nor wool nor milk from the flock. That slaughter is further described in the last verses of the chapter. God there consigns his flock to the care of a foolish shepherd who does not care for the flock and does not even visit it except to kill and eat the sheep.

When God speaks of his flock this way, he shows he has no hope that Zechariah's work will be of any use in the flock. He knew ahead of time that they would abhor Zechariah for his work as shepherd, insult him, and send him away. He knew that as the one who decreed all things from eternity and who carries them out by his sovereign power.

Yet he sent Zechariah to the flock and did so for two reasons. The greater part of the flock, described in chapter 13:8 as two-thirds, would show themselves through the work of Zechariah to be without excuse and worthy of God's judgments. And yet through the flock's rejection of their shepherd the third part would be saved (13:8–9).

When we understand that the word of God is really speaking of Christ, all makes sense and Zechariah and the question of the historical nature of the passage fade into the background. It does not matter whether Zechariah's ministry was rejected by the Jews of his day. Christ, whom he represents, would be despised and rejected of men, and thus every word of God, both of judgment and of salvation, would be fulfilled.

God speaks in chapter 11:3 of other shepherds who had misled and fleeced his flock. These were the priests and prophets who sought only their own well-being, caring nothing for God or for his church. That there were such in the days of Zechariah's prophecy is clear from Nehemiah 5:1–13, where Nehemiah rebukes the nobles and rulers for forcing the people to sell themselves, their children, and their lands in order to pay the king's taxes in a time of famine. The word of God through Zechariah was literally true: their shepherds sold them and were without pity.

The complaint of the people, directed against their own rulers, was as follows:

> 3. Some also there were that said, We have mortgaged our lands, vineyards, and houses, that we might buy corn, because of the dearth.
> 4. There were also that said, We have borrowed money for the king's tribute, and that upon our lands and vineyards.
> 5. Yet now our flesh is as the flesh of our brethren, our children as their children: and, lo, we bring into bondage our sons and our daughters to be servants, and some of our daughters are brought unto bondage already: neither is it in our power to redeem them; for other men have our lands and vineyards. (Neh. 5:3–5)

Such is the historical background of Zechariah's prophecy. What a picture it is of the church world today, full of leaders whose only interest is their own profit. These are the leaders who demand huge fees for bringing lies and nonsense to the people, who are able to fund and support massive television ministries by fleecing the people who follow them, who promise peace and prosperity in order to make themselves wealthy, who sell the grace of God as Rome does for money, who steal the pennies of widows. They say exactly what God puts in their mouths through his prophet: "Bless the LORD, for I am rich."

Nor do they show any mercy or care for the flock. Pastoral work, the work of caring for the spiritual needs of God's people, is beneath their dignity. Caring for and comforting the sick, visiting the widows, helping and assisting God's people in their struggles are beneath their exalted dignity. Indeed, one cannot even get near them, unless it be on a public stage and for their advantage.

Yet the people themselves are also to blame, as chapter 11:6 indicates. They are to blame for following these false shepherds, for being without discernment and knowledge. Their sin is not specifically stated in verse 6 but becomes evident in their rejection of Zechariah's work as shepherd and through him of God's care. They prefer shepherds who feed them with lies, fleece them, and prey on them, prophets who speak smooth things, priests who encourage them in their coldness and formalism, and leaders who lead them astray. They would rather wander and perish than be led in the right way, for that way is narrow and difficult. How true the words of Jeremiah: "A wonderful and horrible thing is committed in the land; The prophets prophesy falsely, and the priests bear rule by their means; and my people love to have it so: and what will ye do in the end thereof?" (Jer. 5:30–31).

The truth of Zechariah's words can be seen in many modern churches. They do not want and would not accept a faithful shepherd but would do to him the same thing these Jews did to Zechariah. They do not want someone who brings them the word of God and who tries to feed them the good spiritual food of the word. They are addicted to spiritual junk food, and that is all they will have.

No one can say, "I am different. I am not like them." We are all as sheep gone astray (Isa. 53:6; 1 Pet. 2:25), and it is only because the Lord has laid on *him* the iniquity of us all that any part at all of the flock is saved. False shepherds and hirelings or strayed sheep, such are we all. Hearing the word of God through Zechariah, we can only hang our foolish woolly heads in shame and humbly thank God for the Shepherd he has given us and for the work of our good Shepherd.

Zechariah is given this work of a shepherd not because there is the possibility that the judgment threatened will be withdrawn if his work is successful, but to show that Israel deserves these judgments. Their rejection of Zechariah's work, prophetic of their rejection of Christ, proves them to be ripe for judgment. The picture would be very dark indeed were it not for the fact, suggested in what follows, that there were a few, referred to in verses 7 and 11 as the "poor of the flock," who would hear and heed Zechariah's words and recognize that he was sent by God.

This elect remnant would be saved and would be in Zechariah's day, as in the days of Christ's ministry and in the history of the apostolic church, the proof of the word of God in Romans 11:5, "Even so then at this present time also there is a remnant according to the election of grace." Though they were poor and few, it was especially for their sakes that Zechariah is sent.

The passage is similar to and has the same message as the parable of the vineyard (Matt. 21:33–46), in which God is represented as a householder who lets out his vineyard to husbandmen (Israel and Judah) and sends his servants (the prophets) to receive the fruits of the vineyard. These servants were beaten and stoned and killed by the husbandmen until "last of all he sent unto them his son, saying, They will reverence my son. But when the husbandmen saw the son, they said among themselves, This is the heir; come, let us kill him, and let us seize on his inheritance. And they caught him, and cast him out of the vineyard, and slew him" (vv. 37–39).

The parable concludes with Jesus' question, "When the lord therefore of the vineyard cometh, what will he do unto those husbandmen?" (v. 40). The answer of the Jews and Jesus' response are telling:

41. They say unto him, He will miserably destroy those wicked men, and will let out his vineyard unto other husbandmen, which shall render him the fruits in their seasons.
42. Jesus saith unto them, Did ye never read in the scriptures, The stone which the builders rejected, the same is become the head of the corner: this is the Lord's doing, and it is marvellous in our eyes?
43. Therefore say I unto you, The kingdom of God shall be taken from you, and given to a nation bringing forth the fruits thereof.
44. And whosoever shall fall on this stone shall be broken: but on whomsoever it shall fall, it will grind him to powder. (Matt. 21:41–44)

Recognizing themselves in the parable and its application, the Jews were all the more eager to kill Jesus, and so again they fulfilled Zechariah's prophecy.

11:7. And I will feed the flock of slaughter, even you, O poor of the flock. And I took unto me two staves; the one I called Beauty, and the other I called Bands; and I fed the flock.
11:8. Three shepherds also I cut off in one month; and my soul loathed them, and their soul also abhorred me.

Having been called by God to feed the flock of slaughter, Zechariah accepts his commission and busies himself with the work. It is he who speaks here to the flock, especially to the poor of the flock, showing himself immediately to be one who does care for them and not only for himself. An important test of the faithfulness of those who are called to be leaders of God's people is their attitude toward and work among the weak, the poor, those who have no other help—those, in other words, from whom they can gain no temporal or financial advantage. It is characteristic of those who are unfaithful shepherds that the rich and those who have a name among their fellow men are their first concern. All shepherds of God's people ought to be like Zechariah.

As part of his shepherd's work among the people, Zechariah takes two shepherd's staves and names them Beauty and Bands, or more literally, Beauty and Unity. The first word is used to describe anything that is pleasant and desirable and is used in Psalm 27:4 and Psalm 90:17 to describe the Lord himself. The second word is from a root that refers to the twisting together of the fibers of a rope. With these names for his staves Zechariah further describes the nature of his work among the people.

His staves would not be used to beat and kill the sheep, but to make them beautiful and to keep them together. He would seek their well-being and promote unity among them. As shepherd he promises in the names of his staves to be a good and faithful shepherd interested only in the prosperity and unity of the flock. He would not let the sheep wander and go astray from the flock, nor would he starve and neglect them, but he would feed them, bind up their wounds, and keep them healthy and beautiful. He assures us too that at least prophetically he actually did that work among the people. "I fed the flock," he says, something every shepherd ought to be able to say when he stands before the chief Shepherd to give account.

In naming one of his staves Bands, Zechariah also promises to seek the unity of the two divided kingdoms, and that in light of God's word in chapter 10, where God shows that this division was the result of sin and not recognized by him. How Zechariah actually did this work we do not know. Perhaps he encouraged the scattered sheep of the ten tribes to join with those of Judah who returned in the work of rebuilding God's house. In any case, he showed himself in all respects a faithful shepherd.

As part of his work he also got rid of some of the unfaithful shepherds who had misled and scattered the flock. Who the three were to whom he refers we do not know, nor do we know what they had done or not done, or how Zechariah cut them off. Perhaps, as priest, he forbad them any part in the work of rebuilding God's house or any part in the worship of God, effectively excommunicating them. What we do know is that he did all he could to deliver the flock from such shepherds.

The reference to three shepherds is understood by many commentators to refer not to three persons but to the three offices of prophet, priest, and king in which the leaders of the people functioned. That may very well be, but the passage nevertheless shows us that Zechariah's work as a faithful shepherd included the work of saving the flock from their rapacious leaders. If that interpretation is correct, then it points also to the coming of Christ, who would come in the place of the kings, priests, and prophets who for so long had led God's people astray. The month is symbolic of the time Zechariah's prophecies were fulfilled during the days of Christ's ministry.

Again we do not even know if this happened in fact or only prophetically, but that such questions are unanswered and unanswerable reminds us again that it is not really Zechariah and what he did that matters, but what Christ, the real shepherd of the sheep, does for the flock. He it is who does everything necessary for the unity of the flock, who feeds them with the word of God and leads them beside the still waters of God's grace. He alone makes the flock beautiful by washing each sheep in his own blood. He forever delivers the flock from hirelings and wolves. He is our unity and peace, our beauty and bands, our glory and salvation. Hengstenberg says:

> The extermination of the three shepherds is not to be regarded as a single act, like the expiation, but as a continuous act, which occupies *some time*. It sets before us in an appropriate manner *the repeated efforts on the part of Christ, to deliver the poor nation, the lost sheep of the house of Israel, from the spiritual tyranny of its blind and corrupt guides.*[5]

Between Zechariah and the unfaithful shepherds and therefore between Christ and such shepherds there exists an implacable enmity, an enmity displayed on both sides. In his love for God's flock, Zechariah could not help but show his loathing for those who were only interested in their own

---

5 Hengstenberg, *Christology*, 4:30.

well-being. In that he pictures the work of Christ in condemning the hypocrisy of the scribes and Pharisees and wicked leaders always. And just as Christ loathed them, so did they loathe him. In their loathing they called him the agent of Beelzebub, rejected him, denied his miracles, stirred up the people against him, and killed him.

It is further fulfilled in the disgust every faithful church leader feels when he thinks of those who abuse and destroy God's flock, and in the contempt that is shown by these spiritual princes for every godly pastor, elder, and leader of God's people.

We do not read that the unfaithful shepherds stirred up the people against Zechariah, but there can be little doubt that what follows, the story of his rejection as shepherd, was at least in part the result of their machinations. People like them do not change and are the same in every age, doing what they can to destroy the reputation of those who are faithful, stirring up the people against them, slandering and despising them. This is implied in what follows, Zechariah's resignation and rejection as shepherd.

11:9. Then said I, I will not feed you: that that dieth, let it die; and that that is to be cut off, let it be cut off; and let the rest eat every one the flesh of another.

It might seem at first that Zechariah, who speaks here, was following the example of the unfaithful shepherds and abandoning the flock, but it is clear in what follows that this was "the word of the Lord," God's judgment on a worthless flock, and the result of the flock's rejection of Zechariah as their shepherd. Verse 9 is Zechariah's resignation. Having put forth every effort to feed them and care for them and having suffered only rejection, Zechariah, with God's permission, resigns his office as shepherd. There is no evidence that this actually happened except symbolically and prophetically, but it was nevertheless a picture of what happens in the church when the church rejects the word of God.

This judgment is expressed first in terms of a flock without a shepherd, the sheep uncared for and perishing, but then also in terms of the Mosaic code, which threatened famine and such famine that the people would resort to cannibalism to stay alive—the sheep would become carnivores and devour each other. God takes away the shepherds and the flock destroys itself.

Not only does the church, in rejecting the work of those whom God sends her, remain unfed spiritually; not only do the people of God perish for lack of knowledge; not only are they cut off from peace and blessing; but eventually they also turn on one another and devour one another. When the word of God is not present, the lies and slanders and evil words of men gain the upper hand, and the warning of Paul, unheeded, comes to pass: "For all the law is fulfilled in one word, even in this; Thou shalt love thy neighbour as thyself. But if ye bite and devour one another, take heed that ye be not consumed one of another. This I say then, Walk in the Spirit, and ye shall not fulfil the lust of the flesh" (Gal. 5:14–16).

Verse 9 does not give leave to every shepherd to resign his work because of its disappointments and discouragements. It is, however, a promise that God will take away from his flock faithful shepherds if the sheep reject and despise the word those shepherds bring. He will send them a famine of the word and will, as the rest of the chapter shows, give them over once again to false shepherds and hirelings.

Calvin's prayer at the end of his commentary on this section of Zechariah is apropos:

Grant, Almighty God, that as thou hast hitherto so kindly showed thyself to be our Shepherd, and even our Father, and hast carefully provided for our safety, —O grant, that we may not by our ingratitude deprive ourselves of thy favours, so as to provoke thy extreme vengeance, but on the contrary suffer ourselves to be gently ruled by thee, and render thee due obedience: and as thine only-begotten Son has been by thee set over us as our only true Shepherd, may we hear his voice, and willingly obey him, so that we may be able to triumph with thy Prophet, that thy staff is sufficient for us, so as to enable us to walk without fear through the valley of the shadow of death, until we shall at length reach that blessed and eternal rest, which has been obtained for us by the blood of thine only Son.—Amen.[6]

---

6 Calvin, *Commentaries on the Twelve Minor Prophets*, 5:314.

11:10. And I took my staff, even Beauty, and cut it asunder, that I might break my covenant which I had made with all the people.

11:11. And it was broken in that day: and so the poor of the flock that waited upon me knew that it was the word of the LORD.

That Zechariah's resignation was the will of God was evident in the breaking of one of his shepherd's staves, the one named Beauty. He resigned his commission, and he did so in such a way that at least some of the flock saw that this was the will and word of God. By cutting that staff in half he broke his covenant with the people, not with Israel but with the nations around them. This covenant with the people can only be a reference to God's protecting care for Israel in protecting them from the nations. That covenant would be broken and the flock exposed to their enmity. Thus too the beauty of the flock would be destroyed.

How some of the people saw the breaking of Zechariah's staff as evidence that he spoke according to God's will is not so easy to understand. Very likely a staff of office, like the staff of Moses, was such an important symbol of God's authority and power that a faithful shepherd would not dare break it except with God's permission or by God's command. Those who knew Zechariah to be a faithful shepherd would know, then, that his resignation was God's will.

When the staff named Beauty was broken by Zechariah, it must have showed the hopelessness, humanly speaking, that characterized his work as shepherd. Apart from a miracle of grace, there was no possibility that the flock would ever be beautiful. Nevertheless, only one staff is broken at first, and though that is not mentioned here, the breaking of only one must have been a sign of hope to those few poor of the flock who waited on Zechariah.

The cutting of this first staff would eventually mean that God's special favor toward the Jews would come to an end. They as a nation would no longer be his chosen people, and the privileges they had so long enjoyed would be taken from them. The breaking of the staff named Beauty indirectly prophesies the sending of the gospel and its blessings to the Gentile nations in the New Testament.

The presence of these poor of the flock and their waiting upon Zechariah also shows that his work had not been entirely in vain. There were those who had been fed, who desired the word of the Lord and recognized Zechariah's prophecies as the word of God. Still sheep, they were nevertheless different from the others as a fruit of Zechariah's work. They are the remnant of the flock described in chapter 13:9, "And I will bring the third part through the fire, and will refine them as silver is refined, and will try them as gold is tried: they shall call on my name, and I will hear them: I will say, It is my people: and they shall say, The LORD is my God."

All this is in direct reference to Christ. He came in obedience to the will of God to be the shepherd of the sheep, but the flock of God, as represented by the nation of Israel, rejected that shepherd except for a few of the poorest of the people, fishermen, tax collectors, and harlots. Thus the judgment of God was pronounced on the nation by Christ himself:

21. Woe unto thee, Chorazin! woe unto thee, Bethsaida! for if the mighty works, which were done in you, had been done in Tyre and Sidon, they would have repented long ago in sackcloth and ashes. 22. But I say unto you, It shall be more tolerable for Tyre and Sidon at the day of judgment, than for you. 23. And thou, Capernaum, which art exalted unto heaven, shalt be brought down to hell: for if the mighty works, which have been done in thee, had been done in Sodom, it would have remained until this day. 24. But I say unto you, That it shall be more tolerable for the land of Sodom in the day of judgment, than for thee. (Matt. 11:21–24)

34. Wherefore, behold, I send unto you prophets, and wise men, and scribes: and some of them ye shall kill and crucify; and some of them shall ye scourge in your synagogues, and persecute them from city to city: 35. That upon you may come all the righteous blood shed upon the earth, from the blood of righteous Abel unto the blood of Zacharias son of Barachias, whom ye slew between the temple and the altar. 36. Verily I say unto you, All these things shall come upon this generation. 37. O Jerusalem, Jerusalem, thou that killest the prophets, and stonest them which are sent unto thee, how often would I have

gathered thy children together, even as a hen gathereth her chickens under her wings, and ye would not!

38. Behold, your house is left unto you desolate. (Matt. 23:34–38)

11:12. And I said unto them, If ye think good, give me my price; and if not, forbear. So they weighed for my price thirty pieces of silver.

Having resigned his place as shepherd, Zechariah also asks for his wages, not because he was interested in monetary gain but as proof of their wickedness and hypocrisy. We know he was not interested in the wages for their own sake by his suggestion that if they preferred not to pay him, that was acceptable. He asks for wages because he understood that the wages they gave him would show their estimation of his ministry among them, as was indeed the case. The fact of the matter was that his ministry was priceless inasmuch as he brought them the word and will of God, full of the promises of the gospel and heavy with its testimony to God's mercy, goodness, and faithfulness.

The price they give him is a calculated insult that shows as nothing else could have their attitude toward his ministry, toward the word of God that he brought, and toward God himself who sent Zechariah. The thirty pieces of silver they gave him were the price of a dead slave (Ex. 21:32). In their eyes he had no more value than that! His whole ministry was not even worth the price of a living slave. It would have been better if they had given him nothing. Their rejection of his ministry could be charitably ascribed to carelessness or forgetfulness otherwise, but the thirty pieces of silver show their hatred of him and all he stood for.

Matthew 26:14–16 and 27:3–10 remind us that this was prophetic, fulfilled in the betrayal of Jesus by Judas.

14. Then one of the twelve, called Judas Iscariot, went unto the chief priests,

15. And said unto them, What will ye give me, and I will deliver him unto you? And they covenanted with him for thirty pieces of silver.

16. And from that time he sought opportunity to betray him.

3. Then Judas, which had betrayed him, when he saw that he was condemned, repented himself, and brought again the thirty pieces of silver to the chief priests and elders,

4. Saying, I have sinned in that I have betrayed the innocent blood. And they said, What is that to us? see thou to that.

5. And he cast down the pieces of silver in the temple, and departed, and went and hanged himself.

6. And the chief priests took the silver pieces, and said, It is not lawful for to put them into the treasury, because it is the price of blood.

7. And they took counsel, and bought with them the potter's field, to bury strangers in.

8. Wherefore that field was called, The field of blood, unto this day.

9. Then was fulfilled that which was spoken by Jeremy the prophet, saying, And they took the thirty pieces of silver, the price of him that was valued, whom they of the children of Israel did value;

10. And gave them for the potter's field, as the Lord appointed me.

The word of God in Matthew 27 and the quotation from Zechariah's prophecy show us that the Jews who crucified Jesus had the same attitude toward his ministry as their fathers did toward the ministry of Zechariah. In Jesus' case as well as in Zechariah's the thirty pieces of silver were a deliberate and calculated insult. Though given to Judas and not to Jesus, though given as the price of betrayal and not wages, the thirty pieces of silver showed the hatred of the scribes and Pharisees and Sadducees for Jesus and showed how completely they rejected his ministry and miracles. He was of no more use or value to them than a dead slave.

Having pronounced judgment on an ungodly nation, Christ receives his wages and the Jews show what they think of him in the price offered Judas, the price of a condemned slave. Through Judas he says to them: "Give me my price." They weigh for his price thirty pieces of silver, an insult to him and to God who sent him, so that the money is cast away, again through Judas as the agent of a sovereign Christ, to the potter for the purchase of his field.

The irony is that in both cases the actions of these unbelieving Jews were prophetic. They meant it as an insult and will have to pay for the insult they gave to God's Son, but in the providence and sovereignty of God there was a terrible truth as well in those thirty pieces of silver. Jesus was indeed, as the sin bearer, of no more value than a dead slave and would suffer the ignominious death of one who was worthless. He was in God's sight as the sin bearer worth no more and was by God himself sold as a dead slave inasmuch as the Lord had laid on him the iniquity of us all. God, however, meant it not as a deadly insult, but as part of his inscrutably wise way of delivering his people, those who are in themselves insulters and despisers of his own, only begotten Son.

There is a difficulty here, however. Matthew ascribes these words to Jeremiah and not to Zechariah, and there is nothing in the prophecies of Jeremiah as we have them that at all resembles this word of God. Those who do not believe in the inspiration of scripture are quick to suggest that Matthew erred, though even if that were possible it is difficult to believe that a Jew like Matthew could make such a horrendous mistake, or having made it would not have quickly corrected it.

Various solutions to the problem have been suggested, but one thing must be clear: there are no mistakes in the word of God, and this is not a mistake. Any acceptable explanation must take that into account. It would be better to admit of having no explanation than to call the inspiration of scripture into question.

Explanations that do take the inspiration of scripture into account say that, though not found in scripture, this prophecy was first delivered by Jeremiah, something not impossible in view of other similarities between Jeremiah and Zechariah. Others say that in the Jewish scrolls various books were written together and called by the name of one of the books. This would have been quoted, then, from a section named "Jeremiah" but including various other prophetic books. The latter is not impossible in that the book of Lamentations was sometimes included in Jeremiah and the books like 1 and 2 Chronicles were written together as one book. A third explanation connects this prophecy with Jeremiah 18:2–6 and says that Matthew is quoting from both Jeremiah and Zechariah, though he only names Jeremiah. Any of these explanations are acceptable in that they do not deny the inspiration of scripture, but the emphasis must fall on what is said, not on the question of who said it, for it is in the end neither the word of Zechariah nor of Jeremiah, but of God.

11:13. And the LORD said unto me, Cast it unto the potter: a goodly price that I was prised at of them. And I took the thirty pieces of silver, and cast them to the potter in the house of the LORD.
11:14. Then I cut asunder mine other staff, even Bands, that I might break the brotherhood between Judah and Israel.

Some might object that Matthew does not even quote Zechariah accurately, for Zechariah is commanded to throw the thirty pieces of silver to the potter, while the money paid to Judas and returned by him was not thrown to the potter but was used to purchase a field in the vicinity of Jerusalem for the burial of strangers, known even today as a "potter's field."

There is no reason to make a division between Zechariah and Matthew and to magnify minor differences in such a way that the message of the word of God is obscured or forgotten. That Zechariah speaks of the potter and Matthew of the potter's field is a very minor difference. Who is to say in light of Zechariah's prophecy that the field purchased with Judas's betrayal money was not purchased from a potter, and by the same token that the money Zechariah gave to the potter was not used to purchase a field?

That Zechariah cast the thirty pieces of silver to the potter in the house of the Lord means that this was a public action designed to show the wickedness of the people. Indeed, that Zechariah cast the silver to the potter in the house of the Lord serves to emphasize even more powerfully the prophetic character of his action, for Judas also cast his thirty pieces of silver down in the temple. How in Zechariah's case they came into the possession of the potter is not stated, but it is not unlikely that they were used to purchase from the potter his field.

The point of the passage is that God recognizes the insult given to his prophet and shows his displeasure by having Zechariah give the money away and by seeing to it that the betrayal money was used to purchase a cemetery for strangers. The reference to a goodly price is ironic, and the punctuation of the KJV is probably correct in indicating that the words "a goodly price that I was prised at of them" are spoken by God. He, not Zechariah, was the one whose value they had assessed at the price of a dead slave. He was the one they had insulted and rejected. He was the one whose words they despised.

To show what he thinks of their actions Zechariah breaks his other staff, prophesying that Judah and Israel would not be united but broken and scattered by the judgment of God. Thus does Zechariah finish his work, and thus does God wash his hands of these wicked and unrepentant Jews. They would be scattered, and the unity pictured in that staff would be found not between Judah and Israel but between the remnant of the Jews and the Gentiles in the New Testament church. Thus also does Christ conclude his work among the unbelieving Jews of his own day.

11:15. And the LORD *said unto me, Take unto thee yet the instruments of a foolish shepherd.*

11:16. For, lo, I will raise up a shepherd in the land, which shall not visit those that be cut off, neither shall seek the young one, nor heal that that is broken, nor feed that that standeth still: but he shall eat the flesh of the fat, and tear their claws in pieces.

In this concluding section God surrenders wicked Israel to the same shepherds who had led them astray, starved them, and oppressed them. He gives them what they wanted, but in so doing brings upon them his wrath. God does this often. When he gave Israel meat in the wilderness, he gave them what they had cried for but gave it in his anger, an anger that brought leanness into their souls while their mouths were filled with meat (Ps. 106:15). "Sin is always folly, and the sinner always a fool, for he secures the great evil of punishment in exchange for the small good of gratification, and therefore always makes a fool's bargain."[7]

There is a lesson in this for those who think that getting what they want is a sign of God's approval and blessing and for those who think that earthly prosperity and health are the only things to pray for and are invariably a sign of God's favor. Psalm 106:15 and the word of God through Zechariah prove that it is not so. We cannot judge God's attitude toward us by what we receive

---

7 Moore, *Zechariah*, 186.

from him in terms of temporal things. His attitude toward us can only be judged in light of his word, and especially that word that promises favor and blessing to those who keep his commandments and walk in his way.

Zechariah, as a sign of what God would do, is commanded to take the instruments of a foolish shepherd to show the people what kind of shepherds they would have from then on. The instruments of a foolish shepherd must have been tools or instruments of such a kind that the man who tried to use them would be unable to do the work of a shepherd, would only harm the sheep, and would bring on himself the ridicule of anyone who witnessed his efforts. Perhaps one can think of a shepherd trying to guide and catch and help the sheep with a broken staff, such as the two staves Zechariah had broken, or to care for them with a club instead of a staff. These staves may in fact be what the passage is referring to, but in any case the instruments would make it impossible for the shepherd to do anything of use for the sheep. As a result of these foolish shepherds and their efforts, the people would not be cared for, helped, or protected, but left to the mercy of their enemies.

These false shepherds not only refuse to care for the poor and sick, they do not even care for the strong and healthy! The words "that that standeth still" mean literally that "which is able to stand" or "the strong." These shepherds are such fools that they bestow no care even upon that which promises to be of profit and that which requires little effort on their part. They are only interested in making themselves fat, and to do that they "tear the claws in pieces," that is, they break the hoofs to extract that last bit of marrow and fat for themselves.

These false shepherds include every religious leader and teacher who teaches anything but the truth of God's word. But ultimately, as Pusey reminds us, that foolish shepherd into whose care God consigns his flock in judgment is antichrist, who comes in the guise of a shepherd but who leads his followers to hell! No wonder the false prophet described in Revelation 13:11 as part of the rise of the antichristian kingdom has the horns of a lamb, though he speaks with the voice of the dragon!

11:17. Woe to the idol shepherd that leaveth the flock! the sword shall be upon his arm, and upon his right eye: his arm shall be clean dried up, and his right eye shall be utterly darkened.

In spite of the fact that these foolish shepherds were the instruments of God's anger, his judgment would come on them also. That is always God's way. He uses the ungodly to chastise and punish, but he punishes them also when they have executed his vengeance and wrath for their own ends and without any thought of his honor. Thus Jeroboam was punished for leading the ten tribes away from Solomon, though he was God's means of chastising Solomon (1 Kings 14:7–11). Thus Baasha was punished in turn for his part in destroying the house of Jeroboam (1 Kings 16:1–4). Thus Jehu and his house were punished for destroying the house of Ahab, and thus the kings of Babylon and Assyria were punished for their part in scattering Judah and Israel. Though Assyria was the axe with which God hewed down Israel, yet because the axe exalted itself against him who wielded it, the axe in turn was punished:

5. O Assyrian, the rod of mine anger, and the staff in their hand is mine indignation.
6. I will send him against an hypocritical nation, and against the people of my wrath will I give him a charge, to take the spoil, and to take the prey, and to tread them down like the mire of the streets.
7. Howbeit he meaneth not so, neither doth his heart think so; but it is in his heart to destroy and cut off nations not a few.
8. For he saith, Are not my princes altogether kings?
9. Is not Calno as Carchemish? is not Hamath as Arpad? is not Samaria as Damascus?
10. As my hand hath found the kingdoms of the idols, and whose graven images did excel them of Jerusalem and of Samaria;
11. Shall I not, as I have done unto Samaria and her idols, so do to Jerusalem and her idols?
12. Wherefore it shall come to pass, that when the Lord hath performed his whole work upon mount Zion and on Jerusalem, I will punish the fruit of the stout heart of the king of Assyria, and the glory of his high looks.
13. For he saith, By the strength of my hand I have done it, and by my wisdom; for I am prudent: and I have removed the bounds of

the people, and have robbed their treasures, and I have put down
the inhabitants like a valiant man:

14. And my hand hath found as a nest the riches of the people:
and as one gathereth eggs that are left, have I gathered all the
earth; and there was none that moved the wing, or opened the
mouth, or peeped.

15. Shall the axe boast itself against him that heweth therewith?
or shall the saw magnify itself against him that shaketh it? as if the
rod should shake itself against them that lift it up, or as if the staff
should lift up itself, as if it were no wood.

16. Therefore shall the Lord, the Lord of hosts, send among his fat
ones leanness; and under his glory he shall kindle a burning like
the burning of a fire. (Isa. 10:5–16)

That the sword of God's justice is upon the shepherd's arm and right eye
is explained by the church father Jerome to signify

the eye, whereby he shall boast to behold acutely the mysteries of
God, and to see more than all prophets heretofore, so that he shall
call himself son of God. But the word of the Lord shall be upon his
arm and upon his right eye, so that his strength and all his boast of
might shall be dried up, and the knowledge which he promised himself falsely, shall be obscured in everlasting darkness.[8]

But there is this too: the eye that did not watch out for the good of the
flock and the arm that made no effort to protect the flock are in exquisite
justice the first objects of God's fury.

In all this God's perfect justice is displayed, his will accomplished, and
by a miracle of grace and mercy the salvation of his people worked out. Thus
all things work together for good to those who love God and for evil to those
who hate him. Thus his sovereign purpose in election and reprobation is
brought to pass, and he receives all the honor. "For of him, and through him,
and to him, are all things: to whom be glory for ever" (Rom. 11:36).

---

8 Quoted in Pusey, *The Minor Prophets*, 2:431.

Chapter 22

THE SECOND BURDEN:
Zechariah 12:1–14:21

The second burden corresponds to and parallels the last three visions, the visions that follow the vision and story of the reclothing of Joshua. There are especially two points of resemblance. First, the Spirit of God is the main figure in the last three visions and in the second burden. In the visions he appears as the Spirit who empowers God's people to their work; here in the burdens he appears as the Spirit of grace and supplication. That is the main difference between vision and burden. Just as Christ appears in the first three visions and in the first burden both in his exalted glory and in his humiliation, so the Spirit appears in all his fullness as the Spirit of glory and of humiliation.

The other similarity is that the second burden, like the last three visions, is concerned more closely with the nation of Israel and the relation between righteous and wicked, believer and unbeliever in the nation, rather than with the relation between Israel and the other nations. Israel and the nations are the subject of the first three visions and the first burden. Redeemed Israel and carnal Israel are the subject of the last three visions and the second burden. This is evident from the introductory words of each burden. The first is the burden of the word of the Lord upon the land of Hadrach; this is the burden of the word of the Lord concerning Israel.

The second burden is divided into three parts that are parallel to the last three visions. Part one of the second burden is parallel to the sixth vision of the flying scroll and the woman in a basket and shows God's judgment on apostate Israel. Part two of the second burden is parallel to the fifth vision of

350

the olive trees and the candlestick and testifies of the presence of God's Spirit in the church. The order is reversed: the work of the Spirit first and then judgment on apostate Israel in the visions and the opposite order in this burden. Part three, the last part of the second burden, is parallel to the seventh and last vision of the chariots coming out from between two mountains of brass and, like that vision, looks ahead to the eternal blessedness of the church and shows in marvelous terms the glory that God has prepared for his own.

The two sets of visions and the two burdens are separated by wonderful revelations of Christ, Christ the justified one in chapter 3, and Christ the rejected shepherd in chapter 11. He, in his saving work, is central to these revelations.

One important feature of the second burden is its emphasis on the day of the Lord, an important theme in these last three chapters. Ten times "that day" is referred to in chapters 12 and 13, and then chapter 14 picks up the theme once again, referring to "that day" another ten times. "That day" is the day of the Lord, the day of judgment and salvation, the short time in which God finishes his work and cuts it short in righteousness (Rom. 9:28). In that day separation is made between the righteous and the wicked even in the nation of Israel, the church. It is the day in which everlasting blessedness is ushered in. That day is the whole New Testament looked at from the viewpoint of God's finished work climaxing in the second coming of Christ.

It is viewed as a day because it is a short time on God's clock of history and because it is all about one event, the coming of Christ for judgment and for salvation. The Old Testament prophets saw that more clearly than we do. We live in the middle of that day and see it stretching backward and forward for thousands of years. They did not see those thousands of years and from their Old Testament perspective could not even distinguish between the first and second comings of Christ, which mark the beginning and end of that day.

The fulfillment of the things prophesied in chapters 12–14 must not, then, be limited to any one period in the history of the New Testament church or one Old Testament event. Jerome says:

For some of the Jews say that these things have already been fulfilled in part from Zorobabel to Pompey who, first of the Romans, took Judaea and the temple, as Josephus relates. Others think that it is to be fulfilled at the end of the world, when Jerusalem shall be restored...But others, i.e. we who are called by the name of Christ, say that these things are daily fulfilled, and will be fulfilled in the Church to the end of the world.[1]

The work of the Spirit of Christ as the Spirit of grace and supplication, however, is the focus of this burden. He is the one who makes the remnant different from the rest and whose work draws the line between those in Israel and in the church who are under God's judgments and those who escape those judgments and receive God's blessing. The difference between the two groups is the work of the Spirit.

As a result of his work not all reject the Shepherd. By his grace the poor of the flock recognize the word of God and obey it. Through him as the Spirit of supplication some, no more worthy in themselves than the rest, distinguish themselves by repenting of their sin and unfaithfulness. In chapter 4:6, God had said, "Not by might, nor by power, but by my Spirit," and lest we forget, he says it again here, though in different words. "Not by might, nor by power, but by my Spirit" is shown here to be the equivalent of "by grace alone in the way of repentance and cleansing of sin."

---

1 Quoted in Pusey, *The Minor Prophets*, 2:432.

Chapter 23

THE SECOND BURDEN, PART 1:
Zechariah 12:1–9

12:1 The burden of the word of the Lord for Israel, saith the Lord, which stretcheth forth the heavens, and layeth the foundation of the earth, and formeth the spirit of man within him.

12:2 Behold, I will make Jerusalem a cup of trembling unto all the people round about, when they shall be in the siege both against Judah and against Jerusalem.

12:3 And in that day will I make Jerusalem a burdensome stone for all people: all that burden themselves with it shall be cut in pieces, though all the people of the earth be gathered together against it.

12:4 In that day, saith the Lord, I will smite every horse with astonishment, and his rider with madness: and I will open mine eyes upon the house of Judah, and will smite every horse of the people with blindness.

12:5 And the governors of Judah shall say in their heart, The inhabitants of Jerusalem shall be my strength in the Lord of hosts their God.

12:6 In that day will I make the governors of Judah like an hearth of fire among the wood, and like a torch of fire in a sheaf; and they shall devour all the people round about, on the right hand and on the left: and Jerusalem shall be inhabited again in her own place, even in Jerusalem.

12:7 The Lord also shall save the tents of Judah first, that the glory of the house of David and the glory of the inhabitants of Jerusalem do not magnify themselves against Judah.

12:8 In that day shall the Lord defend the inhabitants of Jerusalem; and he that is feeble among them at that day shall be as David; and the house of David shall be as God, as the angel of the Lord before them.

12:9 And it shall come to pass in that day, that I will seek to destroy all the nations that come against Jerusalem.

This word of God, the first part of the second burden, parallels Zechariah's sixth vision of the flying scroll and the woman carried in a basket to Babylon. Both are promises of deliverance, not from external enemies but from the carnal and wicked element in the nation, which includes the false prophets, unfaithful shepherds, and a good part of the flock itself. These are often more dangerous than the enemies that come from outside, for they are the enemy within the camp. In Israel, they were the ones who led the nation into idolatry and who neglected the worship of God and sometimes stopped it altogether. They brought on the nation God's anger, and the nation needed deliverance from them as well as from the heathen.

The result of this deliverance would be that a remnant of the flock, a third part, was saved (13:8–9). Deliverance would come in a way that separated the wheat from the chaff, the wheat from the tares, the righteous from the wicked. Only then is true Israel ready to receive the blessings promised in the next chapter, the blessings of Christ's everlasting kingdom.

12:1. The burden of the word of the LORD for Israel, saith the LORD, which stretcheth forth the heavens, and layeth the foundation of the earth, and formeth the spirit of man within him.

The burdens are judgments and blessing, heavy in the one case with God's anger and in the other with his goodness. The opening words of chapter 12 show again that that is the case. Here the burden of wrath and judgment is first for the nations from whom God delivers Judah and Jerusalem and then in chapter 13 upon the apostate and wicked in the covenant nation. That judgment is described in contrast to the blessedness of Jerusalem described in chapter 12 and again in chapter 14.

The mix of blessing and judgment reminds us that in wrath God remembers mercy, that there is always mercy mixed with justice, that Zion is redeemed through judgment. God is the one in whom mercy and justice, righteousness and peace meet together and kiss each other, but only in Christ. Those who are not in Christ by faith and by grace taste only his wrath and justice. That is the purpose of this section: to make sure that those who are wicked and unrepentant have no carnal security. They must not think that they have any share in the blessings described.

God who threatens these judgments reminds the people that he is the creator both of man and of the world in which he lives. Nothing can escape his judgment. Nothing can make void his word. Those against whom he speaks will certainly find to their dismay and terror that the word of God will not come short of fulfillment, though they despised and scoffed at it.

Special mention is made of the spirit of man because the spirit of man is that aspect of his existence that makes it possible for him to live in conscious relation to God. His spirit especially distinguishes him from the brute creatures. Living apart from God he is worthy of God's just judgments, and God, who has created the spirit of man within him, knows every aspect of his existence, searches out all hypocrisy and wickedness, and judges accordingly.

Yet he speaks as Jehovah, the God of the covenant, the faithful and unchangeable one. Twice he uses that precious name here and so reminds us that his judgments are never an end in themselves, but are for the sake of his covenant and his covenant people: "All things are for your sakes" (2 Cor. 4:15). He who stretches out the heavens makes sure that all things under heaven work together for the good of his own. He who lays the foundation of the earth does so according to an eternal plan that includes the election and final glory of those whom he eternally gives to Christ. He who forms the spirit of man within him always has his eye on those whom he has formed for himself in Christ.

12:2. Behold, I will make Jerusalem a cup of trembling unto all the people round about, when they shall be in the siege both against Judah and against Jerusalem.

This graphic figure is found only here and in Isaiah 51:17, 22. Scripture speaks in a similar vein of a cup of wrath or fury (Isa. 51:17, 22; Jer. 25:15) or of a cup of astonishment and desolation (Ezra 23:33), but this figure is unique to Zechariah and Isaiah. It pictures Jerusalem as a basin, filled with the wrath of God. In this case it is the nations who drink that wrath of God and drinking it are filled with trembling. Tasting the terror of the Almighty, they are shaken to their foundations.

What a scene: a huge bowl of wine; several men, representative of Syria, Ammon, Moab, Edom, Philistaea, Phoenicia, crowding around

355

the bowl and setting their lips to it! They are athirst to gulp down Israel. But, strange to say, one after another steps back, reels and staggers as a drunkard, for God has made this to be a bowl of reeling... They are rendered impotent by the wine of the wrath of God and stagger about like drunken fools.[1]

The nations are pictured as besieging Jerusalem when the wrath of God falls on them. To find historical incidents that might be the fulfillment of this word of God is very difficult. There were times in the past history of Jerusalem when God saved the city from a besieging army; the deliverance that God worked in the days of Hezekiah is a wonderful example. But here God speaks of Jerusalem's future deliverance, and there is no single historical incident that can stand as the fulfillment of this prophecy. The most likely event was the siege of Jerusalem by the Roman armies, but God did not deliver the city at that time. Rather he gave it over to the Romans, so that it was completely destroyed as Jesus prophesied in Matthew 24.

Some look for the fulfillment of this prophecy in a future millennial age. They expect that the earthly city will be besieged by nations then existing, identified in scripture as Gog and Magog, and will be miraculously delivered by God. This will bring in an age in which the Jewish theocracy, the throne of David, and the temple will all be restored and Christ will reign on earth over the Jewish nation for a thousand years.

However, this is contrary to the teaching of the whole New Testament, which shows beyond doubt that the nation of God is elect Jewry, gathered from both Jews and Gentiles alike and united to Christ as his church and bride. The fulfillment of Zechariah's prophecy must then be in the church and the church's history during this New Testament era.

Throughout the New Testament the church is besieged by her enemies, not literally but spiritually. This is implied in the words of Jesus in Matthew 16:18, "I will build my church; and the gates of hell shall not prevail against it." Not only in times of persecution but also in times of peace the church is beset by enemies: Satan, who goes about as a roaring lion; the ungodly world, which when it does not persecute the church seeks to infiltrate the

---

1 Leupold, *Zechariah*, 227.

church and destroy her from within; and even the flesh, that is, the weakness and sin of the members of the church, are the enemies that always besiege her. That church God protects and defends until the end of time and then gathers to glory.

> The rising up of God's enemies against Christ's Church, which commenced at the same time, and has been continued in successive persecutions from Jews, Gentiles, and other unbelievers in every age, and which will reach its climax in the great Anti-Christian outbreak of the last times, and be confounded by the Coming of Christ to judgment, is here summed up in one panoramic picture, exhibited at once to the eye.[2]

If there is any specific historical incident that stands out as the fulfillment of this prophecy, it is the last hour when antichrist seeks to destroy the church. This is pictured in Revelation 20:7–9:

> 7. And when the thousand years are expired, Satan shall be loosed out of his prison,
> 8. And shall go out to deceive the nations which are in the four quarters of the earth, Gog and Magog, to gather them together to battle: the number of whom is as the sand of the sea.
> 9. And they went up on the breadth of the earth, and compassed the camp of the saints about, and the beloved city: and fire came down from God out of heaven, and devoured them.

12:3. And in that day will I make Jerusalem a burdensome stone for all people: all that burden themselves with it shall be cut in pieces, though all the people of the earth be gathered together against it.

God uses a second, similar figure to show how he will deliver his people from their enemies. Jerusalem will be like a stone heavy with the wrath of God that will become a burden to those heathen nations. They will take up

---

2 C. Wordsworth, quoted in Pusey, *The Minor Prophets*, 2:432–33.

that stone to destroy it but in the process of trying to destroy it, they will be destroyed. The picture is of a man who tries to move a large stone in a field and in the process he is killed when the stone falls on him, or of a man trying to break such a stone and seriously injuring himself in the process.

As Leupold suggests, the full picture is:

As a husbandman seeks to increase his acreage by removing a stone around which he would otherwise be obliged to plow, so the surrounding nations desire to gain territory by the dismemberment of Israel, which involves lifting Jerusalem out of the way.[3]

The difference between the two figures, the cup of trembling and the burdensome stone, is that in the first Israel's enemies are rendered impotent, while in the second they are actually harmed.

One cannot read this passage without thinking of Christ and what he says of himself as the cornerstone of the church: "The stone which the builders rejected, the same is become the head of the corner[.] Whosoever shall fall upon that stone shall be broken; but on whomsoever it shall fall, it will grind him to powder" (Luke 20:17–18). His presence in the church, here named Jerusalem, is the reason those who seek to destroy the church are themselves broken and destroyed, for the cornerstone is the Son of God himself, and he is laid as the cornerstone by the almighty power of God.

Thinking of Christ the cornerstone, we see the universal application of these judgments. They cannot be confined to one historical incident, in this case the destruction of the city of Jerusalem by the Romans, but reach to the end of time and include every instance of God's judgment on an ungodly world that in one way or another reveals itself as the enemy of his kingdom.

With this verse there begins a series of nine judgment and salvation statements that all include the words "in that day." That phrase is of supreme importance in the prophets and refers to what is elsewhere called "the day of the Lord."

The day of the Lord is the whole New Testament period viewed from the perspective of the Old Testament. In speaking of the coming of Christ,

---

3 Leupold, *Zechariah*, 228–29.

of judgment and salvation, the Old Testament prophets did not see that the coming of Christ in all its aspects reaches over more than two thousand years of history and includes both his incarnation and his return at the end of the ages. They saw it all as one day, just as someone driving into the mountains does not see them from a distance stretching range after range, with many valleys between, but as one range.

Yet the perspective of the Old Testament prophets was not wrong. Through inspiration it is the perspective of the Holy Spirit, which reminds us that from the viewpoint of God's purpose the whole New Testament is a very short time, only one day on God's clock, in which he finishes all his work.

It is the day of the Lord also because the comings of Christ are really one. He does not really come repeatedly but continuously, so that he is never really absent. He is always coming, as the incarnate one, by his Spirit and word, in every act of judgment, and personally and visibly at the very end, but it is all the one coming of the Lord for judgment and for salvation.

It is in that day, therefore, that all the things prophesied by Zechariah and others have their fulfillment, not in one isolated event but continuously, so that no matter when one lives in the New Testament era, he is able to see these things being fulfilled. Always the word of God is relevant and applicable.

This is suggested in 1 Corinthians 10:11, where Paul says that the ends of the ages had already come upon the Corinthian believers, and insofar as his word is directed to us and to every believer, they come upon all of us. The day of the Lord has begun, and every new day is part of the end of the ages and itself another end, for every day is a day of finishing and fulfillment. All culminates in that last hour when Christ appears personally to stop the clock of history and to bring in eternity.

That lends a great deal of urgency to the warnings of scripture, to the call of the gospel, to the demand for repentance, faith, and conversion, for in the New Testament it is always the last day in which only a few hours remain before all must stand in Christ's presence to be judged.

12:4. In that day, saith the LORD, I will smite every horse with astonishment, and his rider with madness: and I will open mine eyes upon the house of Judah, and will smite every horse of the people with blindness.

12:5. And the governors of Judah shall say in their heart, The inhabitants of Jerusalem shall be my strength in the LORD of hosts their God.

Through judgment, by a miracle of grace, the salvation of the remnant and of the true church is accomplished. That was the case in the captivity. That judgment separated the wheat from the chaff in Judah and Israel and was a means for purifying and strengthening the remnant. It is in Christ, however, that this is fully realized, for when at the cross the judgment of God is poured out in all its fury, it is poured out in such a way that true Zion is redeemed and delivered from sin and made righteous before God, while those who are not in Christ are consumed and come under everlasting wrath.

When the nations are gathered against Jerusalem, God, who sovereignly gathered them, executes his judgment on them. The horses and riders are the armies of the heathen, and by smiting them with blindness, astonishment, and madness, God scatters their armies and once again saves Jerusalem, as he so often did during their earlier history. This happens all through the New Testament when God sends renewal and reformation to his church and delivers her from the world and her own sinfulness.

That he opens his eyes on the house of Judah suggests that he had his eyes closed to their plight and only now opens his eyes and, seeing their sad condition, delivers them from their enemies. This does not mean that God changes, but it looks at things from the viewpoint of our experience. To us it seems that his eyes are closed and that he does not see the dangers that threaten his church when things are going badly. Yet he always delivers and saves, and then we know that his eyes were never closed. But only the elect remnant is saved. The rest come under God's fierce anger and are destroyed, and in that also there is no change in God, nor any inconsistency in his word.

The result of God's saving mercy will be that the rulers of Judah have a change of heart, and instead of leading the people astray and destroying them, they will recognize that the people belong to God and find in the people's faith a source of encouragement and strength. They see by faith that the church's strength is in the Lord. The way in which this change of heart comes about is not yet shown and will not be until the end of the chapter, but it will be the way in which God saves not just a few here and there, but the whole city and all the people who are the true citizens of the city.

12:6. In that day will I make the governors of Judah like an hearth of fire among the wood, and like a torch of fire in a sheaf; and they shall devour all the people round about, on the right hand and on the left: and Jerusalem shall be inhabited again in her own place, even in Jerusalem.

12:7. The LORD also shall save the tents of Judah first, that the glory of the house of David and the glory of the inhabitants of Jerusalem do not magnify themselves against Judah.

Verse 6 is another reference to "that day," the third such reference, and more promises now follow. The people are the Gentile nations, the heathen, and God promises that the governors of Judah, having had a change of heart, will be the means by which he destroys the heathen and saves his people. The nations will go up in flames like dried grass, and the leaders of Judah will be the fire with which God burns them up.

The result will be threefold. First, Jerusalem will have her own place secured. Never again will she have to fear destruction and captivity. Second, instead of being hemmed in on every side, the land overrun with enemies and the people unable to return to their own homes and fields, the outlying areas will be delivered also and repopulated, so that Jerusalem with her population and glory will have no reason to think herself more glorious than the rest of the nations. Third, the leaders, who had been the cause of so much trouble and apostasy, will be humbled and will no longer seek their own advantage but the well-being of the whole nation.

This is also fulfilled in Christ, when Jew and Gentile are united in him, when the church is spread throughout the world and earthly Jerusalem no longer has a reason to boast, when the temple in Jerusalem is no longer the only place to worship God but men worship him everywhere in spirit and in truth, and when the church is delivered through her governors and through him those governors serve.

The reference to the tents of Judah, the outlying areas, may be, as some commentators think, a reference to the fact that Zion's deliverance would come not out of Jerusalem but out of little Bethlehem. Certainly Jerusalem had no reason to boast when the King of kings was born in Bethlehem. Laetsch not only makes this suggestion but develops it:

> The Messiah was born not at Jerusalem, but at Bethlehem; He did not grow up in Jerusalem, but in Nazareth; not Jerusalem, but Capernaum and Galilee were the center of His activity, with only occasional visits at Jerusalem. In the Christian Church there is to be no superiority of city over country, of capital city over others, of large congregation over gatherings of two or three (Matt. 18:20). Not locality or size, but Christ and His Word represent the true glory of congregations and churches.[4]

12:8. In that day shall the LORD defend the inhabitants of Jerusalem; and he that is feeble among them at that day shall be as David; and the house of David shall be as God, as the angel of the LORD before them.

In the fourth reference to "that day" of the Lord, God expands on the previous promises, assuring the people of his help and speaking once again of new and godly leaders who are not like those who led them astray. But here he speaks more plainly and clearly of Christ. Christ, the descendant of the house of David, is as God and, ruling over Jerusalem, is as the angel of the Lord before them. Though in prophetic language, the second half of the verse means that God himself in Christ, who gave the throne to David, will be Jerusalem's king in the person of the angel of Jehovah. He will be, at the same time, the representative of the house of David and offspring of that house.

A passage like this must have puzzled the people of God in the Old Testament, who had not seen the miracle of Christ's incarnation as the son of Mary and the Son of God. How could the house of David be as God without being guilty of blasphemy? How could the house of David be as the angel of Jehovah, the revelation of God himself? How could that angel sit on the throne of David and be the rightful ruler of God's people? During his ministry Jesus posed a similar question that puzzled the Jewish leaders. He asked them: "If David then call him Lord, how is he his son?" (Matt. 22:45).

---

4 Laetsch, *The Minor Prophets*, 481.

For us who know the story of the incarnation these questions are easy to answer, though even now it is only faith that can answer them correctly, but it would not have been so easy to give a clear answer in the Old Testament. Perhaps that is why the passage only speaks of the house of David being *like* God and *like* the angel of Jehovah. To say more than that in the Old Testament would have confounded rather than helped the faith of the faithful.

We know, however, that the house of David now *is* God and *is* the angel of Jehovah. Born of the virgin by the overshadowing power of the Holy Spirit, that holy thing who was born of Mary, David's descendant, is also God's Son, come in the flesh, made like us in all things, and higher than the highest heavens. He is capable of being the prince and ruler of God's people who delivers them as even David was not able. Through him Jerusalem is defended forever and becomes the city described in Revelation 21, all glorious and filled with the light of God.

The passage hints, as some suggest, of Christ's atoning work. In his humiliation he is the feeble one who takes as his own all the weakness and sin of the house of David and carries it away. Nevertheless, the main emphasis is on the might of the house of David and the victory obtained by the house of David over Israel's enemies.

In Christ, however, every child of God is like the house of David, everyone strong in the Lord and willing to fight the giant Sin, as David fought Goliath, everyone a hero of faith like David. Everyone is a soldier in the great army of the angel of the Lord, the captain of their salvation, and by them their enemies will be judged and destroyed, none remaining. Even the children are like the house of David. John says: "I have written unto you, young men, because ye are strong, and the word of God abideth in you, and ye have overcome the wicked one" (1 John 2:14).

What a wonderful thing it is when the whole house of David, Christ and his church, are like God and like the angel of the Lord. Then the enemy will not exact upon them, nor the son of wickedness afflict them (Ps. 89:22).

12:9. And it shall come to pass in that day, that I will seek to destroy all the nations that come against Jerusalem.

One last promise of help and deliverance from enemies occurs here, the fifth reference to "that day" before the word of God turns to the main subject of this chapter, the outpouring of the Spirit as the Spirit of grace and supplication. The enemies of God's people, not only the ungodly world that persecutes and seduces them but also Satan, sin, and death, must all be destroyed in order that the Spirit may be poured out. The deliverance and salvation of the church is followed by the gift of the Spirit, for having been redeemed, the church must also be brought back to God and made to live with him forever. The order of the word of God in this verse and what follows is the order of the history of redemption recorded in the gospels and Acts.

Chapter 24

THE SECOND BURDEN, PART 2:
ZECHARIAH 12:10–13:9

12:10 And I will pour upon the house of David, and upon the inhabitants of Jerusalem, the spirit of grace and of supplications: and they shall look upon me whom they have pierced, and they shall mourn for him, as one mourneth for his only son, and shall be in bitterness for him, as one that is in bitterness for his firstborn.

12:11 In that day shall there be a great mourning in Jerusalem, as the mourning of Hadadrimmon in the valley of Megiddon.

12:12 And the land shall mourn, every family apart; the family of the house of David apart, and their wives apart; the family of the house of Nathan apart, and their wives apart;

12:13 The family of the house of Levi apart, and their wives apart; the family of Shimei apart, and their wives apart;

12:14 All the families that remain, every family apart, and their wives apart.

13:1 In that day there shall be a fountain opened to the house of David and to the inhabitants of Jerusalem for sin and for uncleanness.

13:2 And it shall come to pass in that day, saith the LORD of hosts, that I will cut off the names of the idols out of the land, and they shall no more be remembered: and also I will cause the prophets and the unclean spirit to pass out of the land.

13:3 And it shall come to pass, that when any shall yet prophesy, then his father and his mother that begat him shall say unto him, Thou shalt not live; for thou speakest lies in the name of the LORD: and his father and his mother that begat him shall thrust him through when he prophesieth.

13:4 And it shall come to pass in that day, that the prophets shall be ashamed every one of his vision, when he hath prophesied; neither shall they wear a rough garment to deceive:

13:5 But he shall say, I am no prophet, I am an husbandman; for man taught me to keep cattle from my youth.

13:6 And one shall say unto him, What are these wounds in thine hands? Then he shall answer, Those with which I was wounded in the house of my friends.

13:7 Awake, O sword, against my shepherd, and against the man that is my fellow, saith the Lord of hosts: smite the shepherd, and the sheep shall be scattered: and I will turn mine hand upon the little ones.

13:8 And it shall come to pass, that in all the land, saith the Lord, two parts therein shall be cut off and die; but the third shall be left therein.

13:9 And I will bring the third part through the fire, and will refine them as silver is refined, and will try them as gold is tried: they shall call on my name, and I will hear them: I will say, It is my people: and they shall say, The Lord is my God.

12:10. And I will pour upon the house of David, and upon the inhabitants of Jerusalem, the spirit of grace and of supplications: and they shall look upon me whom they have pierced, and they shall mourn for him, as one mourneth for his only son, and shall be in bitterness for him, as one that is in bitterness for his firstborn.

Here, finally, the word of God shows how the promises of the previous verses come to be. It is only through Christ and only by his Spirit that God's people have any blessing. Christ has appeared in the previous burden, meek and lowly, riding on the colt of an ass, but bringing salvation. Now also the promise of the Spirit follows, for it is through the work of the Spirit as the Spirit of grace and supplication that those whom Christ redeemed share in the benefits of his work and experience the blessedness that is promised in him.

Verse 10 describes the actual outpouring of the Holy Spirit and is a prophecy of Pentecost. Though Peter did not quote this passage in his Pentecost sermon, it is evident from the sermon and from his sermon text, Joel 2:28–31, that Zechariah and Joel were speaking of the same thing. That the outpouring of the Spirit on Pentecost resulted in the repentance and conversion of several thousand people makes it even more obvious that Zechariah was looking forward to that event.

When the Spirit is called the Spirit of grace and supplications, he is described as the Spirit who gives grace and who works repentance in the hearts of those to whom he is sent. The supplications are the pleas for forgiveness that rise from a heart overwhelmed by God's grace. These are produced by the Spirit and do not arise naturally from the heart of the sinner.

Sorrow for sin and a changed attitude do not just suggest that a person is under conviction and there is the possibility of his salvation, but prove that the work of grace and salvation has already begun in his heart, even though he may not himself recognize that work for what it is. We shed no real tears for sin, except they be purchased by the blood of Christ and given by the Spirit of grace. There are tears shed for the consequences of sin and because of the judgments of sin, but these are merely the sorrow of the world (2 Cor. 7:10).

When the Spirit of grace and supplication is promised to the house of David and the inhabitants of Jerusalem, we see that salvation is the same in both the Old and New Testaments. There is not one way for the Old Testament, salvation by the works of the law, and another way for the New Testament, the way of repentance and faith, but one way only. Indeed, the house of David and the inhabitants of Jerusalem include the elect Gentiles in the New Testament, who are children of Abraham by faith (Gal. 3) and have the spiritual reality of circumcision (Rom. 3).

The house of David, however, is a reference not just to every child of God but first and foremost to Christ. He is the house of David, the origin, the strength, the offspring, the hope of that house, and the Spirit of grace and supplication is given to him first to be poured out by him upon the church that belongs to him.

He appears in the passage as the one over whom the house of David mourns. It is God himself, of course, whom they pierced by their unbelief and unfaithfulness in the Old Testament and by the crucifixion of his Son in the New Testament. That they mourn means they do the same as those to whom Peter preached on Pentecost. Peter had preached to them that they with wicked hands had crucified Christ, and they responded in repentance with the question, "Men and brethren, what shall we do?" Their repentance is an example of what Zechariah prophesied and pictures all true repentance.

Of the fact that the passage speaks of a divine Messiah, Moore says:

> As God is here the speaker, this passage has always been a stumbling-block to the Jews, for how could God be pierced? The only fact that explains it is that which they have not yet admitted, that they have crucified and slain that prince of peace who was God manifest in the flesh. As soon as they admit this fact they will see the consistency of the passage, and will mourn the guilt of their fathers in crucifying the incarnate Son, and their own guilt in so long rejecting him.[1]

All those who mourn for sin mourn because they have looked in faith on him whom they pierced, on Christ crucified, and their mourning is as sincere and deep as the mourning of a parent for a lost and only child. No one since the days of Christ's ministry is guilty of the actual act of crucifying

---

1 Moore, *Zechariah*, 198.

him, but all who repent are guilty insofar as it was their sins that nailed him to the tree! Seeing that, they mourn: "True repentance is after all only love weeping at the foot of the cross."[2]

Those who mourn therefore include not only penitent Jews, but all who by grace repent of their sins:

> In that penitential sorrow the Gentiles have had their share. Made children of Abraham by faith in Christ Jesus, they, too, have in the long vista of ages been led in thousands and tens of thousands, nationally and individually, to mourn for sin, and to look to the Redeemer, in the sin of whose crucifixion they, too, have had their share.[3]

The passage is full of Christ. He is the great representative of the house of David to whom the Spirit is given. He is the one through whom God pours out the Spirit on the church. He is the one who was pierced and who purchased the gift and graces of the Spirit for his own. He is the one whose wounds cause them to mourn for their sins. And indeed, he is the firstborn for whom they mourn. He is everything.

That this passage is quoted in Revelation 1 in respect to the ungodly and unrepentant must not obscure what we have said. All are guilty of crucifying him, whether in fact or afresh by their unbelief, and so Revelation, describing his return, says: "Behold, he cometh with clouds; and every eye shall see him, and they also which pierced him: and all kindreds of the earth shall wail because of him. Even so, Amen" (1:7).

The verse is also quoted in John 19:34–37 in reference to the piercing of Christ's side by a Roman soldier:

> 34. But one of the soldiers with a spear pierced his side, and forthwith came there out blood and water.
> 35. And he that saw it bare record, and his record is true: and he knoweth that he saith true, that ye might believe.

---

2 Ibid., 203.
3 Wright, *Zechariah*, 397–98.

36. For these things were done, that the scripture should be fulfilled, A bone of him shall not be broken.
37. And again another scripture saith, They shall look on him
whom they pierced.

Quoted in John, the word of God shows that Christ's crucifixion is the
fulfillment of Zechariah's prophecy, but it shows too that the passage has a
broader application than just to the Jewish nation. The very first to look on
the pierced one and mourn was the Roman centurion who was in charge of
the crucifixion. Since then many, both Jews and Gentiles, have looked on
him whom they pierced and mourned for him, repenting of their sins and
seeking forgiveness in his blood.

*12:11. In that day shall there be a great mourning in Jerusalem, as the
mourning of Hadadrimmon in the valley of Megiddon.*

The mourning is so great (it involves all those through the ages who
have seen and repented of their sins) that it is compared to the mourning of
Hadad-Rimmon in the valley of Megiddon. The valley of Megiddon is the
same as the valley of Megiddo, or Armageddon, the place where so many
battles were fought in the Old Testament (2 Chron. 35:22) and where the
last great battle will be fought (Rev. 16:16). Armageddon is the Hebrew
word for "Hill of Megiddo." Hadad-Rimmon is sometimes identified as a
heathen deity, but to quote Laetsch:

> The idea that Hadad-Rimmon here refers to the worship of the Syr-
> ian deity whose cult was similar to that of Adonis, or Tammuz (Ezek.
> 8:14), is preposterous. No prophet of Jehovah would take such an
> abominable, immoral rite as an emblem of the Church's peniten-
> tial mourning. There is no valid reason to doubt Jerome's statement
> that Hadad-Rimmon was a city near Jezreel in the plain of Megiddo,
> called Maximianopolis in his day.[4]

He adds:

---

4 Laetsch, *The Minor Prophets*, 484–85.

At Megiddo, pious King Josiah was slain by Pharaoh Necho (2 Kings 23:29ff.; 2 Chron. 35:20ff.). He was the first king of Judah to fall in battle and leave his country at the mercy of foreign conquerors. (Cp. 2 Kings 23:31–35; 24:1ff.; 2 Chron. 36:1–7, 10–20.) His death was a catastrophic loss for Judah, for with him had passed away (2 Kings 22:15–26) the last bulwark against the flood of wickedness which now swept through the land and carried it to its destruction. The entire nation lamented Josiah's death, and by official decree an annual day of mourning was appointed, still observed when the Book of Chronicles was written (2 Chron. 35:24ff.). Hadad-Rimmon is named as the place or one of the places of such mourning perhaps because it afforded a view of the battlefield, or Josiah may have died here when, mortally wounded, he was being rushed to Jerusalem (2 Kings 23:29ff.; 2 Chron. 35:22ff.).[5]

I agree that Zechariah's prophecy has to do with the mourning of Judah at the time of Josiah's death, though it is not known exactly where Hadad-Rimmon was and why the people mourned there. The event referred to by Zechariah is unrecorded in scripture, but we can have some sense of the greatness of this mourning from the fact that it was still remembered in the days of Zechariah. The weeping of those who are destroyed in God's wrath in the great last day will be like this mourning in intensity and sincerity, but here the weeping, equally great, is pleasing to God, the sorrow of a broken heart that is of more value to him than burnt sacrifice, while the weeping and gnashing of teeth that will be heard in the judgment day he despises, for it is the weeping of those who see their just doom coming upon them.

12:12. And the land shall mourn, every family apart; the family of the house of David apart, and their wives apart; the family of the house of Nathan apart, and their wives apart;
12:13. The family of the house of Levi apart, and their wives apart; the family of Shimei apart, and their wives apart;
12:14. All the families that remain, every family apart, and their wives apart.

---

5 Ibid., 485.

That the different groups mentioned in this section all mourn apart is further evidence of their sincerity. It is not a mere show of sorrow for sin that must be paraded before others but something private and sincere. It is the final proof that their weeping is music in God's ears, proof that they belong to Christ and have his Spirit.

Spurgeon in a sermon on this passage explains the weeping apart thus:

> The watchword of true penitence is this word "apart." How it rings out in the text, "Every family apart; the family of the house of David apart, and their wives apart; the family of the house of Nathan apart, and their wives apart; the family of the house of Levi apart, and their wives apart; the family of Shimei apart, and their wives apart; all the families that remain, every family apart, and their wives apart." Sham repentance can do its work in the mass; it talks about national sin and national sorrow, which generally means the mere notion of sin and the notion of repentance. But when it comes to a true work of the Spirit of God, and men do really mourn for sin so as to obtain pardon, it is a thing in which each individual stands in a personal solitude, as much apart from everybody else as if he had been the sole man that God ever made, and was without father and without mother and without descent, and had himself alone so sinned that the whole anger of God for sin had fallen upon him. A man in this condition gets alone, he bears his sin apart, quitting the company of his fellows, and all the charms that once lured him to destruction; and his lamentation on account of sin is his own sole act and deed. It wells up from his own heart, it is not borrowed from others; but, by the effectual working of the grace of God, everything about it is of himself.[6]

There is a reference also to every class and type of people. David and Levi represent the kingly and priestly families in the nation, and Nathan and Shimei, descendants of David and of Levi (2 Sam. 5:14; Num. 3:18–21),

---

6 C. H. Spurgeon, *Metropolitan Tabernacle Pulpit* (Pasadena: Pilgrim Publications, 1897 reprint), 43:199.

represent those in the nation who held no office, while the wives and families include everyone else, women and children alike. There is no difference before God as far as this weeping is concerned.

13:1. In that day there shall be a fountain opened to the house of David and to the inhabitants of Jerusalem for sin and for uncleanness.

The chapter divisions do not follow the actual divisions here. Chapter 13:1–9 is a continuation of the second part of the second burden and continues to speak of the work of the Spirit. These verses belong with the last part of the previous chapter. The continued repetition of the words "in that day" connects these verses with what precedes, a prophetic record of the blessings that the day of the Lord brings for believers.

The order of these blessings is exactly that of our experience, first deliverance from our enemies, then repentance, and finally sanctification. The deliverance in its spiritual reality is the deliverance that comes through the saving work of Jesus Christ when he delivers us from death, hell, and the devil. Having paid for our sins and won for us the victory, he pours out upon us the Spirit of grace and supplication that we may share in his victory in the way of repentance for sin, and having brought us to our knees in sorrow for sin also through the same Spirit, he opens for us a cleansing fountain in which we are made fit to live in the presence of God and with him, the holy one.

The fountain of living water is really God himself (Jer. 2:13), but God as he reveals himself in Christ as the God of salvation: "If any man thirst, let him come unto me, and drink" (John 7:37), and the water which I shall give him, is a fountain of living water, gushing up to everlasting life (John 4:14). Or as Laetsch says: "This fountain was prepared, dug, by the Lord Our Righteousness when He cried: 'It is finished!' (John 19:30.) By His vicarious suffering and death that fountain, filled with blood drawn from Immanuel's veins, was opened."[7]

The cleansing power of that fountain is the application of the death of Christ to the sinner by the Spirit. Though the Spirit is not mentioned in the verse, he is nevertheless the agent of this cleansing, the one through whom that fountain is opened and the one who puts us into that fountain to be

---

7 Laetsch, *The Minor Prophets*, 487.

cleansed. The day when the Spirit of grace and supplications is poured out is the very same day that a fountain is opened for sin and for cleansing. We are not literally washed in Christ's blood but are spiritually washed when the Holy Spirit applies and gives to us the benefits of Christ's death.

These benefits include cleansing and all the other gifts of grace, faith, forgiveness, adoption as children of God, and finally the glory of heavenly life. They include faith, hope, the love of God, patience, peace, assurance, and every other spiritual blessing, earned by Christ on the cross and received as a gift of God through the work of the Spirit in our hearts. The Spirit in giving us these gifts gives us at the same time the ability to use them, to enjoy and experience them, and to know that they are ours for Christ's sake.

Sin and uncleanness are not two different things, for sin is our uncleanness, and in our sins we are like Joshua in his filthy garments, all our works being nothing but filthy rags and nothing with which to cover our spiritual nakedness before God. Sin is every act of wickedness, and uncleanness is the guilty stain that becomes ours through sin. Cleansing is mentioned here not because it is of more value than all the other gifts of the Spirit of grace and supplication, but because it is only in the way of cleansing that we have and enjoy the other gifts. The gift of cleansing is first.

That this cleansing fountain is opened in "that day" is further proof that the day referred to is the whole New Testament period, for the fountain is opened by the death of Christ and will flow until all the sins of all God's people have been washed away forever, until that day when it is no longer needed in the new heavens and the new earth.

That this fountain is opened to the house of David and the inhabitants of Jerusalem reminds us that before God there is no difference between one person and another: great and small, all are equally in need of this cleansing. Nevertheless, that this fountain is opened to these people does not mean that it is available to all and that their cleansing depends on whether or not they will plunge themselves into that fountain. The hymn is wrong when it says, "Jesus keep me near the cross/There a precious fountain/Free to all a healing stream/Flows from Calvary's mountain."[8]

The house of David and inhabitants of Jerusalem are not all men, not

---

8 Fanny Crosby, "Jesus Keep Me Near the Cross," verse 1, 1820–1915.

even all Jews, but those for whom Christ died, the true Jews, the true children of Abraham by faith, both Jews and Gentiles by birth. They see their need for cleansing from sin only through a gracious work of God in their hearts. Christ died only for the sheep, for those whom his Father had given him, and the faith that brings us to him for cleansing is a gift of God, so that no man comes to him except the Father draws that person.

If that fountain were opened for all if they choose to be washed in it, then no one would be washed, for we are all clean in our own eyes. If Christ died for all, to make salvation a possibility for all, then none would be saved, for then it is not his blood that matters but the will and choice of the sinner. Then his blood flows in vain. Then the fountain is opened in vain, and then it is not really that fountain that cleanses, but the choice of the sinner.

13:2. And it shall come to pass in that day, saith the LORD of hosts, that I will cut off the names of the idols out of the land, and they shall no more be remembered: and also I will cause the prophets and the unclean spirit to pass out of the land.

Included in the cleansing of the nation is deliverance from idolatry and false prophets. These were the bane of Israel's existence in the Old Testament and continue to plague the existence of the church in the New Testament.

We tend to think of idolatry only in terms of worshiping an image of wood or stone, gold or silver, and today of eastern and African peoples and their religions, Buddhism, Hinduism, and fetishism. But modern, civilized western man is no less prone to idolatry than those who bow to sticks and stones. We ought never forget that idolatry is "instead of the one true God who has revealed himself in his word, or along with the same, to conceive or have something else on which to place our trust,"[9] and not only to trust in anything or anyone besides that one true God, but also to love, fear, honor, obey, or know anyone or anything apart from him.

Since idolatry is a matter of the heart, it is not difficult to see that many today who call themselves Christians halt between two opinions, trying to serve God and mammon at the same time, or simply worship mammon openly. Many of them are encouraged to do so by the false prophets who

---

9 Heidelberg Catechism A 95, in Schaff, *Creeds of Christendom*, 3:342.

teach them that health and wealth are all that matter, and who themselves care about nothing else.

These same false prophets are as many today as in the days of Ahab, when four hundred prophets of Baal but only one prophet of God could be found. They not only teach the people to worship other gods, especially gods of gold and silver, prosperity and earthly gain, but also corrupt the worship of God as the prophets did in the Old Testament, teaching the people to ask counsel at their stocks and staffs and to "sacrifice upon the tops of the mountains and burn incense upon the hills, under oaks and poplars and elms, because the shadow thereof is good" (Hos. 4:12–13).

In other words, they teach the people that what God has commanded is not important in the worship of God, but whatever makes them feel good, whatever moves and excites and entertains them. They lead the people away from the word of God, the only place where the will of God may be known, and encourage them to try to discern the will of God through a kind of Christianized sorcery, by signs and wonders. They are no different than the Jews who tried to divine with sticks.

The unclean spirit against which Zechariah prophesies is not something different from the false prophets but the evil spirit that moved them to prophesy falsely, what Leupold calls "the animating principle of false prophecy."[10] It is called the spirit of uncleanness because it does not come from God and because it promotes every form of uncleanness, idolatry, lying, and evil works. It is the unclean spirit that led the Jews to intermarry with the heathen and to adopt their filthy practices. It teaches Christians today to divorce and remarry at will, to live together as man and wife before marriage, to justify homosexuality, and to live like the heathen, so that the lives of Christians are not one whit different from the ungodly in dress, in speech, or in conduct.

God promises that he will also deliver his people from Satan and from all who serve Satan. He begins to do so when he separates his people spiritually from the ungodly: "Wherefore come out from among them, and be ye separate, saith the Lord, and touch not the unclean thing; and I will receive you. And will be a Father unto you, and ye shall be my sons and daughters, saith

---

10 Leupold, *Zechariah*, 246.

the Lord Almighty" (2 Cor. 6:17–18). That separation, sometimes called the antithesis, begins in this life by grace and is finished when God takes his people out of this world forever and into the next. Then their deliverance will be complete, for even the names of the idols will be cut off and no more remembered. What a great day that will be!

13:3. And it shall come to pass, that when any shall yet prophesy, then his father and his mother that begat him shall say unto him, Thou shalt not live; for thou speakest lies in the name of the LORD: and his father and his mother that begat him shall thrust him through when he prophesieth.

13:4. And it shall come to pass in that day, that the prophets shall be ashamed every one of his vision, when he hath prophesied; neither shall they wear a rough garment to deceive:

13:5. But he shall say, I am no prophet, I am an husbandman; for man taught me to keep cattle from my youth.

13:6. And one shall say unto him, What are these wounds in thine hands? Then he shall answer, Those with which I was wounded in the house of my friends.

This part of the passage is very difficult, but it is generally understood to be a further reference to the false prophets and God's deliverance of his people from them. It is addressed especially to those who persist in their errors and in leading others astray: they "yet prophesy." The passage then threatens these false prophets with the penalties of the Mosaic law (v. 3), with the result that the false prophets are afraid to prophesy or even to be identified as prophets (vv. 4–6).

Included in these threats is the suggestion that the people themselves will actively support the law of God and will hate sin with such fervor that even the requirement of the law that a false prophet's relatives be the first to lay hands on him to punish him will be kept. Love for the law will supersede even family feeling. Moore says:

Love to God must be paramount to all other affections, even the tenderest of which the heart is capable. It is, in our present imperfect sanctification, inconceivable to us how we could acquiesce in the perdition of our children, without a pang that would poison all the bliss of heaven, and yet it shall be so. Much as we love them, we shall love God and his law immeasurably more.[11]

The penalties of the Mosaic law are found especially in Deuteronomy 13:1–11, where God's word not only prescribes death as the penalty for speaking lies in God's name, but also teaches that the relatives of a false prophet must be the first to apply these penalties:

1. If there arise among you a prophet, or a dreamer of dreams, and giveth thee a sign or a wonder,

2. And the sign or the wonder come to pass, whereof he spake unto thee, saying, Let us go after other gods, which thou hast not known, and let us serve them;

3. Thou shalt not hearken unto the words of that prophet, or that dreamer of dreams: for the LORD your God proveth you, to know whether ye love the LORD your God with all your heart and with all your soul.

4. Ye shall walk after the LORD your God, and fear him, and keep his commandments, and obey his voice, and ye shall serve him, and cleave unto him.

5. And that prophet, or that dreamer of dreams, shall be put to death; because he hath spoken to turn you away from the LORD your God, which brought you out of the land of Egypt, and redeemed you out of the house of bondage, to thrust thee out of the way which the LORD thy God commanded thee to walk in. So shalt thou put the evil away from the midst of thee.

6. If thy brother, the son of thy mother, or thy son, or thy daughter, or the wife of thy bosom, or thy friend, which is as thine own soul, entice thee secretly, saying, Let us go and serve other gods, which thou hast not known, thou, nor thy fathers;

7. Namely, of the gods of the people which are round about you, nigh unto thee, or far off from thee, from the one end of the earth even unto the other end of the earth;

---

11 Moore, *Zechariah*, 210.

8. Thou shalt not consent unto him, nor hearken unto him;
neither shall thine eye pity him, neither shalt thou spare, neither
shalt thou conceal him:
9. But thou shalt surely kill him; thine hand shall be first upon him
to put him to death, and afterwards the hand of all the people.
10. And thou shalt stone him with stones, that he die; because he
hath sought to thrust thee away from the LORD thy God, which
brought thee out of the land of Egypt, from the house of bondage.
11. And all Israel shall hear, and fear, and shall do no more any
such wickedness as this is among you. (Deut. 13:1–11)

One cannot imagine what it would be like today if everyone who spoke
lies in the name of the Lord were threatened with death. Almost every television ministry would be shut down, and many large churches would be left
without leaders. Arminianism and freewillism, the prosperity gospel, charis-
maticism and all of its excesses, deniers of fundamental Christian doctrines
such as the virgin birth, the bodily resurrection of Christ, justification by
faith alone, the Trinity, and the divinity of our Lord, all would be threatened. What a deliverance that would be for the church and for the people
of God who are blown about by every wind of doctrine, fed a steady diet of
lies in the name of the Lord, and in ignorance follow anyone who claims to
bring the word of God.

Jesus speaks of an abundance of false Christs and false prophets in the
last days, every one claiming to have a word from God and none of them
paying any attention at all to the real word of God in the scriptures: "Then
if any man shall say unto you, Lo, here is Christ, or there; believe it not. For
there shall arise false Christs, and false prophets, and shall shew great signs
and wonders; insomuch that, if it were possible, they shall deceive the very
elect. Behold, I have told you before" (Matt. 24:23–25). They claim to know
the time of Christ's coming, claim to have words of knowledge, claim direct
revelations from God, claim to have been in heaven like Paul, claim to have
seen the risen Lord and spoken to him personally, claim to have the secrets
of success and happiness, but tell only lies.

They spout every kind of nonsense and rubbish imaginable and unimaginable, but they are not the only ones to blame. Jeremiah complains: "A

wonderful and horrible thing is committed in the land; The prophets prophesy falsely, and the priests bear rule by their means; and my people love to have it so: and what will ye do in the end thereof?" (Jer. 5:30–31). Indeed, the people are all too often like those against whom Isaiah prophesies:

> 8. Now go, write it before them in a table, and note it in a book, that it may be for the time to come for ever and ever:
>
> 9. That this is a rebellious people, lying children, children that will not hear the law of the LORD:
>
> 10. Which say to the seers, See not; and to the prophets, Prophesy not unto us right things, speak unto us smooth things, prophesy deceits:
>
> 11. Get you out of the way, turn aside out of the path, cause the Holy One of Israel to cease from before us (Isa. 30:8–11).

Verses 4–6 describe the fear of these false prophets when confronted with the penalties of the law. They are "ashamed every one of his vision," that is, they deny that the words they have spoken are their own and repudiate their own teachings, not out of love of God but out of fear for their own skins. They put away the distinctive clothing of the Old Testament prophets: "Neither shall they wear a rough garment to deceive" (see the description of Elijah in 2 Kings 1:8). They deny that they ever were prophets or had a word from God but claim to have been ordinary working men, husbandmen and keepers of cattle, all their lives: "He shall say, I am no prophet, I am an husbandman; for man taught me to keep cattle from my youth."

When asked about the wounds in their hands, wounds like those of the Baal prophets at Mount Carmel (1 Kings 18:28), they will make lame and unbelievable excuses: "And one shall say unto him, What are these wounds in thine hands? Then he shall answer, Those with which I was wounded in the house of my friends." When asked about the scars that are left, they deny that these were received in Baal's service and claim that they fell down and were injured or were injured in a drunken brawl in the house of a friend. The fear of God will be upon them, the terror of the God of judgment who hates all lies as "the proper works of the devil"[12] and punishes them accordingly.

---

12 Heidelberg Catechism A 112, in Schaff, *Creeds of Christendom*, 3:348.

Some take verse 6 as a reference to Christ, but the word "friends," literally "lovers," is a word that can be used for those who are the "friends of idols and idolaters" (Hos. 2:5–13).

Although false prophets today are not threatened with death, they deserve it, and God will punish them. That they prosper in their wickedness and can gather huge audiences to listen to them does not mean that God will not deliver his people from them. There is coming a day when the new Jerusalem shall descend from God out of heaven and "there shall in no wise enter into it any thing that defileth, neither whatsoever worketh abomination, or maketh a lie; but they which are written in the Lamb's book of life" (Rev. 21:27). No longer will there be any possibility of deception, but only the living and abiding word of God himself to speak life and peace to our souls.

13:7. Awake, O sword, against my shepherd, and against the man that is my fellow, saith the LORD of hosts: smite the shepherd, and the sheep shall be scattered: and I will turn mine hand upon the little ones.

In the last three verses of this section the emphasis, as in vision 6, which it parallels, is still on the removal of the apostate and corrupt element in the nation. The section speaks in unmistakable terms of the death of Christ, but this time from the viewpoint of the judgment that results for the ungodly and unbelieving, those who were Jews in name only. What is pictured in the vision of the curse scroll and the woman in the basket carried away to Babylon is here spoken of more plainly.

The result of this cleansing of the nation, the church, will be the salvation of the remnant. They will be left when the rest are cut off, refined and tried, but through it all they will be able to say, "The Lord is my God." As we would expect, Christ is the reason they survive the destruction of the apostates, and so the verses display Christ and his saving work. Because they show us Christ, they are in the form of a poem, for who, believing in Christ, does not sing when they hear of his death as the shepherd of the sheep?

That this verse refers to Christ cannot be questioned, since it is quoted in the New Testament in Matthew 26:31: "Then saith Jesus unto them, All ye shall be offended because of me this night: for it is written, I will smite the shepherd, and the sheep of the flock shall be scattered abroad." Jesus said this at the last supper, in reference to the disciples who would later that night forsake him and flee when he was captured in the garden of Gethsemane.

Before the quoted part, however, the word of God gives powerful testimony to the sovereignty of God in the crucifixion of Christ. That testimony to God's sovereignty is found first in the name "Lord of hosts," a name that teaches us that the great host of all created things is God's army, which marches in obedience to him, willingly or unwillingly, and thus fulfills his purpose.

It is this sovereign God who calls the sword against Christ, his shepherd and his own only begotten Son. The sword of judgment, up until that time quiet, pictured as sleeping, is wakened by the call of God against Christ. The passage says the same thing therefore as Acts 2:23, which tells us that Christ was delivered to the cross by the determinate counsel and foreknowledge of God, though that never excused the wickedness of those who crucified Christ. Acts 4:27–28 adds that the sword of God's justice was in the hands of Herod, Pilate, the Gentiles, and the people of Israel, who could do nothing with it but what God's counsel, his eternal decree, had determined before to be done.

That in itself is an amazing truth, but the verse says also that God's justice was executed on Christ. He was on trial not only before Pilate, Herod, and the Jews but also before God, and by God he was counted guilty and worthy of death and taken away to the place of execution so that God's justice might be satisfied. "It pleased the Lord to bruise him," Isaiah says (Isa. 53:10), and Christ recognized that, as his cry of agony, "My God, my God, why hast thou forsaken me?" so clearly shows. Moore says:

> There is in the whole compass of human knowledge, nothing more awfully sublime, than this seeming schism in the Godhead. It is as if sin was so dreadful an evil, that the assumption of its guilt by a sinless Mediator must for a time make a division even in the absolute unity of the Godhead itself. It is the most awful illustration of the repulsive and separating power of sin, that the history of the universe affords.[13]

---

13 Moore, *Zechariah*, 211–12.

Christ was counted guilty not for any sin of his own, but because the Lord had laid on him our iniquity. He was condemned before the judgment seat of God, that we might be acquitted. And what makes this even more wonderful is that he was God's only begotten Son, second person of the holy Trinity, a man and yet God's fellow, his nearest kin, as we read here. Though expressed in prophetic language, the verse is a whole theology of atonement and reminds us of all that belongs to our redemption.

That the passage is quoted in reference to the disciples in Matthew 26:31 does not exclude a wider interpretation. When Jesus quoted these words in reference to his disciples, he must have seen them as representatives of the whole nation of Israel and of the church. The reference to little ones suggests this wider application: even the smallest children are part of the fulfillment of this passage.

When the judgment of God falls on the shepherd, therefore, it is also falling on the flock, Israel in the Old Testament and the church in the New. Though the passage does not say as much, looking back to Zechariah 12, we remember that the flock rejects its shepherd and so becomes worthy of God's judgment. The scattering of the flock includes all the judgments of God on Israel, including the captivity in Babylon, the great Old Testament scattering, and the destruction of the temple in AD 70, the final scattering of the flock of the Old Testament. It includes also all God's judgment on the church when the church is unfaithful and disobedient, culminating in the great scattering of the church that will take place in the days of antichrist.

We must remember that though there are both elect and reprobate in the flock, all are equally worthy in themselves of God's judgment. None are guiltless, none unworthy of God's judgment. This scattering of the flock under the judgment of God was seen in miniature in the scattering of the disciples at the time of Jesus' arrest.

Nevertheless, the passage ends on a note of promise, for the phrase, "I will turn mine hand upon the little ones," is not a further word of judgment but a promise that some of the flock will be saved, the part that has already been referred to as "the poor of the flock" (11:7, 11) and "the feeble among them" (12:8). There is a similar promise in Isaiah 1:25: "And I will turn my hand upon thee, and purely purge away thy dross, and take away all thy tin."

Part of the flock upon which God turns his hand will be under the protecting hand of God, its shepherd.

In Matthew 26:31, where the first part of this verse is quoted, Jesus, after having spoken of the scattering of the flock, adds, "But after I am risen again, I will go before you into Galilee" (v. 32). That is the equivalent of "I will turn mine hand upon the little ones" and is a promise that he, the shepherd, will once again lead his flock. Both are promises of the continued care of the shepherd for that part of the flock that is truly his own.

That is the wonder of grace. The shepherd, having been killed by the sword of God, is nevertheless able to lead the little ones of the flock. Indeed, it is through his death and because of his death that God turns his hand upon the little ones and leads them like a shepherd!

> Christians look to a suffering figure for their spiritual cleansing, confessing that, like the remnant, they too have pierced him, and in sorrowful repentance they find in him their redemption.[14]

13:8. *And it shall come to pass, that in all the land, saith the* LORD, *two parts therein shall be cut off and die; but the third shall be left therein.*

Although judgment comes on the flock, the scattering of the flock is not its destruction but its salvation. Through that scattering God removes and destroys the wicked element, those who are not sheep but goats, and by separation of the sheep and goats, the flock is spared, even though two-thirds perish.

The amazing thing is that this comes about through the smiting of the Shepherd. His death is at the same time the reason judgment comes on the ungodly and unrepentant and the reason some escape that judgment. Zion is redeemed through judgment. When God executes the fury of his just anger on sin, there are some who escape because the judgment comes on the shepherd and not on them. Scattered they may be, but they are never lost; wandering and perishing, but never perished.

Nor may the fact that two-thirds of the flock perish hide the truth that

---

14 McComiskey, *Zechariah,* 3:1225.

the flock is saved. The rest are not really Jesus' sheep, though for a time it may appear that they belong. They are those who are of Israel but not really Israel, Jews only according to the flesh and not according to the spirit. They are those who belong to the church on earth but do not belong to Christ, those who have their names on the membership rolls of the earthly organization but whose names are not written in heaven.

The true flock belongs to Christ by election, by atonement, by faith, and by the sanctifying work of the Spirit. The rest, though born in our families and seated with us in the pew, are "not of us" (1 John 2:19). "Ye believe not," Jesus says to the Pharisees, "because *ye are not of my sheep*" (John 10:26, emphasis added).

That flock, chosen in eternity, is redeemed in its entirety. Not one is lost. And that is only to say that when God saves this remnant he not only saves the flock, but he also saves Israel, the world, and mankind. Salvation is not a salvage operation, in which God does the best he can to rescue something out of the world or a part of the flock, but what is saved *is* the flock, the world. The loss of two-thirds does not mean that God fails to accomplish all his purpose. He is never thwarted.

The remnant in scripture is sometimes a tenth (Isa. 6:13), but here a third. That different fractions are used means that we must take none literally. Whether two-thirds or nine-tenths, the thought is frightening: so many who appear to be part of the flock perish in the end under the judgment of God. There is therein good reason for each of us to examine ourselves.

13:9. And I will bring the third part through the fire, and will refine them as silver is refined, and will try them as gold is tried: they shall call on my name, and I will hear them: I will say, It is my people: and they shall say, The LORD is my God.

That the third part that is saved is equally worthy of destruction with the rest is shown in what happens to them. They are spared, but in a fiery way that purges them of their sins. They must be brought through the fire as well, not for their destruction but to purify them. The figures are mixed. We read of the flock and of refining fire and of trying gold and silver, but the mix of metaphors does not make the passage less powerful. The case of the disciples in whose presence Jesus quoted verse 7 illustrates what Jesus would do (Matt. 26:31). They would forsake and deny him, but he would once again lead them. They would be saved in the way of sin and grace as Peter was when he denied his Lord.

One cannot even imagine a flock of sheep being brought through the fire and not destroyed, but that is God's way with his flock, and a necessary way because "all we like sheep have gone astray; we have turned every one to his own way" (Isa. 53:6). The refining of silver and trying of gold, that is, the separation of the pure metal from all impurity, is accomplished only in the hottest fire. The fire of affliction and suffering, persecution and reproach through which the flock must pass in order to be cleansed of the impurity of sin is hot indeed.

But the result of this refining and purifying is good. Through it the flock learns to call on God's name in faith, in repentance, in supplication, in thanks—to call on his name in a way that is acceptable to him and pleasing to him and that he hears. Through this refining fire the covenant of God is realized and his people made holy so that they are able to live in his presence. That covenant is expressed here in terms of the covenantal formula: "I will say, It is my people: and they shall say, The Lord is my God."

This covenant is realized first in the fellowship God's people have with him through Christ: "And truly our fellowship is with the Father, and with his Son Jesus Christ" (1 John 1:3). This is realized finally and forever in the new Jerusalem: "Behold, the tabernacle of God is with men, and he will dwell with them, and they shall be his people, and God himself shall be with them, and be their God" (Rev. 21:3). What a day that will be!

Through all of this the sheep are separated from the goats and the carnal element in Israel and the church taken away and destroyed. Thus God's kingdom comes and his people receive eternal glory with Christ. In that way the curse of God is executed on those who return outwardly from Babylon but whose hearts are still there. In that way the woman, wickedness, is taken away in a basket to Babylon and left there. In that way the remnant comes to enjoy the glory so wonderfully described in the next chapter.

Chapter 25

THE SECOND BURDEN, PART 3:
Zechariah 14:1–21

14:1   Behold, the day of the Lord cometh, and thy spoil shall be divided in the midst of thee.

14:2   For I will gather all nations against Jerusalem to battle; and the city shall be taken, and the houses rifled, and the women ravished; and half of the city shall go forth into captivity, and the residue of the people shall not be cut off from the city.

14:3   Then shall the Lord go forth, and fight against those nations, as when he fought in the day of battle.

14:4   And his feet shall stand in that day upon the mount of Olives, which is before Jerusalem on the east, and the mount of Olives shall cleave in the midst thereof toward the east and toward the west, and there shall be a very great valley; and half of the mountain shall remove toward the north, and half of it toward the south.

14:5   And ye shall flee to the valley of the mountains; for the valley of the mountains shall reach unto Azal: yea, ye shall flee, like as ye fled from before the earthquake in the days of Uzziah king of Judah: and the Lord my God shall come, and all the saints with thee.

14:6   And it shall come to pass in that day, that the light shall not be clear, nor dark:

14:7   But it shall be one day which shall be known to the Lord, not day, nor night: but it shall come to pass, that at evening time it shall be light.

14:8   And it shall be in that day, that living waters shall go out from Jerusalem; half of them toward the former sea, and half of them toward the hinder sea: in summer and in winter shall it be.

14:9   And the Lord shall be king over all the earth: in that day shall there be one Lord, and his name one.

14:10   All the land shall be turned as a plain from Geba to Rimmon south of Jerusalem: and it shall be lifted up, and inhabited in her place, from Benjamin's gate unto the place of the first gate, unto the corner gate, and from the tower of Hananeel unto the king's winepresses.

14:11   And men shall dwell in it, and there shall be no more utter destruction; but Jerusalem shall be safely inhabited.

14:12   And this shall be the plague wherewith the LORD will smite all the people that have fought against Jerusalem; Their flesh shall consume away while they stand upon their feet, and their eyes shall consume away in their holes, and their tongue shall consume away in their mouth.

14:13   And it shall come to pass in that day, that a great tumult from the LORD shall be among them; and they shall lay hold every one on the hand of his neighbour, and his hand shall rise up against the hand of his neighbour.

14:14   And Judah also shall fight at Jerusalem; and the wealth of all the heathen round about shall be gathered together, gold, and silver, and apparel, in great abundance.

14:15   And so shall be the plague of the horse, of the mule, of the camel, and of the ass, and of all the beasts that shall be in these tents, as this plague.

14:16   And it shall come to pass, that every one that is left of all the nations which came against Jerusalem shall even go up from year to year to worship the King, the LORD of hosts, and to keep the feast of tabernacles.

14:17   And it shall be, that whoso will not come up of all the families of the earth unto Jerusalem to worship the King, the LORD of hosts, even upon them shall be no rain.

14:18   And if the family of Egypt go not up, and come not, that have no rain; there shall be the plague, wherewith the LORD will smite the heathen that come not up to keep the feast of tabernacles.

14:19   This shall be the punishment of Egypt, and the punishment of all nations that come not up to keep the feast of tabernacles.

14:20   In that day shall there be upon the bells of the horses, HOLINESS UNTO THE LORD; and the pots in the LORD's house shall be like the bowls before the altar.

14:21   Yea, every pot in Jerusalem and in Judah shall be holiness unto the LORD of hosts: and all they that sacrifice shall come and take of them, and seethe therein: and in that day there shall be no more the Canaanite in the house of the LORD of hosts.

Of this last chapter Luther said, "In this chapter I [surrender], for I am not certain of what the prophet treats."[1] The passage is not so difficult as he thought, however, when viewed in the context of the rest of Zechariah's prophecy and of the book of Revelation.

The third part of the second burden is parallel to Zechariah's seventh vision, but it develops that vision and carries us to the end of time and the final blessedness of the church. In many of the details the chapter is similar to Revelation 21 and 22—no night, no curse, no Canaanite, living waters, an abundance of wealth, perfect holiness, a new Jerusalem—all these are found in Revelation 21 and 22. There are also hints of Revelation 19 and the battle described there, the last great battle in which Christ and his church triumph over all their enemies.

The seventh vision of Zechariah, the vision of the four chariots and the two mountains of brass, also hints at these things, for those chariots come out from between the mountains of brass, out from the presence of God, and the result of their going forth is that all things come to pass according to the will and purpose of God. In that way the things foretold in Zechariah 14 come to pass.

There is also another connection between the two chapters. The two mountains of brass in Zechariah 6 are closely associated with Christ's coming and standing on the Mount of Olives in Zechariah 14:4. The passage between the two mountains of brass from which the chariots issue forth is really the same passage between the two halves of the Mount of Olives through which the people of God escape the coming judgments. Both ways lead into the presence of God and the glory that awaits there.

The main thing in this chapter, however, is the future glory of the church, and thus the cycle of visions and burdens comes to its climax and conclusion. The presence of Christ and his Spirit in the church (visions 1 and 5 and part 1 of each of the two burdens) and the deliverance of the church from her enemies and from the apostate and wicked who are outwardly part of the church (visions 2 and 6 and part 2 of the burdens) lead to a revelation of the present and future blessedness of the church (visions 3 and 7 and the third part of each of the burdens).

---

1 Quoted in Leupold, *Zechariah*, 258.

McComiskey says:

The prophet gives us a glimpse of heaven in symbols that fall far short of reality, but whose emotional force reach a deep level of our comprehension. It is as though we are observing a stained glass window depicting a person or event. The images of colored glass represent objective reality, and while they pulsate with brilliant light, they forever remain symbols. So with apocalyptic [things], for now we must wait to behold its realities. Beautiful as they are, these figures, like pieces of stained glass diffusing the light of the sun, can only suggest "what no eye has seen nor ear heard" (1 Cor. 2:9).[2]

14:1. Behold, the day of the LORD cometh, and thy spoil shall be divided in the midst of thee.

Once again the day of the Lord is in focus. That day is the whole New Testament period as it leads to and ends in the events of the last times. When we read of the day of the Lord *coming*, scripture does not mean that it has not already come. The day is always at hand and will be in the process of coming until history and God's purpose are finished. First Corinthians 10:11 says that the ends of the world have come on us already, no matter when in the New Testament we live, and those ends of the world are identical to the day of the Lord.

The word "behold" says that what follows is a matter of great interest, blessedness, and glory. The day of the Lord is a wonderful day, a day to behold in faith, for it is in the day of the Lord that God, by a miracle of grace, finishes his work and sends in the everlasting blessedness of Christ's kingdom. Only faith can see and behold how wonderful that day is, but the fact that many do not see does not lessen the glory of which Zechariah speaks.

The chapter begins with a reference to the destruction of Jerusalem under the judgment of God. The dividing of the spoil is not Jerusalem's inhabitants' dividing the spoil of their victories over the nations, but the nations' dividing the spoil of Jerusalem after conquering the city. Jerusalem, however, is no longer the city of God, the church, but the false church, Jerusalem that has become Sodom and Egypt (Rev. 11:8). That theme is further

---

2 McComiskey, *Zechariah*, 3:1234.

developed in the verses that follow, but if Jerusalem is spoiled then all the judgment predicted by Zechariah has come to pass and Jerusalem will be on the way to captivity once again for her sins.

All this was fulfilled in the destruction of the city by the Romans, but it continues to be fulfilled when God sends the false church into spiritual captivity. Just as the true church is Jerusalem (Heb. 12:22; Rev. 21:9–10), identical with the Old Testament city of God, so the false church also has that name, though she has that name only and not the reality. There are really two Jerusalems, therefore, the Jerusalem that is above and is the mother of all believers, and the Jerusalem that now is and is in spiritual bondage with all her children (Gal. 4:25–26).

14:2. For I will gather all nations against Jerusalem to battle; and the city shall be taken, and the houses rifled, and the women ravished; and half of the city shall go forth into captivity, and the residue of the people shall not be cut off from the city.

The nations will be God's instrument of judgment against apostate Judah and Jerusalem. God speaks of armies' besieging Jerusalem once again, and he threatens her destruction. Some find in this a reference to the destruction of the city in AD 70 by the Romans, but that interpretation of the passage is too limited, though certainly included. The end of the theocracy in AD 70 was God's judgment on a nation from which he had taken the gospel, a nation that had crucified the promised Messiah and had reached the limits of God's forbearance. The earthly city, when destroyed by the Romans under Titus, was destroyed for her wickedness and rejection of Messiah: "O Jerusalem, Jerusalem, thou that killest the prophets, and stonest them which are sent unto thee, how often would I have gathered thy children together, even as a hen gathereth her chickens under her wings, and ye would not! Behold, your house is left unto you desolate" (Matt. 23:37–38).

Nevertheless, in light of Revelation 11:7–13, there must be a further fulfillment of this prophecy in the end times. Jerusalem will once again be destroyed—not the earthly city, but the false church that she has become:

7. And when they shall have finished their testimony, the beast that ascendeth out of the bottomless pit shall make war against them, and shall overcome them, and kill them.

8. And their dead bodies shall lie in the street of the great city, which spiritually is called Sodom and Egypt, where also our Lord was crucified.

9. And they of the people and kindreds and tongues and nations shall see their dead bodies three days and an half, and shall not suffer their dead bodies to be put in graves.

10. And they that dwell upon the earth shall rejoice over them, and make merry, and shall send gifts one to another; because these two prophets tormented them that dwelt on the earth.

11. And after three days and an half the spirit of life from God entered into them, and they stood upon their feet; and great fear fell upon them which saw them.

12. And they heard a great voice from heaven saying unto them, Come up hither. And they ascended up to heaven in a cloud; and their enemies beheld them.

13. And the same hour was there a great earthquake, and the tenth part of the city fell, and in the earthquake were slain of men seven thousand: and the remnant were affrighted, and gave glory to the God of heaven. (Rev. 11:7–13)

The judgment of God on the apostate church is pictured in terms of a city taken by its enemies without quarter being granted: the slaughter of the inhabitants, rape, and pillage picture the destruction of the false church. No one and nothing is spared, and when God's judgments are finished only the true church remains. As completely as Jerusalem was destroyed first by the Babylonians and then by the Romans, so completely will the apostate church be destroyed.

However, some escape these judgments, and the verse concludes on a note of hope. There will be a remnant, a residue that is not destroyed nor cut off when the old earthly city and all it represents falls. This too finds a partial fulfillment in the destruction of Jerusalem in AD 70, when the Christians escaped to Pella in Syria. It has its complete fulfillment when God's people escape the judgments of God on the false church through history and the destruction of the false church in the last hour of history.

The interesting thing in Zechariah's description of these events is that while Jerusalem is destroyed, a remnant escapes to the last place we would expect, to Jerusalem. The city is taken and spoiled and half of the people go into captivity, while the remainder of the people are forced to flee the city through a way of escape provided by God (vv. 4–5). Yet they are not cut off from the city.

When Jerusalem falls, it is at the same time built and inhabited (v. 11). Given to its enemies for spoil, it is filled with the spoil of its enemies (v. 14). Conquered, it conquers (v. 12), left desolate it is inhabited, and the enemies who destroyed it are gathered into it (v. 16). But there are two Jerusalems (as Paul reminds us in Galatians 4): the Jerusalem that now is and is in bondage with her children, Jerusalem that becomes Sodom and Egypt, Jerusalem that crucifies the Lord of glory and kills his prophets (though she always decorates their graves), and Jerusalem that is above and free, the church of Christ, his bride and body. Delivered from the one Jerusalem, the remnant finds refuge in the other.

14:3. Then shall the LORD *go forth, and fight against those nations, as when he fought in the day of battle.*

God protects his people from their enemies. He has done that always and will do it until there is no more need for such protection, until his and our enemies are destroyed forever. His going forth is a reference to his providential care of his own. It is not as though he is not present always and comes only when needed for their defense, but the verse looks at his care from the viewpoint of our own experience. We are not ordinarily aware of his presence until beset by enemies or troubles, and only then do we experience again his care for us.

Ultimately his going forth refers to the return of Christ at the end of all things. Then he will go forth as a man of war and destroy all the enemies by the sword of his mouth and by the brightness of his coming. Then they will be judged and thrown into hell. His last great battle against his enemies is described in graphic terms in Revelation 19, but every other battle in which God fought for his people pictures what he continues to do for them and will do for them in that last day.

The day of battle is a reference to the whole of history, and especially to the Old Testament. That was the day of battle in that the victory over sin and death had not yet been won. In thinking of the day of battle one ought to think of Abraham's victory over the kings of the East, of Israel's deliverance from Egypt, of their victory over the Amalekites at Rephidim, of the standing still of the sun and moon in obedience to Joshua, of Gideon's victory over the Midianites, of every battle of the Old Testament in which God fought for his people and gave them victory, often in the face of impossible odds. But all of them are only shadows of the battle in which God's enemies are forever defeated, the battle Christ fought at the cross, and of the battle in which God's enemies are given as a prey to birds and beasts and thrown into eternal punishment in hell.

14:4. And his feet shall stand in that day upon the mount of Olives, which is before Jerusalem on the east, and the mount of Olives shall cleave in the midst thereof toward the east and toward the west, and there shall be a very great valley; and half of the mountain shall remove toward the north, and half of it toward the south.

14:5. And ye shall flee to the valley of the mountains; for the valley of the mountains shall reach unto Azal: yea, ye shall flee, like as ye fled from before the earthquake in the days of Uzziah king of Judah: and the LORD my God shall come, and all the saints with thee.

The literalists believe that Christ will actually stand on the Mount of Olives and that it will split in two when he returns a thousand years before the end to establish an earthly kingdom with Jerusalem as its center. The rest of this chapter, when compared with Revelation 21 and 22, shows that this interpretation is faulty. Even in the prophetic language of the Old Testament, the reference is obviously to the end of all things and not to some period a thousand years before the end.

Especially the last words of verse 5 remind us of the end. The coming of the Lord with his saints is not some coming long before the end, but at the very end. In 1 Thessalonians it is announced by the last trump, not a trump that will be followed by many others. In Jude it is part of his coming for final judgment.

What is interesting, though, about such references to Christ's coming with his saints is that they must already have been raised and glorified with

Christ. The exact order of events at the end of the world is difficult to work out, but this and other passages suggest that the resurrection of saints and their glorification precede the end, from which it follows that the awful events of the last hour of the world will be something through which the saints need not pass. They will see these things only as spectators as they come with Christ for judgment.

Christ's standing on the Mount of Olives, as so much of the book of Zechariah, is symbolic. The point is that through the coming of Christ, God's people will escape the judgment that is coming—a way of escape will be provided them, something like their escape from Egypt. The walls of the valley that is made between the two halves of the Mount of Olives will be on each side of them like the waters of the Red Sea, and the presence of the Lord will overshadow them as the pillar of cloud and fire did in the days of Moses. They will be protected on every side.

The Mount of Olives stands on the east side of the city of Jerusalem and guards the city on that side. It also, however, cuts off a quick escape from the city on the east, except that in this case God provides a way. The picture is of Jerusalem surrounded by enemies on the north, south, and west, but God opens a way through the mount so that his people are able to abandon the city and escape the city to the east, toward the rising sun.

The passage does not speak of the place to which they escape. The valley of the mountain is the valley that God makes through the Mount of Olives, part of the way of escape. That they escape to the east suggests that their refuge is finally heaven, for in the east the sun rises, and according to Malachi east is the direction from which Christ also comes as the rising Sun of righteousness.

Having escaped, they find their way back to Jerusalem, not Jerusalem as they knew it, nor Jerusalem as it once existed, nor Jerusalem as it comes under the judgment of God, but a Jerusalem that knows no night, from which flow living waters, a Jerusalem in which even the bells of the horses are holy, a new Jerusalem. The picture is somewhat confusing, but the reality is not. The message is the important thing. One must simply overlook the fact that having escaped Jerusalem they are found again in Jerusalem as a place of refuge. The truth is that, having escaped this world, they find their way to heaven.

The comparison to the flight of the people in the days of King Uzziah and the earthquake that then took place is obscure. There is no record in scripture of this event, except for what we read here, but it must have been a great earthquake, sufficiently terrible that the people of Jerusalem fled the city for fear that they would be caught up in its ruin. The reference to Azal is also obscure, and there is much disagreement among commentators over the meaning and significance of this name. Possibly it means "to stand still" or "to cease" and is not a place name but refers to the fact that God's people will escape completely, that is, to a place where no more danger exists for them, where they will stand still, and where their fear of being caught in the ruin of the city will cease. However, since scripture does not use the name elsewhere, it is best not to speculate, nor is it necessary: the point is that a way of escape and a place of refuge sufficient for all who desire to flee will be provided.

Those who read this word of God should not miss the connection with Zechariah's sixth vision. From between the two mountains of brass, representing the presence of God, the chariots and their horses come to fulfill God's will in all the earth. Now it is between the feet of Christ, representing again God's presence as he comes for judgment, that God's people find a way of escape from old Jerusalem and find their way to new Jerusalem. God's overshadowing presence is the safety of his people as he works his will in all the earth and their refuge and blessedness when his will is fully accomplished.

14:6. And it shall come to pass in that day, that the light shall not be clear, nor dark:

14:7. But it shall be one day which shall be known to the LORD, not day, nor night: but it shall come to pass, that at evening time it shall be light.

Here God begins to describe the glories of the new Jerusalem, the heavenly Canaan-land, in terms that remind us of Revelation 21 and 22. We read of endless day, of living waters flowing from the dwelling place of God, of an end of the seasons, of the everlasting kingship of the Lord, of no more utter destruction, of safety for God's people, and of the complete overthrow of their enemies. Though there are many who look for a literal fulfillment of these promises in an earthly Jewish kingdom, the similarity to the closing visions of John in Revelation show beyond doubt that Zechariah saw and heard the same things as John.

These two verses are similar to Revelation 21:23–24, "And the city had no need of the sun, neither of the moon, to shine in it: for the glory of God did lighten it, and the Lamb is the light thereof. And the nations of them which are saved shall walk in the light of it: and the kings of the earth do bring their glory and honour into it." It is a promise of heavenly light.

Some commentators believe that the words of verse 6, "the light shall not be clear, nor dark," and the words of verse 7, "not day, nor night," mean "that it shall not be a total obscurity, but only a twilight dimness, in which the darkness of the past shall be yielding to the light of the future."[3] However, even these commentators find in the words "at evening time it shall be light" a prophecy of eternal light following this time of gloom, this "great sunset of the world."

It is better to understand verse 6 as a reference to the fading of the heavenly lights. Literally the verse reads: "And it shall be in that day, there shall not be light; the glorious ones will darken." This will be followed by one day that is neither day nor night as we know them, a day in which it will be light at evening time. With the day of the Lord will come a new kind of day known only to God, "one day…known to the LORD," an endless day.

This has nothing to do with this present world but with that which is to come, for God has promised that day and night, summer and winter, seedtime and harvest will not cease while the world lasts. Only in the new creation will these cease. It will be a new world in which righteousness dwells. Neither the death that winter brings nor night that so often becomes a covering for wickedness will last into the new world.

14:8. *And it shall be in that day, that living waters shall go out from Jerusalem; half of them toward the former sea, and half of them toward the hinder sea: in summer and in winter shall it be.*

The literalists believe that a thousand years before the end of the world, Christ will return with those who have been raptured and will establish an

---

3 Moore, *Zechariah*, 224–25.

earthly Jewish kingdom with its center in Jerusalem. Combining this and other prophecies, they believe that a river will flow from the temple mount to the Mediterranean and to the Dead Sea and that the waters of the Dead Sea will be refreshed and will no more be salt and dead. They believe that there will be fruit trees that produce their fruit every month of the year and that the earthly land of Canaan will once again be a land of milk and honey. Only in this way, they say, will the promises God made to Abraham and to his descendants be fulfilled.

The similarity of this passage to Revelation 22:1 makes this view of the dispensationalists and premillennialists an impossible dream. That verse reads: "And he shewed me a pure river of water of life, clear as crystal, proceeding out of the throne of God and of the Lamb." Jerusalem is described in the Old Testament as the throne of God (Jer. 3:17), and when John sees the water of life coming from God's throne in heaven, he sees the same thing Zechariah saw when he saw living water going out from Jerusalem. Revelation 22 is describing nothing in this world but rather the new creation of God, where there will be no more sin (Rev. 21:27) and no more curse (Rev. 22:3), and where the saints reign not for a thousand years but for ever and ever (v. 5). Where this living water flows the word of Christ is fulfilled, "Behold, I make all things new" (Rev. 21:5).

In Revelation 22 these living waters symbolize the fulfillment of all our needs and the satisfaction of all our desires. They are a picture of the waters of salvation that Christ alone provides and that, if anyone drinks, will forever quench his thirst. They symbolize Christ as the source of eternal life and all the blessedness that is in him. Moore says: "To an Oriental in his burning clime, the image of a gushing stream, whose grassy margin was overhung by waving trees, was one of the most significant that could be used to express a divine blessing."[4]

That the waters flow to both the former and the hinder sea means that they flow to all God's people, and that where desolation and death have reigned, life and bliss now rule. There will be no death in the new creation: no Dead Sea and no barren ground. The whole land will be watered from this river of the water of life and will not be as in former days, part fruitful and

4 Ibid., 225–26.

part uncultivated land. It is all figurative and a picture of the new creation and of the things that eye hath not seen nor ear heard, nor have entered into the hearts of men to understand.

14:9. And the LORD *shall be king over all the earth: in that day shall there be one* LORD, *and his name one.*

That the Lord will be king over all the earth in that day does not refer to his universal kingship over all things but to the rule of his grace that will prevail in the day of the Lord, first through the preaching of the gospel to all nations and then perfectly and completely in the new heavens and new earth. He will then be the only ruler in the sense that there will be no other beside himself acknowledged and served. All those who rebel against him will be destroyed, and those who do not bow before him will be taken away.

The repeated use of the name Jehovah makes it clear that the verse has application to his gracious rule over his own, begun when he establishes the throne of his kingdom in their hearts and perfected when he gathers them to himself in the new creation. His name will then be one in their hearts and mouths, and there will be no divided loyalty, no turning away from him, and no more possibility of friendship with the world, for this present world will be destroyed.

As Jehovah, the God of the covenant, his tabernacle will be with men, and he will dwell with them and be their God and they will be his people. The covenant first revealed in paradise will be perfected and lifted up to a greater glory through Jesus Christ, through the resurrection of the dead, and through the making new of all things.

14:10. All the land shall be turned as a plain from Geba to Rimmon south of Jerusalem: and it shall be lifted up, and inhabited in her place, from Benjamin's gate unto the place of the first gate, unto the corner gate, and from the tower of Hananeel unto the king's winepresses.
14:11. And men shall dwell in it, and there shall be no more utter destruction; but Jerusalem shall be safely inhabited.

Zechariah continues to describe the glories of the new creation. Since the earthly land of Canaan was the clearest type of Messiah's heavenly land, it is used in this vivid description to portray what that land will be like when Christ comes again. Included in the picture is a reference to earthly Jerusalem and its inhabitants as a picture of the Jerusalem that is above and her inhabitants.

Here especially the figures used are shown to contradict each other. In verses 4–5 the people of God are seen escaping from Jerusalem, which has been delivered into the hands of her enemies, and in verses 10–11 Jerusalem is inhabited and at peace. This has caused commentators no end of puzzlement, but it is no great difficulty because scripture speaks of two Jerusalems, Jerusalem that is above and free and Jerusalem that now is and is in bondage (Gal. 4), Jerusalem that is spiritually one with Sodom and Egypt and Jerusalem that is the eternal dwelling place of God with his people (Rev. 21:1–3). The saints escape by grace from the one Jerusalem to find their eternal home in the other.

That the land will be turned to a plain can be interpreted in a number of different ways. It may mean something like chapter 4:7, where God promises Zerubbabel that the mountain of difficulties he and the people faced in their work of rebuilding the temple would be removed. It might also mean that the land will be fruitful and blessed with no unfruitful and uncultivated areas, no uncultivated mountainsides, no swampy lowlands, but all one fruitful plain. The latter view seems preferable since the emphasis throughout is on the blessings of the heavenly Canaan.

The rest of the passage confirms that this is a description of the city of Jerusalem. The city was more or less in the form of a blunt triangle, and the description follows the entire circumference of the walls of the city (the gate of Benjamin on the north, the first gate on the east, the tower of Hananeel on the southeast, the wine presses on the southwest, and the corner gate on the west). In other words, the city will be completely inhabited, unlike the days of Zechariah and Nehemiah, when there were not even enough people to live in the city but certain families had to be chosen by lot to fill it (Neh. 11:1–2).

That Jerusalem will be lifted up refers to her final glory when in the new heavens and earth she will be the dwelling place of God. There she will also be free forever from her present troubles. No enemy will come against her again. Never again will her walls be destroyed and her palaces left in ruin. Never again will her inhabitants be deported. She will be called Beulah and her land Hephzibah and never again be called a city forsaken and desolate (Isa. 62:4).

This elevating of Jerusalem is also pictured in Revelation 21, where the city, the new Jerusalem, which is also the Bride, the Lamb's wife, is depicted as a city two thousand miles high. Truly, as Isaiah says, "the mountain of the LORD's house shall be established in the top of the mountains, and shall be exalted above the hills" in that day (Isa. 2:2). God's city will be exalted over all!

Even "no more" can only be understood in light of scripture's promises and revelations of the eternal state. The thousand-year earthly kingdom proposed by the millennialists is no more a complete fulfillment of such promises as these than is the temporary and limited fulfillment found in the history of Israel in Canaan. The literalists insist on a literal interpretation of the promises, but they cannot and will not accept the possibility that the words "no more" may be the only literal part of these verses.

From Geba to Rimmon is from the northern border of Judah (2 Kings 23:8) to its southern border (Josh. 15:32). The blessedness described will be enjoyed by all. None will be missing. Everyone will be included in the promised blessedness. The whole of God's true church will be glorified.

14:12. And this shall be the plague wherewith the LORD will smite all the people that have fought against Jerusalem; Their flesh shall consume away while they stand upon their feet, and their eyes shall consume away in their holes, and their tongue shall consume away in their mouth.

14:13. And it shall come to pass in that day, that a great tumult from the LORD shall be among them; and they shall lay hold every one on the hand of his neighbour, and his hand shall rise up against the hand of his neighbour.

14:14. And Judah also shall fight at Jerusalem; and the wealth of all the heathen round about shall be gathered together, gold, and silver, and apparel, in great abundance.

14:15. And so shall be the plague of the horse, of the mule, of the camel, and of the ass, and of all the beasts that shall be in these tents, as this plague.

Again scripture describes the church's final deliverance in terms of Old Testament victories and judgments. The plagues of verse 12 are similar to those threatened in Deuteronomy. Those plagues were often visited on Israel's enemies in the Old Testament and continue to be visited on the ungodly in the New Testament especially in a spiritual sense. Think of the concluding words of Acts and of the descriptions of hell in the New Testament! Those are the final realization of these judgments. The judgments described are too horrible to imagine, what McComiskey calls "the disgusting description of bodies rotting even before they fall to the ground,"[5] but the crime for which these punishments come is equally atrocious. Those who feel the heavy hand of God are those who fought against Jerusalem, the church of God, which Christ bought with his blood. What a warning to those who despise that church!

The description of verse 13 is of a battle in which the enemies of God's people turn on one another. Of this also there are numerous examples in the Old Testament. Gideon's battle against the Midianites (Judges 7:22) and Judah's battle against a confederation of Moab, Ammon, and Edom in the days of Jehoshaphat (2 Chron. 20:22–23) are some of the more noteworthy examples. The fulfillment, however, is in the end times when the allies of the great whore and the beast turn on her and eat her flesh in the last great battle, the battle of Armageddon. In this battle, which immediately precedes the coming of Christ, the antichristian kingdom begins to disintegrate as the nations who have been at peace with one another turn on each other and destroy one another.

The result of this last battle will be that the people of God take the spoil of their enemies, as Judah did in the Old Testament, only in this case it will be everything the heathen and ungodly have claimed as their own, including all the land. The meek shall inherit the earth, and not the earth only but heaven also, and will live in that glorious land forever.

Verse 15 describes the plague that destroys the church's enemies as coming on the beasts and tents, which is to say that God's judgment comes on everything the wicked have. In this life already the curse of the Lord is in their houses (Prov. 3:33), and in the end they go to the grave and to hell with nothing, "for when he dieth he shall carry nothing away; his glory shall not descend after him" (Ps. 49:17).

14:16. And it shall come to pass, that every one that is left of all the nations which came against Jerusalem shall even go up from year to year to worship the King, the LORD of hosts, and to keep the feast of tabernacles.

5 McComiskey, *Zechariah*, 3:1240.

14:17. And it shall be, that whoso will not come up of all the families of the earth unto Jerusalem to worship the King, the LORD of hosts, even upon them shall be no rain.

14:18. And if the family of Egypt go not up, and come not, that have no rain; there shall be the plague, wherewith the LORD will smite the heathen that come not up to keep the feast of tabernacles.

14:19. This shall be the punishment of Egypt, and the punishment of all nations that come not up to keep the feast of tabernacles.

That this all has a fulfillment in the New Testament and in the gathering of the Gentiles into the kingdom of God is once again evident, for the nations are described as coming to Jerusalem to keep the feast of tabernacles. There are those who look for a literal fulfillment of this prophecy in the reestablishment of the Jewish kingdom for a thousand years in Jerusalem, but its fulfillment is first spiritual and then heavenly.

The feast of tabernacles was the Old Testament feast at which Israel commemorated their deliverance from Egypt and their years in the wilderness under God's protective care by living for a week in booths made of the branches of trees: palms, myrtles, olives, and pines (Neh. 8:15). This feast was celebrated at the same time as the feast of trumpets and marked the end of the ecclesiastical year while pointing to the end of all things. Its fulfillment comes when the last trumpet sounds and when "the tabernacle of God is with men" and he dwells with them as their God and takes them to himself as his people (Rev. 21:1–3).

It also marked the end of the harvest, for when the fulfillment of this feast comes the whole harvest of God will be gathered in, the great harvest of salvation, when the wheat is gathered by the angel reapers into barns and the chaff separated and burnt with fire (Matt. 13:37–43). Each of the Old Testament feasts has its New Testament equivalent. Paul speaks, for example, in 1 Corinthians 5 of New Testament believers' keeping the feast of unleavened bread. The feast of tabernacles is kept in its spiritual reality when Christ comes again.

Coming to that feast in the New Testament is believing in Christ as the one through whom God delivers his people from spiritual bondage and by whom he leads them through the wilderness of this world to eternal rest in the heavenly Canaan. When the Gentiles believe in Christ and look for his return, therefore, they begin to come to this feast as prophesied by Zechariah. Those who do not come will be visited by the plagues mentioned in the previous verses. Their flesh will be consumed by the worm that never dies. They will be cast into outer darkness and will be destroyed in the fire that burns for all eternity.

Revelation 7:16–17, a parallel passage, speaks of hunger and thirst, of tears and of being exposed to the heat of the sun, all of which Israel suffered in the wilderness and all were typical of the child of God's pilgrimage through this world. All of this shall come to an end when the great multitude that no man can number stands before the throne with palm branches in their hands, celebrating the eternal reality of the feast of tabernacles and giving thanks to God as Israel did in the Old Testament when they kept that feast. It is, as Hengstenberg says, a feast "to be celebrated in heaven by those who have ended their dangerous pilgrimage of suffering and temptation through the desert of life, and have safely reached the heavenly Canaan, the place of their repose."[6]

It is celebrated only by those who are left:

> Just as it was not all that came out of Egypt who entered Canaan and celebrated the feast of tabernacles...so the heathen, who formerly marched against Jerusalem, will not all go thither in gratitude and love, but only the remnant, which has been spared by the mercy of God, after the obstinate despisers of His name have been destroyed by the judgment depicted before.[7]

Egypt is mentioned particularly as the nation that held Israel in bondage, but included in Egypt spiritually are all those who are in the bondage of sin and who persecute God's people as Pharaoh did in Egypt. Thus Revelation 11 speaks of the city of Jerusalem itself becoming Sodom and Egypt when it crucifies our Lord. To Egypt, then, belongs every unbelieving Jew and Gentile, and all will be destroyed. Even Egypt, which depended for its

---

6 Hengstenberg, *Christology*, 4:131.
7 Ibid.

fruitfulness not on rain but on the River Nile, will taste the judgment of God when the great day of judgment comes. None will escape.

These judgments are described here in terms of drought because rain was the preeminent sign of God's blessing in the Old Testament. Even then it was a sign nationally. It could not be concluded even in the Old Testament that because an individual had lost his crops, he was without the blessing of God, but nationally that was the case. Rain was an important sign because it symbolized the Spirit and grace of God, and therein lies the fulfillment of this threat. Without the Spirit and grace men perish, and so shall the ungodly perish in every age and at the end when Christ returns. Now God still sends rain on the just and the unjust; then it will be a rain of unquenchable fire.

14:20. *In that day shall there be upon the bells of the horses,* HOLINESS UNTO THE LORD; *and the pots in the* LORD's *house shall be like the bowls before the altar.*

14:21. *Yea, every pot in Jerusalem and in Judah shall be holiness unto the* LORD *of hosts: and all they that sacrifice shall come and take of them, and seethe therein: and in that day there shall be no more the Canaanite in the house of the* LORD *of hosts.*

The book of Zechariah concludes with the most important blessing of the new Jerusalem, the gift of perfect holiness. There will be in that holy city no sin, no sinner, nothing that defiles or makes a lie, and not even the possibility of evil. That the bells of the horses and the common pots in the temple will be holy is scripture's way of saying here what Revelation 22:14–15 say more plainly: all will be holy.

"HOLINESS UNTO THE LORD" was the inscription on the golden plate worn by the high priest on the front of his mitre on ceremonial occasions. It spoke of his complete dedication to God. The Lord was his inheritance, the work of the Lord his only work, devotion to God his sole calling. Thus it will be in the new Jerusalem. All will be priests in the house of God (Rev. 1:6). There will no longer be anything secular or common or unholy.

That there will be no Canaanite is the same truth. Not only will the city itself be holy, but also its inhabitants will be holy with none unbelieving and wicked among them. The Canaanites were those who first filled up the measure of wickedness in the Old Testament and came under the judgment of God. They were notorious for the sins of Sodom and Gomorrah, for their gross idolatry, for sacrificing their own children to their idols, for fornication and uncleanness, and so became worthy of God's wrath. There will be none of them in the new Jerusalem and no one like them.

All this is true and comes to pass through him who rides the red horse and stands among the myrtles in Zechariah 1, through him who takes our filthy clothing as his own and exchanges it for clean garments in Zechariah 3, through him who rides as a meek and lowly king to take possession of his kingdom, through him who appears as the rejected shepherd in Zechariah 12. To him belongs this kingdom. The new Jerusalem is his city and there he reigns. The land is Messiah's land and to his own he gives an inheritance in that land. It is the coming of Zion's king and the work of his Spirit that brings all these things to pass, in the preaching of the gospel and the gathering of the Gentiles in the New Testament and in the everlasting kingdom that is still to be revealed.

MESSENGER
OF THE
COVENANT

THE PROPHECY
OF MALACHI

Behold, I will send my messenger,
and he shall prepare the way before me:
and the Lord, whom ye seek,
shall suddenly come to his temple,
even the messenger of the covenant,
whom ye delight in:
behold, he shall come,
saith the LORD *of hosts.*
—Malachi 3:1

Introduction to Malachi

The prophecy of Malachi, the last voice of the Old Testament, has special significance for those who live at the end of the New Testament era. As a book that describes the end times of the Old Testament and looks forward to better things, it retains its importance for those who live at the end of all ages and who are waiting for the better things of the everlasting and heavenly kingdom of Christ.

The book tells of covenantal unfaithfulness—the unfaithfulness of God's church and of his people in the last days of the Old Testament. The Jews had been cured of the sin of idolatry by the long years of the captivity in Babylon, but they had become unfaithful by falling into other sins. Their unfaithfulness was seen especially in "a spirit of proud and bigoted self-righteousness that claimed the favour of God with insolent haughtiness, at the very moment that this favor was forfeited by unbelief and neglect of duty."[1] In worship their neglect of duty was evident in the mere external performance of religious duties and the despising of God's ordinances for worship, both matters of covenantal unfaithfulness in relation to God. In their daily life they were guilty of unfaithfulness in marriage and thus of covenantal unfaithfulness in their relations to one another.

In a surprising way these instances of unfaithfulness match exactly the unfaithfulness of the church today. There is nothing today that shows the covenantal unfaithfulness of the church as clearly as her complete neglect of what God has commanded for worship and her disregard for God's ordinances concerning marriage. Worship, something that lies at the heart of God's covenant, has been turned into a three-ring circus and the covenant of marriage into a game of musical chairs in the modern church. The divorce rate among evangelical Christians is higher than among the ungodly, and it is difficult in many instances to tell the difference in today's church world between worship and a rock concert. Covenantal unfaithfulness indeed!

---

1 Moore, *Haggai, Zechariah and Malachi*, 350.

Not only does the Jews' unfaithfulness match exactly the unfaithfulness of the church in these last days, but as in Israel, the unfaithfulness of the church is not recognized and all attempts to point it out are met with scorn and disbelief. Indeed, the Jews of Malachi's day, like the church today, charged God with unfaithfulness instead of turning from their own wickedness when they did not receive the blessings he had promised. What Malachi describes, therefore, is so very much like the unfaithfulness of the church today that the book can only have been inspired by the Spirit of God.

This unfaithfulness of the church described by Malachi is the dark background against which God reveals his unchangeable faithfulness and grace. He revealed his faithfulness then in continuing to preserve his church and in promising the coming of Christ as the one who would purge the church of its sins and bring it blessing and glory. Christ's coming was seen by Malachi as the only cure for sin, and the promise of his coming as messenger of the covenant, the purifier of the church, was the central message of the book for Judah. That promise of Christ's coming and of cleansing, given through Malachi, looked forward not only to the first coming of Christ but also to the second, so that the book of Malachi has kept its significance and relevance and continues to be a revelation of God's faithfulness to his church. It is a book of hope looking forward to the church's final purification and salvation.

Because of its relevance the book of Malachi is quoted or alluded to seven times in the New Testament. It is quoted in Matthew 11:10, Mark 1:2–3, Luke 7:27, and Romans 9:13 and alluded to in Matthew 3:3 and Luke 1:17 and 76. In these references the New Testament echoes some of the main themes of Malachi, the coming of Jehovah's messenger and the eternal purpose of God that lies behind all his dealings with his church.

The prophecies of Malachi, then, are words from God that the church very much needs to hear and heed. As much as Israel needed to hear them then, so much more does the church need to hear them now as she waits for the messenger of the covenant and his purifying work. May there be many who do hear and heed what Malachi says.

The Author

Malachi is third and last of the three prophets of the restoration, that is, of the years following the return of Judah from captivity in Babylon. During those years the Jews were busy with the rebuilding of the temple and the city of Jerusalem and their own reestablishment in the promised land. Malachi appears near the end of the period and is later than the other two prophets.

We know next to nothing about him except his name, if Malachi is his name. As in the case of Haggai, no information about his family or history is given, a reminder that the message he brings is not really his but God's. The man himself did not matter much then and really does not matter now. He is only God's instrument or messenger in bringing God's word to God's people. We, like the Jews, must hear his prophecies as the inspired and infallible word of God.

As suggested, there is some dispute about the name Malachi. Some believe that Malachi is the personal name of the author. Others believe that Malachi is not a personal name but a title or description of the author's place in the kingdom of God and of the work that God had given him to do. They believe Malachi is not a proper name because it means "my messenger," is similar to the description of Haggai as "messenger" in Haggai 1:13, and is the same word used in Malachi 3:1 and translated there as "my messenger."

Those who believe that the name Malachi is only a description of the author's office have made numerous guesses about his actual identity. Some, because Haggai is called the Lord's messenger in Haggai 1:13 (the *malach* of Jehovah), believe that Haggai is the author of this book also. Calvin, following Jewish tradition, believed that the book's author was Ezra. But all attempts to name the author, if Malachi was not his name, are pure speculation. It is best to believe that Malachi *is* the name of the book's author, especially because all the other Old Testament prophecies that begin with a superscription like Malachi 1:1 do record the name of the author, that is, Ezekiel, Daniel, Jonah, Haggai, and Zechariah.

If Malachi is his proper name, the meaning of his name, "my messenger," is still important. As a messenger of Jehovah, he prophesies of another messenger, John the Baptist, who would do the same work as himself but at the very beginning of the New Testament era. More importantly, John prophesies of and pictures the great Messenger of Jehovah, the messenger of the covenant who comes to purify the sons of Levi.

"Messenger" and "angel" are the same word in Hebrew, the word "malach." This is of special significance in chapter 3:1, which speaks of the messenger or angel of the covenant and of his coming. Not only does this verse show us that the messenger is Christ, but because messenger and angel are the same word in Hebrew, we know that this messenger is also the *angel* of the covenant or the angel of Jehovah who appears throughout the Old Testament. This messenger or angel of the covenant is the main character in Malachi's prophecy.

The Date

There can be little doubt that the book of Malachi, as its position in the Old Testament suggests, is the last of all the books of the Old Testament. The book itself indicates in Malachi 1:10 and 3:1 that the temple had been rebuilt, making it later than Haggai's and Zechariah's prophecies, and there are other indications that date it to the time of Nehemiah, though no date is given in the book.

The primary evidence for Malachi's being a contemporary of Nehemiah is found in a comparison of the two books, which shows their dealing with the same sins: the sins of mixed marriages, formalism in worship, and neglect of tithes. A comparison of Malachi 1:6–2:9 with Nehemiah 13:4–9, 29–30; of Malachi 2:11–12 with Nehemiah 13:1–3, 23–27; and of Malachi 3:8–12 with Nehemiah 10:32–39 and 13:10–13 shows this clearly. Not only do these parallels show the similarity of the two books, but also both Malachi and Nehemiah mention the covenant with Levi (Mal. 2:4; Neh. 13:29), the only Old Testament books to do so explicitly.

Nehemiah spent two terms in Judah as governor, the two terms separated by a few years. He first came during the reign of the Persian king Artaxerxes, identified in history as Artaxerxes I, to help the Jews rebuild the walls of Jerusalem. This was in the twentieth year of Artaxerxes (approximately 445 BC; Neh. 1:1). He remained in Jerusalem twelve years (Neh. 5:14), during which time he opposed and corrected some of the evils into which Judah had fallen. He then returned to Babylon for a time (Neh. 13:6).

When he returned the second time to Jerusalem, probably around 433 BC, near the end of the reign of Artaxerxes, he found many new evils in Judah. It was then especially that he was forced to deal with the same sins against which Malachi prophesies. Malachi is therefore a contemporary of Nehemiah and so also of Ezra. (Ezra had come to Jerusalem with a second group of returned captives about thirteen years before Nehemiah came [Ezra 7:8] and was still living when Nehemiah arrived [Neh. 8:9].) Malachi must have prophesied about ninety years after Haggai and Zechariah, and between four and five hundred years before Christ.

In that context his prophecy shows the need for Christ's coming and looks forward to his coming as the next great event in the history of redemption. That is its pertinence also for those who believe that the next great event in the history of redemption is Christ's return at the end of all things.

The Divisions

The book of Malachi is divided into six disputations, introduced by a superscription (1:1) and ending with a brief summary (4:4–6). In the first disputation (1:2–5) Malachi speaks in general terms of the unfaithfulness of the people and rebukes them for refusing to love and honor God. In the second (1:6–2:9) he begins to point out specific sins of the people, speaking especially of the sins of the priests. In the third disputation he deals with the sins of mixed marriages and of divorce (2:10–16). In the fourth he prophesies the coming of Christ and of his forerunner (2:17–3:6), and in the fifth he returns again to the sins of the people, this time rebuking them for their neglect of tithes and offerings (3:7–12). The sixth and last section (3:13–4:3) brings more general reproofs and warnings as well as the promise of better things to come. The book concludes with an exhortation to remember the law of Moses, enforced by a reference to the coming day of the Lord (4:4–6).

The English chapter divisions therefore do not follow the actual divisions of the book and are at times misleading. For example, chapter 2:1 divides God's word to the priests into two parts and might leave the impression that there are two different messages for them. Also, that chapter 3 begins where it does separates the promise of the coming of the messenger of the covenant from unfaithful Judah's question in chapter 2:17, "Where is the God of judgment?" The connection between the question and its answer are in that way obscured in our English translation. It would probably be better to read the book following its actual divisions than by following the English chapter divisions.

Chapter 26

THE SUPERSCRIPTION:
MALACHI 1:1

1:1. The burden of the word of the LORD to Israel by Malachi.

Like the greetings in Paul's epistles, the superscription to Malachi's prophecy teaches some important truths besides identifying Malachi as the writer. Most important is the reference to Malachi's prophecies as the "burden of the word of the LORD." That they are the word of the Lord, the inspired and infallible word of God, is beyond doubt in light of the quotations in Romans 9:13 and other passages. That they were and are a burden we shall see.

In identifying himself as the author of these prophecies God uses the name Jehovah (LORD), reminding Judah and us of his covenantal faithfulness. There is no further positive word from God, other than the repetition of this name, from chapter 1:2 through chapter 3:1. Until then, under rebuke and judgment, the mention of Jehovah's name is the only evidence of God's favor.

The covenantal name Jehovah is the most important name of God in the book of Malachi for the same reason. It is found forty-five times in Malachi and very often (twenty-three times) in the form "LORD of hosts," a name that emphasizes God's *sovereignty* as the God of the covenant. In contrast, the name God is found only seven times in the book.

God's great and unchangeable faithfulness as Jehovah preserves Israel and the church in spite of the sins of his people, and that same faithfulness sends the one who will "purify the sons of Levi, and purge them as gold and silver, that they may offer unto the Lord an offering in righteousness" (3:3). The faithfulness of God as Jehovah is expressed most clearly in Malachi 3:6, "For I am the LORD, I change not; therefore ye sons of Jacob are not consumed."

In chapter 1:1, however, God's word through Malachi is described as a burden. This description of God's word, also found in Isaiah 13:1, Nahum 1:1, and Habakkuk 1:1, teaches us three things. It reminds us of the *calling* Malachi had to bring that word. He had to receive it, carry it to the people, and deliver it to them, as any burden is carried. Burden also reminds us of the seriousness or weight of the word that Malachi brings and of our own obligation to hear it. God's word is heavy indeed and may never be ignored. Finally, the description of God's word through Malachi as a burden shows us *why* that word is so heavy, that is, it is very often a word of judgment and rebuke. It is the kind of word that everyone who brings God's word experiences as burdensome and difficult (Jer. 20:9; 2 Cor. 2:16). Here the weightiness of God's judgment is being emphasized.

This word of judgment comes "through Malachi." The name Malachi, as already indicated, is the personal name of the prophet who was called to bring God's word to God's people in troubled times, but the meaning of the name cannot be ignored. In light of the book's emphasis on the *messenger* of the covenant (3:1), it cannot be without significance that Malachi's own name means "my messenger" or "my angel" (messenger and angel are the same word, the word *malach* in Hebrew).

Though Malachi looks forward to and prophesies of the coming of the great Messenger, he is also such a messenger. The connection between them is not just that the one, Malachi, foretold the coming of the other, Christ, but that Malachi was commissioned by Christ and spoke under the inspiration of the Spirit of Christ (1 Pet. 1:10–11). Thus the word he spoke was really Christ's own word to his church, the word of *the Messenger* of the covenant.

Such is always the relationship between the prophets and Christ in the Old Testament and between Christ and his ministers in the New. They are not only those who speak of Christ, but the ones through whom Christ himself speaks to his church (John 10:27; Eph. 2:17). One of the words for a preacher in the New Testament reminds us of this and, when used of a minister of the gospel, is very similar to Malachi's own name. The word usually translated "preacher" refers to the minister of the gospel as a "herald" or messenger of Christ by whom Christ speaks and makes himself known.

This may never be forgotten. When it is forgotten in the church, the preaching of the gospel is seen as nothing different from other forms of teaching and speaking and is soon despised and replaced, as it is today, by all sorts of frivolity and foolishness. When preachers forget that the word they bring is from Christ, the true messenger of the covenant, they no longer see themselves merely as bearers of God's message to his people and begin to bring their own words, none of which have any saving power or value.

The word of God here is addressed to *Israel*, not just to Judah. God never recognized the division between the two kingdoms, just as he does not recognize the divisions that come between Christians today, but views and addresses his church as one. Indeed, by addressing his word to Israel as well as to Judah, God continued to gather a remnant out of the kingdom of the ten tribes. He had done so in the days of Jeroboam and in the time of Hezekiah, and he continued to do it until the gospel was taken from Israel and given to the Gentiles (Luke 2:36–38).

Chapter 27

THE FIRST DISPUTATION:
MALACHI 1:2–5

1:2   I have loved you, saith the LORD. Yet ye say, Wherein hast thou loved us? Was not Esau Jacob's brother? saith the LORD: yet I loved Jacob,

1:3   And I hated Esau, and laid his mountains and his heritage waste for the dragons of the wilderness.

1:4   Whereas Edom saith, We are impoverished, but we will return and build the desolate places; thus saith the LORD of hosts, They shall build, but I will throw down; and they shall call them, The border of wickedness, and, The people against whom the LORD hath indignation for ever.

1:5   And your eyes shall see, and ye shall say, The LORD will be magnified from the border of Israel.

1:2. I have loved you, saith the LORD, Yet ye say, Wherein hast thou loved us? Was not Esau Jacob's brother? saith the LORD: yet I loved Jacob,

1:3. And I hated Esau, and laid his mountains and his heritage waste for the dragons of the wilderness.

God begins the prophecy of Malachi by speaking of his eternal love for his people, and he does so because the people have questioned his love. Probably they had not done this openly, but God who knows men's hearts knew what they were thinking and saying in their hearts:

> [Malachi] expresses the things they feel which perhaps they would never say in public. He exposes that self-deception about our spiritual lives to which we are all so prone. The pious Jew would never sarcastically say, "How has God loved us?" or "It is vain to serve God," in public, while he in fact thinks these things in his heart. Many is the time that, in spiritual weakness, waywardness and blindness, Christians have thought like that, although, of course, they present a different front as they sit in the pew Sunday by Sunday.[1]

In Judah the people had questioned the love of God because they had not received the temporal blessings he had promised them. To this Malachi 3:10–11 alludes. The people had experienced drought, enemies, poor harvests, and many other troubles and had seen this as evidence of a failure on God's part. According to them God's love for his people had failed.

The truth is that temporal benefits are not in themselves the equivalent of God's blessing or proof of his love—it is only a carnal and covetous people who can think so—but the problem was in their own sinfulness. They had no right to expect anything from God when they were hardhearted and formal in their worship and did not acknowledge God's mercies with their tithes and offerings. They expected the most from God for the least amount of effort or expense, and when God in anger gave them nothing, instead of questioning themselves they questioned God's love.

---

1 John Benton, *Losing Touch with the Living God: Malachi* (Darlington, UK: Evangelical Press, 1985), 16–17.

419

This is the usual way with an unregenerated heart. The ungodly world, which never even acknowledges its obligation to be thankful to God, always questions God's love and mercy when God sends his judgments on the world. It insists that he cannot possibly be a God of love and mercy when he sends hurricanes, disease, famine, and other judgments.

The apostate church does the same. Never does she question herself and her own wicked ways, but tells lies about God's love when she comes under God's judgments or when she sees those judgments in the world around her. She says, in the face of disaster and trouble, that God does not send such things but rather the devil, and the belief that these things come from God is inconsistent with the love of God.

We see the same inclination in ourselves. When God sends trials, all of which are designed to purify us and deliver us from our sins, we almost always begin to doubt God's love and to think in our hearts that he does not love us, instead of humbling ourselves before him, examining ourselves, acknowledging our sinfulness, and repenting.

Trials do not always come as a result of some particular sin, but they do come because we are sinners, and God uses them to deliver us from our sins and purify us. When afflicted, we must profit from our afflictions by self-examination and repentance. We must not doubt God's love and mercy. To do so is a grievous sin in the light of God's eternal and unchangeable love for his people revealed in the person and work of the Savior.

In the face of such denials of his love, God speaks of his eternal and unchangeable love for Jacob. The Jews would have known that by the name Jacob, God was referring not only to the man himself but to the nation that traced its ancestry to him, the nation of Israel. They would have known this especially from the prophecies of Isaiah, who often calls the whole nation "Jacob" (Isa. 43:1; 44:1, 23).

God does not, however, speak through Malachi of the love he bore for Israel at the time of Malachi's prophecy, but of his *past love* for Jacob: "I *have* loved you, saith the LORD." Calvinists have always understood the past tense in such statements (Num. 23:21) to refer to *eternity*. When God says, "I *have* loved you," he refers not just to *time* past, but to *eternity* past and therefore to his eternal love, the love that is revealed in election.

The proof for this is found in Romans 9:10–13, where Paul, under the inspiration of the Spirit, quotes from this passage and identifies God's past love for his people as God's election of them in Christ. There the apostle makes reference to the birth of Jacob and Esau and to the word of God concerning them, "The elder shall serve the younger," and tells us that this was said in order that "the purpose of God according to election might stand, not of works, but of him that calleth." He proves his point by quoting from Malachi 1:2–3: "As it is written, Jacob have I loved, and Esau have I hated."

Election is a revelation of the love of God. It is "love before time." Election as sovereign choosing is an expression of God's eternal love. Romans 8:29 says, "Whom he did foreknow [love], he also did predestinate [choose in election]." The love expressed in election is the reason election is complete, decisive, and irrevocable. It is also the reason election is a comfort to God's people. There is no greater comfort than to know that God loves us and loves us from eternity. We may not understand our outward circumstances, but the eternal character of God's love is our assurance that God has not changed and he still loves us.

Malachi speaks of God's eternal love for good reason. For God to say to Judah that he had loved them in *time* past would be no reassurance to them. It is only because he loved them from eternity that his love is proved unchangeable and abiding in spite of what outward circumstances might make them think. He says to them, "Do not say my love has changed or failed when things go wrong. My love cannot fail. It is eternal and abiding and cannot fail. If there is a problem, it is not in me but in you."

Because the love of God is eternal it is also unconditional, that is, the reason for it is never to be found in God's people, either in what they *are* or in what they *will be*. God uses the name Jacob, a name that reminds us of Jacob's weaknesses and sins, to express his unconditional love. Remembering the things Jacob did and the way he behaved as Jacob, we know God could not have loved him for what he was but loved him freely and unconditionally. In the same way, God shows that it was wrong for Israel to say, "Wherein hast thou loved us?" by way of suggesting that God's love was changeable and conditional.

That this love is for Jacob only, that is, for the elect only, is usually glossed over or openly denied. John Benton in his commentary on Malachi goes to great lengths to demonstrate that there is a love of God for non-Christians revealed in the creation and in a genuine offer of salvation to all who hear the gospel, and he quotes 2 Peter 3:9 and John 3:16 as proof.[2]

God also shows the eternal and unconditional character of his love for Jacob and Israel when he speaks of his hatred for Esau. The point here is the same as in Romans 9: God's love for Jacob and hatred for Esau had nothing to do with what they were or would be, but was entirely according to the good pleasure of his own will (Eph. 1:5). He did not love Jacob because Jacob was holier than Esau or had any primacy as far as descent or family was concerned, but he loved Jacob simply because he was pleased to do so.

Thus the reminder in Malachi that Esau was Jacob's brother. In every earthly and outward respect they were equal or Esau was superior, and therefore God's love for Jacob can only have been free and gracious and unconditional. Paul makes this same point in Romans 9:6–13. In order to prove that the difference between the true seed of Abraham and those who are only fleshly descendants of Abraham is all grace, Paul first brings up the example of Isaac and Ishmael, who were both physical descendants of Abraham but of whom only Isaac God counted as the seed of Abraham. Since, however, it would be possible to object that there was a real outward difference between Isaac and Ishmael in that they were half-brothers with different mothers, Paul adds the example of Jacob and Esau, who were not only full brothers but also twins, and whose place in relation to God's covenant and love was revealed before they were born. Their example proves, Paul says, that salvation, including the irresistible calling of some and not others, is according to God's own purpose in election.

The free and eternal love of God for Jacob appears all the more wonderful when contrasted with God's free and eternal hatred of Esau. In speaking of his hatred, God speaks of what is called reprobation, the opposite of election and the eternal decree of God concerning the damnation of some. When God says, "I hated Esau," he is saying he hated and rejected Esau from eternity, just as he loved and chose Jacob from eternity.

There is much opposition to this doctrine, and almost every commentator

---

2 Ibid., 24–26. We recommend to those who are interested in this question "The Meaning of 'Kosmos' in John 3:16," in Arthur W. Pink, *The Sovereignty of God* (Grand Rapids, MI: Baker Book House, 1951), 311–14. This appendix along with much other material is omitted in the Banner of Truth Trust edition.

rejects the idea of eternal reprobation here. Laetsch speaks of the "horrible doctrine of an eternal decree of reprobation" and says God's hatred for Esau only means he loved Esau less than Jacob.[3] Pusey says God could not have hated Esau before he sinned and that Jacob's election and Esau's rejection only have to do with temporal things.[4] Others, regarding Malachi 1:3 and Romans 9:10–13, speak of a national election and reprobation and insist God is only loving and choosing Israel as a nation and hating and rejecting Edom as a nation.

All these efforts to avoid the doctrine of reprobation, the most hated doctrine in scripture, must fail. They must fail because the rest of scripture teaches the doctrine (1 Pet. 2:8; Jude 4). But they must also fail because they do not do justice to what Malachi says here.

If Malachi is only speaking of nations, why does he not use the names of the nations, rather than the names of the two brothers? It cannot be denied that God is speaking through Malachi of his dealings with the two nations. Such is clear from verses 4–5, but those two nations include not only many other individuals, but the two brothers as well. One cannot choose a nation or reject a nation without choosing and rejecting certain individuals. What is more, God's dealings with the two nations are specifically traced back to his attitude toward Jacob and Esau: "Was not Esau Jacob's brother? saith the LORD: yet I loved Jacob, and I hated Esau."

To speak of a lesser love of God for Esau and for Edom is nothing but sophistry. While it is true that the word *hate* is sometimes used in scripture to mean "love less" (Matt. 10:37), it cannot mean that here. For one thing, God not only reveals his attitude toward Esau, but also reveals what the result of that attitude would be. He would lay Esau waste and thwart every effort of Esau and Edom to prosper (v. 4). Indeed, as a result of God's hatred for Edom, Edom would be called "the people against whom the LORD hath indignation forever" (v. 4). That is strange love, even if it is a lesser love than God's love for Jacob.

What is more, if God is saying he loves Esau less than Jacob, there is no comfort in God's love for Jacob, especially when Jacob sees how that lesser

---

3 Laetsch, *The Minor Prophets*, 512.
4 Pusey, *The Minor Prophets*, 2:465.

love for Esau is revealed—in laying Esau's mountains and heritage waste and overthrowing his every effort to rebuild and reestablish himself. Israel would have reason then to say, "That's exactly what we were getting at. That's the kind of love God shows. That's the kind of love he showed for us." Israel's words, "Wherein hast thou loved us?" would become not a wicked complaint, but the truth!

This love and hatred involve more than temporal and earthly prosperity. More was involved in the original case of Jacob and Esau. Already then it involved the promise of Christ, a place in God's covenant, and all the spiritual blessings and privileges that Israel enjoyed in the Old Testament (Rom. 9:4–5). According to Romans 9, the calling and salvation of some and not others was at stake. Being or not being a child of God (v. 8), being counted for the seed (v. 8), and being graciously called (v. 11) were at issue, all of which are traced back to and rooted in God's love and hatred. The very name Jehovah, used in Malachi 1:2, shows that God's covenantal love and covenantal relationship to his people are at stake in God's love for some and hatred of others.

When speaking of the results of God's hatred for Esau, it is easy to miss the spiritual overtones and eternal consequences of this hatred, because this word of God was first fulfilled in the destruction of Edom as a nation. At about the time of Malachi, the territory of the Edomites to the south and east of the Dead Sea was conquered and taken over by the Nabateans, and the existence of Edom as an independent nation ended.

The temporal blessings and judgments of the Old Testament are always pictures of spiritual things. Temporal things in themselves do not necessarily represent the blessing or disfavor of God. If it were so, the wicked would often have more of God's blessing than his own people, and his own people would have no comfort in their trials and troubles. Nevertheless, we can clearly see the destructive power of God's wrath in the judgments he sends on the earth and be warned by them, whether we are believers or unbelievers, whether we are touched by them or only see them at a distance.

Here, then, the laying waste of Edom prefigures the destruction of this present world under the judgment of God and the destruction with it of all the hopes and works of the ungodly. What they have in this world will be laid waste by God, all that they build will be overthrown, and they will be left forever impoverished. It is all a revelation of the eternal hatred of God for some. It is sovereign, unconditional reprobation.

1:4. Whereas Edom saith, We are impoverished, but we will return and build the desolate places; thus saith the LORD of hosts, They shall build, but I will throw down; and they shall call them, The border of wickedness, and, The people against whom the LORD hath indignation forever.

The wicked always refuse to recognize God's judgments. What happens to them in the anger of God they see only as a temporary setback that can with enough time and effort be overcome. AIDS, crime, war, poverty, social inequality, and unrest are all seen as problems to be solved through political action, social reform, and education. Never do they repent of their idolatry, sorcery, murder, and theft (Rev. 9:21). While their world falls to pieces around them they continue to talk optimistically of a better world, even of colonizing the stars. They stubbornly persevere in their rebellion against God. But this is all according to God's eternal purpose and sovereign hatred.

His hatred is reflected in the names that Edom receives as a result of God's judgments. The first name, "border of wickedness," identifies Edom as the wicked world. Edom receives this name from those who witness her judgments. Those who give Edom this name do so because they see that Edom lies beyond the grace and mercy of God. It is a land outside the boundaries and borders of his love and saving purpose. "Border of wickedness" has the same idea therefore as "the world" when that name is used in scripture to refer to the unrepentant and unbelieving world of the ungodly, the world that perishes and for which Jesus does not even pray (John 17:9).

The name "people against whom the LORD hath indignation for ever" describes God's unchangeable and everlasting wrath against Esau and Edom, the opposite of his unchangeable and everlasting love for his people. His wrath, as is always the case, is shown in all his dealings with them, even when he sends earthly prosperity and peace. Even then he is angry with them (Ps. 73:18–20) and is judging them.

Both his wrath and its revelation in Edom's ruin are the outworking of God's eternal hatred and decree of reprobation. This in no wise absolves Edom of her guilt or makes God the author of sin but shows that all things proceed from God's eternal decree: he is indeed sovereign in all his works and ways.

425

This revelation of God's eternal purpose in reprobation is for the purpose of displaying the character of his love for his people. In this respect election and reprobation are not equal, but reprobation serves election. God does not eternally hate and reprobate people as an end in itself, merely because he wants to, but for the sake of election—here for the sake of showing his elect people the nature of his love for them so that they do not question his love for them. Just as his hatred of Esau is eternal and implacable, so must his love for his people also be eternal and unchangeable. Israel may not say, "Wherein hast thou loved us?"

We should not be surprised when this eternal and unchangeable love of God for some, revealed against the frightening backdrop of his eternal hatred for others, is questioned and doubted. It is characteristic of a faithless church now as then to question and doubt the character of God himself and to begin to tell lies about him designed to excuse and cover the church's unfaithfulness and wickedness. His eternal, and therefore unconditional and unchangeable, love for his people through all circumstances and in all times must be emphasized even though it implies his eternal and unchangeable hatred for others. His love is the gospel! Those who understand this will be comforted, not frightened.

1:5. And your eyes shall see, and ye shall say, The LORD will be magnified from the border of Israel.

Why does the prophet speak in this first disputation of the wrath of God and its eternal source (vv. 2–4)? The answer lies in verse 5. God's eternal hatred in reprobation and its results are not an end in themselves. Reprobation is always subordinate and serves another purpose. Here the purpose is described in terms of Israel's seeing God's judgments on Edom, understanding those judgments to be the result of his eternal wrath, learning that his love is also eternal and unchangeable, and thus praising him.

That is the only possible reaction to these judgments and their eternal source, other than disbelief and scorn. Seeing God's fury poured out on the heathen, realizing that the outpouring of his wrath is not a hasty reaction against the wickedness of the heathen but the working out of an eternal and unchangeable decree, we tremble before God and cease to speak carelessly and foolishly of him.

Especially we do not speak as Israel did in the days of Malachi, as though his love is a temporary and changeable thing like ours. Seeing these judgments, we do not say, "Wherein hast thou loved us?" but trust that like his wrath and hatred, his love also is unchangeable and abiding, even when circumstances seem to indicate otherwise. And when we do not experience the height and length and breadth and depth of his love, we do not blame him but examine ourselves and look for the reason in our own sinfulness. We do not say, "Wherein hast thou loved us?" but, "What evil have we done that the Lord should seem so far away in his love and grace?"

The Lord here begins to speak of the fact that it would be no longer in Israel but among the heathen nations, the Gentiles, that he would be feared and honored. "From the border of Israel" does not mean within the borders of Israel but from the border of Israel outward. In Israel, with only a few exceptions, his name would continue to be dishonored and his love for his people questioned. The result would be the removal of the gospel, the good news of God's eternal love for his people, and its privileges from the Jews and the sending of the gospel to the Gentiles.

This becomes clear especially in Malachi 1:11: "For from the rising of the sun even unto the going down of the same my name shall be great among the Gentiles; and in every place incense shall be offered unto my name, and a pure offering: for my name shall be great among the heathen, saith the LORD of hosts." Because of this word of God we Gentiles now know of his eternal love for us and offer up spiritual sacrifices, acceptable to God through Jesus Christ (1 Pet. 2:5).

Chapter 28

THE SECOND DISPUTATION:
MALACHI 1:6–2:9

1:6   A son honoureth his father, and a servant his master: if then I be a father, where is mine honour? and if I be a master, where is my fear? saith the LORD of hosts unto you, O priests, that despise my name. And ye say, Wherein have we despised thy name?

1:7   Ye offer polluted bread upon mine altar; and ye say, Wherein have we polluted thee? In that ye say, The table of the LORD is contemptible.

1:8   And if ye offer the blind for sacrifice, is it not evil? and if ye offer the lame and sick, is it not evil? offer it now unto thy governor; will he be pleased with thee, or accept thy person? saith the LORD of hosts.

1:9   And now, I pray you, beseech God that he will be gracious unto us: this hath been by your means: will he regard your persons? saith the LORD of hosts.

1:10   Who is there even among you that would shut the doors for nought? neither do ye kindle fire on mine altar for nought. I have no pleasure in you, saith the LORD of hosts, neither will I accept an offering at your hand.

1:11   For from the rising of the sun even unto the going down of the same my name shall be great among the Gentiles; and in every place incense shall be offered unto my name, and a pure offering: for my name shall be great among the heathen, saith the LORD of hosts.

1:12   But ye have profaned it, in that ye say, The table of the LORD is polluted; and the fruit thereof, even his meat, is contemptible.

1:13   Ye said also, Behold, what a weariness is it! and ye have snuffed at it, saith the LORD of hosts; and ye brought that which was torn, and the lame, and the sick; thus ye brought an offering: should I accept this of your hand? saith the LORD.

1:14   But cursed be the deceiver, which hath in his flock a male, and voweth, and sacrificeth unto the Lord a corrupt thing: for I am a great King, saith the LORD of hosts, and my name is dreadful among the heathen.

2:1   And now, O ye priests, this commandment is for you.

2:2   If ye will not hear, and if ye will not lay it to heart, to give glory unto my name, saith the LORD of hosts, I will even send a curse upon you, and I will curse your blessings: yea, I have cursed them already, because ye do not lay it to heart.

2:3   Behold, I will corrupt your seed, and spread dung upon your faces, even the dung of your solemn feasts; and one shall take you away with it.

2:4   And ye shall know that I have sent this commandment unto you, that my covenant might be with Levi, saith the LORD of hosts.

2:5   My covenant was with him of life and peace; and I gave them to him for the fear wherewith he feared me, and was afraid before my name.

2:6   The law of truth was in his mouth, and iniquity was not found in his lips: he walked with me in peace and equity, and did turn many away from iniquity.

2:7   For the priest's lips should keep knowledge, and they should seek the law at his mouth: for he is the messenger of the LORD of hosts.

2:8   But ye are departed out of the way; ye have caused many to stumble at the law; ye have corrupted the covenant of Levi, saith the LORD of hosts.

2:9   Therefore have I also made you contemptible and base before all the people, according as ye have not kept my ways, but have been partial in the law.

1:6. A son honoureth his father, and a servant his master: if then I be a father, where is my honour? and if I be a master, where is my fear? saith the LORD of hosts unto you, O priests, that despise my name. And ye say, Wherein have we despised thy name?

In this longest section of the book of Malachi God addresses the priests, not only because they were the spiritual leaders of the people and were responsible for much of the apostasy of the nation, but also because they ought to have been the ones who rebuked the people for their apostasy and tried to turn them from it. When spiritual leaders do not rebuke apostasy but become the leaders in wickedness, they come under judgment for their own sins and for the sins of those who are under them. God points this out in Ezekiel 33:1–6:

1. Again the word of the LORD came unto me, saying,
2. Son of man, speak to the children of thy people, and say unto them, When I bring the sword upon a land, if the people of the land take a man of their coasts, and set him for their watchman:
3. If when he seeth the sword come upon the land, he blow the trumpet, and warn the people;
4. Then whosoever heareth the sound of the trumpet, and taketh not warning; if the sword come, and take him away, his blood shall be upon his own head.
5. He heard the sound of the trumpet, and took not warning; his blood shall be upon him. But he that taketh warning shall deliver his soul.
6. But if the watchman see the sword come, and blow not the trumpet, and the people be not warned; if the sword come, and take any person from among them, he is taken away in his iniquity; but his blood will I require at the watchman's hand.

Thus the judgments Malachi threatened against the priests are especially severe.

The sins of the priests were three. They had polluted God's offerings, they had despised their own position in the church and kingdom of God, and they had been partial in judging the people. These sins are described in chapter 1:6–10, 12–14, and chapter 2:5–8.

Each mention of priestly sin is followed by a statement of the judgment of God upon the priests for their wickedness. For the sin of despising and misusing their office, God would take away their priestly office and give it to the Gentiles (1:11). For the sin of polluting his offerings, the offerings from which they themselves lived and received their sustenance, God would curse the produce of flock and field and thus take away from them everything they had (2:2–4). For the sin of partiality in judgment, the sin of despising God's law, of which they were the caretakers, God would make them contemptible and despised in the sight of the people (2:9).

Those who are the spiritual leaders of God's people always bear a greater responsibility for apostasy and wickedness in the church than do the members. The leaders have this greater responsibility because of their position and calling. They are responsible when they encourage apostasy in the church by their own conduct and example, as these priests did, and when they fail to rebuke the wickedness of the people.

The people themselves are never without fault. They often follow the example of godless leaders blindly and ignorantly, and the people are sometimes a cause of the leaders' wickedness when they refuse good counsel, insist that their leaders tell them only what they want to hear (Isa. 30:10), and stubbornly go their own way.

What usually happens is this: The people become worldly and carnal, as they were in the days of Nehemiah and Haggai, and when they refuse to hear rebuke and to turn from their wicked ways, their leaders, instead of continuing to rebuke them and resist them in their wickedness, begin to cater to it. Eventually, the leaders become the leaders in wickedness and lead the people deeper and deeper into it. So it happened in Israel. So it happens in the church today.

Before pointing out the actual sins of the priests, God speaks of their wickedness as something dishonoring to him. The honor and fear they expected and received from their own children and servants, they refused to give to him. To emphasize the point he speaks of himself as their father and master, which indeed he was, and not just a father and master, but the Father and the Master. Yet they despised his name and never rendered him his due. It was their greatest sin.

God's fatherhood toward his people is a truth not often mentioned in the Old Testament. The explanation of this is found in Galatians 4:1–7, where Israel, though God's child, is compared to an immature child who, under tutors and governors, was treated little different than a servant. Nevertheless, the fatherhood of God *was* known by the people of God (Ex. 4:22–23), and the priests, who were the teachers of the law, ought to have known it and knowing it have honored and obeyed him as a father. Certainly they knew he was their master and Lord and should have feared him at least for that. But they did not. Instead of honoring him as the father of his people, they had behaved as though he was a stranger. Instead of honoring him as their master and owner, they behaved as though the law, the temple, and the sacrifices belonged to them.

Indeed, they did not even recognize their own sin but, when confronted with it, insisted they had not refused to honor him. Thus their question, "Wherein have we despised thy name?" It was not an innocent question but an expression of their doubt and distrust of God and meant: "We have not done so—there is nothing that can possibly be mentioned against us as proof of such a lack of honor." Benton says:

> Filled with a sense of their own importance, leaders and teachers can easily become unteachable. There is always a terrible danger that the man who is so accustomed to ministering the Word of God may foolishly become closed to the Word himself and blind to his own sins.[1]

In Judah neither priests nor people would listen to God's rebukes, a perennial problem in the church and a sure sign of apostasy. Ability to receive rebuke and correction is one of the greatest tests of our spirituality and a test that few today can pass, either as leaders or as members of the church. When one attempts to correct or rebuke a leader in the church, he is solemnly reminded not to touch the Lord's anointed. When members are corrected or rebuked, they simply pack their bags and go elsewhere, even when they have solemnly promised to submit to church discipline.

---

1 Benton, *Losing Touch with the Living God*, 29.

The offerings were the most important part of the worship of God in the Old Testament. In polluting God's offerings therefore, the priests, the spiritual leaders, were corrupting the worship of God. Nor are things any different today, for this is what the leaders of the church almost always do. They do as they please in the worship and service of God and when confronted with their disobedience refuse to recognize their sin. All that matters to them is enthusiasm and a crowd, and the people for the most part agree.

Their appearance, their wealth, their covetousness, their pride, their music, their teachings, their prayers are dishonoring to God, if not openly blasphemous, but when these things are pointed out to them they are shocked. They cannot understand that the music that is indistinguishable from the worst music of the ungodly is an abomination to God, that their own teachings deny every fundamental doctrine of Christianity, that their wealth and covetousness make them the stumbling block to the ungodly and little different from the Pharisees who devoured the livings of the widows and orphans, and that when they speak to and about God they show they know nothing of him.

The people they lead are too ignorant to know the difference, too insensitive to care even if they do know, and only interested in salving their own consciences with an outward show of piety. They care nothing about holiness, know nothing of the glory of God, and will follow anyone who will promise them earthly prosperity and who will keep them entertained. Indeed, their lack of regard for the proper worship of God and their desire for something new are often the reason for the disobedience and wickedness of their leaders. Their leaders are only giving them what they want.

Here for the first time in Malachi, God uses the name Lord of hosts. He does so in connection with what follows concerning the priestly offerings and office. That name identifies God as the sovereign owner and ruler of all things who uses them to fulfill his own purpose and good pleasure—all things are a mighty host, an army, that marches in his service, willingly or even unwillingly. The offerings and offices of the priests belonged to him as the Lord of hosts, not to the priests, and they were not to be used as the priests saw fit, for their enrichment and profit, but for his honor. In the next verse he even speaks of the altar as his own. The priests had acted as though it were not so—as though the offerings did belong to them. They behaved, in other words, in exactly the same way as many ministers, elders, and leaders of the church behave today—as though the worship and service of God and the offerings brought to God in worship belong to them to do with as they please.

1:7. Ye offer polluted bread upon my altar; and ye say, Wherein have we polluted thee? In that ye say, The table of the LORD is contemptible.

1:8. And if ye offer the blind for sacrifice, is it not evil? and if ye offer the lame and sick, is it not evil? offer it now unto thy governor; will he be pleased with thee, or accept thy person? saith the LORD of hosts.

1:9. And now, I pray you, beseech God that he will be gracious unto us: this hath been by your means: will he regard your persons? saith the LORD of hosts.

God charges these priests first with offering polluted bread on his altar. There is some question about whether the word "bread" refers to all the offerings or just to the so-called "meat offerings," which were primarily offerings of meal, flour or loaves, or to the showbread, renewed each day on the table that stood on the north side of the holy place. The "table" may be the table of showbread, the table on which the sacrifices were prepared for the altar, or the altar itself, but it really makes no difference as far as Malachi's point is concerned. Though the word "bread" seems to refer to the meat offerings, the priests in all the offerings were despising the service of God. They could not possibly have polluted only some offerings and kept the others unpolluted.

The priests received their sustenance and support from these offerings. The showbread, when taken from the table, was given to the priests for food. The meat offerings were also theirs, as was a part of every offering, except the whole burnt offering. Malachi addresses this issue, since the priests were not satisfied with the offerings they received. They saw their work not as a calling in relation to God but as a poor-paying job. The contempt of verse 7, therefore, is that of the priests for their work as priests.

This contempt led to a corrupting of the sacrifices. Verse 7 means that the priests allowed the people to bring every kind of unacceptable offering to God, including blind, lame, and sick animals, though forbidden in the law (Ex. 22:31; Lev. 7:24; 17:15; 22:8; Ezek. 4:14; 44:31). What was imperfect was unclean and could not even be eaten by the people. Yet the priests allowed the people to bring such offerings and themselves ate of them, in order to have more than they would otherwise have.

Such wickedness was the fault not only of the priests, but also of the people, in that they did not give willingly to the Lord and begrudged every good thing that was offered to God. Nevertheless, their grudging covetousness and poor giving did not excuse the wickedness of the priests.

This same contempt is often found in those who have the calling to preach the gospel. It usually becomes evident not in an open contempt for the service of God but, as with these priests, in a dissatisfaction with the wages they receive for their work and in the lack of honor they show toward God. Dissatisfied, such men give as little honor to God as they possibly can, changing the worship of God into a sideshow and putting themselves at center stage. And like these priests, they seek to enrich themselves by allowing the people to bring every kind of unacceptable offering, no longer insisting that God must be worshiped as he has commanded.

Also pictured here is every minister of the gospel who finds his work beneath him because he has an inflated sense of his own importance and gifts, every leader who hankers for a position of importance and influence and is reluctant to serve in a small congregation or in any position that requires sacrifice—the man who maneuvers and plays politics in the church for a place in the seminary or some other position of leadership. Here we have a portrayal of every Christian who finds the worship of God and the preaching of the gospel wearisome and who does his Christian duty grudgingly if he does it at all. This is the Christian who can never find time for family worship or private worship of God and who neglects these most important duties because he really is not interested in them.

The worship and service of the temple is a picture and foreshadowing of the worship we bring to God. Many scripture passages speak of our worship as an offering (Rom. 12:1–2; 1 Cor. 5:8; Heb. 13:15). That offering must be brought according to the word of God and in real gratitude and faith. When it is not, it is blind and lame and sick like the offerings of these Jews.

How often is not the offering brought to God in worship poor and lame and sick! Sometimes the act of worship itself is not what he has commanded—when all sorts of things are done in the worship of God that have no place there. Sometimes the offering that is brought is poor and lame and sick not because the act itself is wrong, but because the heart of the worshiper is not right with God. He comes in unbelief, superstitiously, and as a mere formality.

How much more often are not such polluted offerings allowed by those who are God's ministers and representatives in the church as the priests of old! And is it not then most often the case that they allow the people to bring such offerings, though they themselves know better, in order that they may profit—that they may have large congregations, expensive buildings, vestments, larger collections, houses and lands of their own? Few will suffer loss and impoverishment for the sake of maintaining purity in doctrine or in the worship of God. Every reformer whom God has raised up in his church has heard pious words of encouragement from those who appeared to be his supporters but who left him standing alone when their own livelihood and physical well-being were threatened. Every minister of the gospel, every elder and leader in the church who puts himself and his own things before the worship and service of God is as guilty as these wicked priests and is being addressed as well as them.

Such leaders today allow the truths of God's word to be compromised and the worship of God to be corrupted. They allow man-made songs to be substituted for the Psalms contrary to God's command, entertainment to take the place of the preaching of the gospel, and frivolity to take the place of reverence and serving God. They themselves, like these priests, bring such offerings to God as though they will be acceptable to him. What Malachi says is as much for today as for his own times, though most today will say, like the priests, "Wherein have we despised thy name?" "Wherein have we polluted thee?" Such actions, verse 8 reminds us, are evil, acts of rebellion against God because they violate his command and show no regard whatever for his holiness and glory.

To impress upon the priests the seriousness of their sin, God suggests that they bring to their governor, probably Nehemiah (Neh. 5:14), the kind of offerings they brought to God. God's question, "Will he be pleased with thee, or accept thy person?" is a rhetorical question, the answer to which could not possibly be in doubt. Nehemiah took nothing from the people

during his years among them (Neh. 5:15), but even then the kind of offerings they were bringing were unfit and unlawful even for such uses and he,
as governor, would have been insulted by such offerings.

Verse 9 is ironic. Malachi is telling the priests that if the governor would
not accept the kind of offerings they were bringing, then certainly God
would not either. The idea is: "Go with your offerings to God and make
intercession on the basis of these offerings, praying that God will be gracious
to us. Do you really think he will accept your ragged offerings and hear your
silly prayers?" The phrase "this hath been by your means" is part of the irony
and is saying: "You are the only ones who can do these things, the ones who
have been called to do them. Do you think God will be pleased with you
and accept you?"

These priests and the people they led had forgotten God's greatness and
glory. They no longer feared God, something also very much missing in the
church today. The words of Psalm 36:1 are truer today than ever before:
"There is no fear of God before [their] eyes." God has been reduced both in
theology and in practice to an object of contempt. In modern theology he is
portrayed as weak, changeable, dependent on the whims of men: certainly
not a God to be feared. In practice he has become little more than a great
Santa Claus in the sky whose only reason for existence is to satisfy every lust
of the human heart and to justify whatever men wish to do in worship and
daily life, whose commands are meaningless, and whose word is of no more
value than the whining of some poor beggar. He is thought of as someone
who can be manipulated at will and not as someone before whom we ought
to tremble and be reverent. Christians today, including the leaders of the
church, do not even *know* how great he is. If they did they would be terrified.

*1:10. Who is there even among you that would shut the doors for nought?
neither do ye kindle fire on mine altar for nought. I have no pleasure in you,
saith the LORD of hosts, neither will I accept an offering at your hands.*

Verse 10 goes even further in showing God's disgust and displeasure
with the priests. The verse is usually taken to be a further exposure of the
mercenary attitude of the priests: "You will not even shut the doors of my
house without pay." But more in line with the second part of the verse is
the interpretation that sees this as God's rejection of them and their work.

He is telling the priests to shut the doors of his house and to cease offering sacrifices, since that would be better than their continuing to bring the useless, polluted offerings they did bring. "Is there no one," God is saying, "with sufficient zeal for me and for my worship to put an end to this hypocrisy and wickedness?" And lest they would continue deliberately to misunderstand and to stand amazed and disbelieving that God should be so upset with them over nothing, God tells them plainly that he has no pleasure in them and will accept no offering from them.

How the church today needs to hear this. In spite of all the excitement and enthusiasm, the large crowds and huge churches in which they gather, God receives nothing from them and has no pleasure in them. Better would it be if their doors were shut and silence reigned, than that they bring to God the polluted offerings they do: "Christian" rock music, holy laughter, silly miracles, jokes and stories; these are not acceptable to God in place of what he has commanded.

The priests never listened to this word of God, and the doors of the temple remained open and their foolish formal sacrificing continued until God himself shut it all down permanently in AD 70, when temple and altar were destroyed by the Romans. What a warning to all those who offer strange fire and polluted sacrifices on God's altar and who pay no attention when he tells them that he would rather have no worship at all from them!

Moore sums it all up thus:

Then, as now, men sought, as for the philosopher's stone, a cheap religion — one that would insure heaven to them on the easiest terms. Hence they made a shuffling compromise with duty, compounding for the lowest possible percentage of self-denial and effort. God assures them that a cheap religion, like most cheap things, was always dear, since it always cost more than it was worth — for it was worth just nothing. God will not despise the widow's mite, but he will despise the miser's mite — especially when the blinded man is dreaming that by this beggarly shift he is securing the favor of God. As he drops his pittance into the treasury of the Lord, a voice comes forth from the throne, Who is there among you that will close the doors against this insulting mockery, and tell the starveling giver that he had better keep his miserable apology for a gift, for it was worse than thrown away when presented as an offering to God. O! that this voice of indignant scorn could be rung through the laggard Churches of Christendom, who are striving to solve...with how little self-denial and active labor a man may reach heaven at last.[2]

God's name is at stake in the worship of God! Though many do not realize it, his name does not just include the few words with which we address him, but includes everything connected with his glory as God. The Westminster Larger Catechism includes in the name of God "his titles, attributes, ordinances, word, works, and whatsoever he is pleased to make himself known by."[3] The misuse of any of these therefore dishonors and blasphemes his name. These priests were guilty of abusing his name by their offerings and attitude. We can be and often are guilty of the same sin.

All this, though not yet stated, required one who would love the glory and honor of God and who would cleanse the church of its impurity and wickedness and teach God's people to "offer unto the LORD an offering in righteousness" (3:3). The coming of such a one, the Messenger of the covenant, is prophesied in chapter 3.

1:11. For from the rising of the sun even unto the going down of the same my name shall be great among the Gentiles; and in every place incense shall be offered unto my name, and a pure offering: for my name shall be great among the heathen, saith the LORD of hosts.

When we do not cherish spiritual things, God takes them away from us: thus the gift of the gospel to the Gentiles, and thus the movement of the gospel from one Gentile nation to another in the course of New Testament history. Here, because of their lack of regard for the priesthood and offerings, God promises he will take both priesthood and offerings away from the Jews and give them to the Gentiles.[4]

---

2 Moore, *Haggai, Zechariah and Malachi*, 366–67.
3 Westminster Larger Catechism A 190, in *The Confession of Faith and the Larger and Shorter Catechisms* (Inverness, Scotland: Publications Committee of the Free Presbyterian Church of Scotland, 1976), 273.
4 The words "Gentiles" and "heathen" in verse 11, although translated differently in the KJV, are the same word in Hebrew.

Though the gathering of the Gentiles and the preaching of the gospel to them are not specifically mentioned in the verse, it is clear the verse has that in view. The only way God can become great among the Gentiles is by grace, when God graciously forgives the sins of the Gentiles, causes the gospel of grace to be preached to them, graciously gives them the gift of faith that they may believe the gospel, and through the same gift of faith gives them forgiveness and the knowledge of forgiveness, so that they understand what God has done for them and thankfully glorify his name.

All this, however, depends on the coming of the Messenger of the covenant. He alone is able to purify the sons of Levi, whether they be Jews or Gentiles, that they may offer to God a sacrifice in righteousness. Through the coming and work of Christ, God himself makes sure that there are always those who do worship him in Spirit and in truth and do not trifle with his worship and service. He will glorify his name and see it glorified in every age, and the wickedness of men, even in the church, will not defeat his purpose.

The eleventh verse of Malachi 1 is not just a prophecy of the ingathering of the Gentiles, however, but also a prophecy of the priesthood of all believers in the New Testament and the spiritual sacrifices that are offered by that universal priesthood. The glorifying and honoring of God's name by the Gentiles is described in terms of their becoming a priesthood that replaces the corrupt and wicked priesthood of Malachi's day. In the New Testament every believer is a priest, as well as prophet and king, through Christ and under Christ. Except for the priesthood of Christ himself, there is no longer a special and separate priesthood in the New Testament, but a universal spiritual priesthood.

The New Testament priesthood is mentioned and its work described in 1 Peter 2:5: "Ye also, as lively [living] stones, are built up a spiritual house, an holy priesthood, to offer up spiritual sacrifices, acceptable to God by Jesus Christ." Those spiritual sacrifices are described in Romans 12:1–2 as the offering of our bodies in grateful service to God, in Hebrews 13:15 as the offering of our lips in praise, and in Psalm 51:17 as the sacrifice of a broken spirit and contrite heart. These sacrifices are offered, according to 1 Peter 2:9, for the praises of him who has called us out of darkness into his marvelous light.

Such offerings are made both in worship and in the everyday life of

God's people. Believing in Christ requires real sacrifice: the giving up of all pride, all self-sufficiency, all self-seeking, and all fleshly desires. These are true spiritual sacrifices, sacrifices with which God is well pleased and that he accepts. They are not an atonement for sin—that kind of sacrifice was offered and could be offered only by Christ—but they are a thank offering or freewill offering that is the deepest expression of a redeemed and regenerated heart.

As a spiritual and universal priesthood, New Testament believers no longer need to trust in the intercession of an earthly priesthood but go themselves to the throne of grace, praying there for one another and for themselves. As a spiritual priesthood, they bring and offer their own sacrifices. And insofar as their priesthood is universal, their work as priests is no longer limited to one place but is done "from the rising of the sun even unto the going down of the same."

That priesthood of all believers, one of the great doctrines of the Reformation, though seldom remembered or believed today, is an important truth for the daily life as well as for the church life of every believer. Their priesthood requires private prayer and worship as an integral part of their life. As a priest, every believing father has the calling to be an intercessor and teacher in his own family. Holding that priestly office, every child of God, male or female, young and old alike, has the calling to be holy and in holiness to offer himself in all he does as a sacrifice to God. The same priesthood of all believers requires that believers be participants, not spectators, in the public worship of God, and it makes them, not the clergy alone, the church of Christ.

The Heidelberg Catechism identifies this priesthood of all believers with being a Christian. In answer to the question, "But why art *thou* called a Christian?" the catechism answers, "Because by faith I am a member of Christ, and thus a partaker of his anointing; in order that I also may...present myself a living sacrifice of thankfulness to him."[5] In those who fulfill these priestly duties and do so with a true heart, this prophecy of Malachi is fulfilled.

The priesthood of all believers has been replaced today, as it was in the days prior to the Reformation, with a kind of spiritual tyranny, not of pope and bishops but of popular leaders who mislead the people and fleece

---

5   Heidelberg Catechism Q&A 32, in Schaff, *Creeds of Christendom*, 3:318.

the sheep, doing with the ordinary members of the church whatever they wish and saying whatever they please. The words of Luther, written against Rome, echo true today:

> Here, indeed, are the roots of that detestable tyranny of the clergy over the laity; trusting in the external anointing by which their hands are consecrated, in the tonsure and the vestments, they not only exalt themselves above lay Christians, who are only anointed with the Holy Spirit, but regard them almost as dogs and unworthy to be included with them in the Church. Hence they are bold to demand, to exact, to threaten, to urge, to oppress, as much as they please. In short, the sacrament of ordination has been and is a most approved device for the establishing of all the horrible things that have wrought hitherto and will yet be wrought in the Church. Here Christian brotherhood has perished, here shepherds have been turned into wolves, servants into tyrants, churchmen into worse than worldlings.[6]

1:12. But ye have profaned it, in that ye say, The table of the LORD is polluted; and the fruit thereof, even his meat, is contemptible.

1:13. Ye said also, Behold, what a weariness is it! And ye have snuffed at it, saith the LORD of hosts; and ye brought that which was torn, and the lame, and the sick; thus ye brought an offering: should I accept this of your hand? Saith the LORD.

In these verses, which conclude the first chapter but not God's word to the priests, the prophet returns to the matter of priestly sins. Insofar as this section repeats what has already been said in verses 6–10, it does so by way of emphasizing the seriousness of the priests' sins. God could not forget or overlook those sins, though the priests would not recognize them. This section, however, is not just repetition but elaborates on the sins of the priests and on the reason their actions were so wicked.

---

6 Martin Luther, "The Babylonian Captivity of the Church," in *Works of Martin Luther, Philadelphia Edition* (Philadelphia: Muhlenberg Press, 1943), 2:278–79.

Verse 12 and the first part of verse 13 tell us more about the attitude of the priests toward their priestly duties and office. The priests allowed the sacrifices and worship of the temple to be corrupted and in so doing passed judgment on the worship of God, the table and altar and sacrifices, as though they really did not matter. Whether they said this in so many words is beside the point; their deeds certainly spoke very loudly. Their actions made the table of the Lord, that is, the table of showbread, and the food that was offered to God on that table contemptible.

Perhaps they used the excuse that neither the table nor altar were the originals, or that the meat of the sacrifices and the bread of the table were only types and shadows of heavenly things. Perhaps they were complaining that the showbread and meat of the offerings were leftovers—that they received day-old bread and the less desirable parts of the sacrifices for their portion. Very likely they were saying that the sacrifices and temple rituals were only outward things—that what mattered was not the details of what was done in the worship of God, but the sincerity of the worshipers. Whatever they were saying, it was simply an excuse for their own lack of proper regard for the things of God. Thus they found the service of God wearisome, snuffed at it, and treated it with disdain and contempt.

How common these sins are. Many have the same attitude toward those aspects and elements of worship that God commands. When questions are raised about their own practice, their excuse is always that these things do not really matter, that the only thing that matters is that God is worshiped and served sincerely—the *how* is of no account. And when they must endure the things God has commanded, they view them with the same contempt and sneering arrogance as did the priests whom Malachi curses.

This is their attitude not only toward matters of public worship, but also toward the things required of the Christian in his daily life. Only feeling and sincerity matter. The specific details of the Christian life commanded in the word of God do not matter. Blasphemous words, Sabbath breaking, disdain for authority, fornicating, lying, cheating and stealing, speaking evil of others, coveting, and hatred do not matter.

"Torn" in the description of their sacrifices does not mean "torn by wild beasts" but torn away from others by violence, that is, stolen. What a condemnation of the practice of so many self-appointed priests and leaders in

443

the church who use their influence and office to fulfill their own carnal desires, and who by hook and crook, by pleas and tears, by hawking Christ and his grace as the cheapest of all commodities, tear away the living of the poor and of the widows. Such is bad enough, but when they make a pretense of offering it in the service of God, surely they must hear him say, "Should I accept this of your hand?"

What the people were bringing to God in their sacrifices and what the priests allowed them to bring was unacceptable to God. They brought what did not even belong to them, what they had torn from others by violence, and what was of no use to them, the animals that were blemished and diseased, and did this in spite of God's express command to the contrary. In more modern terms, they gave to God only what was left over of their time, their money, their ability and strength and what they did not want anyway, and their leaders allowed it.

1:14. But cursed be the deceiver, which hath in his flock a male, and voweth, and sacrificeth unto the Lord a corrupt thing: for I am a great King, saith the LORD of hosts, and my name is dreadful among the heathen.

In this verse God is not simply speaking again of the way in which the priests corrupted his offerings, but implicating the people as well in their wickedness. Rarely is it the case that the church has bad leaders and good members, or that the wickedness of the leaders cannot be traced to the failings and weaknesses of the people themselves as well as the wickedness of the people to that of the leaders. In Judah the priests polluted the offerings of God, but they did so at the behest of the people, who were themselves covetous and empty of the fear of God.

God is saying something about how evil the practice of both people and priests was when he required so little of them. He did not ask all their flocks and herds, only an occasional beast. He did not expect them to bring the more valuable females but allowed them to bring the more expendable males. So little did he ask, and even that they would not do. Having vowed a male, they brought one that was sick or lame. Obliged to bring a sacrifice, they brought only what they did not want anyway. We are often like them. As one commentator says: "How often do we keep back the firstlings of our flocks, the best of our services, and offer God the shreds of our time, the weary remnants of our thoughts and affections, and the niggardly gleanings of our means!"[7]

For the first time, Malachi uses the name "Lord," or Adonai. This name, not in capitals, is a different name from "LORD", or Jehovah. Lord refers to God's sovereign ownership of all things and is a further reminder that the grudging covetousness of the Jews in giving God only their castoffs was all the worse because everything they had belonged to him. In bringing their offerings, they were only giving him what was already his own. We too, when we forget God's ownership of all things, begin to begrudge everything he asks of us.

This is no small thing in his sight, for he is no beggar to be satisfied with scraps and leavings but is a great king, one whose name is worthy of awe and reverence, one who is offended and angered at our contempt for him. Even the heathen, he says, had shown and would show more regard for his name than do his own people.

The reference to the heathen has to do with those heathen who had in times past acknowledged, some of them under duress, the greatness of God's name (Dan. 4:1–3; Jonah 3:6–9). It is also a prophecy of the coming of Christ, when God's name would be taken from the Jews and given to the heathen who would honor and worship it. God sees to the honor of his name even when his own people do not.

2:1. And now, O ye priests, this commandment is for you.

2:2. If ye will not hear, and if ye will not lay it to heart, to give glory unto my name, saith the LORD of hosts, I will even send a curse upon you, and I will curse your blessings: yea, I have cursed them already, because ye do not lay it to heart.

2:3. Behold, I will corrupt your seed, and spread dung upon your faces, even the dung of your solemn feasts; and one shall take you away with it.

The chapter break here is particularly unfortunate. It comes in the middle of God's word to the priests. The first three verses of chapter 2 record God's judgment on the priests for the sin of despising and polluting his

---

7 Moore, *Haggai, Zechariah and Malachi*, 369.

offerings, the sin just mentioned in the last verses of chapter 1. The end of verse 9 would have been a better place to start chapter 2.

The commandment of which God speaks is not his law concerning the offerings. That law the priests knew, though they callously disregarded it. The word "commandment" is used in a more general sense and refers to the word of judgment and cursing that God speaks against the priests. It is a curse that he commands against them, especially designed for them. That curse comes on them for two things, for their actual disobedience and for their refusal to hear God's rebuke and "lay it to heart."

The curse is referred to as a commandment not only because it comes by the sovereign disposition of the great King and Judge, but also because it comes upon these priests through God's commands to the creation: to the wind and rain, to the fields and crops, to the blight and grasshopper. The commandment therefore is the word by which God exercises his providential control over all things and by which they serve his purposes.

The word "if" does not suggest that there was any doubt about the reaction of the priests—they were so hardened and callous in their disobedient wickedness that God does not even pause before telling them that he had cursed them already. The word "if" has more the force of a strong oath here, as it does so often in the Old Testament, so that the idea is really this: "Since ye most surely will not hear and lay it to heart, to give glory unto my name, saith the Lord of hosts, I will even send a curse upon you, and I will curse your blessings."

God's curse is terrible. It is the powerful and effective word he speaks against the sinner that drives the sinner out of God's presence into hell. This curse God speaks not only against the priests, "I will even send a curse upon you," but also upon their blessings, that is, upon all the good temporal gifts God had given them.

The passage makes it abundantly clear that material things are "blessings" only in a temporal and limited way, for they can be cursed and become a curse to those who have them. They do not, in other words, represent in themselves the favor or love of God for those who possess them.

When God promises to curse their blessings, he means that he would in the end take all those things away from them so that they would be left with nothing. Even while they still possessed them, he would use these "blessings" to bring them nothing but grief and trouble and wrath. Of this Psalm 73 speaks when it reminds us that God uses such things to set the sinner in slippery places (v. 18). Proverbs adds that under the judgment of God even the daily labors of the ungodly are sin (21:4).

Here again God says that he is the Lord of hosts, whom all things serve. If he commands temporal things to be a blessing and mark of his favor, they will surely be that, but if he commands them to bring his disfavor upon those who have them, that too will surely happen.

God does not just speak in general terms of his curse, however, but tells the priests exactly how he will curse them and judge them. His judgment would come both upon the fields and upon their work. The seed referred to in verse 3 is not their children but the produce of the fields. In corrupting it as they had corrupted his offerings (the same word is used), God would take away their very livelihood and leave them impoverished and hungry. Their covetousness and greed, rather than getting them what they wanted, would have the opposite effect. Ultimately the curse would leave them forever desolate in hell. God sometimes leaves the wicked to prosper in their wickedness, but he does not allow them to have what they want and to enjoy it. As Asaph saw in Psalm 73, their end is destruction and desolation.

That God would spread the dung of their solemn feasts upon their faces means he would bring them to dishonor and shame in the eyes of the people, just as the priests had dishonored him before the people. As they had treated their priestly work like dung, so God would make them like dung in the sight of the people. When they appeared before the people to do their priestly work, it would be as though they had dung spread on their faces, and they would be polluted and despised in the eyes of the very people whose favor they curried and whose gifts they coveted and for whom they had forsaken their calling.

The dung would be the dung of their own solemn feasts. Their corrupted form of worship and false feasts, of no more value than dung, would become the reason the people despised them and forsook them as though they had dung on their faces.

How often that happens. For the sake of earthly things and the favor of men, the leaders of God's people forsake their calling and treat God's commands with contempt, doing whatever they please in the worship of God. To their own surprise, the end result is not that they have the support and honor of the fickle multitude, but that they are treated with the same contempt they have shown to God and the people go their own way, no longer supporting them in the work or even coming to them as representatives of God.

This is always the end result of apostasy, that the people no longer come to worship God, nor even to visit the temples in which these men have corrupted the worship of God. The people become wholly secular and worldly, as has our society, so that there are fewer and fewer who show any interest at all in the things these corrupt leaders tout as the worship and the service of God.

And just as dung is carted away and disposed of, so God disposes of this corrupt priesthood, whether it is that of the Old Testament or of the New. In Israel he did that when he brought all the types and shadows of the Old Testament, including the priesthood, to an end. Finally he does that when he throws them and their works into hell.

2:4. And ye shall know that I have sent this commandment unto you, that my covenant might be with Levi, saith the LORD of hosts.

2:5. My covenant was with him of life and peace; and I gave them to him for the fear wherewith he feared me, and was afraid before my name.

2:6. The law of truth was in his mouth, and iniquity was not found in his lips: he walked with me in peace and equity, and did turn many away from iniquity.

2:7. For the priest's lips should keep knowledge, and they should seek the law at his mouth: for he is the messenger of the LORD of hosts.

In the closing section of God's word to the priests, he examines their sin from the viewpoint of his covenant with Levi. God calls the covenant with Levi a covenant of life and peace and speaks of the duties of the priesthood as their covenantal obligations. That covenant the priesthood had violated and broken by their wickedness. Their sin, in other words, was covenantal unfaithfulness.

The covenant with Levi is first mentioned when the Levitical priesthood, through Phinehas the son of Aaron, showed great zeal for God and for his holiness by killing in the act a man of Simeon and a woman of Midian who were openly committing fornication. This happened at Shittim on the borders of Canaan. God said of Phinehas and his descendants at that time: "Behold, I give unto him my covenant of peace: And he shall have it, and his seed after him, even the covenant of an everlasting priesthood; because he was zealous for his God, and made an atonement for the children of Israel" (Num. 25:12–13).

The covenant with Levi goes back, however, to the time God gave the priesthood to Levi and his descendants. All the priests were part of that covenant in that God promised to dwell among the children of Israel through the tabernacle and the priesthood that served in it:

> 44. And I will sanctify the tabernacle of the congregation, and the altar: I will sanctify also both Aaron and his sons, to minister to me in the priest's office.
> 45. And I will dwell among the children of Israel, and will be their God.
> 46. And they shall know that I am the LORD their God, that brought them forth out of the land of Egypt, that I may dwell among them: I am the LORD their God. (Ex. 29:44–46)

This covenant with Levi is part of the same covenant mentioned elsewhere in scripture, as is evident from the fact that God speaks of it as "my covenant." It is not a different covenant, nor different in nature from God's covenant with Abraham, with Israel, or with David. It is the relationship between God and his people, as is clear from Malachi 1:6, which speaks of Levi's walking with God.

This covenant and relationship between God and his people is described in three ways in scripture. Sometimes one finds the covenantal formula or a variation of it: "I will be thy God and ye shall be my people" (Gen. 17:7). At other times scripture speaks of walking with God and of fellowship with God (Gen. 5:22; 6:9), and of friendship between God and his people (James 2:23), but the idea is always the same: a very close relationship between God and his people.

That covenant of God is always viewed in scripture as one and everlasting, and therefore also as an unconditional covenant that is made and preserved by God alone without man's help. That is true here also. Levi's unfaithfulness, though it can be described as covenant breaking, is not the end of the covenant but shows the need for a priest, a Messenger of the Lord who would not break the covenant and through whom God's covenant with Levi would be kept forever.

The covenant with Levi was part of God's covenant with Abraham and with Israel in which Levi represented Israel to God and God to Israel. Levi's unfaithfulness in the covenant was Israel's unfaithfulness, and the calling that Levi had in the covenant was Israel's calling, fulfilled through Levi as their God-appointed representative.

God's word in this passage begins therefore with a reminder that God had sent Malachi to call Levi and the nation back to covenantal faithfulness. It is his commandment, requiring repentance. It was sent in order that the priests might repent of their wickedness and return to God and that through them the people might do the same, and thus both God and his people might once again enjoy together the blessings of his relationship to them.

Even though God's covenant is unconditional and everlasting, a covenant that cannot be broken and destroyed, a covenant that depends only on God and his grace, God's people have obligations and responsibilities in that covenant. The covenant does not depend for its existence on them and on their faithfulness, but their duties are nonetheless important in that they are evidence of God's relationship to them and proof of the power of his covenantal grace.

Indeed, though the covenant itself does not depend on the faithfulness of God's people, their own enjoyment of covenantal blessings and their own assurance of their place in God's covenant do. When they are unfaithful, they cannot possibly have any assurance of a place with God. When they walk in sin, their own consciences testify that they are God's enemies, not his friends. As the Canons of Dordt put it:

> By such enormous sins, however, they very highly offend God, incur a deadly guilt, grieve the Holy Spirit, interrupt the exercise of faith, very grievously wound their consciences, and sometimes lose the sense of God's favor, for a time, until on their returning into the

right way by serious repentance, the light of God's fatherly countenance again shines upon them.[8]

In Malachi 1:4–7 God speaks of the covenantal responsibilities that belonged to the priests and through them to all Israel. Some of those duties, the worship of God through the sacrifices and offerings and the duty of being separate and holy to God, have already been mentioned. These duties the priests had neglected and despised. Now God speaks of a third responsibility, that of knowing and teaching the law of God and of judging Israel according to that law.

We see this priestly duty in Deuteronomy 17:8–11 and 19:17–18. The first of these passages reads:

> 8. If there arise a matter too hard for thee in judgment, between blood and blood, between plea and plea, and between stroke and stroke, being matters of controversy within thy gates: then thou shalt arise, and get thee up into the place which the LORD thy God shall choose:
> 9. And thou shalt come unto the priests the Levites, and unto the judge that shall be in those days, and inquire; and they shall shew thee the sentence of judgment:
> 10. And thou shalt do according to the sentence, which they of that place which the LORD shall choose shall shew thee; and thou shalt observe to do according to all that they inform thee:
> 11. According to the sentence of the law which they shall teach thee, and according to the judgment which they shall tell thee, thou shalt do: thou shalt not decline from the sentence which they shall shew thee, to the right hand, nor to the left. (Deut. 17:8–11)

The priests were not the ones who ordinarily and actually executed the law as Phinehas did. That was usually the duty of the judge or king. But the priests were the ones who interpreted the law and who told all Israel what it said and meant.

---

8 Canons 5.5, in Schaff, *Creeds of Christendom*, 3:593.

Their duty had three parts, all mentioned here. First, the priests had to know the law. This is implied in what God says of Levi: "The law of truth was in his mouth." The priest's lips were to "keep knowledge." The idea is that the priest, through knowledge of the law, had to have it ready to hand: it had to be in his mouth and he had to be ready to speak it. Second, he had to be a teacher of the law. Seeking the law at the mouth of the priest did not just mean seeking a judgment from the priest, but learning the law from him. There is an example of this being done in 2 Chronicles 30:22, where the Levites in the days of Hezekiah are referred to as those who "taught the good knowledge of the Lord." Last, the priest was a judge who interpreted and applied the law to the people. Ministers, elders, and deacons all share something of this priestly office in the New Testament and are unfaithful priests when they neglect these duties as did Judah's priests.

In all of this the priest was the messenger of the Lord of hosts. He was bringing the word of the great King to the people of the King. He might therefore bring nothing but the word of the King as he had given it, not taking away from or adding to the message. He had to do this because the word of the king is always the law by which the citizens of the kingdom are governed and under which they prosper.

In the Old Testament this meant that the priests were always also prophets. Even wicked Caiaphas could prophesy of Christ because he was high priest. Of this we read in John 11:51: "And this spake he not of himself: but being high priest that year, he prophesied that Jesus should die for that nation."

In the New Testament this is the responsibility that every teacher and minister of the word of God has. He must bring only the word of the King. He must add nothing to it nor take anything away from it. He may not do that with the scriptures themselves (Rev. 22:18–19), and he may not do that in preaching the scriptures.

This is also the priestly duty of every believer. Holding the office of a priest (Rev. 1:6), every Christian is also a prophet and as prophet must know, teach, and judge according to the word of God. He must do that in his own home as a married person and as a parent. He must do that in his daily calling as a witness. He must do that in the church and in relation to the other members of the church. Always and everywhere he is God's prophet.

He may not add to the word and he may not take away from it in thought or in conduct.

The value of the knowledge of God cannot be overestimated. Scripture speaks of its value in Proverbs 1:7, Proverbs 2:6, Jeremiah 22:16, Hosea 4:6, and elsewhere, but it is John 17:3 more than any other passage that shows us that this knowledge is indispensable, for it is eternal life. This knowledge the priests of Malachi's day had despised and withheld, and so it is today. The famine of hearing the words of the Lord prophesied by Amos has come (Amos 8:11).

At the heart of these priestly duties was and is the calling to "turn many away from iniquity." That is the purpose of the preaching, of the gospel itself, of our witness as Christians, and of our parental duties. Who does that today? Sin is seldom mentioned and rarely rebuked or disciplined. Everything but sin and repentance is emphasized. Being a Christian is about being happy, feeling good about oneself, having what one wants, health and wealth, changing the world, but seldom about turning from iniquity. No one could possibly describe either the leaders or members of the church today, today's priests, as those who turned many from iniquity.

Levi himself had been faithful in his duties, but these priests and many others today have been unfaithful. For their unfaithfulness God always judges them.

2:8. But ye are departed out of the way; ye have caused many to stumble at the law; ye have corrupted the covenant of Levi, saith the LORD of hosts.

God continues to rebuke the unfaithfulness of the priests as teachers of the law. Instead of judging the people according to the law of God, they judged falsely, causing the people to stumble at the law. They had protected evildoers by misinterpreting the law and been a bad example by their refusal to keep the law of God. Verse 9 speaks of partiality in judging, that is, the taking of bribes and the favoring of the wealthy and influential. They were involved in the sins of contracting heathen marriages and in divorcing for any cause. Not only did they allow divorce for any cause, as Jesus' controversies with the Pharisees demonstrate (Matt. 19:3), but also they themselves had married heathen wives. Nehemiah 13:28 mentions especially one of the grandsons of Eliashib the high priest, who was son-in-law to

Sanballat the Horonite, one of Israel's enemies. The priests were the leaders in wickedness.

By their wickedness they corrupted the covenant of Levi, that is, they were unfaithful to their covenantal responsibilities and to the great God of the covenant and led the people astray as well, so that the people were unable to enjoy the blessings and privileges of fellowship with God. The covenantal relationship between God and his people was harmed and interrupted by the evil deeds, the evil example, and the evil teachings of these false priests.

Such unfaithfulness is common today. The leaders of the church teach a gullible people lies and false doctrine instead of the wholesome doctrines of God's word. They encourage them in wickedness instead of teaching them God's precepts. The whole matter of divorce and remarriage addressed in the next section of Malachi 2 is a good example. Today, as then, the leaders are the ones who justify the people's hardheartedness and insistence on doing as they please in divorcing and remarrying, finding them the excuses instead of teaching them the Lord's hatred of divorce. They cause many to stumble at the law in this and in other matters.

Such unfaithfulness corrupted the covenant of God with his people but did not destroy it, for even though Phinehas and his descendants eventually lost their priestly office, the covenant was continued and fulfilled in Christ. These verses hint of that, for he alone is the one in whose lips is found no iniquity (v. 6); he only is able truly to turn many from iniquity (v. 6); and he, as we shall see in chapter 3:1–3, is the true messenger of the Lord of hosts (v. 7) who faithfully teaches the law of God not only by his mighty word but also by the work of his Spirit in the hearts of his people.

2:9. Therefore have I also made you contemptible and base before all the people, according as ye have not kept my ways, but have been partial in the law.

In the justice of God, his judgments are always fitting: the punishment always fits the crime. Because the priests polluted the offerings of God, he would pollute them by spreading the dung of their solemn feasts on their faces and destroy their place and reputation among the people (v. 3). Because they turned away from his law and would not uphold it, he pronounces a law of judgment and cursing against them. Here, because they had treated not only his offerings but also his law with contempt, God promises to make them contemptible in the eyes of the people.

This is usually understood to mean that God would take away their credibility and honor in the hearts and lives of the people, so that the priests would more and more lose their influence. We see something like this happening today through the wickedness and corruption of the Romish priesthood, and it often happens as well with other church leaders who have departed from God's ways. Sometimes this comes about when God leads them into falls and sins that destroy their credibility. Sometimes it happens simply because they begin teaching and preaching such nonsense that even the fools who listen to them begin to see folly.

God is not mocked. What a man sows, even in church office, he also reaps. He who sows to the flesh, as these priests did and as many priests do today, of the flesh reaps corruption. What he gains is itself corruptible and does not deliver his soul from eternal corruption. The same is true of those believers who sow to the flesh. They, a New Testament priesthood, reap unrighteousness, indignation, wrath, tribulation, and anguish and do not profit from their covetousness, for they too are unfaithful.

In the last day, the great day of judgment and wrath, every unfaithful priest will receive a just reward. Though in this life he may have had the adulation of men, he will be made contemptible and base, and not just before the people whom he cheated and deceived and to whom he lied. Before all nations he will be told by Christ, the true messenger of the covenant, "Depart from me; I never knew you."

Chapter 29

THE THIRD DISPUTATION:
MALACHI 2:10–16

2:10   Have we not all one father? hath not one God created us? why do we deal treacherously every man against his brother, by profaning the covenant of our fathers?

2:11   Judah hath dealt treacherously, and an abomination is committed in Israel and in Jerusalem; for Judah hath profaned the holiness of the LORD which he loved, and hath married the daughter of a strange god.

2:12   The LORD will cut off the man that doeth this, the master and the scholar, out of the tabernacles of Jacob, and him that offereth an offering unto the LORD of hosts.

2:13   And this have ye done again, covering the altar of the LORD with tears, with weeping, and with crying out, insomuch that he regardeth not the offering any more, or receiveth it with good will at your hand.

2:14   Yet ye say, Wherefore? Because the LORD hath been witness between thee and the wife of thy youth, against whom thou hast dealt treacherously: yet is she thy companion, and the wife of thy covenant.

2:15   And did not he make one? Yet had he the residue of the spirit. And wherefore one? That he might seek a godly seed. Therefore take heed to your spirit, and let none deal treacherously against the wife of his youth.

2:16   For the LORD, the God of Israel, saith that he hateth putting away: for one covereth violence with his garment, saith the LORD of hosts: therefore take heed to your spirit, that ye deal not treacherously.

2:10. Have we not all one father? hath not one God created us? why do we deal treacherously every man against his brother, by profaning the covenant of our fathers?

Verse 10 begins the third disputation and seems to have little connection either with what precedes or with what follows. It is an important introduction to the third section of the prophecy. Though one of the most difficult verses in the prophecy, it is the premise on which the following condemnation of divorce and mixed marriage is based.

Many find in this verse proof of the universal fatherhood of God. He is supposed to be the father of all men, who loves them all and is gracious to all without exception. This universal fatherhood is the result of God's creating all, so it is thought. The context shows, however, that this is not what Malachi's words, "Have we not all one father? hath not one God created us?" mean. The point in the following verses is this: the Jews were not allowed to marry heathen wives because those heathen girls and women were daughters of a strange god (v. 11), *not* daughters of Jehovah. The passage in a somewhat round-about way states that the heathen are not God's children, nor is he their father, but they are strangers and foreigners. The passage speaks of the "covenant of our fathers." It was not some universal covenant that was being violated by the sins of the Jews. They were not acting against a universal love and grace of God but against his covenant with the Jews and his very exclusive love for them, revealed in his covenants with them. "We" in the passage is the Jews, and in the Old Testament that did not include the Gentile nations, who were excluded from God's covenants with the Jews and from all the privileges of those covenants.

Nor is there any love of God for all or any kind of universal fatherhood of God. The first verses of the prophecy of Malachi teach that God's love for some and hatred of others are eternal and unchangeable. It is only when the doctrine of God's sovereignty in election and reprobation is discarded that one can even begin to speak of a universal love of God, a love that makes him helplessly dependent on the will of the sinner in salvation and that vitiates all that scripture says about his wrath and judgments against sin.

Instead, the verse is speaking of God's gracious covenantal relationship with Israel as something violated and profaned by the marital sins of the Jews, that is, by the sins of marrying heathen wives and callously divorcing the wives God had given them. By their sins they profaned God's covenant and dealt treacherously against their own brethren.

The sin of marrying heathen wives was an act of treachery against brethren both because it brought the heathen into a relationship that had been established only with Israel, and because the bringing in of these heathen threatened the very existence of God's covenant with Israel, for those heathen brought with them their wicked and idolatrous practices. It was a profaning of God's covenant because marriage is supposed to reflect God's covenantal relationship with his people, something these mixed marriages could not possibly do.

The other sin, the sin of divorcing, was an act of treachery against brethren because it was an act of violence against both a bosom companion and a fellow member of God's covenant. It was a violation of the covenant because it broke off a relationship that was a reflection and part of God's own unbreakable covenantal relationship with his people.

However, God's covenant with Israel was not with every individual Israelite. Those who were wicked and unbelieving like the heathen were not even counted as Israel (Rom. 2:28–29; 9:6–8). True Israel in scripture is not an earthly nation with geographical boundaries but a spiritual nation of those who believe the promises, love God, and walk in his ways. God is not the father and covenant God of the heathen. He is not even the father and covenant friend of every physical descendant of Abraham.

In the New Testament the Gentiles who believe are also counted as Israel by God and are among the true children of Abraham (Gal. 3:29). The dividing line between Jew and Gentile, between God's people and the heathen, is not drawn along the lines of earthly parentage and descent but along spiritual lines, the lines of election and of grace. As in the Old, so in the New Testament: those who have the name and who are born into the families of these true Israelites are not all Israel, but only those to whom God gives grace and who believe by grace. That is why the word of God in a passage like this is so sharp. It makes separation between true Israel and that which has only the name, between those who belong to God's covenant and those who do not, between those whom God the Father loves and those he does not love, between those who keep God's covenant and those who do not.

The Old Testament, with its promises and warnings, including this prophecy of Malachi, is addressed to God's people in every age, to us as well as to them. We too are forbidden to intermarry with the "heathen" and to divorce for fear of profaning the covenants of our fathers and of acting treacherously in God's covenant.

However, the true Israel, the people of God, are found mingled with the unbelieving and ungodly. When the ungodly sin, there is the danger that God's people participate in those sins and become guilty of them. There is an even greater danger that they look the other way. In either case they become guilty and with the rest of the church or nation suffer the temporal consequences of these sins.

Malachi speaks of "we" not excluding himself, because he understood that there is a corporate responsibility for these sins, especially sins against God's covenant. When mixed marriages and divorcing for every cause are allowed in the church, the whole church comes under the judgment of God and all suffer, not only those who are directly implicated in these sins. Covenantal sins are punished covenantally, not only individually.

2:11. Judah hath dealt treacherously, and an abomination is committed in Israel and in Jerusalem; for Judah hath profaned the holiness of the LORD which he loved, and hath married the daughter of a strange god.

Before we look at this verse and what follows, let us notice that the two great examples of covenantal unfaithfulness mentioned in Malachi are faithlessness in office and in the worship of God by the church's leaders and faithlessness in marriage on the part of the ordinary people. It is difficult to miss the similarity between Malachi's days and ours. If one had to pick two areas in which the church today is unfaithful, it would be exactly these two—on the part of the leaders, great unfaithfulness in knowing, teaching, and worshiping according to the word of God and the practice of using offices in the church for personal advantage and profit, and on the part of the people, a complete abandonment of all that the Bible teaches concerning marriage.

The first sin that Malachi condemns is intermarriage with the heathen.

That God speaks of Judah, Israel, and Jerusalem is intended to show how widespread this sin was, and the books of Ezra and Nehemiah confirm it, showing that it was not only the common people who had committed this sin, but also their priests and leaders. Nehemiah mentions the grandson of the high priest, and Ezra gives a long list of names, including twenty-seven priests and Levites and eighty-six others (Ezra 10:18–44).

The sin was not that these women were foreigners and from other nations but that they were unbelieving and idolatrous. It was not wrong in itself to marry a woman from outside Israel. Many Old Testament marriages of that kind God blessed, Joseph and Asenath, Salmon and Rahab, Boaz and Ruth, but these were marriages with women who had learned to fear and worship Jehovah and had renounced their idolatry and the idolatrous nations in which they had been born. "Thy people shall be my people, and thy God my God" was Ruth's confession before she married Boaz (Ruth 1:16). She and others like her had become Israelites not only in name but also in heart.

It was unbelieving and idolatrous women who might not be married to God's people. These heathen women are described as daughters of a strange god. Heathen gods were their spiritual parents, and they were still lost in unbelief and idolatry. People love and honor and serve their gods, whether they be statues of Baal and Buddha, unbelieving philosophies, wealth and honor, possessions, or persons of influence, as children honor and obey and serve their parents. They really do become the children of their false gods.

When they are described as children of a false god, we are reminded of the exclusiveness of God's love. He is not their father. He does not love Esau but hates him. He loves Jacob as a father loves his children—loves him with an everlasting love and loves him alone!

When the heathen women intermarried with the Israelites, their sin became Israel's sin. Through Ahab's marriage to Jezebel, Baal worship was introduced into the northern kingdom and eventually also into Judah. Nehemiah, Malachi's contemporary, mentions Solomon's sin and its evil fruits for all Israel: "Did not Solomon king of Israel sin by these things? yet among many nations was there no king like him, who was beloved of his God, and God made him king over all Israel: nevertheless even him did outlandish women cause to sin" (Neh. 13:26). Jeroboam is forever remembered in God's word as the one who made Israel to sin with his idolatry.

This sin of mixed marriage is condemned also in the New Testament. In 1 Corinthians 7:39, the rule for Christian marriage is "only in the Lord." It is as wrong for a Christian to marry an unbeliever as it was for the Jews to marry Moabites, Philistines, and Ammonites (Neh. 13:23). Such marriages, contracted deliberately and against the express command of God, cannot have his blessing. Nor may young Christian men and women ever think that in marrying an unbeliever they have the opportunity to convert them and be a good influence on them. The passages in Ezra, Nehemiah, and Malachi show what will actually happen—the heathen will not be converted but God's people will become idolatrous.

The greatness of this evil is seen in the words Malachi uses to describe it: abomination, treachery, and profaning the Lord's holiness. The word "abomination" is commonly used in the Old Testament to describe idolatry. To abominate is to hate. Mixed marriages are something God hates and an act of hatred against God.

Mixed marriage is also treachery. It is committed against God in forsaking his friendship for union and friendship with those who do not love him, and against God's people in bringing into the church those who will surely lead the church astray: treachery, indeed! For this reason too it is a profaning of his holiness, for it will always be cause of apostasy and failure in the church. It is no small sin!

The matter can be put very bluntly: when a Christian marries a non-Christian, such cannot be an act of love for God, for there is nothing of God in the non-Christian. What the Christian loves in that case is the worldliness, the sexuality, the fleshliness of the non-Christian. As Benton says, "What you love about them is their *ungodliness*, and your attachment to that person only betrays the true desires of your own heart, covered with a flimsy film of church attendance!"[1]

Christian marriage is a covenant—a relationship of friendship and fellowship that is part of God's relationship with us. Paul, speaking of Christian marriage, says, "But I speak concerning Christ and the church" (Eph. 5:32).

---

1 Benton, *Losing Touch with the Living God*, 75.

Marriage is not only a reflection of the blessed and wonderful relationship that we have with Christ, but it is also part of that relationship, so that the two cannot really be separated. In marriage man and woman experience and enjoy something of God's relationship to us.

Nor is the sin of idolatry a danger that no longer exists. Idolatry is committed not only by bowing down to a stick or a stone. It is the sin of loving, fearing, wanting, serving anything or anyone as much as or more than God. It is committed when a man or woman loves and wants an unbelieving partner at the expense of obedience to God. Even in marrying we and our children must be warned, "Thou shalt have no other gods beside me."

2:12. The LORD will cut off the man that doeth this, the master and the scholar, out of the tabernacles of Jacob, and him that offereth an offering unto the LORD of hosts.

In Israel the sin of marrying heathen wives made the sinner worthy of being cut off, that is, of death or banishment. In the New Testament it makes one worthy of excommunication. Nor ought the elders of the church hesitate to censure and if necessary put out of the church those who are guilty of these sins. The principle set out in 1 Corinthians 5:6 applies here also: "A little leaven leaveneth the whole lump." Excommunication in such cases is simply recognition that a person, by such sins, has shown himself to be one who despises God's covenant and friendship. To this covenant and friendship with God the "tabernacles of Jacob" refer (Rev. 21:1–2).

God speaks of master and scholar because both the common people and the leaders were guilty of this sin. Perhaps he even means to point out that those who held such positions in Israel used their influence and study (in the case of scholars) to justify their actions by misinterpreting and misapplying the word of God. It certainly is the case today that theologians and scholars go to great lengths to justify divorce for any cause, remarrying of divorced persons, even such abominations as homosexuality, and it would have been no different then.

God speaks of those who offered an offering because these Jews were doubly guilty, not only of forsaking God's covenant in intermingling with the heathen, but also of maintaining a hypocritical pretense of loving God and fearing him by continuing to bring their offerings to the temple. None of them, however prominent, would escape God's judgment.

2:13. And this have ye done again, covering the altar of the LORD with tears, with weeping, and with crying out, insomuch that he regardeth not the offering any more, or receiveth it with good will at your hand.

With these words the prophet begins to deal with the other sin of which the Jews were guilty, the sin of divorcing. "This have ye done" refers not to what has just been said, but to what follows.

Some take this verse as referring to heathen and idolatrous worship and take the verses that follow not as a reference to actual divorcing and a condemnation of that sin, but as a reference to pagan worship. In other words, the Jews committed the sin of divorce only by forsaking God and worshiping idols. It is true that idolatry and intermarriage with the heathen are a kind of spiritual fornication (Ezek. 16), but there is no reason at all to take Malachi 2:13–16 as anything but a literal and explicit condemnation of divorce. Those who take it otherwise usually have a hidden agenda and do not accept the teaching of the word of God about divorce and remarriage.

The tears referred to, therefore, are the tears and weeping of the Jewish wives who had been injured by this sin, tears that are as often shed today as then, not only by wives who have been forsaken, but also by husbands and children who have suffered as a result of this sin and whose tears are a testimony against everyone who commits the sin of divorcing. Today a climbing divorce rate and a divorce rate among evangelical Christians that is higher than among the ungodly are the source of these many tears.

The warning of verse 13 is especially forceful since God refuses to receive the worship of those who commit this sin or to show them any good will or favor in their attempts to placate him. How many there must be today whose worship is unacceptable to God on account of this unrepented sin!

2:14. Yet ye say, Wherefore? Because the LORD hath been witness between thee and the wife of thy youth, against whom thou hast dealt treacherously: yet is she thy companion, and the wife of thy covenant.

As always the Jews refused to see their sins and to hear the word of God through Malachi, and so God elaborates on their sins and speaks of the *treachery* of the Jews against their wives. Each of these mistreated wives is referred to as "the wife of thy youth" not only because the Jews married young, but also because they were divorcing the wives to whom they had been married for many years, who had born their children, and whom they were now forsaking. No less common and no less treacherous are such deeds today.

God shows the seriousness of this sin also by describing each wife as "thy companion" and "the wife of thy covenant." By describing a wife as a companion he refers to the intimacy, fellowship, and love that ought to characterize a marriage and usually does in the beginning but that often, through sin, wanes and disappears. By describing her as "the wife of thy covenant," he speaks of marriage not only as a covenant, but as part of God's covenant also. The intimacies of marriage picture the intimacies of God's relationship to us, and the bond of marriage is part of the bond between God and his people.

What could be more important? When we are dealing with marriage, we are not just dealing with a temporary human relationship that is of no real spiritual significance, but we are dealing with God's covenant. It is gross hypocrisy, then, for someone to say that he or she loves God and is a friend of God while doing nothing to live in marriage as an institution of God.

God describes himself as a witness between the Jews and their divorced wives because he alone was able to see and know the real motives behind their actions. There can be no doubt that the Jews excused themselves by saying that they had married young when they did not really know what they were doing and therefore could not be responsible for their actions and could not be expected to live anymore with their wives; that they no longer loved their wives and that they were sure God wanted them to be happy; that circumstances had changed and though they had done all they could to maintain their marriages, there was nothing left but to divorce—the same vapid excuses that are heard today.

God knew better. He knew, as the one who searches the heart, that their real motives were selfish and wicked—that they were moved only by lust—and that all their excuses were just that and nothing more. He had seen not only their actions but their hearts also and was witness against them, a witness who would make sure they suffered just punishment for their crimes. As Jehovah, the Lord, the unchangeable and faithful God of the covenant, he would deal severely with those who despised the covenant of marriage.

2:15. And did not he make one? Yet had he the residue of the spirit. And wherefore one? That he might seek a godly seed. Therefore take heed to your spirit, and let none deal treacherously against the wife of his youth.

Verse 15 is by all accounts the most difficult verse in the whole prophecy. One commentator even gives up and says "the worst thing that could be done would be to assume that it *can* be understood."[2] The questions are many: What does it mean that he made one? What is the residue of the spirit and who had it? Who was seeking a godly seed and how? The verse is indeed difficult, but it is not impossible. In fact, the questions must be answered and the verse interpreted, for it lies at the heart of what God is saying in this part of the prophecy.

Perhaps the most common interpretation is that God is holding up to the Jews the negative example of Abraham, their first father, who was married to Sarah, one flesh with her, but took Hagar as his concubine, seeking a godly seed in doing so. However, Abraham did not divorce Sarah or deal treacherously with her. In fact, it was Sarah's idea that Abraham marry Hagar. The example would have had no force, therefore.

Another common interpretation, that of Calvin among others, refers the verse to God's creation of Adam and Eve as man and woman, as one flesh in marriage. The example would then be positive and an implicit condemnation of the Jews who were acting against God's original marriage ordinance in divorcing and remarrying and in separating what God had joined together. That interpretation has little against it exegetically and would parallel what Jesus says in Matthew 19:1–9.

Better, though, is the interpretation that understands the verse in the context of what God has just said about his relationship to the Jews. The making one is God's establishing his covenant with the Jews and taking them as his peculiar people. The seeking of a godly seed is his reason for doing so: they among all the heathen nations would be his dear children.

The reference to "the residue of the spirit" means that God by his Holy Spirit dwelt among the Jews but that the riches of his Spirit had not been poured out even on them. The passage then reads something like this:

> Did not God make us one? Did he not separate us from other nations into an isolated unity? Yet this was not done because the blessing was too narrow to be spread over other nations, or because infinite

---

2 Douglas Stuart, "Malachi," in McComiskey, *The Minor Prophets*, 3:1340.

fulness was exhausted; for the residue of the Spirit was with him. There remained an inexhaustible fulness of spiritual blessing that might have been given to other nations. Why then did he choose but one? It was that he might make a seed of God, a nation which he should train to be the repository of his covenant and the stock of his Messiah, a people in which the true doctrine of the unity of God should be cherished amid surrounding polytheism and idolatry, until the fulness of time should come.[3]

The verse therefore picks up on some of the themes already introduced and develops them.

There is good application of the verse to the church and to believers today. As New Testament Christians, we are separated by God in marriage from the wicked world in which we live in order that we might be holy to him. Any violation of what God has commanded for marriage is a contradiction of what God has done for us in Christ. God has made us separate in order to fulfill his own promise to be our God and the God of our children—has separated us, in other words, in order that the seed of the covenant might be brought forth and preserved among us, that his promise might not fail, that his purpose might be accomplished and his name glorified and honored in the seed of the covenant.

All this leads to the conclusion: "Therefore take heed to your spirit, and let none deal treacherously against the wife of his youth." Divorce is treachery: a gross betrayal of husbands and wives and covenant children! God's word is unchanging in spite of the wicked efforts of men to justify divorce. It is treachery not only toward other persons but also toward God. Thus we must take heed to our "spirits." The spirit of man is that aspect of man's creation that enables him to know God and to live in fellowship with God. Not only is a man's relationship to others damaged by marital treachery, but also his relationship to God. May we hear and heed this warning!

2:16. For the LORD, *the God of Israel, saith that he hateth putting away: for one covereth violence with his garment, saith the* LORD *of hosts: therefore take heed to your spirit, that ye deal not treacherously.*

---

3 Moore, *Haggai, Zechariah and Malachi*, 383.

Attempts to deny the plain teaching of this verse are legion. One commentator lists four basic interpretations, three of which turn the passage on its head: first, that it concerns only pagan worship and has nothing to do with divorce; second, that it permits or even requires divorce; third, that it prohibits only "aversion" divorce, that is, divorce for no other reason than the husband hates his wife and no longer loves her; and fourth, that it actually does prohibit divorce. The fourth interpretation is the only correct interpretation since the words "putting away" always refer in scripture to divorce (Matt. 19:3, 8–9).

That the Jews were given to divorce is evident from the question of the Pharisees in Matthew 19 and from Jesus' response. Many of them believed in putting away "for every cause." In answering their questions about putting away, Jesus speaks of the hardness of the hearts of the Israelites going all the way back to the time of Moses: "Moses because of the hardness of your hearts suffered you to put away your wives" (v. 8). Things are no different now. The same hardness of heart that Jesus condemned allows for, practices, and even blesses divorce today.

The truth is, Malachi says, God hates divorce. He hates it because it is a violation of his original marriage ordinance, when he brought together one man and one woman in marriage, and because it is he who joins married persons: "What therefore God hath joined together, let not man put asunder" (Matt. 19:6). Especially, however, he hates divorce because marriage is both picture and part of his relationship to his people. Divorce is a violation of the covenant of marriage and of God's covenant of grace with his people.

God is not just condemning what one commentator calls "aversion" divorce. It is not just putting away out of lack of love that is condemned here, but all putting away, and it is condemned exactly because the very act of putting away is something God never does. As we will learn in chapter 3:6, God never puts away, never divorces his people, but is forever faithful to them even though they are often unfaithful to him.

Divorce is an act of violence against those who are put away, to be sure, and it is an act of violence against God himself, an act of violence usually covered up with a cloak of hypocrisy and piety. "God wants me to be happy. God cannot expect me to live singly. It is impossible for me to get along with this woman (or this man). I no longer love her (or him). If I no longer love her (or him), God cannot expect me to maintain a marriage that is only a sham. That would be hypocrisy and lies." Or on the part of church leaders: "Your marriage has broken down irretrievably, and therefore I as your minister and counselor advise you to get a divorce. You are not able to serve God as you should under the present circumstances, and if you separate and divorce you will be able to do so once again happily and thankfully."

In connection with this condemnation of divorce, the question is, does not the word of God in Deuteronomy 24:1–4 approve of divorce? Deuteronomy 24:1–4 reads:

1. When a man hath taken a wife, and married her, and it come to pass that she find no favour in his eyes, because he hath found some uncleanness in her: then let him write her a bill of divorcement, and give it in her hand, and send her out of his house.
2. And when she is departed out of his house, she may go and be another man's wife.
3. And if the latter husband hate her, and write her a bill of divorcement, and giveth it in her hand, and sendeth her out of his house; or if the latter husband die, which took her to be his wife;
4. Her former husband, which sent her away, may not take her again to be his wife, after that she is defiled; for that is abomination before the LORD: and thou shalt not cause the land to sin, which the LORD thy God giveth thee for an inheritance.

The Deuteronomy passage does approve of divorce but only lays down certain rules for divorcing in the face of Israel's insistence on divorcing contrary to God's ordinance. Jesus, in Matthew 19:7–9, says that in Moses' day divorce was only "suffered," and that because of the hardness of heart the Jews had shown. They had hardheartedly insisted on divorcing, even though the word of God was against it. God's original ordinance established marriage as a permanent bond between man and woman, a bond that is broken only by death.

Jesus says therefore, "From the beginning it was not so," and lays down the law for all time: "What therefore God hath joined together, let not man put asunder" (v. 6). Deuteronomy 24 therefore does not contradict Malachi but rather confirms it, especially when interpreted in light of Jesus' words in Matthew.

Against all this nonsense and hypocrisy God tells the church both of the Old Testament and of the New: "Take heed to your spirit." "Your relationship with God himself is at issue in all this. Do not deal treacherously with your spouses and do not deal treacherously with me. What I have joined you must not dare to put asunder. The wife (or husband) you have is the wife (or husband) I have given you. Instead of divorcing, take heed to your spirit, repent of your sins, and seek my grace and help, for only in that way can you be blessed."

How this needs to be heard today! Divorce is an act of violence and treachery. Putting away is displeasing to God. "He hateth putting away" ought to be written over the door of every church in Christendom, though it is doubtful that it would be heeded even then, for most will do their own will and fulfill their own lusts, no matter what admonishments, warnings, and threatenings God sends.

Chapter 30

THE FOURTH DISPUTATION:
MALACHI 2:17–3:6

2:17   Ye have wearied the LORD with your words. Yet ye say, Wherein have
we wearied him? When ye say, Every one that doeth evil is good in
the sight of the LORD, and he delighteth in them; or, Where is the
God of judgment?

3:1   Behold, I will send my messenger, and he shall prepare the way before
me: and the Lord, whom ye seek, shall suddenly come to his temple,
even the messenger of the covenant, whom ye delight in: behold, he
shall come, saith the LORD of hosts.

3:2   But who may abide the day of his coming? and who shall stand when
he appeareth? for he is like a refiner's fire, and like fullers' soap:

3:3   And he shall sit as a refiner and purifier of silver: and he shall purify
the sons of Levi, and purge them as gold and silver, that they may
offer unto the LORD an offering in righteousness.

3:4   Then shall the offering of Judah and Jerusalem be pleasant unto the
LORD, as in the days of old, and as in former years.

3:5   And I will come near to you to judgment; and I will be a swift witness
against the sorcerers, and against the adulterers, and against false
swearers, and against those that oppress the hireling in his wages, the
widow, and the fatherless, and that turn aside the stranger from his
right, and fear not me, saith the LORD of hosts.

3:6   For I am the LORD, I change not; therefore ye sons of Jacob are not
consumed.

2:17. Ye have wearied the LORD with your words. Yet ye say, Wherein have we wearied him? When ye say, Every one that doeth evil is good in the sight of the LORD, and he delighteth in them; or, Where is the God of judgment?

Though this last verse of chapter 2 is connected with what precedes, it really belongs to what follows. It is not a conclusion to the discussion of marriage in 2:10–16 but an introduction to the next section, in which God continues to rebuke the people's sins and to promise the coming of Christ as the only possible answer to the people's sins. What God says in chapter 3 about the Messenger of the covenant is in answer to Israel's question in chapter 2:17: "Where is the God of judgment?" The chapter division therefore is not very helpful.

Once again Judah and Israel refuse to hear what God says about their sins. The question "Wherein have we wearied him?" arises not from a regenerated heart that knows its own sinfulness, but from the pride and blindness of unbelief. When God speaks of the sins of his people in his word, one whose heart is softened by grace and who by grace knows his own depravity always says, "It is I the word of God is describing." Those who know their sins do not try to excuse them and hide them. They do not look at the sins of others instead of their own, but acknowledge their sins before God.

Here God accuses the Jews of calling evil good and of saying that God delights in evil. Very few have ever had the courage to do this in so many words, but it happens all the time nevertheless. In Israel it was happening in various ways. In relation to the sacrifices, the people were saying such things as: "Since God has not kept his word to us in blessing us, he has no reason to be dissatisfied with the sacrifices we are bringing." "The priests have approved of what we are doing, so it must be right." Thus they called evil good.

In the whole matter of marriage, they were also calling evil good by approving both of mixed marriages and of divorcing and by practicing these sins. In some cases they called evil good simply by not condemning evil; in others by saying that a particular sin, such as that of divorcing, was not displeasing to God and not a violation of his commands. Or, as so often happens today, they called evil good by actually arguing that a particular sin is pleasing to God.

There is a good example of the latter in the interpretation of those who say that Malachi 2:16, instead of forbidding divorce, is actually approving it and even requiring it in certain circumstances. Those who interpret the passage this way translate it: "If he hates, let him divorce!" an interpretation that fits neither the context nor the grammar of the passage but is simply an attempt to call evil good.

That sin of calling evil good is committed today when the church says that homosexuality and women serving in church office are not sin, and especially when the church says that these things are pleasing to God—that he loves homosexuals because they "love" one another and loves women in teaching positions and positions of authority in the church because they are doing good work. Others approve of forms of worship that are not commanded in God's word and argue that such things are good because they bring in members, please the people, and arouse people's emotions, even though they are contrary to what scripture reveals about God.

More often this sin is committed when sins are not dealt with in the church but overlooked and allowed to prosper—when elders and ministers and members allow gross sins to remain unrebuked: cursing and swearing and gossip and fornication and theft and Sabbath breaking and gambling, and disobedience to authority, and hatred and drunkenness and dabbling in the occult, and a thousand other sins. Seldom are such sins disciplined. Rarely are those who commit them admonished, and so, by default, the church and its members call evil good.

Not only did Israel commit this sin, but they also argued that the sins of which they were guilty could not be sins because God, the God of judgment, did not punish them. They said, in the words of the passage, "Where is the God of judgment?" They were like the people of whom God speaks in Psalm 50 and whom he condemns for adultery, theft, lying, and slander, adding: "These things hast thou done, and I kept silence; thou thoughtest that I was altogether such an one as thyself: but I will reprove thee, and set them in order before thine eyes" (v. 21).

This sin too has not disappeared in the church. Every one of us commits it when we go on in sin, thinking that because we prosper in sin and because God keeps silence and does not uncover our sin, therefore we can sin with impunity. We commit it when we think that because sinners are not punished, God is no longer a righteous judge. We commit it when we put all thoughts of the coming judgment out of our minds and do not live as those who must soon stand before the judgment seat and give an account of every deed and word.

Such excuses and lies weary God, Malachi says. He does not mean God is at first tolerant of such sins but grows tired of them. God hates all sin unchangeably and eternally. Malachi means that in committing these sins the ungodly bring on themselves the judgment of God. They say, "Where is the God of judgment?" while they develop in sin and become ready for judgment. When they have filled up their cup of sin, God will reveal himself as the God of judgment and punish them with everlasting desolation.

Although his people are also guilty of such sins, God does not destroy them but sends the Messenger of the covenant to save and deliver them. This too is answer to the question, "Where is the God of judgment?" for salvation comes in the way of judgment for sin, judgment that falls not on the sinner but on God's Messenger. It falls on him in such a way that the sons of Levi, the true spiritual priesthood of both the Old and New Testaments, are purified.

3:1. Behold, I will send my messenger, and he shall prepare the way before me: and the Lord, whom ye seek, shall suddenly come to his temple, even the messenger of the covenant, whom ye delight in: behold, he shall come, saith the LORD of hosts.

Here the word of God through Malachi becomes not just a word of rebuke and judgment but also the gospel of God's grace. Malachi 3:1–6 is the prophecy of Christ's coming that lies at the heart of all the prophet says, for Christ's coming delivers Israel, both priests and people, from their sins and provides redemption and cleansing.

All this is in answer to Israel's question, "Where is the God of judgment?" In sending Christ as the messenger of the covenant, God reveals himself as the God of judgment and as the one who brings salvation through judgment, as earlier through Isaiah he had promised to do: "Zion shall be redeemed with judgment, and her converts with righteousness" (Isa. 1:27).

This is always the way salvation comes. Salvation comes through judgment first of all because God's judgments against sin must be executed, and the salvation of God's people is possible only because those judgments are executed on Christ rather than on them. But salvation also comes through judgment because the cross brings God's judgments on the unbelieving and unrepentant world. Jesus himself announced this in John 12:31 when he said, "Now is the judgment of this world." Because God pours out his wrath against sin in all its fury at the cross, those who are not in Christ and protected by him come under the wrath and judgment of God and are condemned and destroyed by it.

In this passage, which speaks of salvation through Christ, he is the messenger of the covenant of whom the text speaks. However, the text speaks not only of him but of another messenger who prepares his way, whom we know from the New Testament to be John the Baptist. In fact, verse 1 is quoted in the New Testament especially in reference to John the Baptist.

John, like Malachi (1:1), bears the same name and office as Christ. They are all God's messengers. That is true because every priest and prophet is sent by God and brings the same divine message concerning salvation in Christ, but it is true also because every messenger of God speaks by the Spirit of Christ. We read of this in 1 Peter 1:10–11 (emphasis added):

10. Of which salvation the prophets have inquired and searched diligently, who prophesied of the grace that should come unto you:
11. Searching what, or what manner of time *the Spirit of Christ which was in them* did signify, when it testified beforehand the sufferings of Christ, and the glory that should follow.

John, as the first messenger of whom the text speaks, prepared the way for *the* Messenger of the covenant. John did this by preaching repentance and by speaking of him who would follow—by announcing him as the Lamb of God. He preached and prepared the way also by his appearance and doing his work in the wilderness, all of which were a testimony against the formalism and disobedience that characterized Israel. He even prepared the way by his baptizing, which pointed to the work that Christ, the messenger of the covenant, would do to cleanse God's people from their sins.

In this way the preaching of the gospel always prepares the way for the

coming of God's Messenger. The preaching of repentance and of Christ crucified is the means the Spirit uses to give faith in Christ and the blessing of
salvation in Christ. In giving salvation he gives Christ, who comes to live by
his Spirit in the hearts of his people: "I am crucified with Christ: nevertheless I live; yet not I, but Christ liveth in me: and the life which I now live
in the flesh I live by the faith of the Son of God, who loved me, and gave
himself for me" (Gal. 2:20).

The verse shows us too that the one whose way he prepared would be
able to save because he would be God himself come in the flesh. The messenger of the covenant is also called here the Lord. The name, of course, is
not the same as the name "LORD". The first name means "sovereign owner
and master" while the second is the name Jehovah. Nevertheless, the use of
the name "Lord" here identifies Christ as God, for this Lord is called "the
Lord whom ye seek." He is, in other words, the God of judgment, whose
coming the Jews had doubted and questioned.

Only as the God of judgment, the one who is equal to the Father, fully
and completely God, is he able to do what no mere man can do: suffer the
judgments of God and finish them, and so bring in everlasting righteousness.
Only he can cleanse the sons of Levi, whom even the word of God through
Malachi did not turn from wickedness.

When Malachi predicts that the Lord would come to his temple, Malachi is not so much speaking of the building, usually referred to as Herod's
temple, to which Jesus did come and that he cleansed twice. Malachi is
rather speaking of the true temple, Christ's own body, the church, for whom
and to whom Christ would come in order that it might be redeemed and
delivered. Jesus himself made that clear at the time of the first cleansing of
the temple. When he said, "Destroy this temple, and in three days I will raise
it up" (John 2:19), he was speaking "of the temple of his body" (v. 21).

He is identified not just as God's messenger, but as *the* Messenger of the
covenant. This identifies him both as the fulfillment of all the promises, the
one of whom every other messenger was only a type and forerunner, and also
as the one who would by his work bring God's people into the full enjoyment
of their covenantal relationship with God and who would establish that
covenant on everlasting foundations, so that the relationship between God
and his people could never again be interrupted.

But Christ is the messenger of the covenant not only because he takes away that which separates God and his people, that is, their sin; not only because he, by his Spirit, actually receives them into fellowship with God; but also because he is in his own person the one who unites us to God. He is the one in whom dwells the fullness of the Godhead bodily and the one whose bone and whose flesh we are, so that in him we live and walk with God and are joined to God. He is Immanuel, God with us.

That he is the one in whom we delight stands in stark contrast to the unbelieving question of chapter 2:17. When he does come, unbelief is cured, doubt is turned to faith, and disbelief becomes delight, by his gracious work as God's messenger.

This is all promised by Jehovah of hosts, the one whom all things serve and in whose army they march. Nothing, therefore, can prevent the coming of the Messenger of the covenant. Nothing can stand in the way of his work. Nothing can spoil or interrupt his work, not the rise of the Roman Empire, not the apostasy of Judah in the days following Malachi's prophecy, not the rise of Pharisees who would be his bitter enemies, not even the temptations of Satan. All things would serve him.

3:2. But who may abide the day of his coming? and who shall stand when he appeareth? for he is like a refiner's fire, and like fullers' soap:

Christ's work is presented here under two similar figures. He is compared to a refiner's fire and to fuller's soap. A refiner's fire is the very hot fire of the man who purifies precious metals by burning away the dross and impurity. Fuller's soap is the soap used to bleach and whiten linen and other cloth, and a fuller is the man who does that work. The emphasis therefore is on purifying and cleansing.

Christ does the work of fuller's soap and of fire by his death on the cross, for in dying he removes the guilt of those who were given him by his Father and legally purifies them. He does that work also through his Spirit when he sanctifies them, for then he through the work of the Spirit removes the dross and corruption of sin in them and delivers them from the power of sin. He does that work finally and forever in the judgment day, when he through death and the resurrection removes even the presence of sin in his people and welcomes them into everlasting habitations.

In that work not only are his people purified and delivered from the dross of sin, but the wicked world and its ungodliness are also burned up and destroyed by the coming of Christ. The people of God are purified and cleansed, for they are then delivered from all temptation and from the possibility of sin. This work begins at the cross, for as Jesus says: "Now [at the cross] is the judgment of this world" (John 12:31), and it ends in the great day of judgment.

The question that is asked about abiding the day of his coming is asked not only about his first coming but also about his return at the end of the world, when the final judgment begins to come on the ungodly:

15. And the kings of the earth, and the great men, and the rich men, and the chief captains, and the mighty men, and every bondman, and every free man, hid themselves in the dens and in the rocks of the mountains;
16. And said to the mountains and rocks, Fall on us, and hide us from the face of him that sitteth on the throne, and from the wrath of the Lamb:
17. For the great day of his wrath is come; and who shall be able to stand? (Rev. 6:15–17).

Verse 17 quotes Malachi 3:2.

No one of himself is able to abide the day of Christ's coming or to stand when he appears. All are sinners and are worthy of being destroyed by the judgment of God. Through the coming of Christ judgment always comes on the wicked world, whether it be the false church or the secular world. It came on Bethlehem. It came on the whole Jewish nation at the time of Christ's death. It came on Jerusalem through the Romans when the city was destroyed and the nation scattered. It comes today through the preaching of the gospel when under the gospel men and women are hardened in unbelief. It comes finally and forever when this old world is destroyed and the new kingdom of Christ is brought in.

That some do stand is not because they are different in themselves, but because they are given to Christ and are hidden in him when these judgments come. They are in him by faith and in obedience to the call of the

477

gospel. All who hear must believe, for who shall abide the day of his coming otherwise? All who hear must come to him, for in no other way can they stand when he appears.

3:3. And he shall sit as a refiner and purifier of silver: and he shall purify the sons of Levi, and purge them as gold and silver, that they may offer unto the LORD an offering in righteousness.

Now Malachi speaks in further detail of Christ's work as savior under the figure of a refiner of gold and silver. He adds something about the ultimate purpose of Christ's work as refiner and shows that it will be for the purifying of "the sons of Levi."

Who are these sons of Levi? In the Old Testament, of course, they were the Aaronitic priesthood and the rest of the tribe of Levi, including the temple singers, porters, and others who assisted the priests in their work. Even in the Old Testament, however, Malachi did not have them in mind exclusively when he spoke these words, but the whole nation, which was in great need of purifying. He speaks of the priests, therefore, as the leaders and representatives of the people and through them of the whole nation. Israel was a nation of priests: "And ye shall be unto me a kingdom of priests, and an holy nation" (Ex. 19:6).

Insofar as this looks ahead to the New Testament, it is a prophecy of the cleansing of God's people in every nation, for all believers are "sons of Levi," priests and prophets. Exodus 19:6 is quoted in 1 Peter 2:9, "But ye are a chosen generation, a royal priesthood, an holy nation, a peculiar people; that ye should shew forth the praises of him who hath called you out of darkness into his marvellous light." We have here in Malachi another allusion to the priesthood of all believers.

The great result of this purifying of the sons of Levi would be, God says, that his offerings would no longer be polluted and defiled and despised, but an "offering in righteousness" would be brought to him by these previously disobedient sons of Levi. Whether or not there was a true and complete purifying of the Old Testament priesthood following these prophecies of Malachi, we do not know from the sacred record. Nehemiah and Ezra speak of their efforts in this direction, but there is no indication of the extent to which these efforts were successful (Ezra 10:18–44; Neh. 13:1–31). In the

New Testament they *are* successful in that God's people are by grace a "holy priesthood, to offer up spiritual sacrifices, acceptable to God by Jesus Christ" (1 Pet. 2:5).

Those sacrifices are not offerings of beasts to be slain and burnt, but the sacrifice of ourselves to God in worship and holy obedience, a sacrifice that is designed to "shew forth the praises of him who hath called you out of darkness into his marvellous light" (1 Pet. 2:9). Such sacrifices are offered in the offering of the heart to God and of the lips, the hands, and the mind in his service and in thankfulness to him.

This offering is called an offering in righteousness because it is acceptable to him, being offered by righteous hands, hearts, and lips. The righteousness that makes these offerings acceptable is not, however, inherent in those who bring this offering but is the free gift of God's grace in Jesus Christ, a righteousness that is ours not by works but by faith only. It is a righteousness that is ours through the work of the Messenger of the covenant.

3:4. Then shall the offering of Judah and Jerusalem be pleasant unto the LORD, as in the days of old, and as in former years.

The offering brought to God by a cleansed and renewed priesthood is acceptable to him, as the prophet now states more plainly, speaking of God's delight in their offerings. He would delight in them, Malachi says, as in the days of old and as in former years, referring both to the early history of the nation when the priesthood and sacrifices were first instituted and to more recent times, those immediately following the return to Canaan, when the offerings of the people were brought with a willing heart and without hypocrisy.

That their offerings were and would be pleasant to him does not mean that there is anything of value in the blood of calves and goats, but that the sacrifices of the people would be offered in obedience to God and not carelessly as before. They would be offered in faith, looking to the coming of Christ as the one who fulfills all sacrifices by the offering of his own body on the tree of the cross. This the people had not done but would by the grace of God do once again.

We bring that same pleasing offering in the truest sense of the word, no longer bringing the sacrifices that were types and shadows of Christ, but through him offering ourselves to God. We do that not as an atonement for sin, for atonement has been made and no other atoning sacrifice may now be offered, but we do it in grateful acknowledgment of that perfect sacrifice of Christ: "I beseech you therefore, brethren, by the mercies of God, that ye present your bodies a living sacrifice, holy, acceptable unto God, which is your reasonable service" (Rom. 12:1).

3:5. And I will come near to you to judgment; and I will be a swift witness against the sorcerers, and against the adulterers, and against false swearers, and against those that oppress the hireling in his wages, the widow, and the fatherless, and that turn aside the stranger from his right, and fear not me, saith the LORD of hosts.

Although Christ will come and purify the sons of Levi, his work is limited in its extent. He will not purify everyone, but only those God has given to him. The rest will perish through the judgment that he brings. Indeed, he will be the dividing line between those who are purified and those who perish. In him and through him God comes as a swift witness against the sinners mentioned in this verse.

As a swift witness he always comes quickly. That may not have seemed to be true in the days following Malachi's prophecy, when four hundred years of spiritual darkness came to separate Malachi's prophecy from its fulfillment. It does not always seem so now as we wait through the ages of the New Testament for Christ's return. Nevertheless, he comes quickly.

He comes quickly first because he comes not according to our clocks and reckoning of time, but according to the reckoning of God, to whom a day is as a thousand years and a thousand years as a day. He also comes quickly in that he does not delay a moment beyond the fulfillment of all that God has planned—he comes as soon as he can. He comes quickly too in that when the time is ripe he appears suddenly and without warning, the joy of his people and the terror of his enemies.

The sins he judges are sins not previously mentioned in the book of Malachi, but Malachi shows here that the wickedness of the people was not just in a few matters but was very widespread, as it always is. Though his main concern was covenantal unfaithfulness in the corrupting of the sacrifices and the matter of marriage, he does not overlook that the people were guilty of many other sins.

These sins are not uncommon today in the church. There are many who dabble in the occult, in fortune telling, astrology, and demonology, the sins Malachi is speaking of when he mentions sorcerers. Indeed, many who practice what they call "spiritual warfare," exorcism and healing, are dealing in an unbiblical way with dangerous and wicked things.

The sin of adultery is committed not only in divorcing and remarrying, but also in the cohabiting of those who are not married, in fornicating, in homosexual behavior, and in the widespread use of pornography. Today as then, these sins often have the tacit if not the open approval of the leaders of the church, just as they did in the days of Malachi.

False swearers are not only those who tell lies under oath but all those who do not keep their pledged word—those whose word cannot be trusted in business or in the church, whether they are officebearers who do not keep the promises they made when ordained to office or members who have a reputation for untruth and for dishonesty. God hates such sins because he is the Truth.

Those who oppress and steal from the hireling, the widow, the orphans, and the strangers are not only found in society at large but are those "Christian" employers who do not pay their employees a decent wage and those who take advantage of others, especially when those they cheat are easy prey because they do not speak the language or know the customs of the country to which they have come. They are the televangelists who use every opportunity to enrich themselves with the pennies of the widows and even claim revelations from God in order to bilk the people.

Such are as common today as they were in the days of Malachi, and the word of God through Malachi shows how much God hates such sins as well as those that are still socially unacceptable—robbery, murder, perjury, and such like.

The fear of which Malachi speaks is that holy fear and reverence of God that is the true source of obedience. It cares to please God more than it cares to please men, because it knows how great he is. It counts God's favor of more value than all the pleasures and treasures of this world. It knows that life with him is the only guarantee of blessing and prosperity, for it knows him as the Lord of hosts, and it knows too that the only prosperity that matters is spiritual and heavenly.

3:6. For I am the LORD, I change not; therefore ye sons of Jacob are not consumed.

God concludes this part of the prophecy with a reminder of his own immutability (unchangeableness). This may seem out of place at first, but most certainly it is not. It is important both for those who stand in jeopardy of God's judgments and for those to whom he promises salvation through the coming of Christ to know that he is unchangeable.

Those who continue to live wickedly and show no fear of his judgments must know that he is unchangeable especially because his judgments do not always come immediately. When they do not see those judgments, they begin to think that God is not going to judge them at all, and they become hardened in their rebellion and disobedience.

Those to whom God promises salvation—the true sons of Jacob—must also know that he does not change, because the revelation of their salvation does not always come immediately. The believing Jews in these last days of the Old Testament had to wait another four hundred years for the fulfillment of God's word, and we too, who have seen the beginning of that fulfillment, are still waiting for its completion. We must know that "the Lord is not slack concerning his promise, as some men count slackness" and that "the day of the Lord will come" (2 Pet. 3:9–10).

We must know his unchangeableness also as the great God of our salvation. We deserve to be consumed, for we are in ourselves no different from the ungodly among whom we live. We also are guilty of the sins mentioned in the previous verse, but we are not consumed because God is unchangeable. He is unchangeable as the God of election who has chosen his people as his own from eternity and whose eternal love for them cannot fail. He reveals his unchangeableness in the sending of the Messenger of the covenant when he does not allow the sins of his people to separate them from himself, but redeems and delivers them by his Messenger. He shows his unchangeableness in giving them his Spirit and causing the gospel to be preached to them, so that through faith the righteousness of Christ becomes theirs and they stand justified before him.

Although Israel and Judah thought that God had changed because they were not enjoying his promised blessings, it was not he but they who had changed in departing from him. Nevertheless, he would save among them the remnant according to election whom he had eternally loved and whom he would not cast away; would save them for the glory of his own name and to show that he is Jehovah, the God of the covenant, the one who does not change. That he did do, and he continues to do the same today in his unchanging faithfulness.

Chapter 31

THE FIFTH DISPUTATION:
MALACHI 3:7–12

3:7   Even from the days of your fathers ye are gone away from mine ordinances, and have not kept them. Return unto me, and I will return unto you, saith the LORD of hosts. But ye said, Wherein shall we return?

3:8   Will a man rob God? Yet ye have robbed me. But ye say, Wherein have we robbed thee? In tithes and offerings.

3:9   Ye are cursed with a curse: for ye have robbed me, even this whole nation.

3:10   Bring ye all the tithes into the storehouse, that there may be meat in mine house, and prove me now herewith, saith the LORD of hosts, if I will not open you the windows of heaven, and pour you out a blessing, that there shall not be room enough to receive it.

3:11   And I will rebuke the devourer for your sakes, and he shall not destroy the fruits of your ground; neither shall your vine cast her fruit before the time in the field, saith the LORD of hosts.

3:12   And all nations shall call you blessed: for ye shall be a delightsome land, saith the LORD of hosts.

3:7. Even from the days of your fathers ye are gone away from mine ordinances, and have not kept them. Return unto me, and I will return unto you, saith the LORD of hosts. But ye said, Wherein shall we return?

In this fifth section of Malachi's prophecy, he returns again to the sins of the people, this time rebuking them for the sin of robbing God in their tithes and offerings. By this sin also they were guilty of gross covenantal unfaithfulness.

Israel had long been guilty of this sin. Other sins they had been cured of by the long years of the Babylonian captivity, especially the sin of idolatry, but of this sin they had not been cured. Hezekiah in his reforms had reestablished the law's system of tithing (2 Chron. 31:4–10), but after Hezekiah there is little evidence that the law's demands regarding tithing continued to be observed.

In speaking of their fathers, God reminds them that these sins were of long standing. They had learned these sins from their disobedient fathers and were really no different from their fathers. Perhaps they prided themselves in having forsaken the sins of their fathers, but it was not so. Their fathers had been covetous and worldly and so were they.

This is the way God visits the sins of the fathers upon the children as he threatens to do in the second commandment. He does not punish the children for the sins of their fathers. Ezekiel 18:20 is clear: "The soul that sinneth, it shall die." But God visits the sins of the fathers on the children when in his just judgment the children learn the sins of their fathers and walk in them and come themselves under the judgment of God. There is a corporate responsibility for sin. Our sins have consequences, as did Adam's and as do every man's, not only for ourselves, but also for others including our children.

What a warning to believing parents! What an incentive to careful godliness! Not only out of the love of God, but out of fear for their children also they ought to walk in God's ways with all their heart. And what grief it is— greater grief there is not—when they see their own sins in their children. Then they pray the more fervently that God will deliver both them and their children from those sins, and that he will be gracious and remember his covenant.

God speaks of ordinances rather than just of one single ordinance concerning tithes for several reasons. There were many laws concerning tithing and none of them were being kept. The apostasy of the people both at this time and in times past was widespread. They neglected not only the law concerning tithes, but also all the ordinances concerning the worship and service of God. So it is always. Never does the church in her calling to serve and worship God go astray only at a few small points, but apostasy once begun continues until the whole of obedience to God's ordinances and laws erodes away.

This widespread apostasy also shows the insolence of the question asked by the Jews, "Wherein shall we return?" Not only had they departed in a few minor matters, but they needed to return at every point. Yet they could not and would not see their sin. So it is with those to whom God has not given his grace. Not only does the unredeemed sinner continue in his sin, but also he cannot and will not see his sin or turn from it. How we must beware, therefore, of the temptation to make excuses, to play down our sins and the sins of our children, to give no heed to the warnings of the word of God and of others. We may not pretend that those warnings apply to others and not to ourselves!

Yet God identifies himself as Jehovah of hosts, the God of the covenant. As the Lord of hosts, he was the lawgiver whose laws they broke and the one to whom all their sacrifices belonged, the one against whom they sinned. He also hints, however, at his covenantal faithfulness to them, for though they had often been unfaithful, niggardly, and hardhearted, he would never be unfaithful to them.

Of this same faithfulness he speaks when he tells them to return to him and promises that in so doing he would also return to them. That promise, like all God's promises, is sure and was surely fulfilled in Christ. Never does God cast away his people whom he foreknew.

His returning to them when they returned to him does not mean that his returning depended on theirs. Then there could be no hope of his ever returning to them. Their returning to him, though he does not say so here, would be, when it happened, an evidence that he had already returned to them! Nevertheless, it was only in the way of their returning that they would experience again his favor and blessing. As long as they continued hardhearted and impenitent, their experience would be that he was far off as a God of mercy and love, and near only in wrath and judgment.

Of this relationship between our returning to God and our experience of his lovingkindness the Canons of Dordt speak beautifully in an article quoted before:

> By such enormous sins, however, they very highly offend God, incur a deadly guilt, grieve the Holy Spirit, interrupt the exercise of faith, very grievously wound their own consciences, and sometimes lose the sense of God's favor, for a time, until on their returning into the right way by serious repentance, the light of God's fatherly countenance again shines upon them.[1]

Because repentance is always a work of God, the Canons say that:

> by his Word and Spirit, he certainly and effectually renews them to repentance, to a sincere and godly sorrow for their sins, that they may seek and obtain remission in the blood of the Mediator, may again experience the favor of a reconciled God, through faith adore his mercies, and henceforward more diligently work out their own salvation with fear and trembling.[2]

Such is the great incentive to repentance—the knowledge that God receives and blesses those who are sorry for their sins. He always forgives them and never turns away his face from the tears of those who weep for their sins. He assures us that "though we oft have sinned against him, yet his love and grace abide."[3] There is, however, no mercy or experience of God's favor for those who continue to say, "Wherein shall we return?"

3:8. Will a man rob God? Yet ye have robbed me. But ye say, Wherein have we robbed thee? In tithes and offerings.

3:9. Ye are cursed with a curse: for ye have robbed me, even this whole nation.

---

1 Canons 5.5, in Schaff, *Creeds of Christendom*, 3:593.
2 Canons 5.7, in ibid., 3:594.
3 No. 280:3, in *The Psalter*.

God now proceeds to show why the neglect of tithes and offerings was such a serious sin by accusing the Jews of robbery, robbery of himself. What God says about robbery was needed then and is needed now, for both Israel and the church today are guilty of gross unfaithfulness to God in this matter. The church today is no more eager to acknowledge its sin than it was in the days of Malachi. Instead, with callous indifference, it brushes aside the complaints of God's word: "Wherein have we robbed thee?"

The tithes of which God speaks were of various kinds. Moore distinguishes them thus:

> The tithes required by the Mosaic law were, first, a tenth of all that remained after the firstfruits, (which belonged to God and must be given to him,) which tenth was God's, as the original proprietor of the soil, and was paid to the Levites for their maintenance. (Lev. 27:30-32.) Secondly, from this tenth the Levites paid a tenth to the priests. (Num. 18:26-28.) Thirdly, a second tenth was paid by the people for the entertainment of the Levites and their own families at the tabernacle. (Deut. 12:18.) Fourthly, another tithe was paid every third year for the poor, widows, orphans, etc (Deut. 14:28–29.)

Moore adds: "The first three classes of tithes are specially referred to here, as appears from the context, though the fourth was also withheld, as we would infer from chap. 3:5."[4]

Strict tithing is not obligatory for New Testament Christians, as 2 Corinthians 9:6–7 indicates: "But this I say, he which soweth sparingly shall reap also sparingly; and he which soweth bountifully shall reap also bountifully. *Every man according as he purposeth in his heart, so let him give*; not grudgingly, or of necessity: for God loveth a cheerful giver" (emphasis added). These verses require freewill giving on the part of God's people, not giving that is regulated by law, because we live in the New Testament, not in the Old. Nevertheless, even these verses show that giving is an important part of the service and worship of God (Rom. 12:8). God *loves* a cheerful giver! And the practice of tithing, even if not obligatory, remains a good guide for our

---

4 Moore, *Haggai, Zechariah and Malachi*, 405.

giving. If a person is not giving at least a tithe of what he has, he is probably not giving as he should.

Giving is not a matter of repayment, for who can repay God for his abundant mercies, but is rather an expression of thankfulness. We give a little of what we have received in order to demonstrate our conviction that God has given us all things in Christ, and to show that we understand that we have only the use of what he gives. It all remains his, for he is the sovereign creator and owner of all.

Failure in these obligations is covenantal unfaithfulness, for those who do not give as they should do not acknowledge God's goodness and faithfulness and do not recognize that all they have belongs to him and is given them for their use because they are his covenant friends. In this way too, sins committed by lack of giving or grudging giving are robbery. They are robbery not only because they are a refusal to give him what he requires, but also because they are a refusal to recognize that all we have is his. When we do not give or give cheerfully, we are not stealing just the tenth from him but *everything*.

Romans 1 condemns the heathen nations for ingratitude, for though they know God through the things that are made and by his own testimony within them, they are not thankful (Rom. 1:20–21). If God condemns them for ingratitude, how much greater will our condemnation be for the same sin, aggravated by our knowledge of him as Savior and our confession that we are his covenant friends!

For this reason, God's curse is upon those who fall under the condemnation of these verses. Though poor giving may seem a small thing to us, it is no small matter to God. His curse is a word of his anger by which he sends the sinner to hell. He speaks here therefore of damnation for such sins.

3:10. Bring ye all the tithes into the storehouse, that there may be meat in mine house, and prove me now herewith, saith the LORD of hosts, if I will not open you the windows of heaven, and pour you out a blessing, that there shall not be room enough to receive it.

Israel's sin was primarily not giving the tithes at all or giving only part of what God required. These sins are found in the church today as well. God often receives only what is left over after we have gotten what we wanted, and what is left over is usually just a pittance. Nevertheless, there are other ways in which this sin is committed. When we give grudgingly, even if we give liberally, we rob God, for our grudging covetousness is a failure to recognize that everything we have is his. Viewing it as our own, we rob him to whom it all belongs.

The same is true of those who give only to get. Those leaders who promote giving only to enrich themselves and those who believe the lie that giving is primarily a way of getting even more in return from God (they speak of casting their bread upon the waters, Eccl. 11:1) are also robbing God. They give not out of gratitude to God for his great mercy, but only to fill their own pockets at his expense.

When God promises to be liberal to those who give liberally, he does not contradict what we have said. Indeed, his liberality precedes our giving and is the reason for it. We do not, cannot, give anything to him unless he has first given us all things in Christ, and then we give not to get more from him, for what more can he give, but to acknowledge his great goodness and to show our gratitude.

Yet in the way of showing our gratitude to him in giving, we experience and enjoy his goodness to us. The person who gives sparingly or grudgingly shows that he has experienced nothing of God's great goodness. The person who gives from the heart and in gratitude shows that he is already enjoying God's goodness, that he knows it and appreciates it. He has seen the windows of heaven opened and blessings poured out greater than he would ever ask or think, and he will see it again.

We may not conclude from this verse that material prosperity is promised to all those who give liberally. Even if it were promised it could not be the motive for giving, but it is not promised. In the Old Testament it was true in a limited way, especially for the nation as a whole, that faithfulness in these matters brought material prosperity, but even then it was not necessarily true on an individual basis. What is more, material prosperity, though it can picture the blessing of God, does not in itself constitute that blessing. If it did, the poor would have to conclude that they have forfeited the blessing of God, and the rich would be able to think they had his favor in a special way. Indeed, we would all conclude that the ungodly have more of his favor than his people, for the experience of God's people is often that of Asaph in Psalm 73: "*Their* eyes stand out with fatness: they have more than heart could wish...All the day long have *I* been plagued, and chastened every morning" (vv. 7, 14, emphasis added).

The blessings promised therefore are in principle spiritual and heavenly. They are the blessings of salvation: what the New Testament refers to as the riches of God's grace and the blessings that are in Christ Jesus (Eph. 1:3, 7).

"Prove me now herewith" is not said in the bad sense of tempting God by doubting him and his goodness (Ps. 78:18; 106:14), but in the sense of putting his mercy and goodness to the test by doing as he commands. Israel would find in doing this, Malachi says, that God is full of lovingkindness and tender mercy; that he is abundantly good to those who fear and serve him. Then the word amounts to a promise and guarantee of God's goodness.

There is some dispute about the last phrase of verse 10. Some understand it to mean that God promises to give more than enough, more than is sufficient for the needs of his people. Others understand it to mean that he promises to give perpetually and without end. The latter interpretation seems to be more correct in that a similar phrase is translated in Psalm 72:5, "as long as the sun and moon endure." In any case, God is promising blessing beyond what we would ever ask or think (Eph. 3:20). He promises blessing as Jehovah of hosts, the covenant God of his people, the one to whom belong all the hosts of heaven and earth, all of which serve him and accomplish his purpose and all of which he will use to give blessing to his people.

We learn here also that our giving is primarily directed to the work of the church, the ministry of the gospel, and the well-being of God's people. "Give," he says, "that there may be meat in mine house." In the Old Testament the tithes were for the maintenance of the priests and Levites, for the upkeep of the temple, and for the support of the poor. So it is in the New Testament. Our offerings are not first of all for world relief or world hunger, but for the maintenance of the ministry of the gospel, to provide a living (not an enrichment) for the ministers of the gospel, and for the care of the poor and widows. We give to God by giving to the work and support of his church, and we give that way for we can give him nothing directly. He is, after all, the one who is "dwelling in the light which no man can approach unto; whom no man hath seen, nor can see" (1 Tim. 6:16).

3:11. And I will rebuke the devourer for your sakes, and he shall not destroy the fruits of your ground; neither shall your vine cast her fruit before the time in the field, saith the LORD of hosts.

Apparently the Jews were suffering the judgments of God on the crops and fields for their unfaithfulness. The verse speaks of disease, probably a blight of some kind that was destroying the produce of the vines, as well as of the devourer. The latter refers to plagues of crop-destroying insects described by God as "my great army," an army in which the cankerworm, the caterpillar, and the palmerworm marched (Joel 2:25).

We should note the difficulty in seeing specific acts of God's providence, such as diseases, plagues, famines, poverty, war, and so on, as well as material prosperity, as evidences of his disfavor or favor. The difficulty arises out of the fact that events and occurrences and providences are not themselves the favor or blessing of God. Thus sickness, poverty, and trouble can be blessings to God's people and wealth and health a curse to the ungodly.

It is impossible in both the Old and New Testaments to make any such consistent connection on a personal level, and it is only on a national or worldwide scale that this can be seen. In other words, viewed at large, earthquakes, war, famines, and plagues are signs of God's judgment, even though the individual child of God need not fear when he is caught up in these things. God's displeasure does not then rest on him personally.

Here, *as a nation*, Israel would see God's favor in material prosperity and in a withdrawal of the plagues that were destroying their livelihood. In the New Testament we see God's displeasure with our own nations and with the whole world of the ungodly in that such plagues are not removed, but rather increase.

Nevertheless, the judgments God sent on Israel's fields and vineyards are fulfilled in the spiritual plagues he sends on an unfaithful church in the New Testament. The result of these plagues was prophesied by Amos: "Behold, the days come, saith the Lord GOD, that I will send a famine in the land, not a famine of bread, nor a thirst for water, but of hearing the words of the LORD" (Amos 8:11). In such times of famine the church is dry, barren, and unfruitful—terrible times for those who remain faithful. Such famine is the worst of all and a sure sign of God's displeasure.

3:12. And all nations shall call you blessed: for ye shall be a delightsome land, saith the LORD of hosts.

God promises Israel through Malachi renewed prosperity as an evidence of his blessing, something even the nations around them would see. The difficulties they had previously experienced would vanish and their life in Canaan would be a life of ease and plenty, and they would be envied by those who witnessed their prosperity.

This promise was never fulfilled literally. God is speaking of the future spiritual prosperity of his people. Stuart says:

> The Israel of Malachi's day was a defeated little remainder state under Persian domination consisting of some of the former Judah and some of the former Benjamin, much of it still in ruins, its capital city still largely unpopulated (Neh. 11) and its people eking out a hardscrabble existence in an area of the world that no one could ever call "lush." But the future would hold for them things that they had never experienced, expressed here, as is typical in the prophets, in grand materialistic terms, though surely having their ultimate import in terms of the people's spiritual relationship to God.[5]

Because of this lack of literal fulfillment, there are those who believe in a fulfillment of these promises in a future earthly millennial kingdom. We know, however, from the word of God that Israel is a spiritual people (Rom. 2:28–29; 9:6–8; 1 Pet. 2:9–10) and that the promises concerning the land and their prosperity in the land are fulfilled in their blessed salvation and in the eternal blessedness of heaven (Heb. 11:9–10, 13–16).

The spiritual prosperity of the church therefore is prophesied as a fulfillment of the prophecy of Malachi. The church is a delightsome land, for there are the promises of God in Jesus Christ. There Christ rules as the everlasting king of his people. There his people enjoy the forgiveness of sins, the promise of eternal life, and the work of the Holy Spirit. There they are separated, as Israel was in Egypt, from the spiritual plagues of the ungodly:

---

5 Stuart, "Malachi," 1372.

terror, a troubled conscience, hopelessness, separation from God, the failure of marriage and family, violence, deceit, and all the other judgments of God upon this present world. A delightsome land indeed!

Malachi also speaks of heaven and its blessings. There can be no doubt of this in view of the word of God in Hebrews 11:16, which speaks of a better and heavenly country, and Revelation 21 and 22, which give us a glimpse of the most delightsome land of all:

22. And I saw no temple therein: for the Lord God Almighty and the Lamb are the temple of it.
23. And the city had no need of the sun, neither of the moon, to shine in it: for the glory of God did lighten it, and the Lamb is the light thereof.
26. And they shall bring the glory and honor of the nations into it.
27. And there shall in no wise enter into it any thing that defileth, neither whatsoever worketh abomination, or maketh a lie: but they which are written in the Lamb's book of life. (Rev. 21:22–23, 26–27)

1. And he shewed me a pure river of water of life, clear as crystal, proceeding out of the throne of God and of the Lamb.
2. In the midst of the street of it, and on either side of the river, was there the tree of life, which bare twelve manner of fruits, and yielded her fruit every month: and the leaves of the tree were for the healing of the nations.
3. And there shall be no more curse: but the throne of God and of the Lamb shall be in it; and his servants shall serve him:
4. And they shall see his face; and his name shall be in their foreheads.
5. And there shall be no night there; and they need no candle, neither light of the sun; for the Lord God giveth them light; and they shall reign for ever and ever. (Rev. 23:1–6)

Chapter 32

THE SIXTH DISPUTATION:
MALACHI 3:13–4:3

3:13   Your words have been stout against me, saith the LORD. Yet ye say,
       What have we spoken so much against thee?

3:14   Ye have said, It is vain to serve God: and what profit is it that we
       have kept his ordinance, and that we have walked mournfully before
       the LORD of hosts?

3:15   And now we call the proud happy; yea, they that work wickedness
       are set up; yea, they that tempt God are even delivered.

3:16   Then they that feared the LORD spake often one to another: and the
       LORD hearkened, and heard it, and a book of remembrance was writ-
       ten before him for them that feared the LORD, and that thought upon
       his name.

3:17   And they shall be mine, saith the LORD of hosts, in that day when I
       make up my jewels; and I will spare them, as a man spareth his own
       son that serveth him.

3:18   Then shall ye return, and discern between the righteous and the
       wicked, between him that serveth God and him that serveth him not.

4:1   For, behold, the day cometh, that shall burn as an oven; and all the
       proud, yea, and all that do wickedly, shall be stubble: and the day
       that cometh shall burn them up, saith the LORD of hosts, that it shall
       leave them neither root nor branch.

4:2   But unto you that fear my name shall the Sun of righteousness arise
       with healing in his wings; and ye shall go forth, and grow up as calves
       of the stall.

4:3   And ye shall tread down the wicked; for they shall be ashes under the
       soles of your feet in the day that I shall do this, saith the LORD of hosts.

3:13. Your words have been stout against me, saith the LORD. *Yet ye say, What have we spoken so much against thee?*

This last main section of the prophecy of Malachi is more general than what precedes. Its purpose is to make a distinction between God's people in Israel and the unrepentant wicked. It speaks therefore of the spiritual difference between these two groups, of how that difference is manifest in the conduct of each, and of how each group will be blessed or cursed by God.

This distinction between two groups in Judah is to be traced back ultimately to God's eternal decree of election and reprobation as that is set forth in chapter 1. It is not just that one group was repentant, loved the name of the Lord, and obeyed him, while the other group was hardhearted, would not repent, and sneered at God's word. Then the difference would be of works. Instead the difference lies in God's eternal and exclusive love for Jacob and hatred for Esau.

The love of God for Jacob did not include all of his descendants. There were many in Judah who were spiritual Edomites. They behaved like Esau and were counted by God as his descendants, not as Jacob's. They would be dealt with by God as Esau was. For them there would be no place of repentance (Heb. 12:17). They would be rejected by God (Heb. 12:17) and would be far off from the blessings of his covenant (Gen. 27:39). What they built God would tear down, and they would be called "The border of wickedness, and, The people against whom the LORD hath indignation forever" (Mal. 1:4). So it is with all those who prove themselves the spiritual descendants of Esau, though they be born in the lines and families of God's people and of his covenant.

In this opening verse of the section, God speaks again of their stubborn impenitence. Always they resisted his word. Never did they see themselves as the object of God's rebukes and threats. Endlessly they excused themselves. And even when God through Malachi rebuked them for this stubborn impenitence, they refused to see that they had done any wrong.

It is never any different. It is not only the heathen who are guilty of impenitence, but always there are those in the church who, with a comforting sense of their own importance and righteousness, never see themselves

496

as the sinners described and admonished in the word of God. Though they will make a vague and general confession of sin and acknowledge the truth of total depravity, they forever excuse themselves. When the admonitions of the word are preached, they always think of someone else. When their sins are pointed out, they have a thousand arguments and always point the finger at others. When their children are accused of wrongdoing, they refuse to believe their children could be guilty. No specific sins are ever confessed by them to God or to others. They do not know what it is to mourn for one's sins and to humble oneself before God. And if God presumes to judge them for their hardheartedness, immediately they are filled with complaints about him, doubting his goodness and mercy, complaining of his injustice, and further excusing their wickedness. How very near these sins are to all of us! If it were not for the work of the Messenger of the covenant and of his Spirit, there would be no one at all who did not come under the condemnation of these words of God.

The Israelites were exactly like their fathers, and so are all who follow in their footsteps. God had spoken against them long before this by saying to Ezekiel:

30. Also, thou son of man, the children of thy people still are talking against thee by the walls and in the doors of the houses, and speak one to another, every one to his brother, saying, Come, I pray you, and hear what is the word that cometh forth from the LORD.
31. And they come unto thee as the people cometh, and they sit before thee as my people, and they hear thy words, but they will not do them: for with their mouth they shew much love, but their heart goeth after their covetousness.
32. And, lo, thou art unto them as a very lovely song of one that hath a pleasant voice, and can play well on an instrument: for they hear thy words, but they do them not. (Ezek. 33:30–32)

The Jews of Malachi's day, Malachi says, resisted God with their words. Their words are recorded in the last part of verse 13 and in verses 14 and 15. Those words expressed doubt that God's word applied to them. They included charges against God himself and excuses for sin, but all those words

497

were only the outward manifestation of hard, unregenerated hearts. What a warning for us! Such words of excuse, of doubt, of complaint, the evidences of hardhearted and stubborn impenitence, ought never be found in the mouths of God's children.

What is more, their words had been spoken against the Lord, the God of the covenant, the God who had established his everlasting covenant with their fathers and who had repeatedly told them that covenant people must fulfill their obligations in the covenant and show by obedience, humility, and repentance that they are friends of the living God. This they had not done.

The word "stout" suggests that they had, at least in their own minds and hearts, "overruled" God and his word. In reality they could not overrule God any more than they could rob God. This overruling of God must not be understood, then, in the sense suggested by one commentator, who asks: "Can people actually overrule God? Of course they can. God has chosen to restrain his own actual sovereignty so as to give to human beings autonomy, which they may use for or against God."[1] That is simply a denial of God's sovereignty and goes hand in hand with the wicked notion that salvation and damnation depend on the will of the sinner and not on the eternal, unchangeable, and sovereign will of God.

Their words "overruled" God because they justified themselves at God's expense. As far as they were concerned the words God had spoken were defeated and gone. What a striking description of a very common sin! By excuses, by accusing others, by misinterpreting and misapplying the word of God, by stubbornness, by disobedience we "overrule" God's words to us, put them away from us, and set ourselves in his place as though we were rulers and lawgivers in our own right.

3:14. Ye have said, It is vain to serve God: and what profit is it that we have kept his ordinance, and that we have walked mournfully before the LORD of hosts?

In these words, which God quotes from the mouths of the people themselves, the real reason for their hardheartedness and impenitence comes out.

---

1 Ibid., 1376.

It was all the result of their covetousness. If there was no material profit in the service of God, they were not interested. They had tried the service of God and found it profitless and so had abandoned it.

Like these covetous Jews are all the people, leaders and followers, who preach a health and wealth gospel, a name it and claim it gospel, and who are interested in the things of God only for what they can get out of it. They include those who seem to think that the name of Jesus is a kind of magic cure for all their earthly ills and who turn to him only in their need for help with family troubles, sickness, and other trials. Included too are all those whose sole interest is enriching themselves, even if it is at the expense of the widows and the poor.

Nor are those who sell religious junk excused. The books, the trinkets, the superficial piety they sell make merchandise of the gospel and are an abomination in their shallowness and silliness. WWJD bracelets, miracle anointing oil, genuine pewter pocket tokens, and a thousand other such things not only are as silly and superficial as the relics of Roman Catholicism but become a substitute for God's word, for the true worship of his name, and for repentance and holiness.

These sins are not that far from us. When we turn to God only in our need, as though he exists only to give us what we ask, we are equally guilty. When we are disappointed that our efforts and service do not bring praise and are not noticed, we are no different than these Jews. When we are discouraged because our service of God brings no earthly advantage or profit, we too fall under the condemnation of this word.

When these people said, "It is vain to serve God: and what profit is it that we have kept his ordinance, and that we have walked mournfully before the LORD of hosts?" they meant what many mean today: "No one notices what we have done. No one praises us for our obedience. God doesn't love us in spite of the fact that we have served him. The proof is in the troubles he sends us. He cannot be a just and righteous God. What is the matter with him anyway?"

There is no profit in the service of God, not in the strict sense of that word: nothing earned, nothing ever merited. What we do receive from him is always more grace, and all of it undeserved. Even the reward promised in his word to his people is only grace upon grace. Yet God's grace in its abundant blessedness puts the lie to those who think that the service of God is vain. It is the way of everlasting peace, eternal wealth, and gracious reward beyond what we would ever ask or think.

3:15. And now we call the proud happy; yea, they that work wickedness are set up; yea, they that tempt God are even delivered.

Verse 15 continues their haughty complaint. The Jews were suggesting that the heathen who did not serve God were happier than they were, though idolaters; to them the prosperity of the heathen was proof that it was of no value to fear and obey God. They thought God was building the heathen up while tearing Judah down. The proof of it all, according to these Jews, was that the heathen escaped any punishment for their wickedness.

This too is often suggested today, though perhaps not in such blatant terms. When theologians speak of a love and grace of God for all, when they promote universalism in any form as many do, they are saying that there is no real profit in the service and worship of God. God loves everyone anyway. Nor do those who listen to such theologians miss the point of what they say. Their actions show they have understood the "gospel" that is preached to them to mean that they can continue in their wickedness and unbelief. After all, God loves them no matter what. And so the urgency and seriousness of the gospel are destroyed.

Moore sums it up thus: "This atrocious insinuation, that God favored evil-doers, was the highest insult they could have uttered, and was that which, as it were, drove God to inflict his judgments upon them."[2]

Those judgments are not actually mentioned until chapter 4:1. God pauses before speaking of those judgments to describe the attitude of his redeemed people and the blessings that they would enjoy in verses 16 and 17 of chapter 3.

3:16. Then they that feared the LORD spake often one to another: and the LORD hearkened, and heard it, and a book of remembrance was written before him for them that feared the LORD, and that thought upon his name.

As God had shown Elijah that there is always a remnant, when Elijah thought he was the only one left who feared God, so he speaks of the same

---

2 Moore, *Haggai, Zechariah and Malachi*, 411.

remnant here through Malachi. That there was such a remnant in the closing days of the Old Testament suggests that there will be a remnant also in the last days before Christ's return, when the church is scattered and it seems as though there is no longer faith upon the earth (Luke 18:8).

The word "then" has the force of "but" or "in contrast," for the character and attitude of those who are described in this and the following verse are spiritually the opposite of those described in the previous verses. As one commentator suggests, however, the word also implies that these faithful deliberately and consciously spoke to one another as a witness against the skepticism and unbelief of the majority.

It is well worth noting that twice in the verse the faithful are described as those who feared the Lord. In this way especially they were different from the rest. Surely the whole nation with few exceptions claimed to know and honor God, but what was lacking was the awe and reverence that comes from a real spiritual and personal knowledge; what is so often referred to in scripture as "fear."

Among those who make a show of religion and piety and who claim to love and serve God, this is what is most often missing. It becomes evident, as it did with the majority of the Jews, in a lack of carefulness in worship, in quickness to doubt God and even to accuse him of evil, and in a refusal to pay any heed to what he says. If there is one thing that is obviously missing in the prayers, the worship, and the obedience of church members today, it is this fear.

This fear is not a terror of God—not a slavish or guilty fear—but a fear that knows from experience both the majesty of God and his lovingkindness and while trembling before him nevertheless fears to be separated or alienated from him. It produces holiness of life, reverence, true piety, and a deep consciousness of the amazing love of God.

The faithful are also described as those who thought upon his name. They knew his majesty and glory and could not possibly join with the ungodly in speaking evil of him and of his works. God's name not only includes the titles by which he is addressed, but as the Westminster Larger Catechism points out, also includes everything by which he reveals himself: his attributes, works, ordinances, and word. These faithful few knew his name and did not misinterpret his dealings with Judah. Nor will anyone who knows his name—really knows it—ever think wrongly of him whatever outward circumstances may be.

The speech of these faithful few is in contrast to the speech of the ungodly, who were questioning among themselves all that God had revealed of himself. Though the passage does not tell us what the faithful said, there can be no doubt that they spoke, as God's people always do, of his covenantal faithfulness, of his unchangeableness as the only reason for Judah's continued existence, of their own sins and of the sins of the nation that deserved all of and more than the judgments God had sent, and of their desire to be faithful to God and to keep his law.

That God hears their speech is of great comfort, for the world and the false church will not hear. No matter what the faithful church says of God, the world turns a deaf ear and the apostate church mocks. But God hears and remembers and counts their words of great value.

There are two possible explanations of the "book of remembrance" to which Malachi refers. The first says that this book of remembrance was a book the people themselves wrote recording their desire to be faithful to God and to keep his covenant. In that case Nehemiah 9 and 10 may very well record the substance of all that they said to one another and refer to this book, for Nehemiah was a contemporary of Malachi. Nehemiah 9 and 10 record Nehemiah's prayer on behalf of the people, but at the end of chapter 9 the word of God speaks of a written covenant that was made by those of the leaders and people who were still faithful. It is an attractive idea and not impossible that the book of remembrance of which Malachi speaks is the same as the written and signed covenant of which we read in Nehemiah 9:38–10:39. The book of remembrance, then, would be a written covenant of the same sort as that which was drawn up in the days of Josiah (2 Kings 23:3).

The other interpretation is that the book is the book of life or the "books" of judgment mentioned in Daniel 7:10 and Revelation 20:12, or some other book written by God himself, perhaps a figurative book in which God remembered the fear and obedience of the remnant. This book cannot, however, be the book of life since the "book of life" was written before the foundations of the world and will never have anything added to it. Nor is it written as God's response to the obedience of his people, but according to the eternal good pleasure of his own will.

That it is a book of judgment in which the obedience of his people is recorded is possible, and so is the similar idea that it is simply a figurative way of saying, "Jehovah remembers." This is Calvin's explanation and is to be preferred. Calvin says:

> Our Prophet wished especially to show, that God *attended*; and hence he uses three forms of speaking. One word would have been enough, but he adds two more; and this is particularly emphatical, that there was a *book of remembrance written*. His purpose then was by this multiplicity of words to give greater encouragement to the faithful, that they might be convinced that their reward would be certain as soon as they devoted themselves to God, for God would not be blind to their piety.[3]

3:17. And they shall be mine, saith the LORD of hosts, in that day when I make up my jewels; and I will spare them, as a man spareth his own son that serveth him.

The book of remembrance just described is the book in which God records the faithfulness of his people, and this verse describes the reason for the writing and keeping of that book. It is written that the faithful may be God's in the day when he makes up his jewels and that they may be spared in the judgment. The book, though not a literal book, shows that they are God's possession (the word "jewels" is literally "possession") and his dear children.

The day referred to is evidently the day of judgment since the prophet speaks of the faithful being spared. It is the day so often referred to in scripture as the day of the Lord. But what a wonderfully comforting description of that day is given! For God's own it is the day when he makes up his possession and takes his people as his own, takes them into his presence and into his heavenly house to live with him there forever. It is the day in which the tabernacle of God is with men and he dwells with them and is their God (Rev. 21:3).

They are his "possession," something very valuable and especially prized. The KJV by its translation "jewels" exactly catches the sense of the word. So

---

3 Calvin, *Commentaries on the Twelve Minor Prophets*, 5:603.

once again God uses the name Jehovah of hosts to speak both of their place as his covenant people and that among all the "hosts" of which he is Lord, they are most valued.

God makes up his possession by taking his people as his own and by separating them from all others in the judgment: "In that great day of final adjustment...God shall make up his own peculiar people from the assembled millions of the earth."[4] He will finally gather them in one in Christ for the greater glory of his great name (Eph. 1:10).

They are his here and now. They most certainly are his by election, by the blood of atonement, and by the indwelling of the Holy Spirit. But the word of God clearly refers to the day when God's covenant with his people will be lifted up to a new and greater level of blessedness. Then they will be his in ways that now can only be imagined.

In the day God makes up his jewels, he will spare them from wrath and judgment. When the ungodly and impenitent are sent away into everlasting fire, his people will receive eternal life. When the wicked are banished from God's presence, his people will see his face. The judgments that fall on the world will not fall on them.

All this is true not because of anything in them, but because of the work of the Messenger of the covenant. The Lord remembers them for the Messenger's sake and for the sake of his work in them. They are his possession by right of purchase and price paid. They are a valuable possession because he is in them by his Spirit. They are spared because he was not spared (Rom. 8:32). They are God's because the Messenger is God's messenger and his work God's own redemptive work.

3:18. Then shall ye return, and discern between the righteous and the wicked, between him that serveth God and him that serveth him not.

This concluding verse of chapter 3 (though not the concluding verse of the section) answers the evil slanders of those who suggested there was no profit in serving God and no difference between God's people and the heathen. Though the difference may not always be evident in this life, it will be evident in the day of judgment. "Then" refers back to the day of verse 17,

---

4 Moore, *Haggai, Zechariah and Malachi*, 413.

the day of judgment, but suggests also that *now* it "doth not yet appear what we shall be" (1 John 3:2). Now we cannot always clearly see ourselves as the righteous. Nor can the ungodly see, who sneer at the claims of God's people and accuse them of thinking they are better than others when they refer to themselves as God's children.

Now both because of our sinfulness and because the work of grace is unfinished, there is not always a clear distinction between those who are righteous and those who are wicked. Now because God's work of grace begins in the heart and because there are many hypocrites, we cannot always tell who serves Jehovah and who does not serve him. But it will not always be so. As Calvin says:

> Ye shall see how much the good differ from the evil; God indeed spares the wicked, but he will at length rise to judgment, and come armed suddenly upon them, and then ye shall know that all the deeds of men are noticed by him, and that wickedness shall not go unpunished, though God for a time delays his vengeance.[5]

And the Belgic Confession says:

> The faithful and elect shall be crowned with glory and honor; and the Son of God will confess their names before God his Father, and his elect angels; all tears shall be wiped from their eyes; and their cause, which is now condemned by many judges and magistrates as heretical and impious, will then be known to be the cause of the Son of God. And, for a gracious reward, the Lord will cause them to possess such a glory as never entered into the heart of man to conceive.[6]

4:1. For, behold, the day cometh, that shall burn as an oven; and all the proud, yea, and all that do wickedly, shall be stubble: and the day that cometh shall burn them up, saith the LORD *of hosts, that it shall leave them neither root nor branch.*

---

5 Calvin, *Commentaries on the Twelve Minor Prophets*, 5:612.
6 Belgic Confession 37, in Schaff, *Creeds of Christendom*, 3:435–36.

This prophecy of the destruction of the wicked is undoubtedly a reference to the end of the world and the eternal state that follows for the wicked. It must refer to their end because its opposite, the salvation and blessedness described in chapter 3:16–17, refers to the end and to eternity. "The day" referred to will be for those who fear the Lord a day of salvation and bliss, but for those who do wickedly a day of terror. It is the day that ends the long history of this world.

Almost all prophecy, however, has a continuing or successive fulfillment, and the day of the Lord described here includes the whole New Testament age. It is described as a day because on God's calendar it is the short time in which he finishes all his work and cuts it short in righteousness (Rom. 9:28).

Because the prophecies of the Old Testament have an ongoing fulfillment, this word of God is fulfilled *throughout* the New Testament. Moore describes it well:

> It is true that the deluge, the destruction of Sodom, Babylon, and Jerusalem, and all subsequent visitations of God's wrath, were days of the Lord, and in each one of them the proud and evil-doers were as chaff. But as each one did not exhaust these ominous predictions, so all together have not yet met the full reach of the terrors, which will only be done in that future day in which the Lord shall descend from heaven with a shout, with the voice of the archangel and the trump of God, and the drama of earth shall be ended. All previous judgments were but reddenings of the dawn, that betokened the coming, but did not unfold the terrible brightness of that awful day. As the prophet in this verse gazes upon its distant rising, he exclaims, as if in breathless emotion, It comes! burning like a furnace! the wicked proud are chaff! the day burns them! There is something very forcible in these abrupt exclamations, as if the prophet was elevated on some mount of vision, and actually beheld this terrible pomp come rolling up the distant skies, on its reddening pathway of fire and blood.[7]

Peter speaks of blood and fire on the day of Pentecost and Jesus of judgment in connection with his cross. The proud are living not just under the

---

7 Moore, *Haggai, Zechariah and Malachi*, 416–17.

threat of judgment but in the midst of judgments already begun and increasing as the final hour approaches. They live in a world already on fire with the conflagration that will finally consume it (2 Pet. 3:7). Already now before the judgments of the Lord they are as chaff, as recent newsworthy disasters have shown.

The rising Sun of righteousness who comes with healing in his wings also comes for judgment. The same glories that will be the everlasting healing and peace of his people will burn the ungodly with unquenchable fire. The righteousness that is our hope and peace will be their terror and everlasting destruction.

Not only shall they themselves, the wicked and the proud, be consumed, but also that day, as the prophet reminds us, will leave them neither root nor branch. "The earth also and the works that are therein shall be burned up," Peter says (2 Pet. 3:10). Even the elements shall melt with fervent heat and "the heavens being on fire shall be dissolved" (v. 12). Nothing will be left to show that wicked men ever lived on this planet. All their vaunted works and culture will be burned and destroyed as a bit of hay flares and is gone in the fire.

Then the difference between the righteous and the wicked will be evident, the difference that is the result of God's gracious work upon and in his people. When all is consumed, they shall endure. When all is destroyed, they shall stand. When the wicked call for the mountains and the hills to fall on them and hide them from the face and wrath of the Lamb, they will with uplifted heads and outstretched arms be waiting for their redemption.

4:2. But unto you that fear my name shall the Sun of righteousness arise with healing in his wings; and ye shall go forth, and grow up as calves of the stall.

Those judgments of Malachi 4:1 are part of the coming of the Sun of righteousness. The fire is the fire of his holiness (Heb. 12:29) and the brightness the brightness of his coming. What a contrast verse 2 presents therefore: instead of destruction, healing; instead of judgment, righteousness.

This Sun of righteousness is Christ. Moore says, "We cannot think that the prophet here meant to predict Christ personally,"[8] but he is wrong. Even

---

8 Ibid., 418.

those who prepared the KJV, as the capitalization of the word "Sun" shows, understood Malachi to be giving a specific prophecy of the coming of Christ. And when Jesus calls himself the light of the world (John 8:12) and is seen by John on Patmos with his countenance "as the sun shineth in his strength" (Rev. 1:16), we know it is him of whom Malachi speaks. Because he is the Sun of righteousness, there will be no need of sun or moon in his everlasting heavenly kingdom (Rev. 21:23).

Christ is called the Sun of righteousness because by bringing in everlasting righteousness, he brings light into our dark night of sin and dispels the darkness of our unbelief, ignorance, and depravity. He is called the Sun because his righteousness is the righteousness of God and shines with the glory of God. His coming is described as the rising of the sun because when he comes the awful night of sin will be over and the darkness of unbelief banished forever.

Those who wait for him are described as those who fear his name. They know how great he is—that without him we sit in darkness and in the shadow of death. They know who he is as the Son of God: the one in whom dwells all the fullness of the Godhead bodily. They know what he does in God's name and by God's power to save those whom God loved, and knowing these things, they tremble in adoring awe and humble reverence.

The wings are an allusion to the apparent movement of the sun as it "flies" through the heavens, and in this case to Christ's swift coming. Like the sun he brings light, the light of life, and with it spiritual healing and peace, for just as no man can live without the light of the sun, so we cannot live without his light. Apart from him we know only pining sickness and death.

The joy that shall be ours is described in terms of the young calves running and leaping in the fields when first released after the long confinement of winter. Moore calls it "a striking image of the joy that the righteous shall feel after being kept so long waiting for deliverance."[9]

4:3. And ye shall tread down the wicked; for they shall be ashes under the soles of your feet in the day that I shall do this, saith the LORD of hosts.

The righteous shall not only see the destruction of their enemies, the ungodly, but they shall also have a part in the judgment and destruction of

---

9 Ibid.

their enemies. The righteous shall sit in judgment with Christ over their enemies (Jude 14–15). The day of judgment is also a day of victory. The victory will be Christ's but will be theirs with him. It will be a complete victory, for every wrong shall be righted, every tear avenged. This promise gives heart and patience to God's people as they live out their lives here and suffer for the kingdom's sake. They know, though the ungodly seem not to know, that there is a God of judgment (Mal. 2:17) and that he judges in perfect righteousness.

The Belgic Confession, in the article previously quoted, expresses the very same sentiments as Malachi and shows how the word of God in Malachi 4:3 is a comfort to God's people:

> And, therefore, the consideration of this judgment is justly terrible and dreadful to the wicked and ungodly, but most desirable and comfortable to the righteous and the elect; because then their full deliverance shall be perfected, and there they shall receive the fruits of their labor and trouble which they have borne. Their innocence shall be known to all, and they shall see the terrible vengeance which God shall execute on the wicked, who most cruelly persecuted, oppressed, and tormented them in this world.[10]

This recurring emphasis on the coming judgment in the last chapters of Malachi is an important part of the message of the book, for it is the final revelation of God's faithfulness to his elect and of the unfaithfulness of many.

---

10 Belgic Confession 37, in Schaff, *Creeds of Christendom*, 3:435.

Chapter 33

THE CONCLUSION:
MALACHI 4:4–6

4:4   Remember ye the law of Moses my servant, which I commanded unto him in Horeb for all Israel, with the statutes and judgments.

4:5   Behold, I will send you Elijah the prophet before the coming of the great and dreadful day of the LORD:

4:6   And he shall turn the heart of the fathers to the children, and the heart of the children to their fathers, lest I come and smite the earth with a curse.

The last three verses of the book form a conclusion to the whole and are in the form of a double admonition to remember the law of Moses and to look for the coming of Elijah the prophet. The first admonition is a reminder that covenantal faithfulness is a matter of obedience to the law of God (v. 4), and the second admonition is a reminder of how this covenantal faithfulness comes about, that is, by the work of God's messenger (vv. 5–6).

Many modern so-called scholars believe these concluding verses were not written by Malachi but were added later. There is no proof for this, and it reflects the prevailing unbelief of modern Bible scholarship, which does not see scripture as the word of God. In fact, even a child can see the similarity between Malachi 4:5 and Malachi 3:1 and can see therefore that these verses not only belong to Malachi but are also an important part of the book.

4:4. Remember ye the law of Moses my servant, which I commanded unto him in Horeb for all Israel, with the statutes and judgments.

In the admonition to remember the law, the key is the relation of the Mosaic law and God's covenant with Israel. The relation is stated in Deuteronomy 4:13. All the sins that Malachi admonishes were violations of the law, therefore, and of God's covenant with Israel.

The covenant is God's and the making or breaking of that covenant does not in any way depend on the obedience or disobedience of his people. He makes and he keeps his covenant without any help from them. Nevertheless, through their obedience they show they are God's friends and have a place in his covenant. It is impossible to do so in any other way but the way of obedience. The law therefore, which shows them the way of obedience, is part of God's covenant with them, an essential part.

The law is referred to in three ways: as law, statutes, and judgments. Each of these words has a slightly different but important emphasis. The word "law" says that the commandments of God are a "way," and the word is so translated in many passages. The law, then, not only encompasses one's whole life, but it is also only in the "way" of the law that covenantal fellowship and friendship with God is possible.

The other two words emphasize, respectively, the permanent character of the law and the law as a code according to which all shall be judged. God is saying by these three words, "Walk in my ways. In spite of the changing circumstances of your lives, I do not change and this is the only way that you can know and love me. And do not forget that you must stand before me someday and give an account of what you have done in keeping or not keeping my law. Those who walk in my ways shall experience the eternal healing that my Messenger will bring when he comes. Those of you who do not shall be as ashes under his feet."

Always God's judgment is according to works. Works are not meritorious and we do not earn our way into his favor, but works are nevertheless the evidence of whether we belong to Christ and are among the sons of Levi who have been purified by him, or whether we are among the proud and impenitent who say in words or deeds that it is vain to serve God. Those therefore who by grace keep his commandments will live forever before him and enjoy him into eternity. Those who do not will be banished from his presence.

4:5. Behold, I will send you Elijah the prophet before the coming of the great and dreadful day of the LORD:
4:6. And he shall turn the heart of the fathers to the children, and the heart of the children to their fathers, lest I come and smite the earth with a curse.

The coming of Elijah in these last verses of Malachi is a reference to John the Baptist and his work as forerunner of the Messiah. This is beyond doubt in light of Jesus' words in Matthew 11:14: "And if ye will receive it, this is Elias, which was for to come." In Matthew 17:12 he says the same: "But I say unto you, That Elias is come already, and they knew him not, but have done unto him whatsoever they listed. Likewise shall also the Son of man suffer of them"; to which scripture adds, "Then the disciples understood that he spake unto them of John the Baptist" (v. 13).

It may seem strange that the prophecy ends with a reference to John as God's messenger and not to the great Messenger of the covenant. Nevertheless, there is good reason for this ending.

John was Elijah not because he was some reincarnation of Elijah the prophet, but because he came "in the spirit and power of Elias" (Luke 1:17) and because he preached the same message of judgment and repentance as

Elijah did. In the same way all the prophets of the Old Testament were "Elijah" and all prepared the way of the Lord. John was only the last and greatest of them all. Even the ministers of the word in the New Testament bear a certain resemblance to Elijah and stand in his place when they preach the same message as Elijah and point to Christ as the one who fulfills all the promises of God.

But why does God speak of this messenger (and of all who stand with him as messengers and preparers of the way) and not of the great Messenger himself, especially here at the end of the prophecy? There are two reasons. First, those who heeded God's messengers in the persons of John and Malachi and the prophets would also heed the Messenger of the covenant, and those who did not heed the lesser messengers would not heed the greater either. As Jesus said later to the scribes and Pharisees, "If they hear not Moses and the prophets, neither will they be persuaded, though one rose from the dead" (Luke 16:31).

Second, through such messengers the Messenger himself speaks. They do not just speak about him, but he speaks through them. To hear and heed them is to hear and heed Christ as the great Messenger. Those who would not hear John would not hear Christ, nor any of the others who stood in the long line of prophets of which John was the last and greatest. Nor today will those who refuse to hear God's messengers hear Christ, though they may piously protest otherwise.

To Israel God is saying, "Give heed to Malachi and to the other prophets who have gone before him, who were part of the long line of prophets." To us he is saying that we too must give heed to those who come in the spirit and power of Elijah, to John and all the rest who bring his message of repentance and judgment. In heeding and repenting we must also "Behold the Lamb of God, which taketh away the sin of the world" (John 1:29).

Along with verse 4, the passage very strikingly sets before the people Moses and Elijah, the two who appeared to Jesus on the Mount of Transfiguration. They appeared there and are mentioned here for the same reason. They represent the whole Old Testament, the law and the prophets, all of which testified of Christ. Search the scriptures, Jesus said to the Jews, for they are they that testify of me (John 5:39). In the New Testament the testimony is also of Christ, but of him as the fulfillment of all the promises and as the one who is coming again. In the Old Testament that testimony kept the church looking for the coming of Christ and the fulfillment of the promises in him. In the New Testament it keeps us "looking for and hasting unto the coming of the day of God" (2 Pet. 3:12), the day when he shall come again.

Testifying of the coming of Christ, therefore, the law and prophets prepared the way of the Lord. Moses did so by setting before the people the demands of the law, which would become a "schoolmaster to bring [them] unto Christ" (Gal. 3:24). Elijah and the prophets did so by calling the people to repentance in view of the coming day of wrath, and their spirit lives on in all those who preach the law and the prophets, pointing to Christ as the one in whom alone salvation is to be found. As Moore says:

> Indeed, to every regenerated soul there is essentially this coming of Elijah, this summons, "Repent, for the day is coming!" And as the faithful minister of Christ goes forth, it must be ever in the same spirit, calling on men to repent, and pointing to the lurid flashings of that *dies irae*, which, when once perceived by the startled eye of the soul, will lead it to flee to the only refuge from this wrath to come.[1]

This sending of Elijah, fulfilled over the whole course of history in the testimony of the law and the prophets, in Malachi, in John, and in every preacher, is not for the purpose of giving men a chance to repent, but to *work* repentance in the hearts of God's elect—to *turn* the hearts of the fathers to the children and the hearts of the children to the fathers. The language of the passage is the language of sovereign grace and a wonderful testimony to the truth that the gospel is indeed the "power of God unto salvation" (Rom. 1:16).

Verse 6, then, describes the fruit of "Elijah's" work through the ages. It is the good fruit of repentance and conversion. Although expressed in language that may seem strange to us, this is clear from the quotation of the passage in Luke 1:16–17. There the second phrase is interpreted by the angel Gabriel to mean "the disobedient to the wisdom of the just." The idea must therefore be that by Elijah's preaching of repentance, the hearts of the pious

---

1 Moore, *Haggai, Zechariah and Malachi*, 422.

and faithful fathers of Israel would live once again in their children and the children would be restored to the piety of their fathers.

To the piety of the fathers Malachi had referred repeatedly (1:2; 2:5–6; 3:4). It would live again and does live again not only in the hearts of their Jewish children but also in the heart of every spiritual child of Abraham, that is, in the hearts of those who are children of Abraham by faith (Gal. 3:29).

This fruit would be produced by Elijah's message, whether preached by Elijah himself or by those who followed him. The message produced such fruit in the Old Testament because the Spirit of Christ spoke through the prophets (1 Pet. 1:11). It produces the same fruit in the New Testament because Christ speaks through the preaching (John 10:27; Eph. 2:17).

That promise of good fruit was God's encouragement to Malachi in a time when it seemed as though no one listened or gave heed. It would be an encouragement to John when he was a "voice of one crying in the wilderness" (John 1:23). It is an encouragement to everyone who brings the word of God in times of apostasy, coldness, and wickedness.

The encouragement is the promise of salvation as God's own work, the promise that therefore his people will surely be saved. God through Malachi gives the same assurance given to Elijah many years before when God assured him in his despondency that he had reserved in Israel seven thousand who had not bowed the knee to Baal. It is given in the New Testament when the word of God assures us that even today there is a remnant according to the election of grace (Rom. 11:5).

All this is reinforced by the threat of God's curse. The curse came on Israel as a nation when they were cut off and destroyed and when the gospel was sent to the Gentiles. But just as the word of God concerning the conversion of many continues to be fulfilled throughout the New Testament, so does this threat of curse still hang over the heads of all who do not repent: "Be not highminded, but fear: For if God spared not the natural branches, take heed lest he also spare not thee" (Rom. 11:20–21).

With these words of verses 4–6, Malachi's prophecy and the whole Old Testament ends, and what an ending! As Pusey says:

After the glad tidings, Malachi, and the Old Testament in him, ends with words of awe, telling us of the consequence of the final

515

hardening of the heart; the eternal severance, when the unending end of the everlasting Gospel itself shall be accomplished, and its last grain shall be gathered into the garner of the Lord. The Jews, who would be wiser than the prophet, repeat the previous verse, because Malachi closes so awfully. The Maker of the heart of man knew better the hearts which He had made, and taught their authors to end the books of Isaiah and Ecclesiastes [and Malachi] with words of awe, from which man's heart so struggles to escape.[2]

Or as Laetsch puts it:

The Masoretes [early Jewish editors of the Old Testament] repeated v. 23 after v. 24, and the LXX [the Septuagint, a Greek translation of the Old Testament] reversed the order of the last two verses in order to have the last book of the Bible close, not with a curse, but a blessing. That is not the way for unbelief to escape the curse. None but Jesus saves! (Acts 4:12; 10:43.)[3]

The concluding prayer of Calvin certainly expresses, therefore, what everyone who reads and understands the prophecy of Malachi must feel:

Grant, Almighty God, that as nothing is omitted by thee to help us onward in the course of our faith, and as our sloth is such that we hardly advance one step though stimulated by thee,—O grant, that we may strive to profit more by the various helps which thou hast provided for us, so that the Law, the Prophets, the voice of John the Baptist, and especially the doctrine of thine only-begotten Son, may more fully awaken us, that we may not only hasten to him, but also proceed constantly in our course, and persevere in it until we shall at length obtain the victory and the crown of our calling, as thou hast promised an eternal inheritance in heaven to all who faint not but wait for the coming of the Great Redeemer.—Amen.[4]

2 Pusey, The Minor Prophets, 2:503–4.
3 Laetsch, The Minor Prophets, 547.
4 Calvin, Commentaries on the Twelve Minor Prophets, 5:632.

BIBLIOGRAPHY

Augustine. *The City of God*. Translated by Marcus Dods. In *The Nicene and Post-Nicene Fathers*, 1st ser. Grand Rapids, MI: Eerdmans, 1988.

—. *Confessions*. Translated by J. G. Pilkington. In *The Nicene and Post-Nicene Fathers*, 1st ser. Grand Rapids, MI: Eerdmans, 1988.

Bentley, Michael. *Building for God's Glory: Haggai and Zechariah Simply Explained*. Darlington, UK: Evangelical Press, 1989.

Benton, John. *Losing Touch with the Living God: Malachi*. Darlington, UK: Evangelical Press, 1985.

Berkhof, Louis. *Systematic Theology*. 4th ed. Edinburgh, UK: Banner of Truth Trust, 1958.

Calvin, John. *Commentaries on the Twelve Minor Prophets*. Translated by John Owen. Grand Rapids, MI: Eerdmans, 1950.

The Confession of Faith and the Larger and Shorter Catechisms. Inverness, Scotland: Publications Committee of the Free Presbyterian Church of Scotland.

Hengstenberg, E. W. *Christology of the Old Testament and a Commentary on the Messianic Predictions*. Translated by Theod. Meyer and James Martin. N.p., 1872–78; repr., Grand Rapids, MI: Kregel Publications, 1956.

Hoeksema, Herman. *Behold He Cometh: An Exposition of the Book of Revelation*. Grand Rapids, MI: Reformed Free Publishing Association, 1969.

Hoeksema, Homer C. *Unfolding Covenant History: An Exposition of the Old Testament*. Vol. 3, *From Jacob to the Exodus*. Grandville, MI: Reformed Free Publishing Association, 2003.

Keil, Carl Friedrich. *The Twelve Minor Prophets*. Translated by James Martin. Biblical Commentary on the Old Testament. Grand Rapids, MI: Eerdmans, 1954.

Kline, Meredith G. *Glory in Our Midst: A Biblical-Theological Reading of Zechariah's Night Visions*. Eugene, OR: Wipf and Stock, 2001.

Laetsch, Theo. *Bible Commentary on the Minor Prophets*. St. Louis: Concordia, 1956.

Leupold, H. C. *Exposition of Zechariah*. Grand Rapids, MI: Baker Book House, 1974.

Luther, Martin. "The Babylonian Captivity of the Church." In *Works of Martin Luther, Philadelphia Edition*. Philadelphia: Muhlenberg Press, 1943.

Moore, Thomas V. *A Commentary on Zechariah*. Edinburgh: Banner of Truth, 1958.

—. *A Commentary on Haggai, Zechariah and Malachi*. Edinburgh: Banner of Truth, 1979.

Motyer, J. Alec. "Haggai." In *The Minor Prophets: An Exegetical and Expository Commentary*, edited by Thomas Edward McComiskey. Grand Rapids, MI: Baker Books, 1998.

Newton, John. *Olney Hymns*. Vol. 1, hymn 77. N.p., 1779.

Ophoff, George M. "The Prophecy of Zechariah." *Standard Bearer* 32, no. 18 (July 1, 1956): 443; 33, no. 5 (Dec. 1, 1956): 106.

Pink, Arthur W. *The Sovereignty of God*. Grand Rapids, MI: Baker Book House, 1951.

The Psalter with Doctrinal Standards, Liturgy, Church Order, and Added Chorale Section. Reprinted and revised edition of the 1912 United Presbyterian *Psalter*. Grand Rapids, MI: Eerdmans, 1927; rev. ed. 1995.

Pusey, E. B. *The Minor Prophets: A Commentary Explanatory and Practical*. Grand Rapids, MI: Baker Book House, 1974.

Schaff, Philip, ed. *The Creeds of Christendom with a History and Critical Notes*. 6th ed. 3 vols. New York: Harper and Row, 1931; repr., Grand Rapids, MI: Baker Books, 2007.

Smith, Ralph L. "Zechariah." In Word Biblical Commentary, vol. 32, *Micah-Malachi*. Waco, TX: Word Books, 1984.

Spurgeon, C. H. *Metropolitan Tabernacle Pulpit*. Pasadena: Pilgrim Publications, repr. 1897.

Tertullian. *Apology*, 37. Translated by S. Thelwall. In *The Ante-Nicene Fathers*. Grand Rapids, MI: Eerdmans, 1980.

Von Orelli, C. *The Twelve Minor Prophets*. Minneapolis: Klock and Klock, 1977.

Wright, Charles Henry Hamilton. *Zechariah and His Prophecies*. London: Hodder and Stoughton, 1879.

Index of Scripture